W9-ATS-168

U.S.A.—
SECOND-CLASS
POWER?

by Drew Pearson
and Jack Anderson

SIMON AND SCHUSTER · NEW YORK · 1958

ALL RIGHTS RESERVED
INCLUDING THE RIGHT OF REPRODUCTION
IN WHOLE OR IN PART IN ANY FORM
COPYRIGHT © 1958 BY DREW PEARSON AND JACK ANDERSON
PUBLISHED BY SIMON AND SCHUSTER, INC.
ROCKEFELLER CENTER, 630 FIFTH AVENUE
NEW YORK 20, N.Y.

SECOND PRINTING

LIBRARY OF CONGRESS CATALOG CARD NUMBER: 58-13168
MANUFACTURED IN THE UNITED STATES OF AMERICA
BY AMERICAN BOOK-STRATFORD PRESS, INC., NEW YORK

To our children
and grandchildren
and all the other children
who will have to pay the consequences—
if we fail

Contents

Foreword

It is inescapable that this book will arouse a great deal of criticism. We hastily add that is was not written for that purpose. It is only human to prefer praise to criticism, and the authors, despite some things said about them, are not inhuman. But they are convinced that the emergence of Russia from the wheelbarrow age to the atomic age is the greatest miracle of modern times. And while the American who says this publicly is likely to be blasted as pro-Communist by the Un-American Activities Committee, yet if America doesn't recognize this fact, it is likely to get blasted off the face of the earth.

We will go one step further and venture the opinion that the American who states that Russia's emergence as a first-class power may be a healthy stimulus to the United States runs the risk of being considered a betrayer of the American way of life and an admirer of the Soviet system. He may even come under scrutiny by the FBI. Yet if we are frank with ourselves, we have to admit that for too long have we been confident, fat, and complacent. Too long have we put self-interest ahead of national interest, ease before duty, luxury before sacrifice, golf before decisions, Thunderbirds before missiles, Madison Avenue camouflage before truth.

It is sometimes difficult to face the truth. It is much easier to accuse a critic of our shortcomings of not telling the truth, to brand him a liar or a headline-hunter, or even a pro-Communist, if he comes up with unpleasant facts about the waning power and prestige of the U.S.A. Yet it is a fact that for some time we have been slipping. Not only have we been slipping, but we have been afraid to admit the fact that we were slipping. The shameful desertions and surrenders of American troops in Korea were the first sign that something had gone wrong. They were also the first sign that we were afraid to face the degree to which we had put materialism ahead of patriotism. The American public still does not know that the shocking confessions made by American prisoners in Korea were by no means all exacted by torture; that Turkish, British, Canadian and other United Nations troops did not turn their backs on their countries to anywhere near the same degree. The American public does not know that General William F. Dean, captured commander of the 7th Infantry Division, gave twelve different statements to the enemy. Never in all history have so many Americans, including high-ranking officers, disgraced the uniform of the country which spawned them, protected them, and gave them the freedoms of which they should have been proud—but which they took for granted.

After the Korean War came a deluge of defeats, diplomatic and otherwise, culminating with the events of 1957-58 when the world woke up to find Russia occupying outer space while the United States occupied Central High School in Arkansas.

The world recognized our defeats, but, generally speaking, the American people did not. We played up defeat in Korea as if it were a victory. We pussyfooted so long in Indochina that most of it went Communist. We bungled so badly in the Near East that its vast oil reserves are slipping through our fingers. We have affronted and antagonized and alienated our allies in Western Europe until the North Atlantic Treaty Organization has become a military shell. The world knows this, but we do not.

It is not pleasant to criticize the United States of America. He who does so is accused of losing faith in his country. But the American people cannot meet the challenge of the powerful, tireless government that threatens them if they are fed sugar-coated half-truths and soothing syrup. They must know the facts.

We cannot sit back and wait for bickering inside the Kremlin to deliver Russia into our hands. The walls of the Kremlin are not like the walls of Jericho. They will not come tumbling down after seven statements by John Foster Dulles. Nor will they yield to a civilization in which an Elvis Presley makes more than the President of the United States, in which truck drivers in Chicago are paid more than many schoolteachers, in which one third of all prescriptions filled at drugstores are for tranquilizing pills. The road to Miltown is not the road to victory over the vigorous and unscrupulous government that rules Russia. We cannot win the battle for freedom or the great goal of peace if we keep our heads in the sands of ignorance.

The ingredients of greatness, however, have not gone out of the bones of the American people. They are equal to great challenge—if they know the facts. It is in order that they may know the facts that this book is written.

The material that has gone into its chapters has been obtained from scores of Army, Navy, and Air Force officers, civilian defense experts, scientists and diplomats who have the welfare of their country at heart. The material is also based on several years of covering foreign affairs and the defense news of Washington. It is based on six trips abroad during the past two years.

We are indebted to many for advice and guidance in the preparation of this book—to the former Secretary of the Air Force, now Senator from Missouri, Stuart Symington; his assistant, Edward Welch; to Senators Estes Kefauver of Tennessee and Henry Jackson of Washington of the Senate Armed Services Committee; to Senator William Fulbright of Arkansas of the Foreign Relations Committee; to Trevor Gardner, the former Assistant Secretary of Defense; Wernher von Braun of the Army Ballistic Missile Agency; Lt. Gen. James Gavin; Admiral Hyman Rickover; Dr. Harold Urey of the University of Chicago; former Senator William Benton of Connecticut; John Kennedy, publisher of the Sioux Falls (S.D.) Argus-Leader, *who gave us the results of his several trips to Russia; Eric Berghaust, editor of* Missiles and Rockets; *Clay Blair, author of* The Atomic Submarine; *Louis Johnson, former Secretary of Defense; Tom Wilcox, formerly of the Air Force Office of Scientific Research; Don Ludlow, Washington Correspondent for the London* Mirror; *Herschel Schooley, formerly of the Defense Department; Captain William Chambliss, U.S.N; and Col. John R. Nickerson, whose explosive memo first revealed some of the basic defects of our missile program.*

Finally, we are indebted to a hundred or so officers of the armed services who cannot speak out in public but who believe that without imitating the Soviet Union as to methods we can meet its challenge; who believe that the United States does not have to become a second-class power.

To that end, this book is written.

i

OPERATION SOOTHING SYRUP

When the first Russian sputnik began beeping across the heavens on October 4, 1957, President Eisenhower was stunned. A barrage of bitter criticism was hurled at him by newspapers and commentators, a barrage to which he was completely unaccustomed. Once before, early in his Administration, he had confided to a friend that he might have made a mistake in running for President. He had attained the highest pinnacle of achievement as a military man, he said, and might have gone down in history alongside General George Washington and General Robert E. Lee. But in politics, he feared he might become another Ulysses S. Grant.

Once more this haunting fear came over him as he read the bitter outpouring of criticism over the fact that he, Dwight D. Eisenhower, a military man, had allowed the United States to lag behind Russia.

The President had known, of course, that Russia was likely to launch its satellite ahead of the United States. He had known also that Russia was forging ahead of the United States with its intercontinental ballistic missile. He had known, and yet in a way he had not known. The clear warning that Russia would launch a satellite in the autumn of 1957 had come as early as the preceding June. The date was even fixed in one Russian scientific journal—September 17.

Despite this warning, the Administration had blandly continued cutting defenses. It was only two months prior to October 4 that Secretary of Defense Wilson, at the order of the President, had sent a letter to Republican Senate Leader Knowland of California, advising that the Senate should accept a two-billion-dollar economy cut passed by the House of Representatives. The Senate had been all set to restore the cut, and Senator Leverett Saltonstall of Massachusetts, spokesman for the Administration, had been arguing eloquently for the two billion dollars inside a joint conference of House and Senate committee members. He looked flabbergasted when handed the Administration letter.

"My friend," jibed Congressman Harry R. Sheppard, California Democrat, "it looks to me as if you're riding on a train that has lost its caboose."

"I will concede," replied the blueblood Senator from Back Bay Boston, "that the nap of my rug has been sheared from under my feet."

The Administration also knew three months before the Russians announced it at the end of August that they had successfully tested an intercontinental ballistic missile, and further, that the test had been amazingly successful. Washington knew this because the American radar network which has been set up all around the Soviet recorded the missile as fired in May 1957 from Kolguev Island in the Arctic to the Sea of Okhotsk, a distance of 4,500 miles.

Assuming that President Eisenhower did not read the carefully prepared intelligence reports which Allen Dulles, Director of Central Intelligence, was giving him, he could have been forewarned by reading the newspapers. On August 31, the "Washington Merry-Go-Round" said: "Russia will launch the artificial satellite ahead of us. This may be shot into space as early as September 17, the one hundredth anniversary of Konstantin Tsiolkovsky's birth. Tsiolkovsky has been publicized in Russia as father of space flights. . . ."

Also on August 31 in the Washington *Post*, which is placed daily on the desk of the President, the authors warned: "Our top officials have known for three months that Russia has successfully fired an intercontinental missile about 4,500 miles from Kolguev Island in the Arctic to the Sea of Okhotsk in the Northwest Pacific."

Nearly a year and a half before this, on May 31, 1956, the "Washington Merry-Go-Round" reported: "U.S. experts admit Russia will launch an earth satellite ahead of us—probably in 1957. This will be one year in advance of the U.S.A."

Again on the same date, the authors warned: "Central Intelligence reports flatly and categorically that Russia is ahead of us in guided missiles. This means Moscow will probably build the dread intercontinental ballistic missile capable of flying from Moscow to Washington before we do." The Alsop brothers also published repeated warnings that we were falling behind in the missile-satellite race. No journalist's intelligence was as complete as that placed upon the desk of President Eisenhower weekly. Unfortunately, he paid little attention to either press reports or confidential reports.

Though it was later announced at the White House that we were in no satellite race with Russia, actually we were in a desperate race. And both the White House and the Defense Department had been fully informed of the tremendous psychological advantage of getting a satellite into the air first.

However, and for reasons still inexplicable, the Administration actually slowed down missile production and did nothing about speeding up satellite production. The Air Force had been turning out the Thor intermediate-range ballistic missile at the rate of four per month. But in August 1957, Secretary Wilson cut back production to two per month.

All this took place before the fateful satellite-launching day of October 4, 1957—actually only seventeen days off from the Russians' September 17 target.

Therewith began the first big debate inside the White House—whether to tell the American public the full truth.

The proposed policy was called Operation Candor. It was chiefly advocated by Vice-President Nixon and got some help from Secretary of State Dulles. It got a great deal of opposition from Sherman Adams, then the most potent man in the White House, from Director of the Budget Percival F. Brundage, and from Admiral Lewis L. Strauss, Chairman of the Atomic Energy Commission.

Long before Sputnik, Nixon had been battling behind the scenes to meet the Soviet challenge and damn the cost. But the budget-balancing forces, led at that time by Secretary of the Treasury Humphrey, had far more influence with Eisenhower. Easily they overruled Nixon. Early in his Administration, President Eisenhower had taken a dangerous but calculated risk. Under pressure from the budget-first advisers, he had gambled that Russia would not start a nuclear war. This ruling automatically gave the budget-balancers priority over national defense. In addition, during the fateful summer of 1957, as intelligence warnings of Russian progress increased, the President found his defense expenses bumping up against the $275,000,000,000 debt ceiling set by Congress. The debt ceiling, plus earlier Republican charges that the Democrats had no respect for it, had been a major issue in the 1952 campaign. A Republican Administration, the public was told, would lower the debt ceiling, not raise it. So the summer of 1957 found Mr. Eisenhower more worried about crashing through the debt ceiling than about a crash program to keep ahead of the Kremlin. In addition, the Defense Department, during the fiscal year 1957, had spent $2,400,000,000 more than it had anticipated. This shook the Eisenhower Administration to its fiscal foundation.

All these political and personal factors piled up to defeat Operation Candor. For Eisenhower to have delivered a Churchillian blood-sweat-and-tears speech to the nation, as part of Operation Candor, would have opened the door to extremely embarrassing inquiries. Why had intelligence warnings regarding Russia's mushrooming military might been ignored? The warnings had come direct from Allen Dulles. He had sent report after report to the President's desk—warnings that Russia was climbing ahead of the United States on missiles and satellites with alarming speed. Why were they ignored? Why was the warning of General James H. Doolittle ignored? Early in the Eisenhower Administration, April 5, 1953, he had warned that research conducted then would determine the quality of planes and missiles five and ten years hence. Or the warning of Dr. James R. Killian, later to become White House scientific adviser, who in 1955 told the Administration, "Only seven per cent of the Government's research and development funds are allocated to basic research." And there was the discreet but pointed warning of General Donald L. Putt, Deputy Air Force Chief of Staff, also in 1955, that "our work could have progressed faster . . . there just were not enough resources to go around."

Why also did the President ignore the appeal of Dr. Courtland D. Perkins, Chief Scientist of the Air Force, January 29, 1957, for more "understanding of our research and development in our higher political echelons"? "Higher political echelons," of course, was a polite way of referring to the White House. Why, instead of recommending action, did Frank D. Newberry, Assistant Secretary of Defense for Research, blandly alibi on March 21, 1957, "Photographing the other side of the moon is not a Pentagon responsibility"? Why was the warning of the President's own Special Assistant Air Force Secretary for Missiles, Trevor Gardner, ignored, when after repeated private warnings to the White House he resigned and on February 19, 1956, stated publicly, "I felt that we were not making enough progress relative to our possible enemies, and further, I felt that the level of support for air power and missiles was not adequate"?

Why had the President deliberately lulled the public regarding the reasons for Gardner's resignation? Why, instead of pushing missile development, did he calmly assure the public immediately after Gardner resigned, "I think over-all we have no reason to believe that we are not doing anything that human science and brains and resources can do to keep our position in proper posture"?

These were questions the public was bound to ask if the President went on the air with a fighting, frank admission that the United States was tragically behind Russia and that it would take great sacrifice, great effort, great dedication by the American people to catch up. These were the reasons why Operation Candor, after great debate inside the White House, was junked.

Thus the tragic decision of 1953 to put economy ahead of security was followed by a second decision after October 4, 1957, to put syrup ahead of truth. Thus Operation Soothing Syrup was born.

The President's first chins-up speech was delivered on November 7. Originally scheduled to be delivered in Oklahoma City on November 13, it was pushed ahead when Arthur Larson, newly appointed psychological-warfare adviser to the President, warned that the Russians might pull a new and spectacular sputnik development on November 7, the date of their fortieth anniversary. Actually, the American Embassy reported that the second dog-carrying sputnik had been scheduled for launching on November 7 during the gala celebration of the Russian Revolution. But Khrushchev also was having problems. Just as Ike was worried over domestic reaction to our lag in science, Khrushchev was worried over domestic reaction to his ousting of Marshal Zhukov. So he pushed the launching of Sputnik II ahead three days.

Ike's sudden decision to advance the date of his speech had White House ghost writers scurrying all over the Pentagon. Assistant Defense Secretary Murray Snyder, formerly White House assistant for public relations, directed the search for new American "scientific accomplishments."

"We must have something definite and significant," Snyder instructed. He was particularly interested in the Air Force's Operation Farside, which had just shot a research rocket from mid-Pacific into outer space, and even hinted that the Air Force should exaggerate its achievements. Snyder also pounced upon a Jupiter-C nose cone which the Army had recovered from mid-ocean and had intended to exhibit at the Army Association convention in Washington as evidence that missiles could now re-enter the dense atmosphere surrounding the earth without disintegrating. The Pentagon was opposed to having the President show the nose cone on his telecast, first because this particular nose cone had re-entered the atmosphere at a cockeyed angle which slowed it down to less than one-third the speed of a normal ballistic missile, so that it was not a real test of re-entry into the atmosphere; second, because the problem of re-entry had not only been solved five months earlier, but had been previously publicized by the United Press in May 1957 when an experimental X-17 three-stage rocket was fired 650 miles straight up at Patrick Air Force Base, Florida, and the nose cone recovered intact.

Nevertheless, those who favored Operation Soothing Syrup over Operation Candor trundled the nose cone up to the President's study, where he dramatically displayed it to the American public as a major American missile achievement. The public, listening to him that night, did not realize that having a resistant nose cone did not compensate for not having a long-range intercontinental ballistic missile to launch a nose cone any great distance. The public also had no way of knowing that the speech fell far short of being Operation Candor. The aviation experts, however, unlike the public, were able to detect the following glaring misstatements of fact:

Though the President referred to the B-52 jet bomber as standard in our Strategic Air Command and told how it "can carry as much destructive capacity as was delivered by all the bombers" in World War II, actually it was not standard. At that time only two wings had been produced and many Strategic Air Command bases were clamoring for them. Far from being an adequate defense against Russia, there were just not enough B-52's to go around.

"The B-52," said the President, "will in turn be succeeded by the B-58, a supersonic bomber." Actually, the B-58 will supersede the B-47, and at the time he spoke there were only two B-58's finished in the entire United States, with only twenty more on the production line for completion in 1958. They were by no means an adequate future defense against an enemy.

Referring to the tremendous production of Corporal missiles, the President said, "Four battalions of Corporal missiles alone are equivalent in fire power to all the artillery used in World War II on all fronts." What he didn't say, however, was that the Corporal missile was then out of date and being junked.

"One U.S. atomic submarine," said the President, "ran almost sixteen days recently without surfacing." But what the President didn't mention was that the United States has only three atomic submarines, and no other modern submarines. Russia has 600 new submarines.

The air-breathing Snark, said the President, "traveled over a guided course for 5,000 miles and was accurately placed on target." The President did not point out that the Snark travels slowly, can be easily shot down, and is a long way from being an intercontinental ballistic missile.

"What concerns us most," said editor Wayne Parrish of *American Aviation*, after reviewing the errors in the Eisenhower speech, "is that *at the top* there may still be no real understanding of what this vast new space era is all about."

Thus was defeated Operation Candor. Thus began Operation Soothing Syrup. Remarked one high officer at the Pentagon, "There's nothing to fear except annihilation itself."

Vice-President Nixon had got out of a sickbed to come to the White House shortly before the President's first chins-up speech. He begged that the speech be tougher. While he lost the battle, he continued to urge an emergency full-speed missile program. By this time Sherman Adams, under public pressure, had backed down a bit and conceded that more money must be spent on missiles. He even abandoned his dream of a tax cut. But he stoutly insisted that taxes must not be raised, and he proposed taking the extra money for missiles out of other programs, particularly veterans' aid, public housing, farm aid, public works, reclamation, and welfare.

Nixon argued that the United States must catch up with Russia by 1960—if the Republicans wanted to have any hope whatsoever of being re-elected. Nixon also fought for a two-billion-dollar increase in foreign aid and got some real support from John Foster Dulles. He got little support inside the National Security Council.

This battle, which raged back and forth inside the White House and spread at times to the Pentagon and Capitol Hill, was merged into a much more important, more personal battle immediately after the President suffered an occlusion of the brain on November 25. The battle after that was not merely over national defense and the budget. It was over whether Nixon should take over the administration of national defense and the budget.

Because of the early mystery surrounding the President's illness, it was impossible to ascertain at that time whether he would recover.

Not even his doctors dreamed his recovery would be so rapid. During those first days, especially the day when Vice-President Nixon camped for ten long hours inside the White House, some of the White House staff had resented the manner in which the Vice-President and his friend, Attorney General Rogers, seemed to constitute a death watch.

After Eisenhower's first illness at Denver in October 1955, Nixon had spent most of the night with Rogers, wondering what might happen, discussing what he would do if he became President. Later when the Vice-President made some discreet moves toward taking over part of the President's powers, Sherman Adams rushed out to Denver and grabbed the reins. This had followed a meeting in the office of Secretary of the Treasury Humphrey, at which it was decided Nixon should be permitted to preside over the Cabinet and the National Security Council—both strictly ceremonial functions —but that he was not to be given any temporary power to act as President.

After Eisenhower's third illness, in November 1957, Nixon was the height of discretion and diplomacy. Nevertheless, resentment against him boiled inside the White House as the silent struggle for power intensified.

Jim Hagerty, Sherman Adams' strongest ally against Nixon, was in Paris preparing for the NATO Conference. It took several hours' search of the night spots of Paris to locate him at 4 A.M., load him aboard a plane and fly him back to Washington. Before Hagerty could rally to the support of his friend Sherman Adams, however, Secretary Dulles had moved in on the side of Nixon and decided that the Vice-President would substitute for Eisenhower at the Paris Atlantic Pact Conference. Nixon also let it be known that he, not Adams, would preside at the meeting of Congressional leaders which Eisenhower had called for the following week. And to bolster his hand, Nixon had his good friend Senator Styles Bridges of New Hampshire, dean of Senate Republicans, telephone the White House and threaten to stay away from the meeting unless Nixon, not Adams, presided. Bridges added that he was speaking for Senator Lyndon Johnson, leader of the Democrats, as well. Bridges was so emphatic that Adams was conspicuously absent when the Congressmen gathered at the White House the next week.

By this time Jim Hagerty had flown back from Paris, and came charging into the White House in defense of Sherman Adams. He aligned himself vigorously against Nixon in the struggle to see who was to take over control of the government of the United States.

Dramatically and unexpectedly Eisenhower's condition improved. Hagerty promptly persuaded Dulles to make no final decision as to whether Nixon should attend the Paris meeting until Eisenhower could pass on it personally. This was the first block placed under the wheels of the rapidly rolling bandwagon of the Vice-President.

Nixon, however, scored a counterpoint when he persuaded Hagerty to let him hold a press conference in the White House. This was unprecedented. A Vice-President of the United States had never before held a press conference in the White House but Nixon did so. He chose the occasion to announce that he would preside in Cabinet meetings and at the meeting of legislative leaders in place of Eisenhower. This was bad enough for the anti-Nixon bloc; but what really infuriated them was that Nixon told newsmen Eisenhower was having difficulty finding words to express himself as a result of his illness. This directly contradicted what Hagerty had been saying, namely, that the President was having difficulty only in pronouncing certain long words.

The White House is not only the most powerful institution in the United States, but one of the most secretive. Few outside its walls knew the struggle for power that went on inside its walls for control over the man who sat upstairs in his bathrobe, palette in hand, recuperating from a stroke.

Hagerty and Adams retaliated against Nixon immediately. Hagerty told newsmen that Eisenhower might go to Paris after all. He even persuaded Eisenhower to preside over the Cabinet meeting and the conference of Congressional leaders. The President talked very slowly at both. He stayed at the meeting of Congressional leaders only a short time. But the White House staff was determined that he stay on the job and fight. It was like the heroic battle of a great, over-age boxing champ, egged on by his managers to go in there and slug it out. The champ had taken three bad falls, but each time the managers were in there splashing water in his face, rubbing his arms, massaging the biceps, telling him he had to get back in the ring.

Twice before, the champ had got up from the mat when he was ill. In one case he had been sent off to Panama almost from his sickbed to prove that he was better. It made no difference that the champ, at Panama, told the President of Brazil, himself a doctor: "I feel sick and tired all the time." The wobbly knees, the tired feeling made no difference. The managers were in there to win. They knew how to drown out the murmurs of protest from the champ. They knew all too well how difficult it was to get the champ to tackle major problems. They'd been with him at Newport when the champ didn't want to tackle Little Rock, when he almost had to be hauled off the golf course to do it. They knew that the champ was finding it difficult to concentrate; they knew the medical history of older people when less blood flows to the brain, how it's difficult for older men to make decisions under stress and strain; and they knew how distressed he had been over the headaches and heartaches of the past year—over Little Rock, the missile failures, the bickering inside his own Cabinet. He had writhed in surprise when his good friend the Secretary of the Treasury, George Humphrey, publicly lambasted his budget. He had been hurt too when Charlie Wilson, visiting the White House to differ with him on the National Guard, told newsmen: "This is not my dunghill." Later Mrs. Wilson slapped the champ hard as only a woman can slap and get away with it.

These things were not what the managers had promised the champ when they urged him, after two bad spills, to stay on in the ring; when they told him they could handle things for him, not to worry.

But once again the managers rushed in with the bucket of water, the quick massage, the megaphone, the statement to the public that everything was fine. And for better or for worse, once again the champ got up off his knees and into the ring again. This time he decided to go to Paris, decided like an old soldier to die, if necessary, with his boots on. It was a heroic gesture. But was it good for the national defense and the safety of the American people?

ii

GRAVITY OF THE CRISIS

WHEN THE AMERICAN PEOPLE first received the news that Russia had developed a long-range ballistic missile and also had launched the first man-made moon into outer space, there was a studied effort to minimize the full impact of the news. "The Administration is not interested in serving a high score in an outer space basketball game," said Assistant to the President Sherman Adams in San Francisco. . . . "We never thought of our program as one which was in a race with the Soviets," explained James C. Hagerty. . . . "The real danger of the Sputnik is that some too eager people may demand hasty and sensational action regardless of cost and relative merit in an attempt to surpass what they have done. Americans must never lose their sense of balance and proportion," cautioned Secretary of the Treasury George M. Humphrey. . . . "Nobody is going to drop anything down on you from a satellite while you are asleep, so don't worry about it," soothed Secretary of Defense Wilson. . . . "There has been no race to launch the satellite between us and the USSR, unless we create one now, which is directly contrary to our policy," opined Republican Senator Jacob L. Javits of New York. . . . "The superiority of the free world is not materially affected by Sputnik, which is a scientific achievement rather than a military one," was the advice of Maxwell M. Rabb, White House aide and secretary of the Cabinet.

Regardless of this steady ooze of soothing syrup, however, two reports prepared by the Rockefeller Brothers Fund and the Ford Foundation after careful study of American defenses showed that the United States was well on the way to becoming a second-class power.

Concluded the Rockefeller report: "It appears that the United States is rapidly losing its lead over the USSR in the military race.

For perhaps the next two years, we still possess a superiority in strategic striking power, and any Soviet attack on us would meet a crushing reply. But our position a year or two hence depends on decisions which must be taken immediately. Unless present trends are reversed, the world balance of power will shift in favor of the Soviet bloc. If that should happen, we are not likely to be given another chance to remedy our failings."

Again, the Rockefeller report found: "The USSR will continue to gain in overall military strength, greatly aided by Communist China and some of its other allies. . . . The economic superiority of the West will become less and less significant militarily at our present levels of effort. Sacrificing the civilian sector of its economy, the Soviet Union has caught up with the United States in major fields of technology. In certain areas assigned high priority by the Kremlin, the Soviet Union has surpassed us qualitatively as well as quantitatively. Unless we greatly increase the pace and level of our military effort, the Soviet Union will achieve superiority in other fields as well."

The second report, prepared under the direction of H. Rowan Gaither of the Ford Foundation, was never made public. It was too frightening. It showed the United States facing the most dangerous peril in all history, cataclysmic catastrophe from push-button ICBMs operated in the Arctic Circle by a nation which in a few short years had miraculously strengthened its economy and its industrial production. This was why the White House asked that only two copies of the report be typed. It did not want extra copies even in confidential circulation. However, 100 copies of the report were typed, and the Gaither Committee did its best in a quiet way to make sure that the general content of its warning was known to key people. A private dinner was even held at the home of William C. Foster, former Under Secretary of Defense, who succeeded Gaither as chairman, for the purpose of discussing the grave situation with Vice-President Nixon and considering the possibility of making the report, at least in general terms, public. The White House, however, was adamant. President Eisenhower sent a firm letter to Senator Lyndon B. Johnson, chairman of the Senate Preparedness Subcommittee, refusing even to let members of Congress see the report.

The authors, however, have seen the essential portions of the Gaither report. It was prepared in the summer of 1957 before Russia launched its first satellite but at a time when American intelligence knew that Russia had made tremendous strides in developing an intercontinental ballistic missile. It showed that Russia was stronger than the United States following our disarmament after V-J Day; that we caught up and jumped ahead of Russia during the Korean War; but that since then we have dropped back. As of the summer of 1957, the report showed, the United States and Russia were about equal. However, the Soviet was forging ahead so rapidly that as of this writing she is ahead of the United States. The Gaither report solemnly warned that the fate of the American people rested almost solely on the Strategic Air Command and that this vital war weapon was so seriously vulnerable to enemy attack that it must be dispersed immediately. It also recommended an enormous increase in military spending, a five-billion-dollar civilian shelter program, a sweeping reorganization of the Pentagon, and an immediate strengthening of our big-bomber method of retaliating against the Soviet—until the United States could catch up with the tremendous Soviet lead in missiles. It recommended increased foreign aid to friendly governments abroad and outlined a five-year program of armament which would cost approximately twenty billion dollars.

Finally, and most awesome of all, the Gaither report suggested, though it did not flatly recommend, that the United States desert its 181-year-old policy of never becoming the aggressor. The weapons of war had become so devastating and the advantages accruing to the nation with one hour's jump so great, the Gaither report said, that the United States should consider taking the initiative. If we waited to be attacked first, most of the major cities of the United States would be wiped out. It was the first time preventive war had ever been seriously advocated by highly responsible persons as a matter of official government policy.

In the Congressional investigations which followed the alarming developments of 1957–58, witness after witness bore out the pessimism of the Gaither and Rockefeller reports. Much of their testimony is still secret. However, the United States has encircled the Soviet Union with the most elaborate series of listening devices ever established to ferret out the developments of another nation. Radar stations in Turkey, Pakistan, and Japan can spot every major missile launching inside the Soviet Union. Airplanes equipped with electronic detection devices have flown over many parts of the satellite nations. Airplanes flying around Soviet borders can and do pick up radioactive dust after any Soviet nuclear explosion and by measuring that dust can ascertain the nature and strength of the bomb that has been detonated.

In this manner and through the Central Intelligence network operated by Allen W. Dulles, brother of the Secretary of State, the United States government has a depressingly accurate knowledge of the full might of Soviet military strength. From these reports, from the Congressional hearings, and from the Gaither and Rockefeller reports, it is possible to summarize the relative military power of the U.S.A. and the U.S.S.R. without any sugar-coating:

The Red Army is ten times the size of that of the United States. Its 175 divisions outclass our seventeen divisions not only in manpower, but in firepower as well. The Russian divisions are highly mobile, armed with rockets, and trained for atomic warfare. They are a match for our much-vaunted Petomic Divisions, which also have been streamlined for atomic warfare. The Red Army relies on helicopters and armored personnel carriers for mobility. It is equipped with fast-moving, self-propelled assault artillery and heavy tanks more rugged than ours.

On the high seas Russia in ten short years has built up the second-largest navy in the world—second only to that of the United States. It now surpasses in size and strength the British Navy, upon whose flag the sun never sets. Although Russia now has a fleet of powerful new cruisers, by all odds the most potent part of her Navy is the submarine, with an estimated undersea fleet which is the largest in naval history. Russia's 600-submarine fleet is ten times greater than that which Hitler used at the start of World War II when his U-boats almost knocked out Allied merchant shipping. Soviet shipyards have been turning out new submarines every three weeks, six for every submarine launched in this country. The known Soviet goal is 1,200 subs.

In contrast, the American Navy has only 110 subs on active duty, another 80 used for training or stored in moth balls. Russia's main submarine weapon is now the stub-nosed supersonic Comet, which can be launched under the ocean for distances up to 700 miles. Significantly, 30 per cent of our key targets in the United States are located within 150 miles of the Atlantic, Pacific, or Gulf coasts. Russian submarines could knock out such cities as Pittsburgh, Birmingham, Cleveland, Akron, Cincinnati, to say nothing of the coastal cities of New York, Philadelphia, Baltimore, Washington, Los Angeles, and San Francisco. The United States in contrast has less than two dozen missile submarines carrying winged Regulus missiles and they must be fired from the surface. Our first sub equipped to fire the 1,200-mile Polaris missile will not be completed until 1960.

The United States today is still ahead of Russia in building atomic submarines, though Naval Intelligence estimates that Russia will have several deep-diving, missile-bristling atomic subs by 1962.

In the air the odds are more nearly even, though the Soviet Union today numerically has the world's largest air force. She has many more combat planes than the United States and her factories are producing them faster. U.S. technical intelligence has made detailed examination of several Soviet planes that have fallen into our hands, and these airplane autopsies show that, while Russian technology lagged behind us from 1945 until 1952, the Russians have equaled our best efforts in air weapons since.

In airplanes that count, Russia has over 13,000 sleek, modern jets assigned to combat units. Our total, counting both Air Force and Navy, adds up to less than 9,500 jets. Russia has more than twice as many intercontinental jet bombers, though we have more medium bombers.

In nuclear power, Russia, whose first atom bomb was four years behind ours, has now practically caught up with us in nuclear firepower. Our stockpile is larger, but Russia has enough bombs to cripple the United States. Although we have reduced the hydrogen bomb to a more compact warhead and designed a so-called "clean" bomb relatively free of radioactive hazard, Russia also has hydrogen warheads and has improved the trigger mechanism for both H- and A-bombs.

Russia is known to be ahead of us in developing an atomic rocket necessary for long-distance space flight. Russia is also completely outdistancing us in building atomic power plants. By 1960 Soviet plants will be producing 2,500,000 kilowatts, American plants only 689,000 kilowatts. The Russian program calls for several small portable atomic plants mounted on caterpillar tractors. These will not only carry precious power into the Siberian hinterlands, but will be used for "peaceful" penetration of undeveloped Asia and Africa.

In the field of missile power, Dr. Wernher von Braun, the German missile expert, warns that it will take us five years to catch up with Soviet missiles. Russia has successfully tested a dozen intercontinental ballistic missiles capable of raining H-bombs on American cities. As of the time when the American people first began to realize their weakened status, the United States had attempted to fire only two ICBMs, both duds.

The Soviet arsenal is bristling with medium-range missles—T-4s which glide on thin wings to targets 1,000 miles away, and T-2s which hurtle like giant artillery shells for distances up to 1,800 miles.

These are pointed right at our overseas bases in Europe, Africa, and Asia and could be launched at the press of a button. In contrast, the United States was still testing medium-range missiles at the time of the Soviet sputnik. Soviet missile production is estimated at about 2,000 per month, with emphasis on two qualities: simplicity and reliability. Our own production figures, which can't be published, are alarmingly lower. The Russians have built a rugged rocket engine with an astounding 820,000-pound thrust. Our largest engine produces only 135,000 pounds thrust.

The Russians have built twenty major missile bases in the Arctic, each with a string of twenty or more launching sites. These are equipped to launch long-range missiles over the North Pole, the shortest route to major American targets. At several sites, the launching equipment is known to be underground. Yet the United States for a long time had only one testing site at Cape Canaveral and it is worthless in hitting Russia. Our first ICBM launching site in Wyoming was not announced until the fall of 1957. The Air Force wanted to build this base underground but it didn't have the money.

Such are the cold facts faced by the American people. Unfortunately they are not the facts which have been given to the American people.

When the Air Force predicted that the United States would produce an ICBM by the end of 1958, Thomas G. Lanphier, Jr., the vice-president of the Convair Division of General Dynamics, which is building the Air Force's ICBM, the Atlas, was more realistic.

"We will have to rely upon conventional forces for the next five years," Lanphier warned. "We will be walking a very tight wire with our lives for the next five years."

During the first week of October 1957, John Foster Dulles had invited Andrei Gromyko, Foreign Minister of Soviet Russia, to visit him privately at the Dulles mansion overlooking Rock Creek. It was the first time the Secretary of State had invited the Foreign Minister of Russia to his home for a personal conference, and Dulles did not know at the time he issued the invitation that momentous events would be happening later in the week.

Mr. Dulles comes from one of the oldest and most renowned law firms on Wall Street, and from one of the oldest diplomatic families in the United States. His grandfather, John W. Foster, was Secretary of State under President Benjamin Harrison, and his uncle, Robert Lansing, was Secretary of State under Woodrow Wilson. Mr. Gromyko had first come to Washington an uncommunicative, un-co-operative, belligerent secretary of the Soviet Embassy on Sixteenth Street. Judging from his dour expression and his public statements, he had never liked the United States, scorned men with such financial and social background as Mr. Dulles.

Those were not easy days for John Foster Dulles. At that very moment, Nikita Khrushchev was threatening to invade Turkey, while Turkey had been making menacing motions in the direction of Syria. The peace which Mr. Dulles had labored so patiently to construct, and which he had boasted about saving after war broke around Suez in 1956, seemed on the verge of going down the drain. So, remembering the criticism leveled at his predecessor, Dean Acheson, that he had not warned the Communist world in advance that the United States would go to war if Korea was attacked, Mr. Dulles decided to give such a warning to the Soviet world in regard to the Near East. This was why he invited Foreign Minister Gromyko to his home in Washington.

When he issued that invitation Mr. Dulles had not the faintest idea that a Soviet sputnik would be launched into the heavens on October 4. He had been warned repeatedly that Russia would launch a satellite and that she was ahead of the United States in preparing a satellite. But Mr. Dulles did not dream that the launching would take place on October 4, one day before his meeting with Gromyko.

The meeting lasted for two and a half hours. Mr. Dulles called attention to Soviet threats in the Near East which he feared might lead to war. He urged the importance of co-operation between the United States and Russia. He emphasized the fact that the American people and the American government devoutly wanted peace. He added that the United States had certain historic interests and a great financial stake in the Near East and had given commitments to some of the governments there. Mr. Dulles had received a report on the Russian timetable for penetrating not merely Syria, but Lebanon, Saudi Arabia, Jordan, and Iraq, until all the vast oil reserves of the Near East—70 per cent of the world's known reserves—were under Communist control. With this in mind, he spoke to Gromyko eloquently and forcefully.

The public never knew the outcome of that personal conference between the foreign ministers of Soviet Russia and the United States. But the diplomats did know. Shortly after returning to New York, Gromyko called a meeting of delegates from Egypt, Syria, Yugoslavia, India, Poland, Czechoslovakia—all friendly to the Soviet Union—and reported on his talk with Dulles. When he told of Dulles' threat to use force to keep the Soviet out of the Near East, he laughed. It was obvious that the Soviet Foreign Minister considered the Eisenhower Doctrine guaranteeing the sovereignty of pro-Western nations in the Near East to be as limp as the mop used on the waxed floors of the Dulles mansion.

Nine months later, and because Mr. Dulles himself realized how limp the Eisenhower Doctrine had become in the eyes of the world, he undertook a desperate move to stiffen it by landing Marines in Lebanon.

The snicker of Andrei Gromyko and the braggadocio of Nikita Khrushchev resulted from just one fact: They had the balance of power, we did not. Mr. Dulles could no longer negotiate from strength. The diplomats of the world knew this, but the American people did not. After spending $99,666,000,000 between 1947 and 1957 reconstructing Europe and revitalizing the two nations which sit astride the entrance to the Black Sea; after training a NATO army for the defense of Europe; after sending technical assistance to almost every corner of the world, the United States faced the possibility that this investment of money and friendship might have been in vain. The reason: The race in power politics goes to the swift and the strong.

The fact that howling mobs in Venezuela almost murdered the Vice-President of the United States; the fact that most of South America has turned against its onetime respected friend in the North; the fact that Generalissimo Franco in Spain began getting restless about American bases; that Premier de Gaulle began flirting with Russia; that British opinion in by-election after by-election has swung away from the United States; that the Scandinavian countries and a growing majority of Germans are skeptical regarding American missile bases; the fact that nation after nation in the Near East, once friendly to us, went over to Nasser—all this did not happen overnight or by accident.

And when, during the Lebanese crisis, Saudi Arabia, which the United States had wooed and courted, would not answer a request to permit American military planes to use the Dhahran Air Force base; when Greece, which we had saved from starvation, demurred at permitting military planes to refuel in Athens; when Austria, which we saved from Soviet clutches, sent jet fighters to keep American transports from flying over a corner of her Tyrol; when Japan, which we reconstructed as an ally, turned against us in the United

Nations; when American diplomats had to twist more arms and collect more due bills than ever before in history to rally United Nations support for our intervention in Lebanon, it was not entirely that these nations disapproved of that intervention. It was also because the world knew, even if the American people did not know, that the United States appeared on the way to becoming a second-class power.

What has been the reason for our downhill skid in power and prestige? The Gaither report puts the blame on bickering between the armed forces. This, of course, was true but it is an understatement. There are many reasons. They go back to the terrorism of the McCarthy era when we drove scientists out of government. They go back to the easygoing complacency of our educational system, our concentration on football and snap courses rather than science, and our failure to pay teachers a living wage. They go back to the passionate budget-cutting of Secretary of the Treasury George Humphrey and his willingness to put a balanced budget ahead of national security. They go back to the scramble for orders by the defense contractors who have almost more influence inside the Pentagon than the President of the United States and who, consciously or unconsciously, have sometimes put profits ahead of patriotism. They also go back to the dangerous American political system of raising tremendous amounts of money to elect candidates and then paying off the contributors with defense contracts. They involve personal jealousy and rivalry of the type that almost prevented Admiral Hyman Rickover from building our first atomic submarine. They involve the genial personality of a Secretary of Defense who wanted to be loved more than he wanted to crack military heads together.

But perhaps as much as any other fact, the reasons why we fell behind Russia go back to the personality of the Commander in Chief. He too wanted to be loved. And during the course of his military career in Europe and his campaigning for the Presidency, he had built up a public love and devotion and prestige that amounted to a father image. Because of that image and because of his long service in the army, the nation trusted him. He could do no wrong. They did not know that he was complacent, easygoing, unwilling to spend the long hours of grueling grind which any President must spend if he is to lead the nation. That Dwight D. Eisenhower was not willing to do these things, that he honestly believed he could serve as a part-time President, that he did not have the courage to deal forcefully with his old buddies in the Pentagon or the budget cutters in the Treasury Department is one of the chief reasons why the United States today finds itself in the gravest danger in all history.

And to the press of the United States, which failed to report both the inadequacies of our national defense and the inadequacy of our Commander in Chief, must go part of the blame.

iii

RED TAPE, RANK AND PROTOCOL

WHEN PRESIDENT EISENHOWER took to television to reassure the American people that the first weird beeps of the Soviet sputnik had not left us too far behind in the great space race, he reported that the Air Force had just launched a rocket from a balloon in the mid-Pacific a probable distance of 4,000 miles into outer space. What he did not tell the people, because he probably did not know, was that this record flight was concocted by three young Americans in a restaurant in Rome; that it was concocted because Russian scientists had drunk and talked too much; and that the flight was almost killed a half-dozen times by red tape, rank and Pentagon protocol before it finally soared from 2,500 to 4,000 miles in the direction of the moon.

The dramatic, inside story of that rocket, officially known as Operation Farside, can now be told for the first time. It is the story of America's first real reach into space, a grab for the stars by scientists who refused to be held down by their superiors. It is also the story of a bumbling general who was more concerned about parking space than outer space, yet who directed the Air Force's vital exploratory research. Most important of all, the story illustrates why the United States has fallen behind Russia in the satellite-missile race and why the nation is in grave danger of becoming a second-class power.

The story begins in the late summer of 1956 in an obscure restaurant in Rome. Three young Americans, pleasantly stuffed with Chianti and calories, were talking earnestly over their coffee. They were intense and subdued. They did not look like the usual Americans enjoying the romantic atmosphere of a Roman evening.

They were rocket scientists who had come to Rome to attend the annual conference of the International Astronautics Congress and a few hours earlier had held a revealing conversation with delegates from the Soviet Union. With that extraordinary frankness of which they are sometimes capable, the Russians had described their plans to take the first great step into space. They had discussed earth-circling satellites with a scientific authority that was convincing.

To the young Americans, intimately concerned with their own space projects and acutely aware of how these were being neglected, the implications were appalling. Unless the United States could head off the Russians and get into space first, they could foresee a catastrophic decline in American prestige and power.

So under the shadow of the Palatine Hill, where Romulus, the son of Mars and founder of Roman armies, was suckled by a she-wolf, they sketched on paper napkins a plan to beat Russia into outer space.

Around them as they planned were the relics of an empire which once ruled the world, whose armies under Scipio Africanus and Julius Caesar had reached out to Egypt and Syria, to Spain and Germany. But the short swords and short spears of Rome's intensively trained infantry had become outmoded, and during the rule of Constantine X historians noted that "the military budget was ruthlessly cut, lack of a profitable career stopped the flow of officers, and the Emperor thought to meet dangers from external enemies by diplomacy." This was one reason for the ruins of ancient Rome.

The three young Air Force experts were not profound historians. Yet something of this historic atmosphere influenced the urgency of the plan which they sketched on napkins in that little restaurant in the shadow of Palatine Hill.

Thus was born Operation Farside, an operation which was to bear fruit one year later and fifteen thousand miles away. If the three Americans had not been slightly flushed with Chianti, if the Russians with whom they fraternized had not been even more flushed, Operation Farside never would have been born. And if a hundred and one other obstacles had not been overcome during the year that followed, President Eisenhower would not have been able to boast on television that the United States had made at least some penetration of outer space.

The three men in Rome knew what some of these obstacles would be and that the most formidable would be money. They also knew that the chief danger to their plans would come not from Soviet agents but from their own superiors, including their own Secretary of Defense "Engine Charlie" Wilson, whose impatience with scientific research had already been proclaimed to Congress with the words "I am not much interested as a military project in why potatoes turn brown when they are fried."

For that reason, the three conspirators took a pledge of absolute secrecy. If they could get their project well started before Pentagon economizers discovered it, they might have a real chance of success.

Farside was a comparatively simple conception. It was based on the fact that the greatest obstacle to rocket flight is air friction. To overcome that obstacle, a plastic balloon was planned which would carry the rocket above the dense atmosphere, above the air friction.

From a precarious perch 100,000 feet high, a rocket could be launched with a minimum of drag, and the trio calculated that a multistage rocket would soar 4,000 miles, perhaps farther, toward the moon. The project's two great advantages were its cheapness and its simplicity. It was cheap because only the balloon would have to be specially made. A multistage rocket could be assembled from Air Force equipment already "on the shelf." This had the additional advantage of being quick. It would reduce the risk of technical delays.

The young scientists had more in mind than a simple space stunt. They hoped to poke a finger of science into space, to sample the strange magnetic tides, meteoric streams and cosmic rays that surge and swirl around the planets. With sensitive, rocket-borne instruments they hoped to explore the invisible trails that future space travelers may some day follow.

Their plan was not entirely new. On previous occasions the three scientists had talked about the theoretical possibility of a balloon-launched rocket. But in Rome they boiled their ideas down to a positive plan and resolved to go ahead with it. They shook hands across the table and shortly returned to the United States to begin their great gamble.

Two of the three conspirators, Colonel William Davis and Dr. Morton Alperin, both of the Air Force Office of Scientific Research, had been classmates at New York University. The third was Dr. Fred Singer, who had fled to the United States after tasting Nazi totalitarianism, graduated from Ohio State University and joined the faculty of the University of Maryland.

Davis and Alperin, the two main conspirators, are a contrasting pair. Davis is a handsome, forceful, articulate combat pilot, a man of action as well as science. Although a nuclear physicist with a Carnegie scholarship at Cambridge University, England, then the Mecca of physics, Colonel Davis flew bombers in World War II. He still sails sloops and drives sports cars as a hobby. At the age of twelve he made up his mind he would command the first space expedition, and he still hasn't given up that dream. Alperin is a scholarly, soft-spoken scientist, most at home in a laboratory, who brings test-tube mannerisms to his desk as director of advanced studies for the Air Force Office of Scientific Research.

Back in the United States, the three dinner companions made their first cautious moves. Alperin, in his Pasadena office, began to fit together a workable blueprint with Singer's technical advice. Davis, at headquarters in Washington, brought his influence to bear on the meager research budget.

First he had to win over his commanding officer, Brigadier General Hollingsworth Gregory, a lean, loose-limbed Southerner whose blanched face and graying, wavy hair gave him a look of fading dignity. Once a crusader in his own right—when he fought the Air Force brass for more helicopters—Gregory had his fingers so badly scorched that much of the fight had gone out of him. In space matters he found it easier to please than to oppose his superiors. He also was a stickler for red tape, spic-and-span floors and the accouterments of high command, which may make for parade-ground precision but not for progress in the scientific race against Russia.

Gregory directed the scientific teams that were doing exploratory research for the Air Force, the pioneers of test tube and slide rule who, in research laboratories around the world, were exploring the frontiers of science. They were looking beyond the present and above the earth, seeking answers that might have special significance for the Air Force. Gregory's office had awarded over seven hundred research contracts to universities, foundations, companies and government agencies throughout the free world.

The bewildered Gregory might have been excused if he felt a little like the football coach who suddenly found himself dean of science. He understood too little of what his scientists were doing to interfere with their work. So he occupied himself making big problems out of the little problems he did understand. He was given to delivering military ultimatums on such subjects as parking space, telephone bills and press releases.

On at least one occasion, Gregory seemed more anxious to pursue a missing can of floor polish than the goals of outer space. He had admired the shine on the floors of a Los Angeles hotel, and the pleased manager had presented him with a sample of the wax. Unfortunately for the peace of the Air Force Office of Scientific Research, the forgetful Gregory left the wax aboard the plane he shared with an Air Force doctor, Brigadier General Donald Flickinger.

Several days passed before Gregory suddenly remembered the wax and sent an aide to retrieve it. "That's an order," the General said sternly, a phrase he frequently used to emphasize important assignments. The unhappy aide, Lieutenant Robert Hill, put in three days of detective duty tracing the can of polish. It had been forwarded mistakenly to General Flickinger, whose floors were already shiny enough to suit him. So, by default, the wax remained in the possession of Flickinger's chauffeur. Lieutenant Hill finally located it on the chauffeur's kitchen floor. It had been spread with professional care and rubbed to a high sheen.

When the aide reported this fact to General Gregory, the General grabbed the phone and called General Flickinger. "Where's my wax?" he bellowed. "What wax?" asked the puzzled Flickinger. Gregory, his voice rising in terrible temper, explained that an aide had shrewdly traced the gift of wax to Flickinger's office. The space surgeon didn't know what he was talking about. Gregory declared the wax was his rightful property and accused Dr. Flickinger of stealing it. The annoyed doctor hung up.

Gregory, left sputtering into a dead phone, summoned an attorney from the Judge Advocate General's office and ordered him to draw up formal charges against Flickinger. The incredulous lawyer tried to dissuade him, but Gregory would not be mollified. He actually started court-martial proceedings. When Flickinger heard about it he threatened, "As staff surgeon, I'll declare Gregory mentally incompetent." This closed the incident. By undeclared truce, Flickinger was spared a criminal record and Gregory retained his legal sanity.

Such were the problems considered more important than beating the Russians into outer space; such were the personalities involved in the effort of three young scientists to launch Operation Farside before Moscow launched its first sputnik.

General Gregory's co-operation was absolutely necessary if Operation Farside were to proceed, and it took all Colonel Davis' enthusiastic salesmanship to persuade the reluctant dragon of

AFOSR to give the green light. To his credit, he finally gave the project his feeble but nonetheless definite blessing.

Beyond General Gregory, Davis and Alperin took elaborate care not to share their confidences with a single soul more than was required by the fact that they were working with government funds on a government project. Every piece of paper concerning Farside was marked "Secret" and carefully guarded. Their fear was not of subversive agents but of their own economy-first superiors in the Pentagon.

Perhaps because of this secrecy they got off to a good start. Aeroneutronics Inc., a Ford Motor Company subsidiary, accepted the prime contract; General Mills of Minneapolis agreed to build the giant balloons. Work began. Davis and Alperin prayed that it would attract no attention. They recognized, of course, that stealth and secrecy could not protect them indefinitely. It was amazing, however, how far three determined young men were able to get inside that vast and inscrutable beehive called the Pentagon without the men at the top, supposed to be running the Defense Department, having any inkling of what they were doing.

Inevitably the leak occurred. It was inevitable because by now contractors were involved, other government agencies had to participate, vouchers had to be signed. The selected launching site, Eniwetok Island in mid-Pacific, for instance, was run by the Atomic Energy Commission, garrisoned by the Army and serviced by the Navy. They had to be let in on what was happening. Thus it was that news of Operation Farside got to the press, and through the press to the top man in the Pentagon.

Charles E. Wilson, Secretary of Defense, read the news at breakfast one morning and it nearly ruined his digestion. It didn't help his digestion that the story was more glamorous than the facts warranted. The name Farside, for instance, was interpreted as signifying an attempt to explore the mysteries of the moon's unseen side.

To Secretary Wilson, this smacked of rank mutiny. He had already rapped one AFOSR project, the regeneration of air in confined areas such as spaceship cabins. Now, he fumed, the incorrigible eggheads were at it again. His reaction was immediate. He decreed that the Air Force was not in the business of flying to the moon and arbitrarily lopped $50,000,000 off the Research and Development budget.

The three young men got a hurry-up call that "Charlie wants to know all about Farside." Actually, they never saw "Charlie," never had occasion to justify their dream to him. Actually, there was some doubt that Operation Farside was specifically canceled by Wilson. But in any event, the Air Force brass, subservient to the Secretary's wrath, scratched the offending project off their list. The Farside budget amounted to a mere one per cent of the $50,000,000 slash. But at AFOSR headquarters, General Gregory wrung his hands. To him this was the end. To Colonel Davis, however, it was the beginning. Hurrying to the Pentagon, he cornered Richard E. Horner, Assistant Air Force Secretary in charge of research, and made such a good case that Horner, sticking out his own neck a giraffe's length, ordered the project continued. He agreed to take full responsibility with "Charlie."

Horner's courage was not shared, however, by the Air Force brass. Mindful of Wilson's crack about the moon and anxious not to invite any more financial retaliation, they put a gag on space talk. On July 29, 1957, teletyped orders went to all commands:

"For all Commanders: Recent news stories which described certain Air Force Research and Development projects as space flight projects have resulted in unfavorable reaction at Air Force and Department of Defense. It is suggested that any speeches or public releases planned by you or your staff avoid mention or discussion of space, space technology and space vehicles. No statements can be made which might in any way cause the national news media to describe valid Air Force projects as efforts to 'fly to the Moon.'"

The real target of this guided missive, of course, was AFOSR. With a staff of fewer than 150 people and a budget barely large enough to buy two $8,000,000 B-52 bombers, the Office of Scientific Research was low man on the Air Force totem pole, and there were some Pentagonians who would have been happy to crowd it off the totem pole altogether.

Farside, now on famine rations, began to falter dangerously. It probably would have foundered except for the financial backing of the prime contractor, Aeroneutronics Inc. Dr. Joe Karsch, the company's project director, saw the value of the project both to the country and to his company. He got permission from Ford, the parent company, to go fifty-fifty with AFOSR on further financing. If it had not been for Ford's foresight in becoming a partner of the government, Operation Farside never would have got off the ground.

By the end of June, General Mills delivered the first giant balloon, and the Farside crew prepared to test their theory. They knew the balloon would become brittle and burst at 68 degrees below zero.

They also knew the balloon would have to pass through temperatures ranging from 78 to 85 degrees below zero. The air gets colder up to a point known as the tropopause. This is the name given to the dividing line which separates the troposphere from the stratosphere at about 50,000 feet above the earth. On both sides of this dividing line, the temperatures would be below the balloon's freezing point. But just as the temperature would drop as the balloon approached the tropopause, the air would gradually warm up after the balloon crossed into the stratosphere. The danger zone would extend for several thousand feet on both sides of the tropopause. The Air Force scientists hopefully calculated that the balloon would retain enough heat from the lower, warmer air to get safely through this cold zone.

The Farside crew made prayerful preparations for the crucial test. They poured iron filings into an empty rocket chamber until the scales registered over 2,300 pounds, the calculated weight of the equipment that would be hauled aloft at Eniwetok. Then they pumped helium into the mammoth balloon and watched it float gently upward. In addition to the dummy rocket, the balloon carried instruments which reported its progress as it passed slowly, safely through the cold zone and soared to a record altitude of 104,000 feet. The crew was elated.

But their elation turned to gloom in September when, even as the first Farside tests began at Eniwetok, Colonel Davis was suddenly and ignominiously transferred to an inappropriate post at Wright Field, Dayton, Ohio. In his tenacious pursuit of the stars of space, Davis had offended men who wore stars on their shoulders. Was this their revenge against him?

We have never been able to get a satisfactory answer. The Air Force offered only the bleak explanation that the transfer of officers was routine. That the right man had been removed from the right job at the wrong time made no sense whatsoever. But it was "policy," which to many military minds is ample excuse for the worst blunder. In this case, "policy" finally forced the brilliant but discouraged Colonel Davis to resign from the service.

However, he had not been bucking the top brass in vain. Though he was not present to witness it, the late summer of 1957 saw six balloon and rocket assemblies—all that the available money would buy—on their way to Eniwetok. Alperin was on hand and for him it was a time of tension. Looking at his six assemblies and adding up the odds against him, he must have groaned. If any one of them was lost, damaged or destroyed—whether by accident on the ground or by conditions in the air—it meant one less chance of beating the Russians into space.

By this time the weather, not the Pentagon, was the chief enemy. Conditions had to be precisely perfect. The wind had to be under ten knots and from the correct quarter. A stronger wind would drag the rocket gear along the ground and make it impossible to launch the giant balloons. A gentler wind from the wrong direction would send the rocket gear crashing into Eniwetok's housing facilities. Alperin also knew that a mile over his head the trade winds were howling and that they would descend at a rate of a few feet each day until they reached the surface. This would make the launching of Operation Farside completely impossible until another year rolled around. By that time, Russia would be in outer space. In this atmosphere of mingled hope and desperation, the first American attempt to penetrate outer space began.

That first attempt met with failure. The balloon, pumped full of helium gas, was launched from a truck. In a cradle hung under the balloon was the rocket, to be launched by radio when the balloon reached an altitude of 100,000 feet. The balloon sailed up a few thousand feet, then, for reasons nobody could ascertain, slowly descended. It was swallowed up by the Pacific.

The second attempt was made October 4, even as Soviet scientists on the lonely steppes of central Russia were launching their first sputnik. The American balloon rose to 90,000 feet before it started to drop. As it settled down to 70,000 feet, the ground officer desperately pressed the firing button and the rocket leaped into space. But by this time the balloon had started to collapse, and the rocket, piercing through the collapsing balloon, broke off its instrument head. This hurtled on for 370 miles, a small abortive satellite sending signals to the ground. What happened to the rocket is not known, but it may still be out there somewhere in outer space.

By now, the whole world was hailing the pronged metal ball that Russia had sent spinning into space. Its weird beep-beeps, as if from an alarm clock in space, woke up the Pentagon. Suddenly Operation Farside, a white elephant nobody wanted, became the white hope of the nation. Urgent messages were flashed to Alperin, urging him to get a rocket up somehow, some way, as some sort of answer to the Russians.

With the score two down and four to go, Alperin hurried preparations for the third test. The sputnik had been whirling around the world for two days when another balloon rose over Eniwetok. At

60,000 feet, a short in the firing mechanism triggered the rocket prematurely. Rocket number three sprang into space as if eager to chase the sputnik, but the instrument head was damaged and never let out a bleat.

Balloon number four never made it through the cold layer on each side of the tropopause. The other balloons had survived the frigid temperatures, but number four didn't get past 56,500 feet. It froze solid like a great, fragile light bulb and shattered into millions of tiny plastic flakes which floated down on the tropical ocean like a strange, glittering snowstorm. Four down and two to go.

At this point, Colonel Eugene LaVier arrived at Eniwetok to replace Colonel Davis. LaVier, an able physicist, tried to be helpful. But it was impossible for him not to appear in the role of the man from headquarters, dispatched posthaste to find out what was wrong and put it right. That his presence did not produce a disastrous decline in morale was due largely to the determination and vision of the scholarly Alperin.

With LaVier watching over Alperin's shoulder, balloon number five was launched on October 19. It ascended slowly and dramatically to 96,500 feet, carrying Alperin's hopes with it. The rocket firing button was pressed just as the balloon, like a distant blob of filmy white protoplasm, passed behind a stratocloud. But once again, the instrument head, fired from the balloon's basket below the balloon's bag, caught on the rigging overhead and was damaged. After transmitting only four-tenths of a second, the mute rocket soared into space. How far can only be guessed.

There remained just one assembly—one more balloon, one more rocket, one more chance to answer the sputnik. After months of planning, months of secrecy, months of bucking the top brass, after traveling seven thousand miles to the mid-Pacific, the Farside team had only one balloon with which to carry out the dream etched on paper napkins in a restaurant in Rome the summer before.

Not only was there only one of the balloon-rocket assemblies left, but the weather was turning against them. The trade winds were falling closer and closer to earth.

Desperately anxious that this last try succeed, the scientific team racked their brains to figure what they had done wrong. They concluded that the rocket cradle should be tipped slightly for the final try. This would keep the rocket from tangling with the apparatus hung under the balloon but immediately above the launching basket.

It now remained for Lieutenant Colonel Robert Bugard and Commander Jack Masterson to scare up some favorable weather. Everything focused on them. Bugard and Masterson are two of the most skilled weathermen in the business. But they couldn't manufacture the weather; they could only observe it. The next two evenings they came up with the doleful report, "Sorry boys, no luck for tomorrow."

The weather necessary for that one last try was a combination of wind from approximately 110 degrees blowing at less than ten knots. Finally on the night of October 21, Bugard and Masterson stuck a pinwheel on the bulletin board and wrote the figures 110-5 all around the circumference.

"Just spin the wheel," they said, "and you'll get tomorrow's weather."

It was their way of announcing the good news that the weather next day would be perfect. Wherever the pinwheel stopped it would be at 110-5—in other words, wind from 110 degrees on the compass blowing at five knots.

That last balloon, that last rocket, that last chance to catch up, in part, with Sputnik were launched early the next morning. The silvery plastic balloon, shimmering in the sunlight, climbed up and up, carrying enough heat to get through the subzero temperatures of the troposphere and the early stratosphere until it reached an altitude of 96,500 feet. From there the gleaming yellow rocket climbed into space in four mighty spurts, like a sunbeam returning home.

It transmitted radio signals for eight minutes before they faded. The sensitive ground instruments, straining for sounds, picked up another faint signal after forty-five minutes. The scientists were convinced it was Farside's distant voice, but there was a bare possibility it could have been caused by cosmic conditions. After analyzing the recorded signals, the scientists concluded that the rocket had penetrated at least 2,500 miles, probably 4,000 miles and perhaps much farther into space. Later President Eisenhower, grasping for straws of American space achievement, used the 4,000-mile figure. Whatever the correct mileage, it was at the time a distance record.

Back in Washington, the Air Force called a press conference to boast of the achievements of its once-scorned project. Two latecomers, Colonel Eugene LaVier and Colonel William Bowers, met the press. There were all the trimmings—floodlights, microphones, TV cameras, popping flashbulbs. But the men who could have told the whole story were not present. The three young scientists who, flushed with Chianti and worried over Russian confessions, had dreamed the fantastic operation in an Italian restaurant, were not invited to the celebration.

Scientifically, Operation Farside was a disappointment. The eight minutes of clear radio signals did not produce much new knowledge about outer space. The Air Force collected valuable data about the performance of balloons at high altitudes and the launching of rockets above the atmosphere. But the real triumph was more psychological than scientific. As the three scientists had foreseen, Farside was important to show the world that America also had a finger in space.

The tragedy is that the lesson has not penetrated the Administration as successfully as the rocket penetrated outer space. A few weeks later, Secretary of State John Foster Dulles shrugged off the importance of beating Russia to the moon. "I don't know what it is going to cost to get to the moon, or whether it is possible for us to beat the Russians at it," he told the House Foreign Affairs Committee. "How much we want to spend in an effort to be second, I don't know."

Thus, the same troubles which bedeviled Operation Farside continue to bedevil this nation's space projects. Whereas the Kremlin has relaxed its tyranny to spur its men on, in this free country a tyranny of rank and protocol, of red tape and budget worship holds its best men back. It's a tyranny of laziness, ignorance and complacency in high places; of political opportunism and cynicism; a tyranny which places vote-getting above national security. It's one reason why the United States is on the way to becoming a second-class power.

iv

THE AMERICAN MAGINOT LINE

The Maginot Line, erected in the 1930s to protect France from German attack, extended from the Swiss border to Belgium. The American Maginot Line, erected in the 1950s to protect the West from Soviet attack, extends from the deserts of North Africa to the icecaps of Greenland. Its construction cost billions in money and even more in man's ingenuity, sweat, and blood. Unlike the massive French fortress of concrete with its maze of secret caves, tunnels, and gun emplacements, the American Maginot Line is largely in the air. It has been kept highly mobile. Hitler's armies laughed at the Maginot Line as they skirted round it. They laughed because the Maginot Line could not be moved.

The American Maginot Line can be moved. But is it any more effective? Will Soviet missile bases in Albania make it just as ineffectual as the Maginot Line of France? Will Soviet missiles launched from submarines in the Mediterranean make it, too, the laughingstock of the world? Will it, meanwhile, give the American people the same false sense of security that the Maginot Line gave to France, that the Great Wall gave to the people of China?

If you visit segments of the American Maginot Line you get the impression of intense and efficient activity. In the early, murky mornings at Wheelus Air Force Base in Tripoli, fighter planes roar over your barracks. The barracks tremble as jet after jet takes off over the Mediterranean on the alert for enemy planes, or to drop live bombs on a make-believe enemy over the Libyan desert. Jet pilots, dozing or playing cards alongside their planes, suddenly spring to life, slide down a pole, clamp on their helmets, are strapped into cockpits, and shoot out of the hangar in less than three minutes to meet a simulated enemy.

Or fly up to Thule, Greenland, northernmost extremity of our

Maginot Line, 700 miles from the North Pole, nearer Leningrad than Washington. For hours you are alone in the Arctic night, nothing but ice below, ice floes, icebergs, ice mountains. They are beautiful in the moonlight, cruel in the moonlight—no place to land, not a single light, not a single sign of human habitation.

Then suddenly in the moonlight an F-86 comes out of nowhere and pulls alongside the wing of your plane in an eerie demand to know who you are, whether friend or enemy has dared encroach on this strategic end of the American Maginot Line at the top of the world.

Spread out below, a few minutes later, are a thousand lights—not the aurora borealis, but the lights of man, a city that grew out of nowhere, a city without trees or vegetation, where man had never lived, where wolves howled and bears fished, but where today the lights of a modern aluminum city built on stilts mark one of the miracles of man.

It is impossible for anyone sitting warm and comfortable in his home in Brooklyn or Chicago to realize what infinite expense and infinite care have gone into the construction of the American Maginot Line. Half a dozen power plants light up the never-ending Arctic night for the six thousand men and three women at Thule Air Force Base. During the summer when the sea is open enough oil has been shipped in to last several years in case of war. Every gallon of water is hauled by truck because pipes freeze unless buried more than a hundred feet in the ground. A million truck miles a year are necessary to haul water to Thule, and almost as many to haul the sewage out.

There is nothing simple about the American Maginot Line. It is the most complex, most far-flung piece of defense mechanism ever devised by man. A few hundred miles south of Thule stretches another segment, the DEW line (Distant Early Warning system), 3,000 miles from Baffin's Bay to Cape Liburne on the tip end of northern Alaska—a line of men sitting in the snow watching the skies. They are trained technicians, radar experts, telephone men, paid up to $14,000 a year to sit in the Arctic. They sit in darkened rooms watching the skies through radarscopes which, far better than man's eye, scan the Arctic horizon all the way to Greenland. This network is linked with other observer networks and with Air Force headquarters by a complicated electronic telephone mechanism constructed at a cost of $2,400,000,000 by American Telephone and Telegraph. Operating almost faster than man can think, it puts the whole radar communications network on a sort of dial system. It can sort out all the radar blips on the radarscope, supply instantaneous information as to which are scheduled, which are unidentified. Then in split seconds it can put the whole intricate defense machinery of the Arctic Maginot Line in high gear.

Several hundred miles south, across Canada, extends the second line of Arctic watchers—the mid-Canada line. Below that, the Pine Tree line runs parallel to the American-Canadian border, from Maine to British Columbia, ready to guide the fighters and bombers of the American Maginot Line should an enemy attack. Out at sea, a fleet of Navy destroyers cruises constantly; another fleet of Navy Constellations patrols back and forth along the coast; hunter-killer submarines, a member of the crew listening twenty-four hours a day to the ships' sonar, lie off the Atlantic Coast; Navy blimps join the lookout; off Cape Cod, Texas towers house lonely men who sit as the waves lash the underpinnings of their man-made islands and watch the skies for an enemy approach.

All this is part of the American Maginot Line.

A more destructive part, calculated to deter the enemy, sits at bases in Labrador, Newfoundland, Maine, Nebraska, Louisiana—big bombers of the Strategic Air Command, also on the alert to carry the offensive to Moscow, Leningrad, and Odessa. Instead of secret passageways burrowing through blocks of concrete through which French artillerymen passed to fire their guns, the American Maginot Line is connected by an intricate communications system, no part of which must be out of gear. Snowed in at Harmon Air Force Base at Newfoundland one Christmas one of the authors watched the Base Commander sweat over orders from General Curtis E. LeMay, SAC Commander in Omaha, to get Harmon runways free of snow and do it fast. Sanding the runways would mean that pebbles might be sucked into jet engines and put three million dollars' worth of airplanes out of commission at one whack. Bulldozing the runways to remove the snow takes hours; yet that SAC runway at Harmon is vital. It has to be kept open in case the men sitting on the DEW line, or the men watching from Thule, or the men patrolling the seas in Super Constellations should give the word that the fatal day had arrived.

So operates the far-flung American Maginot line.

Great diplomatic shrewdness and considerable sacrifice by the taxpayer went into the acquisition of the bases which make up the

American Maginot Line. It has been necessary to negotiate special agreements to buy fish from Iceland; it has required several billion dollars of aid to Turkey and Greece, great diplomatic finesse plus the Marshall Plan in Italy, and a whole series of bizarre incidents with General Francisco Franco, the dictator of Spain.

Unlike some of the other governments of Western Europe, which didn't enthuse over American bases, Dictator Franco yearned for them. He yearned for them so badly that he hired as his Washington lobbyist Charles Patrick Clark, onetime minor bureaucrat on the Senate investigating committee which first catapulted Harry Truman to public attention, who had received from Truman an autographed photo which he, Clark, displayed on his office wall as evidence that he was on intimate terms with the man who became President. Charles Patrick Clark was paid $100,000 a year by Franco to try to get Spain in on Marshall Plan–American-base gravy. Franco paid high because he was in desperate need of American dollars. His economy was slipping. His people were restless. If he did not get Americans busy building bases in Spain with an accompanying golden stream of dollars, Franco faced revolution.

President Truman and his Secretary of State, Dean Acheson, however, did not look with favor on aid to Spain. They did not look with favor first because both had a deep-seated aversion to dictatorship; second, because our allies in London and Paris were dead opposed to Franco. Nevertheless, a Congress which preached economy and which was highly critical of sending the taxpayers' money to foreign countries proceeded to appropriate a total of $187,500,000 for Franco in 1950–52. The White House and the State Department argued that this money was not necessary; so in the end they spent only $59,800,000 out of the $187,500,000 appropriated. Yet Congress, while trying to cut down on money for other friendly governments, continued to appropriate more money for Franco. All of which led to the creation of one of our most politically uncertain segments of the far-flung American Maginot Line.

The political miracle whereby Congress appropriated money which was unwanted and unwarranted was performed through the pure and simple expedient of lobbying. Lobbyist Clark, with Max Truitt, son-in-law of Vice-President Barkley, also retained by Franco, proved themselves more effective than the President and his Secretary of State. Franco also had the support of Senator Owen Brewster of Maine, astute and able chief money-raiser for the re-election of Republican senators; and of Senator Pat McCarran of

Nevada, who was determined that a group of Germans should get contracts to build bases in Spain. McCarran even got the Spanish Minister of Public Works, Conde Vallellano, on the transatlantic telephone, and according to the secret recording made by U.S. Intelligence, the following conversation took place:

OPERATOR: I have Conde Vallellano on the line. He does not speak English.

MCCARRAN: I have an interpreter here.

OPERATOR: Conde Vallellano is ready now.

MCCARRAN: As you know, I have always been a champion of Spanish causes in this country. I would like to have my mind so clear as to be able within my own conscience to make decisions most advantageous, both to my country and to yours.

VALLELLANO: It is a great honor that you should take the trouble to telephone me, and I appreciate your sentiments greatly, as all Spaniards appreciate them.

MCCARRAN: What I would like to bring up is the question of building military bases in Spain. I know of various plans which offer great advantages. The one that appeals most to me proposes that wherever necessary, Spanish construction capacity should be supplemented by West German technicians and facilities.

VALLELLANO: I personally am of the same opinion as the Senator that Germans should be used in the construction of these bases. I am familiar with this idea of using Germans. Many of the details of such a program have already been furnished to me. Of necessity, it must be received by me and by Spaniards with the utmost sympathetic and favorable consideration.

MCCARRAN: I wish to receive an opinion from some high Spanish officials to guide my thinking.

VALLELLANO: I can state that I know of no objection of any kind to such a procedure.

What McCarran did not tell the Spanish Cabinet officer was that the German contractors had agreed to reach all the way to Nevada to buy their heavy machinery—to the Reno office of Wells Fargo, a group with which the Senator had the most intimate relations. This was one reason he summoned first Herbert E. Gaston, head of the Export-Import Bank, later Assistant Secretary of State Livingston T. Merchant, to demand more money for Spain.

In the end, McCarran got the Grand Cross of Isabella the Catholic from Dictator Franco. What he got from the Germans is not known. But the United States got a segment of the American Maginot Line without any commitment whatsoever that it could be used in war, without any commitment that Spain would fight on the side of the United States in case of war, without any guarantee that the U.S. Navy and Air Force would not be thrown out of Spain after expiration of the ten-year lease.

This unprecedented contract was not signed, however, until after one of the most extraordinary lobbying jobs ever seen in Washington. An instrument in the job was Congressman Eugene J. Keogh of Brooklyn, who, after eleven humdrum years in the House of Representatives during which he took no interest in Spain, suddenly became the great champion of Dictator Franco. Keogh littered the *Congressional Record* with statements and editorials favorable to Spain. He interrupted Congressional debates to defend Spain. He offered an amendment to include Spain in Marshall Plan generosity.

This began in 1949. It was in that same year that Congressman Keogh was seen frequently in the company of Franco's lobbyist, Charles Patrick Clark. On October 8, 1949, Congressman Keogh paid a visit to Dictator Franco in Madrid in company with Clark and Senator Brewster; and while traveling on a Spanish train, Congressman Keogh hung his pants too near the window of his sleeping car and, according to Spanish newspapers, lost $5,000. That much cash is not normally carried by tourists in foreign countries. They use traveler's checks. Congressman Keogh has never adequately explained where the cash came from.

Nor has he adequately explained the fact that in March 1950 he began receiving a series of checks from lobbyist Clark. The checks were listed as payments by Clark for legal advice on a tax case which the federal government had brought against Silas E. Chambers of Miami. The first check, dated March 6, 1950, was for $1,500; another, on March 24, 1950, for $1,000; April 5, $500; May 3, $500; and June 15, $1,000. As a member of Congress, Keogh had no business accepting a law fee in connection with a tax case. Such law practice against the federal government by a member of Congress is illegal. And some months later when the receipt of these checks was reported to the Justice Department, Congressman Keogh wrote a letter to lobbyist Clark dated October 31, 1950, abruptly withdrawing from the tax case. He did not, however, return the money.

Then there was the case of Senator Brewster's gin-rummy game.

It took place in April 1950, just as the Spanish lobby staged its first big drive to include Spain in the Marshall Plan, and coincided with the exact time lobbyist Clark began paying Congressman Keogh checks averaging about $1,000 a month.

On April 25, 1950, the Spanish Embassy sent Clark a check for $5,000 to cover "expenses." On the same day, April 25, Clark wrote a check for $1,000 made out to cash and asked his secretary to cash it at the Mayflower Hotel in $100 bills. Clark told his secretary that he had a date that evening to play gin rummy with Senator Brewster. He also remarked, "Hurry up and get that check cashed or Brewster will be hopping mad." He did not say that he was paying Brewster the thousand dollars. Possibly he meant he would arouse Brewster's ire if he were late to the gin-rummy game.

Clark had instructed his secretary to cash the check in $100 bills. She could not get that denomination at the hotel and had to take tens and twenties.

Two days later, April 27, Senator Brewster introduced an amendment to the Marshall Plan appropriation to include Spain. He made the motion on the Senate floor, delivered a speech supporting it, and then entered into the debate which followed. Near the conclusion of the debate Senator Brewster asked permission for an additional two minutes to speak in support of the Spanish amendment and was given the time. The Senate, however, voted him down 42–35. But four months later, after continued efforts by Keogh, Senator McCarran, Max Truitt, and Clark, the Senate finally tacked a rider on an appropriation bill okaying $62,500,000 for Spain through the Export-Import Bank.

Thus did the United States lay the first foundation for one segment of the American Maginot Line.

Ironically, after Franco received American bases, following the most amazing lobbying operation which a foreign government ever put across in Washington, he was the first to threaten a walkout. Less than a week after the first Russian sputnik was launched in October 1957 and it became well known that Russia was developing a long-range ballistic missile, Franco began badgering American representatives about the withdrawal of American bases—unless we could defend them against the Russian ICBM, or unless more American aid was forthcoming.

The Spaniard who had always considered "Red" a dirty word suddenly began flirting with the Communist bloc. He dickered with Czechoslovakia regarding trade and began angling for closer relations with East Germany. His moves so alarmed Washington that John Foster Dulles, en route home from the NATO Paris meeting in December 1957, went out of his way to stop in Madrid—officially for the purpose of informing Franco on what had happened at Paris, actually to keep the wavering dictator in line. Franco finally made it clear that the American multimillion-dollar investment in Spain, made because of his own lobbying, might remain there—if the United States would raise the ante. He suggested as a starter that we double economic aid.

Other segments of the American Maginot Line may rest on the summer-melting icecap of Greenland, but they rest on firmer political relations. They were not foisted on an unwilling White House by Congress. They were sought after frantically by the Truman Administration, most of them as the terrific onslaught of Russian-armed Chinese Communists in Korea raised fears that Moscow was planning to move in on the Mediterranean and Europe. Today they are not only amazing American oases on the edge of the Sahara Desert and unique aluminum cities on the ice of the Arctic, they are also for the most part modern miracles in human relations. Base commanders drill their men in the technique of getting along with the people of Morocco, Libya, Turkey, Italy, France, Germany, England. On the whole they do well.

Greatest wrecker of American friendship is the American automobile. Driven sometimes at breakneck speed by American GIs along roads crowded with donkeys and camels, women with water jugs on their heads, people whose ears and reflexes do not respond to klaxons, fatalities are inevitable. At one time in Athens, American relations were so strained that it was a question of either curtailing traffic accidents or giving up American bases in Greece. The Air Force finally imported Colonel William Allen, native of another Athens—Athens, Georgia—whose heroic measures stopped automobile accidents almost overnight.

In Morocco every airman under twenty-five is required to take a compulsory driver-improvement course every Saturday for three weeks—a total of ten hours' driver-training. There are also courses in the language of the country, and special courses in English, safety, and technical skills for native personnel employed on each base. A Moroccan or Libyan can work for eighteen months in an American machine shop and graduate a skilled mechanic.

The American soldier's ability to adjust himself to his surroundings is just as much a miracle as the construction of these American cities on deserts and icecaps. In Africa, three to five thousand miles from Washington or Wichita, Shreveport or San Bernardino, you will see basketball and baseball games played with just as much enthusiasm as in the United States and with the same league competition between different air bases. You will see men studying for high-school diplomas and university degrees thousands of miles away from their prospective alma maters. You will see touch football, tennis, swimming, soccer, and at Christmastime as you walk down the main street of Wheelus Air Base in Tripoli, you will see each barracks competing for the best Christmas decoration as avidly as, and sometimes more effectively than, any community back home; while over the maintenance shop at Nouasseur Air Base in Morocco you will see Rudolf the Red-nosed Reindeer picked up by an Air Force wrecker-truck which has rescued Santa Claus and is towing his sleigh against the desert skyline in a display as dazzling as any electrical extravaganza illuminating Times Square.

All this is part of the American Maginot Line.

Also a part of the Maginot Line are such Madison Avenue gimmicks as the American tour of King Mohammed the Fifth of Morocco, accompanied by twelve Moroccan newspapermen who cabled thousands of inches of space to Moroccan newspapers telling about the wonders of Washington, New York, and Los Angeles; also the visit of the Crown Prince of Morocco to the U.S.S. *Forrestal* to witness the amazing efficiency of American jet planes as they land on and take off from a giant airplane carrier; also the opening up of American bases to native visitors to learn that American military men can be as proficient at hospitality as at dropping hydrogen bombs.

But while men work at influencing friends and winning natives, there are lined up on the runway at Sidi Slimane, Morocco, two dozen sleek, speedy, wind-swept B-47s, each loaded with a hydrogen bomb. They are poised and ready to take off. Destination: Moscow. Flying at a speed of 600 miles an hour, Moscow is just four hours away. This is what our Moroccan bases are really for, and this is the most important part of the American Maginot Line.

In November 1957 General Thomas S. Power, Chief of the Strategic Air Command, announced in Paris that since October 1 the Air Force had had giant bombers loaded with hydrogen bombs on a twenty-four-hour alert, ready in fifteen minutes to take off toward enemy targets in case of war. General Power did not specify where these planes were, but he was referring to Sidi Slimane, the 8,000-

acre American oasis between Rabat and the foothills of the Atlas Mountains where B-47 bombing crews go about their business as if nothing were happening, with one ear always listening for the klaxon alarm which could send them speeding toward "the target." There are thirty-eight klaxons on the base. There are three men in each B-47 crew. Each crew has a jeep. They must stick together with that jeep ready to rush to their plane. If one goes to call on his girl friend, the other two go with him. They must be ready night and day for the sound of those klaxons.

An armed Air Force policeman stands beside each B-47 on the runway, and even Base Commander Colonel John Kunkel of Indianapolis had to show his identification before the guard would let him crawl up into the cramped cockpit of a giant bomber. Only a few feet away in another compartment of the plane was the hydrogen bomb containing more explosive power than all the bombs, all the artillery shells, all the other firepower detonated in all of World War II. Every minute of the day one or more of these bombs is in the air ready for eventualities. Every minute of the night and day these B-47s are lined up on the runways of Morocco ready to strike.

This is the most deadly, most destructive segment of the American Maginot Line.

When the Great Wall of China was constructed along the Manchurian border north of Peking, historians record, it lulled the people of China into a false sense of security. And when the city of Peking finally fell, it was the rocket, first forerunner of the modern missile, which finally subdued that mighty fortress.

Today it is Russian missiles which can make the most modern and ramified defense system ever conceived by man just as out-of-date as the Great Wall of China.

Wheelus Air Force Base in Libya is the biggest American air base in the world outside the United States. But it could be wiped out in just a few minutes. It could be wiped out not by an air attack, as the Japanese attacked Pearl Harbor, but by intermediate-range missiles based just behind the Iron Curtain in Bulgaria.

Russia has the missiles and she has the bases. While the United States argued as to which missiles to build and who should build them, the Soviet proceeded to turn out several thousand ballistic missiles with a range of 1,000 to 1,800 miles. Carrying, as they do, hydrogen warheads, one missile could wipe out an entire base. And Russia has enough missiles to fire more than one missile at each base.

There is nothing the lonely watchers in the Arctic DEW Line can do to warn of missile attacks. Their approach is too fast. The elaborate machinery, the intricate electronic equipment, the phone lines, the snowbank houses of the northern Maginot Line costing a total of $18,000,000,000, all are now mere monuments to our frantic, futile search for safety.

Nothing the heroic Air Force pilots who scramble into their jets every dawn could do would save Wheelus. Nothing the 7,000 airmen who dutifully go about their job of supporting a little piece of America in North Africa could do would save Wheelus. Its wooden barracks and concrete installations, its hangars and its gas tanks, its theaters and its churches, its officers' club with the bougainvillaea climbing over the veranda, its neat rows of married men's quarters with gay marigolds in front and children's perambulators on the back porch—all would go up in a pillar of smoke over the desert.

This is a desert where fifteen years ago a German general named Rommel wheeled and maneuvered. For months he dodged, ducked, and eluded the British. But even in the brief period since then, warfare has changed. In this same desert, a whole tank corps once could hide. But not any more. The ancient rocket which once humbled the Great Wall of China and the city of Peking has come back, sleek, modernized, armed with a hydrogen warhead, to revolutionize military power and make obsolete the American Maginot Line.

The water of the Mediterranean is blue and beautiful along the North African coast. Men swim along the beaches—when they can duck modern man's habit of fouling his nest with his own sewage. But blue and beautiful as that water is, it harbors the possibility of even greater danger than the IRBM—namely, Russian submarines. It is only about a hundred feet from the sea to the home of the commander of Wheelus Air Base. The entire base is built along the sea. One missile from a submarine lying low in the blue and beautiful Mediterranean could knock Wheelus out. The sub wouldn't even have to surface. And it wouldn't have to come all the way from Russian waters. As Harry Truman remarked, "For two hundred years the Czars wanted to penetrate down through the Bosporus to the Mediterranean, but failed. Today the leaders of the Kremlin have three submarine bases in the Mediterranean—one in Albania, one in Syria, and one in Egypt. Stalin must be laughing in his grave."

Further west in Morocco, our big bomber bases at Sidi Slimane are 2,000 miles away from the Iron Curtain and out of range of Russian IRBMs. But feverishly in the little country of Albania the

Kremlin is constructing three huge missile bases—launching sites for new IRBMs to be aimed squarely at Sidi Slimane and the row of sleek wind-swept B-47s lined up on the runway, each guarded by an air policeman with cocked revolver and each carrying a hydrogen bomb the equivalent of all the explosives dropped in World War II. When those Albanian bases are finished, when those new IRBMs are installed, those B-47s will not be able to remain on the runway any more.

When the Russian sputnik was first launched on October 4, 1957, and when the first dread news seeped in on the American public that Russia had developed an intercontinental ballistic missile, President Eisenhower took pains to emphasize the importance of our Strategic Air Command and the ring of bases surrounding Russia which make up the American Maginot Line. His was a public statement.

But privately General Thomas D. White, Chief of Staff of the Air Force, simultaneously warned Secretary of Defense McElroy that our Strategic Air Command was falling apart. He predicted Russia would surpass us in strategic bombing power by the end of 1958. He begged for more big bombers until such time as American ballistic missiles would be in production. Secretary McElroy gave him the alternative of fifty-two more B-52s or forty-seven faster, short-range B-58s. White insisted the Air Force needed both. The Secretary of Defense claimed there wasn't enough money in the budget. Reluctantly, White chose the B-58s, but with a warning that by 1959 Russia will be ahead of the United States in both bombers and missiles, able to destroy all overseas bases with a shotgun salvo of atomic-tipped missiles.

V

SLUM IN THE SUN

On July 8, 1947, a decision was taken that was to transform a scrubby, mosquito-infested sand bar, jutting out into the Atlantic from Florida's sunny east coast, into the most crucial installation in our defense complex. The name of that sand bar is Cape Canaveral, starting point of the missile test range that stretches 5,000 miles to a bleak, volcanic island called Ascension deep in the South Atlantic.

What goes on at Canaveral, known less formally as the Cape, is vital to the free world. Upon the success of the missiles tested there, upon the efficiency of its operations, largely depends the answer to that terrifying question: Can the United States catch up with Russia in the race to dominate outer space? All our strategic missiles, from the ocean-leaping Atlas to the underocean-launched Polaris, must pass through the Cape. Every hour squandered there represents an equivalent gain for Russia—a gift of time on a platter of dollars.

At first the range was operated by all three armed forces, an arrangement bedeviled by interservice rivalry. But on May 15, 1950, the Air Force took charge of the nest and began adding island bases to test and track missiles in flight. To patrol the watery space between the islands, a fleet of white picket ships was acquired. A dozen electronic outposts, backstopped by as many floating stations, trace the great metal "birds" during their supersonic migrations from the Cape.

Suddenly in 1953, just as the Air Force had settled down to a highly efficient operation of this all-important testing ground, its management quietly passed to a private contractor, as curious a cuckoo as ever invaded any nest: Pan American Airways.

Immediately Pan American began recruiting missile managers on a jobs-for-buddies basis, hiring former pilots, mechanics, ticket agents and baggage handlers. Its motives weren't alone patriotic.

The contractor was paid a fixed fee as its profit for managing the base, and this fee quickly jumped to a million dollars a year. The company also foresaw a commercial future in the missile business. "Indeed," its literature happily boasts, "when guided missiles open the way for space travel, Pan Am's Guided Missile Range may emerge as the pioneer of commercial space-lines."

Pan Am advertises that it is "the world's most experienced airline," and beyond any question it is second to none in its champagne-and-orchids service to travelers. But whether it should be allowed to cut its space-age teeth on so critical a project as the missile-launching base from which we must compete with Russia is another matter. The record so far revealed shows that Pan American Airways and the operation of Cape Canaveral must accept some responsibility for America's drastic drop in power.

The Air Force justified the Pan Am contract in a confidential memo, composed by Lieutenant General Orval Cook and dated October 26, 1953: "The Air Staff favors contractor operation at the Air Force Missile Test Center because of the conviction that a more efficient and effective operation will result. (Private) contractors are able to obtain better quality and stability of personnel than the Air Force. . . . They do not depend on proselyted Air Force personnel to fulfill their requirements." Cook added another ominous argument: "Ineptness or inefficiency in testing could have dire consequences not only from the cost standpoint, but also in the effectiveness of the weapons as finally adopted."

The warning was sadly prophetic. After the Soviet sputniks had humbled American pride almost to the panic point, one of the authors investigated conditions at the Cape. Unhappily, Pan Am's rule of the range has not fulfilled Air Force hopes. Its management has been plagued with the very "ineptness and inefficiency" the Air Force was trying to avoid. Its motley staff does not qualify as "better personnel." The turnover rate, exceeding 50 per cent a year, is far worse than the Air Force average, far worse also than that of the average industrial plant. It does not provide "better stability of personnel."

Pan Am may not have been proselyting Air Force personnel, but it has ended up with a startling number of retired colonels and generals. These pastured officers, who enjoy the Florida sunshine and the opportunity to supplement their pensions with Pan Am paychecks, got their jobs through Pentagon cronies whom the company wanted to please. This nepotism has reached such proportions and produced such inefficiencies that even Pan Am is worried.

How did a commercial airline, whose only claim to missile know-how is the coincidence that both airplanes and missiles fly, end up operating the free world's most important missile center? The evidence indicates that an important factor was reward for a worthy Republican contractor.

The Secretary of the Air Force who turned the missile range over to Pan American Airways was the late Harold E. Talbott, one of the most likable rough-and-tumble businessmen ever to serve in the Pentagon, but also one of the worst misfits. He owed his appointment under Eisenhower to the fact that he was one of the most indefatigable money-raisers for the Republican Party, just as Louis Johnson owed his appointment as Secretary of Defense under Truman to the fact that he was an ardent money-raiser for the Democratic Party.

Talbott had been Eastern chairman of the Republican Finance Committee in 1934 at about the same time another young money-raiser, Samuel F. Pryor of Connecticut, later a top executive for Pan American Airways, was emerging in Republican ranks. Pryor was Eastern treasurer of the Republican National Committee from 1936 to 1938, then became Republican National Committeeman from Connecticut and manager of Wendell Willkie's Eastern campaign headquarters. Harold Talbott served as chairman of the Metropolitan New York GOP Finance Committee and then became chairman of the over-all Republican National Finance Committee for the 1948 campaign that almost elected Tom Dewey but didn't. It was a terrible blow to Talbott. He had been promised the job of Ambassador to the Court of St. James's, and his daughters had all but picked their court dresses.

During these years, both Talbott and Pryor helped raise thousands of dollars for the Grand Old Party and, like all political money-raisers, believed that to the victor belongs the spoils. One of the most lucrative spoils was defense contracts, and Talbott did not hesitate to try to cancel an aluminum-extrusion-press contract with Kaiser Aluminum at Halethorpe, Maryland, in favor of the Harvey Aluminum Company, which had contributed handsomely to the Republicans. He did not hesitate to cancel the military-plane contract with Kaiser in favor of his old friend Grover Loening and Fairchild Aircraft. And he also suddenly switched an Air Force heating contract to a newly organized, completely inexperienced company formed by the brother of Governor J. Caleb Boggs of Delaware.

Talbott had been forced to resign from the Aircraft Procurement

Office of the War Production Board during the Roosevelt Administration and had been severely castigated by Charles Evans Hughes as guilty of "conduct of a reprehensible character" in connection with the award of airplane contracts during World War I. The airplane scandal was so serious that Woodrow Wilson appointed Hughes, former Governor of New York and candidate for President of the United States, to investigate. Despite Hughes's scathing indictment of Talbott and his father, of Charles Kettering, and of Colonel Edward Deeds, head of Delco Battery, which became part of General Motors, Talbott was picked by Eisenhower to head the Air Force.

Such is the power of political campaign funds.

Eventually, Talbott's partisanship toward favored companies, particularly Paul B. Mulligan & Company, in which he was a partner, brought a Senate investigation and forced his resignation as Secretary of the Air Force. But in the interim, he had switched Cape Canaveral from operation by the Air Force to private-contract operation under his old political comrade in fund-raising, Sam Pryor of Pan American Airways.

Curious facts about this contract have been dug out of Pentagon files. The man directly concerned with the negotiations under Talbott was Assistant Secretary Roger Lewis, who received General Cook's memo quoted earlier. In his own handwriting, Lewis scrawled his approval of the memo: "I concur in General Cook's endorsement of contractor operation as opposed to A.F. (Air Force). Have some questions about contract details however." Finally, on December 21, 1953, Lewis signed the order authorizing General Cook to draw up the contract.

From his office in the Pentagon, Lewis watched the bustle going on down at the Cape as the airline took over. On September 21, 1955, he resigned from the Air Force and the very next day joined Pan American Airways as executive vice-president.

His starting salary was a comfortable $28,000 per year plus bonuses, almost double his Air Force pay. He was also let in on a company plan that permitted him to buy 15,000 shares of Pan Am stock over a ten-year period at the market value on December 6, 1955. Only three vice-presidents, all company veterans, were offered this amount of stock. Other vice-presidents who had been with the company several years were offered as little as 6,000 shares.

Outlining Lewis' new duties, Pan American president Juan T. Trippe wrote: "Your initial assignments will include supervision of company projects relating to the national defense, including operating supervision of the Guided Missile Range Project." Trippe was careful to add that Lewis would *not* participate in any negotiations with the Air Force. It was an obvious and minimum caution. Anything less would probably have landed the airline in legal difficulties.

Trippe has since sworn that Lewis had no discussions with Pan Am while he was considering the missile-range contract and that Lewis had actually submitted his resignation to the Air Force before he was invited to join the company. These protestations, however, have not dispelled the cloud that hangs over the strange transfer of Cape Canaveral to Pan American Airways.

The main subcontract for technical work on the missile range went to the Radio Corporation of America. This cut of the Canaveral pie was dished out to RCA by Air Force Secretary Harold Talbott at the same time he was collecting an engineering fee indirectly from RCA through Paul B. Mulligan & Company. In 1954, RCA tried to back out as a Mulligan client. This brought a long-distance phone call from Talbott in the Pentagon to Sam Ewing, RCA general counsel, demanding to know why RCA was acting "so high and mighty." Talbott pocketed $67,000 profit a year from the Mulligan firm while he was running the Air Force. Although a generous share of this came from Air Force contractors who considered it wise to retain the Secretary's firm, Talbott later protested in blue-eyed innocence that his actions had been "within the bounds of ethics."

So it came to pass that a private airline undertook to show the generals how to get their rockets in the air. That those rockets did not get into the air in quantities equaling the Russian effort may be attributed, in part, to delays at Cape Canaveral. After nearly five years of Pan Am control, the administration of the missile range presented a record of meddle and muddle, of wasted time and money sufficient to cause profound dismay.

Colonel Paul Cooper, the contract officer who probably works more closely with Pan Am than anyone else in the Air Force, has found it necessary to write a confidential memo to the range commander, Major General Donald Yates, declaring in angry candor: "Within the past two years it has become increasingly apparent that planning for range expansion and the implementation of this planning is accomplished in a random fashion. This random planning has led to confusion . . ."

Cooper also complained about a "decided lack of coordination" between Pan Am and its chief subcontractor, Radio Corporation of America. For example, secret films of the first Vanguard failure—

which had the world calling it the Sputternik and the Kaputnik—were supposed to be rushed to Washington but were delayed for two hours because Pan Am, in a fit of jealousy, would not permit RCA to deliver them directly to the Air Force. It insisted they go through "the proper channels." In early 1957, RCA needed an extra infrared tracking device, but Pan Am made no provisions to house it until three months later. Result: The device was listed in the budget for fiscal year 1958 but its shelter wasn't listed until fiscal year 1959. Again, when the telemetry buildings at the Cape were modified to accommodate some new equipment, it was found while the redesigning was in progress that technical advances had made it possible to eliminate some obsolete instruments. This made extensive building unnecessary. But nobody told the designers to curtail. They went ahead with their original plans. If they had been told, one whole receiver building could have been eliminated.

Of this topsy-turvy planning, Colonel Cooper reported: "Increase in personnel adds to the inefficiency by increasing the number of planners with an attendant increase in the variety of philosophies of planning. . . . In other words, the Air Force spends more money to buy greater inefficiency."

Too many cooks at the Cape are not only spoiling the missile broth but making an already expensive commodity more costly. Or to put it in Colonel Cooper's words: "The efficiency of the planning and programming activities within the Air Force Missile Test Center is seriously impeded by the management structure as now constituted. This efficiency will continue to decrease as the workload increases unless action is taken to revise management philosophies. Introduction of more effective management could reduce the size of the Range Contractor's (Pan American's) planning groups by 50 per cent. It is estimated that this reduction would effect a yearly saving of possibly one million dollars . . ."

Pan Am has shown a schizophrenic attitude toward the taxpayers' money—a curious combination of extravagance and economy. For instance, one Pan Am technician lost a $2,000,000 Thor missile by carelessly crossing the wrong wires in the Dovap system, which shows the ground officer whether the missile is on or off course. The big, 1,200-mile Thor headed out over the Atlantic perfectly, but the crossed wires made it appear to be looping in the opposite direction, not toward the Antarctic but toward Orlando. Frantically, the safety officer pushed the "destroy" button. The Thor was blown to smithereens. For this $2,000,000 mistake, Pan Am gave a mild reprimand to the inept employee.

To save money, however, Pan Am refused the extra expense of stationing medics on the picket ships that patrol the Atlantic. Inevitably, a crewman developed an abscessed tooth. With no one on board qualified to administer penicillin, the ship was forced to leave the range and steam 300 miles to the nearest Brazilian port to have the man treated. This contributed to the delay in firing a 5,000-mile Snark. Another Pan Am employee drew $600 in advance expenses for a trip to the missile station at Recife, near Brazil, but spent the whole bankroll before he got out of town. His boss, F. E. Bruhn, refused to fire him, explaining at a staff meeting: "This man will have to be kept on as an employee so we can get back the $600."

There is also the case of the gleaming yellow technical laboratory completed in 1957. Before the experts were through inspecting it, they had ordered revisions costing another $490,000. On the other hand, Pan Am was allotted $4,500,000 to construct a new missile station. Inflation increased the costs by an estimated $2,000,000, but the company was able to cut corners and hold the price of the finished base to a remarkable $3,100,000.

Pan Am is not responsible for all the pocketbook capriciousness connected with the missile base. In 1951–52, the Air Force wound 136 miles of plastic cable around the Cape as the nerves of the vital communications network. The Florida damp seeped through the insulation, causing a bewildering rash of short circuits. Result: The whole tangled maze had to be replaced at a cost of $630,000. Yet any local electrician, knowing Florida's humid climate, could have forewarned the experts.

On economy orders from higher up, the Air Force also abolished all overtime and directed a 5-per-cent personnel slash at the missile center—*after* Russia had shaken the world with the first intercontinental missile and its space child, Sputnik I. Yet at the height of this economy wave, the top brass sent a C-54 to Trinidad to pick up a troupe of calypso entertainers for their officers' club. The plane developed engine trouble in the Dominican Republic, where the crew spent a happy seven-day holiday waiting for another C-54 to be flown to the rescue.

Of all the waste, however, none is more insidious than that of festering morale. The incredible 50-per-cent personnel turnover not only has helped put us behind Russia but costs the taxpayers an estimated $4,000,000 a year. General Yates complained at a staff meeting that it costs $5,000 to replace *one* engineer. This is the amount of money spent to hire, train and investigate him *before* he can start work.

Surrounding the test center are all the ingredients for carefree tropical living—gently sloping, surf-washed beaches, fish-choked rivers, golden orange groves, graceful palms. To while away their leisure hours, the workers can indulge in anything from horse racing to big-game fishing. These travel-folder attractions have lured many job seekers but have held few after they have encountered the realities of Cape Canaveral. Some improvement in morale took place following the sputniks, but this was generated more by patriotism than by any effort to help the newcomers, and it will take more than a few successful flights of the intercontinental Atlas to lift these sagging spirits out of the Florida sand.

Discontent breeds in three areas:

Working Conditions. The converted barracks which serve as office buildings at Patrick Air Force Base, headquarters for the missile range, are the worst sweatshops this side of New York City's garment jungle. Summer temperatures hit 105 degrees in some offices; the supply building became so stifling in the summer of 1957 that the health inspector shut it down temporarily because of insufficient oxygen. General Yates told us, "These working conditions are the worst I have ever seen." After badgering the Pentagon for three years, he finally got air conditioning installed in the worst buildings.

Family Conditions. For many the Cape has become a slum in the sun, a dreary existence of teeming trailer camps and squalid high-rent bungalows. Some people have even been found sleeping on car seats and in open concrete pipes. Yet this primitive living costs almost Gold Coast prices. Schools are hopelessly overcrowded. Two-lane highways leading to the base are jammed during rush hours with bumper-to-bumper traffic that backs up as far as twenty miles. Undrained swamps breed swarms of mosquitoes which force families to lead a birdcage existence behind screens.

Salaries. These are shockingly low for the caliber of men required to run so complex a project. Top administrators are paid between $9,250 and $12,500 a year—little more than what carpenters and bricklayers make in some northern cities. The best men are constantly quitting the Cape for better-paying jobs. Two dozen left to work for the Martin Aircraft Company in nearby Orlando. Others have gone to West Palm Beach, where Pratt-Whitney has opened an office. Still more have switched over to the contractors who manufacture the missiles. The pay scale is topsy-turvy, too. In some cases Pan American paid janitors more than highly trained nurses on the emergency crews.

Pan Am's range boss, shy, burly Richard Mitchell, argues that the turnover is not so depressing as it seems because the figures include transient laborers. Yet four key men resigned and one was fired from administrative jobs during a two-month period in 1957. In nine months, four civilian chiefs rotated through the missile station on Eleuthera Island, and in less than a year fifteen top changes were made in the personnel division itself. One management expert, Dan Sullivan, when he resigned, left behind a critical analysis of Pan Am's administration. He shook a stern finger at the supervisory personnel—the airline buddies and Pentagon cronies—who had no business running a missile range. He warned that one weak supervisor has been estimated to cost a company more than a hundred hourly workers.

He also discovered the intracompany mailing system was so slow and haphazard that many instructions had to be given orally. The supply system for the range is so clogged that requisitions often aren't filled for several months. There are ten different requisition forms, and no supply officer is familiar with them all. It took eighteen months to fill requisition number 62536 for a sandblasting machine and another eighteen months to fill requisition number 9330 for dish racks. It took twelve months to fill number 93450 for a steam table and the same time for numbers 79888, 65662 and 79869 for air-conditioning gear. These examples are only too typical.

The missile watchers atop bleak Ascension Island had to wait forty days for such basic supplies as soap. But they got two fancy lawn mowers, though there isn't a single blade of grass to mow. With wry humor, they assembled the mowers as monuments and hung over them a sign, "Rust in Peace." A requisition for fuel oil for Ascension was mysteriously misplaced. Happily it was possible to divert a Navy tanker to the island just as the vital missile station was on the point of closing down. Then, after Ascension had all the oil it needed, the original requisition showed up, dumping an extra supply on the island.

Pan Am's safety record on the range has also been poor. The accident frequency rate is much higher than American industrial standards. The cause of most of its accidents: "lack of knowledge or skill." The company which advertises its excellent safety record as an airline has had to warn its supervisors, "Many injuries have been reported as resulting from unsafe method or procedure, but later investigation disclosed that no standard method of procedure had been set up for the jobs. The method was declared hazardous only after it resulted in an accident."

Thus did Pan American admit confidentially what it denies publicly, that inexperienced and inefficient personnel are doing much of the work at the missile center.

The little episodes of fumbling and bumbling are almost numberless. An October 1957 test of the Vanguard rocket had to be "scrubbed"—postponed—because the ground crew couldn't pump alcohol into the missile. They tinkered with the pump for eight hours before they discovered that its motor had simply run out of gas. Also in 1957, six $10,000 recorders were stacked at the test center upside down. Oil drained from their motors, almost ruining them. A strict order was issued that this kind of carelessness must not be repeated. Four months later, six more recorders were again stacked upside down with the same result.

On a typical project, workmen were ordered to reconstruct the concrete blockhouse which had been used in the Navaho missile test. A jackhammer crew showed up with only one jackhammer, though later two more were rounded up. Then it developed that only one of the four jackhammer men knew his trade. Meanwhile a crew of machinists sat in the shade from 7 A.M. to 3 P.M. waiting for the carpenters to build their forms. On top of this, the laborers left their shovels in the trucks and it took them half a day to get the shovels back. These are the men supposed to be engaged in work of utmost urgency—keeping the United States abreast of Soviet Russia.

Pan Am's boss man at the Cape, Dick Mitchell, a veteran of thirty years in aviation, graduated from flying (he was once personal pilot to William Randolph Hearst) to high-level administration. He is dedicated to his work. So is the missile range's commanding officer, General Yates. Yet all their efforts have failed to get the range running at anything like peak efficiency. There has also been a disturbing tendency to sweep embarrassing facts about waste, mismanagement and stupidity under the convenient carpet of secrecy.

Perhaps as you read this, the sun is going down over that extraordinary blend of the tropics and the Arctic—swaying palms and igloo-style concrete blockhouses—that is the Cape Canaveral missile range. Twilight is always a good time for reflection. Reflect then that the Cape is entrusted with testing the new sword and shield of American defense against the remorseless and increasing menace of Soviet Russia. There we are battling for time in a race against war. We are not supposed to be helping one company gain experience to become the world's first spaceline at the price of the security of the free world.

vi

WHO WAS TO BLAME?

Apologists for America plead somewhat mournfully that we fell behind in the science of rocketry because the Russians started first. They say this with an air of hurt surprise as if the Russians should not have jumped the gun on us. Yet buried in the Pentagon, as if in some mammoth tomb, are dead papers which tell a different story; secret records which, like bad memories, have come back to haunt the guilty.

These all-but-forgotten files reveal that our scientists were thinking in terms of satellites and missiles as far back as 1945. Hardly had the last echoes of World War II faded than they designed the first satellite, which could have beaten the Soviet sputniks into space by half a decade. They also drew up blueprints, for an intercontinental missile not unlike today's mighty Atlas. That these projects were allowed to mildew in their Pentagon pigeonholes can be blamed partly on the budget blight, partly on lack of foresight. Actually foresight was present. But in the budget battle between money and brains which constantly plagues the world's wealthiest nation, money—or lack of it—always won.

Horseshoe nails do not appear on any list of components for long-range missiles or earth satellites, but the old proverb, "For want of a nail the shoe is lost; for want of a shoe the horse is lost; for want of a horse the rider is lost," applies today as it did when knights rode to war in clanking armor. A passion for saving a handful of dollars became a deadly handicap against a potential enemy which threw its full resources into the race to become lords of space.

Scores of speeches have been made and scores of mimeographed statements have been issued by the Republican and Democratic national committees attempting to show that Louis Johnson or Charles E. Wilson, Truman or Eisenhower was responsible for our lag on missiles and satellites. The responsibility cannot be fixed so easily. But the beginning of the story can be dated October 1945, when the first proposed intercontinental ballistic missile, the Atlas, became a gleam in the eyes of Air Corps planners. The war was only one month over at that time. Harry Truman had been in the White House only six months, Henry L. Stimson was just leaving as Secretary of War, and General George C. Marshall was Chief of Staff when the air strategists sent out a call to the aircraft industry to submit proposals for a ballistic missile of up to 5,000 miles range.

The proposed new ballistic missile was in contrast to the slower concept of air-breathing missiles with which the Air Corps was also experimenting. The air breather, because it uses oxygen from the atmosphere to operate its propulsion engines, had to stay within the atmosphere to breathe. Therefore, the friction generated from traveling through the atmosphere would reduce its flight to a relative snail's pace. But the ballistic missile, to be propelled by its own liquid oxygen, would not be dependent on the atmosphere to breathe; therefore it could fly far above the friction-pulling atmosphere at speeds up to 15,000 or 20,000 miles an hour. At this speed it could reach Moscow from Washington in less than thirty minutes.

It was this fast-as-lightning intercontinental ballistic missile that was proposed in 1945, and which Convair immediately offered to build. Karel J. Bossart, a Belgian-born expert working for Convair, came up with the design of a metal monster resembling a giant artillery shell which, he claimed, could hurdle the ocean at the speed of a shooting star.

A detailed design was forwarded to the Air Corps on January 10, 1946. The generals were so impressed that on April 22 they awarded a $1,400,000 contract to Convair to begin the project. Two months later they allocated another $493,000 to speed up the work.

That was the start of the Atlas, the King Kong of American missiles. It was the start, but not the end. Ten years passed, one whole decade, and the Atlas still was not operational—one decade during which Russia jumped far ahead. And on July 15, 1958, twelve years later, as American foreign policy floundered on the beaches of Beirut and as Nikita Khrushchev coupled a bulldozing demand for a summit conference with a bulldozing threat of Russian missiles, the giant Atlas failed in another series of tests which were still behind Russia.

Convair, of course, had no way of knowing back in 1945 that its first test missiles would be stillborn, not to be reborn for ten crucial years. And had it not been for Bossart and his boss, Floyd B. Odlum, chairman of Convair, the Atlas would have been abandoned earlier and altogether on the New Mexico desert. It was Bossart's faith and Odlum's bold use of company money that kept the project alive long after it had been left to die by the defense cuts of 1947. Not until 1951 did the Air Force come back with government funds to rescue the project.

The MX-774, as the big ballistic baby was known in 1947, belonged technically to the Army, whose chief overlord was General Dwight D. Eisenhower. He had come back from the Supreme Allied Command in Europe to replace General Marshall in the most important military post in the continental U.S.A., Chief of Staff of the Army. It was a time of postwar reductions when he and most of the American people were more concerned with budgets than ballistics. The world was hoping for peace. So less than six months after the speed-up order, reverse instructions were delivered to slow down the MX-774. Convair was told that it would have to get along for two years on the funds allotted for one year. This brought a written objection from Albert Lombard, a project engineer, that the MX-774 "must receive backing financially on a scale somewhat of the magnitude of the German (rocket) activities at Peenemunde."

This objection is one of the secret papers that has arisen from the dead files of the Pentagon to haunt the planners charged with keeping the United States ahead of Russia. The tragedy is that component parts of the first MX-774 missiles were already in the machine shops when on July 1, 1947, their death notice arrived from Washington. Economy was in the air. Because of it, the air generals decided that they could concentrate on only one intercontinental missile and that a slower, air-breathing missile, subsequently called the Snark, would be easier to construct and surer of success. Work had already been started on the Snark. It had wings and therefore was more comprehensible to the men who believed in wings.

It was General Eisenhower, then Chief of Staff, who approved the order killing off Project MX-774. He acted, of course, on the advice of his experts who faced budget cuts.

His former chief, Henry L. Stimson, when Secretary of War in 1944, had once telephoned the senior author, saying, "I read your story about the light tank and its failures. You're right that it's costing us some extra money. But I have learned that it sometimes pays to spend extra money experimenting with a new weapon. That's how new weapons are made."

Unfortunately, Dwight D. Eisenhower lacked either the foresight or the courage of Henry L. Stimson.

As an act more of penitence than of perspicacity, the Air Corps did permit Convair to continue with its contract until all the money had been spent. Bossart's engineering crew squeezed out the last penny to complete three test missiles less than half the size of the present-day Atlas but almost as complex. All three were fired with astonishing success at White Sands, New Mexico, on July 13, September 27, and December 2, 1948. Since they were simply designed to test propulsion and configuration, they were fired straight up and not over a range. The pattern of flight proved excellent. It should have, because the MX-774 was almost identical with today's Atlas design. The fuel in each missile, however, cut off prematurely, and later the trouble was traced to a valve jarred by the intense vibration. This was easily eliminated in the next tests. But they had to wait almost a decade—nine agonizing years—until June, September, and December of 1957.

During those bleak years in between, a disappointed but undaunted Bossart refused to give in. He built a miniature of the Atlas and shipped it to Washington for a final appeal to the generals. Convair's Washington representative, Richard Swanson, worked hard to get the brass lined up for a meeting to consider more appropriations for perfecting the embryo Atlas. For some reason the model of the Atlas was delayed and didn't arrive until 1:50 P.M., ten minutes before the Air Force brass were scheduled to arrive.

"Get that crate open!" ordered Swanson anxiously. But the crate had been put together with long screws driven into the wood by machine. The model was almost as secure as in a bank vault. For an hour, as the generals fumed and fretted, workmen, stripped to the waist, struggled to pry the crate open. When at last they succeeded, they found the missile had been broken during their battle with the box. The impatient generals snorted and walked out. So did a disconsolate Swanson. When air officers asked what they should do with the model, he replied bitterly, "It's your personal property." Thus Convair lost the reprieve for the Atlas, not for lack of a nail but because of too many screws. Thus also the United States took one step downward on the path to becoming a second-class power.

In desperation Bossart turned to his boss, Floyd Odlum, who nodded his balding, freckled head. "Keep the project going," he ordered. So Convair dipped into its own treasury while the generals poured out money on the Snark, a nonballistic, air-breathing weapon which proved to be relatively obsolete before it became operational. Although usable if it flies so close to the ground that it can't be shot down, the Snark, at around 600 miles an hour, is slow as a milk truck compared to the Atlas, which flies some 19,000 miles an hour. The Snark is not a weapon of the future.

Floyd Odlum, chairman of Convair, came in for a lot of criticism from the Navy when he built the giant B-36, which in 1946 was the biggest long-range bomber ever produced. The admirals charged—unfairly—that he had got the contract because of his friendship with Stuart Symington, then Assistant Secretary of War. This criticism got plenty of headlines. But getting no headlines, in fact kept secret until this day, is the fact that Odlum spent around $20,000,000 of Convair's own money to construct the Atlas and that this expenditure materially helped the long-range development of an intercontinental ballistic missile.

By 1951, however, Convair's directors were pressing Odlum to run a red-ink line through the entire Atlas project. It was costing too much money. So Swanson was sent back to the Pentagon to see what he could do. He managed to corner Lieutenant General Don Putt, the Air Force's research chief, during the December round of pre-Christmas parties. The quiet, competent Putt had never doubted the Atlas. He had urged Convair to keep the project going and had done his best to interest his superiors in it.

He listened grim-faced as Swanson explained that Convair directors felt the firm was scraping the bottom of its cash register. Without authority from superiors, the General promised to turn over $500,000 of his research funds to Convair to save the Atlas from extinction. "I have just found half a million dollars," he said with a Christmassy twinkle, "in the bottom of the drawer."

The tribulations of the Atlas were not over by any means. Although its life was saved, it had to survive on the most meager of diets. Convair invested more of its own money in the construction of the huge Atlas plant in San Diego at the same time the Air Force was providing free plants for Boeing to build bombers. Bombers would soon be out of date. Missiles were the weapons of the future. But it was much easier at that time to get appropriations for conventional bombers than for unconventional missiles. Another company, North American Aviation, dipped into its own treasury for $1,000,000 to erect the first great rocket-engine test stand at Santa Susana, California. Because of its willingness to pioneer, North

American developed the mighty motors which now power not only the Atlas but the 1,200-mile Thor and Jupiter missiles.

Despite this pioneering, it remained for the Russian scientists to win the argument that the devoted engineers at Convair and North American lost. Not until Assistant Secretary Trevor Gardner opened the Pentagon's eyes in 1954 to what was going on inside Russia did the Air Force begin a major push on ballistic missiles. By late 1955, the Air Force still hadn't built a single launching pad for its own ballistic missiles at the Cape Canaveral testing center. As of that date, it was equipped to launch only the much slower, air-breathing missiles.

Thus, through lack of foresight, lack of money, and lack of a nail did we fall behind Russia in developing the ballistic weapon of the future.

The detailed story of how we fell behind Russia in launching a satellite also goes back to the Forrestal and Johnson regimes in the Defense Department, and even beyond. Officially Louis Johnson was to blame for killing the American sputnik. But the story is more complex than that and once again involves lack of foresight, lack of money, and no lack of red tape. It also involves the manner in which our Secretaries of Defense are usually picked.

James V. Forrestal was picked as Under Secretary of the Navy because Tommy Corcoran, famed member of the Roosevelt Brain Trust, had been the lawyer for Forrestal's investment firm, Dillon, Read and Company, during pre-New Deal days. It was Corcoran who persuaded Roosevelt to bring Forrestal to Washington as a White House assistant, then as assistant to Secretary of the Navy Frank Knox, at a time shortly before Pearl Harbor when F.D.R. needed big-business backing for his defense build-up.

Louis A. Johnson, a small-town West Virginia lawyer with a big-business practice, first got into government after, as commander of the American Legion, he swung the veterans' vote to Roosevelt in 1932 and 1936. He was rewarded for his pains with the then relatively innocuous job of Assistant Secretary of War, with the promise—or so he thought—that he would later become Secretary of War. Pathos and pain have marked the governmental career of Louis Johnson—pain to himself and pain to the government—but also a certain amount of heroic achievement.

The achievement came in the pre-Pearl Harbor days when a great many Americans never believed the Axis was out to take over the world, never believed the United States would be drawn into war, never believed it was necessary for the United States to prepare for war. One of those who thus believed was Johnson's chief, the Secretary of War, Harry H. Woodring of Kansas. And while Woodring opposed American rearmament, Johnson worked blatantly and brazenly behind his back to encourage rearmament, including the ordering of planes for France and England, virtually without authorization from Congress. It was Johnson's forthright action which helped save England when Hitler finally struck.

After Hitler struck, however, Franklin Roosevelt, knowing the United States was also in for war, proceeded to appoint a bipartisan Cabinet. Johnson went to the Democratic convention in Chicago in 1940 completely confident that he was to be promoted to the post of Under Secretary of War. Henry L. Stimson, a Republican, former Secretary of War under Taft and Secretary of State under Hoover, had just been appointed Secretary of War in Roosevelt's coalition Cabinet. Despite this, Johnson was serenely confident that he was to be promoted to be Stimson's right-hand man. He was not. The Democratic convention ended July 10. On July 25, Johnson was forced to turn in his resignation. John J. McCloy, a New York attorney and an old friend of Stimson's, took his place.

From that time on, Louis Johnson nursed an unquenchable, corroding ambition to stage a comeback. He was a good soldier. He continued to serve Roosevelt whenever and wherever needed. And in 1948, when no one else would undertake the disagreeable and apparently hopeless job of raising money for the re-election of Harry S. Truman, Louis Johnson volunteered. He was chiefly responsible for financing the campaign that put Truman back in the White House, and Harry Truman, who never forgets his friends, was grateful.

These were the circumstances which led to the appointment of Louis Johnson to be Secretary of Defense in the spring of 1949. The appointment caused considerable resentment, first because it was political, second because James Forrestal was popular both in the Pentagon and with the newspaper corps in Washington.

A change in the office of Secretary of Defense would have been necessary, however, regardless of Johnson, and regardless of the hundreds of thousands of dollars he raised for the 1948 campaign. For Jim Forrestal was fading. He was fading mentally. His wife had all but left him. He had been working under great strain. He had been an excellent Secretary of the Navy. But the job of putting the unwieldy, unwilling, antagonistic Army and Navy and Air Force together under one department, as ordered by the new unification act, was too much for him. He forgot appointments. He telephoned Attorney General Tom C. Clark to complain that FBI agents were in his outer office hounding him. He labored under the hallucination that he was being persecuted. He seemed fixed with the obsession that his own government was investigating him. It was obvious at Cabinet meetings that Forrestal did not have all his mental faculties with him, and although he was slated for retirement on May 1, President Truman pushed the date forward to March 3.

Many people, including Mr. Truman, Louis Johnson, and Drew Pearson, have been blamed for Forrestal's subsequent suicide. The fact is that the deterioration of his mind started six to nine months before his forced resignation and long before the tragic night in Hobe Sound, Florida, when he ran outdoors in his pajamas screaming that the Red Army was after him. He was given an injection, carried to an ambulance, and flown to the Bethesda Naval Hospital outside Washington. Later, when a guard left him for a moment, James Forrestal jumped out the window.

It was under these unhappy circumstances that Louis Johnson became the second Secretary of Defense in American history. The circumstances had a direct bearing on his work. He felt compelled to make a name for himself. He was determined to knock heads together in the armed services. This was necessary and important. Under Forrestal the generals and the admirals had had their own way. Forrestal was a likable, pliable figurehead. Johnson was determined to be the opposite.

One of the surest ways Johnson could make a name for himself was by cutting the budget. Taxes were high. The country was complaining. The war was over. The United Nations was talking about disarmament. Johnson cut, and cut ruthlessly.

One of the projects he cut was the American satellite. The cutting was largely accidental and might have occurred regardless of Johnson. For the satellite was badly bogged down.

The story of the early efforts to build a sputnik has never been fully told. In fact, it took nearly three years for even a whisper to leak out; then it was quickly hushed up again. In preparing his 1948 annual report, Secretary of Defense Forrestal cast around for examples of interservice co-operation. He badly needed something to offset the headlines that the generals and the admirals were at each other's throats. So he slipped into his annual report a paragraph which never should have been published. It may have given the Russians the tip-off regarding our satellite. The paragraph which Pentagon censors let slip into the report read:

> The earth satellite vehicle program which has been carried out independently by each military service was assigned to the Committee on Guided Missiles for coordination. To provide an integrated program with resultant elimination of duplication, the Committee recommended that current efforts in this field be limited to studies and component designs; well defined areas of research had been allocated to each of the three military compartments.

Newsmen immediately spotted this paragraph, started to ask questions. Pentagon censors immediately brought out the blue pencils. From that day to this, not another word has been said officially about the early attempt to build a satellite and how we didn't build it.

The untold story goes back to October 3, 1945, and a secret meeting within the Navy's Bureau of Aeronautics. At that meeting it was decided that a satellite vehicle was not only desirable but *feasible*. At that meeting a satellite became more than a scientist's dream of opening up new vistas to mankind.

The estimated sum for the proposed satellite was trivial: somewhere between five and eight million dollars. The actual amount spent in the next three years was smaller still: a bare million, despite the high priority which had been urged. This is less than is now being spent every day on American satellites. If we had spent it then, the nation would have been spared the extravagance of crash efforts today.

Yet even on a shoestring, valuable work was accomplished on essential theory. A Committee for Evaluating the Feasibility of Space Rocketry, set up by the Bureau of Aeronautics, visualized a vehicle with a gross take-off weight of between 100,000 and 200,000 pounds, carrying a one-ton satellite. The California Institute of Technology set to work on a study of the interrelationship of orbit, rocket motor, and fuel performance. All the calculations pointed to success. The Aerojet Company was given the job of studying fuels, including liquid hydrogen. The largest hydrogen liquefier in the world was put into operation. Other studies on design were made by the North American Aviation and Glenn L. Martin companies. All this excellent work, carried out with great enthusiasm, produced an identical conclusion. An earth satellite was possible; it required only the green light.

At this stage, the Navy's purse strings were drawn so tight they threatened to strangle the project. James V. Forrestal was then Secretary of the Navy and Harry Truman was in the White House. So the Army Air Corps was approached by the Navy to put up part of the funds and establish a joint project. On March 7, 1946, the first of several meetings was held. It was an example of attempted interservice co-operation. Present for the Navy were Captain W. P. Cogswell and Commander H. Hall; for the Air Corps, Major General H. J. Knerr, Major General H. M. McClelland, and Brigadier General W. L. Richardson. The results seemed encouraging. A memo was drawn up stating: "It was agreed at the conference that the general advantages to be derived from pursuing the satellite development appear to be sufficient to justify a major program, in spite of the fact that the obvious military, or purely naval applications, in themselves may not appear at this time to warrant the expenditure. On this basis, the Army representatives agreed to investigate the extent of Army interest by discussions with General LeMay and others . . ."

But hopes for co-operation were short-lived. That gruff old air warrior, General Curtis LeMay, had done a dramatic job of building up the Strategic Air Command, charged with taking the offensive against Moscow and Leningrad. But he appeared to resent Navy interest and asked bluntly what the Navy was doing in this field of celestial navigation. The sailors, he implied, should be content with the oceans they already had at their disposal, should not be seeking to sail into space.

The project hung fire for several weeks until another joint conference in the summer of 1946. Major General Laurence C. Craigie, director of Air Corps research and development, produced a study report on which the ink was hardly dry, setting out the bargaining position of the Air Corps. Officially, the Air Corps wanted to be a full partner in the project. Unofficially, the Navy construed this to mean Air Corps domination. With the last flutter of this document, as the General gestured with it to emphasize his point, the spirit of service teamwork to lead the way into space was shooed out the window. Yet two years later, in 1948, the new Secretary of Defense, James Forrestal, was to cite the satellite project as an example of interservice harmony.

By this time the Army, the Navy, and the Air Corps, which had now become the Air Force, were amalgamated into one unified command, into one supposedly harmonious Defense Department. But they did not act as if they had read the unification act so recently passed by Congress. For a while the Navy and the Air Force, just separated from the Army, pursued their separate satellite research, and in 1948 they presented it to the civilian Technical Evaluation Group of the Research and Development Board Committee on Guided Missiles. No help came from that quarter. While the civilian technical experts conceded that "the feasibility of an earth satellite vehicle is clearly established," they joined the most reactionary brass in adding that "neither the Navy nor the USAF has as yet established a military or scientific utility commensurate with the presently expected cost of a satellite vehicle. We believe that no satellite vehicle should be built until utility commensurate with cost is clearly established."

In brief, the satellite had to pay its own way.

For the Navy, Rear Admiral Daniel V. Gallery made a last sally to try to win a partnership with the Air Force to produce the satellite. He was thrown back by the air generals, who were suspicious of the harpoons Gallery had thrown into air strategy in the past. He had written an article for *The Saturday Evening Post*, extolling the virtues of the airplane carrier as against the long-range bomber, which raised the blood pressure of the Air Force. So he was not the best equipped pacifier to try to bring harmony to satellite research.

There was a further attempt to get funds for a superperformance "sounding" rocket which would reach a height of 400 miles. The hope was that if it were successful, the fanfare would make it easier to get money for the satellite project. This too came to nothing.

It was the old story of no cash without a pay load; of buck-passing instead of bucks. The fact that somewhere on the lonely steppes of central Russia plans were proceeding for the sputnik seemed of secondary concern to those manning the ramparts of the Pentagon.

On September 12, 1950, Louis Johnson was abruptly called in by Harry Truman and fired. He should have known it was coming, but he didn't. He took a long walk up Sixteenth Street, trying to figure out what had hit him, trying to figure out what he had done wrong. Just what his own conclusions were, history does not record. But the conclusions of the authors are that he was fired, first, because of the failures of the Korean War; second, because he had alienated too many generals and admirals in the Pentagon. He was not fired because he had killed the American sputnik. Actually, the appropriations squeeze had started its death before he took office; and although an Admiral Rickover or a Henry L. Stimson might have had the vision and the courage to rescue the satellite, Louis Johnson did not. It should be noted in fairness that he can be blamed only for his failure to foresee Russia's rapid technological advance. The Eisenhower Administration had ample evidence of this advance. He did not. The Eisenhower Administration had positive proof that Russia had caught up with us in A-bomb and H-bomb design, had even surpassed us in developing a trigger mechanism, and was pushing ahead of us on missiles. Johnson did not. Johnson was a West Virginia lawyer who, when he saw the perils of Hitler, acted with vigor. When he faced the complacency of peace, he did what his friend the Chief of Staff, later President of the United States, also did. He cut the budget at the expense of national safety.

vii

THE BULL IN THE MILITARY SHOP

CHARLES E. WILSON's appointment as Secretary of Defense was the National Association of Manufacturers' greatest opportunity to make good its perpetual boast that businessmen can put efficiency into government.

Wilson tackled this golden opportunity full of cocky conceit. As the head of the world's biggest corporation, he sincerely meant it when he said, "I thought that what was good for the country was good for General Motors and vice versa." He figured he could run the Army, the Navy, the Air Force, and the Marine Corps with one arm tied behind him, spending his weekends in Miami and Detroit. The eyes of the entire business world were upon him. Businessmen were not worried about the outcome.

Four years later, Charlie Wilson came out of his experience a less cocky, more human man. "They are trying to make me the goat," he said plaintively, when the Eisenhower Administration blamed him for the disastrous defeat on Sputnik and the tragic lag on long-range missiles.

He was right. The Eisenhower Administration badly needed a goat. Charlie Wilson did not deserve to be that goat. But neither was he a success as Secretary of Defense. The great labyrinth of corridors and red tape called the Pentagon, the military caste system, the generals and admirals who had either broken or taken a long line of Secretaries of Defense in the past, took him. Wilson became a captive Secretary of Defense. Business efficiency did not take over our Defense Department. The military system took him.

Everybody liked him at the end. They gave him columns and columns of praise as he departed, plus farewell party after farewell party. He had come to know the military services. He had worked hard at his job. He was probably a better Secretary of Defense than his predecessors. Nevertheless, history will show that under him the United States suffered its worst technological defeat—right in the field where big business is supposed to excel.

That this defeat was suffered was partly the fault of Wilson's budget-pruning colleague, the Secretary of the Treasury. But Wilson, too, must take some of the blame. If he had not kept insisting, "The Russians are not nine feet tall"; if he had not pooh-poohed science with "Someone else should look into what makes the grass grow green"; if he had fought for missile efficiency with the same drive he once fought for better Chevrolets, the country which he loves might not be a second-class power today.

When Eisenhower appointed Charlie Wilson as Secretary of Defense, the politicians acclaimed it a political ten-strike. They knew how General Motors had pulled wires to switch Michigan delegates and Chevrolet dealer Summerfield away from Senator Robert A. Taft to Eisenhower at the 1952 convention in Chicago, also how much money General Motors had raised for Ike's election. They were a little dubious, however, when Eisenhower appointed four General Motors men to places of power. In addition to Wilson there was the new Postmaster General, Arthur E. Summerfield, largest Chevrolet dealer in the world; the new Secretary of the Interior, Governor Douglas McKay of Oregon, a prosperous Cadillac dealer; and Roger M. Kyes, Wilson's right-hand man at General Motors in Detroit, who became his right-hand man as Under Secretary of Defense in Washington. At that time, however, the worshipful American press was ready to let Eisenhower steal the copper off the dome of the Capitol. There was no critical comment.

"I'm going to give this job the darndest whirl it ever had," Wilson said as he was sworn in as Secretary of Defense. He carried out his promise. That he didn't know what tracer bullets were when he saw them fired in Korea made no difference. That he didn't know that under the law he could not handle General Motors contracts himself also made no difference. That Arthur Godfrey is one of the most difficult prima donnas in the world also made no difference. Godfrey had long helped him sell Chevrolets, so Wilson wanted to appoint him Assistant Secretary of Defense for Information.

Wilson was so ignorant of the routine of Washington that he couldn't understand when Thomas E. Stevens, White House appointment secretary, phoned to tell him he would have to change his regular weekly conference with Eisenhower from Tuesday to Wednesday.

"The President is receiving the Disabled War Veterans on Wednesday," Stevens explained, "and therefore he wants to golf on Tuesday. Accordingly, he would like to see you a little early on Wednesday before the veterans' garden party."

But the Secretary of Defense didn't understand. Stevens gave the instructions a second time, then a third time. Finally, as Wilson looked at his calendar, Stevens, cupping the telephone receiver with his hand, remarked to his secretary, Roberta Barrows: "Just how did they ever explain the Chevrolet to this guy?"

At first Wilson dodged the press. He even ordered his subordinates to avoid public speeches and interviews. There were times when he wished he had followed the advice himself, especially after his famed 1954 press conference in Detroit. "I've always liked bird dogs better than kennel-fed dogs," he said, referring to men out of work in Detroit. "You know one will get out and hunt for food rather than sit on his haunches and yelp."

Wilson probably doesn't know to this day that if it hadn't been for Walter Reuther, his remark would have been unnoticed by the then quiescent press. But Reuther immediately issued press releases, wired the White House demanding to know whether this represented the view of the President, made sure Wilson's views were headlined from coast to coast.

He never lived down that remark. But he did turn it around as a good joke on himself. When the Association of American Cartoonists presented him with a miniature doghouse as the "outstanding cartoon subject of the year," Wilson told the cartoonists, "I'm more complimented than offended. Mostly it's my fault for sticking my neck out. As long as I have an opportunity to be your victim, it's all right with me. I tell my friends I'm no politician, and they say they know it, but can't understand why I have to keep on proving it over and over again."

Wilson put his collection of doghouse cartoons on the walls of his Pentagon office and took great delight in showing them to visitors. Once when the Defense Department was under Congressional fire over buying too many hamburgers, Wilson turned to his press chief, C. Herschel Schooley, and remarked: "If this business of the hamburgers stays on, I'm going to propose that we feed this hamburger to my bird dogs."

On another occasion, when General Lauris Norstad's blunt testimony on Capitol Hill caused Soviet Foreign Minister Gromyko to remark that U.S. generals should keep their mouths shut, Wilson remarked: "Unaccustomed as I am, I can't agree with him more."

There were times, however, when his foot-in-mouth *faux pas* really upset international apple carts. One was when he remarked that there was no danger that Russia could deliver the hydrogen bomb. President Eisenhower was so upset that he spent the weekend in bed from hypertension. That was the first time Ike tangled with his Secretary of Defense. The second was over Wilson's announcement that the United States was pulling one division out of Europe at the very same time Secretary of State Dulles was assuring Europeans just the opposite. As a result of Wilson's *faux pas*, the United States had to slow up the previously planned withdrawal of land troops.

"Maybe I should remember what the mama whale told the cub," he said later. " 'Son, it's only when you're spouting that you're liable to be harpooned.' "

Eventually he got the hang of the technique of the press conferences and seemed to enjoy them. He held more than any other member of the Cabinet. He struggled with his answers, twisting and wriggling his feet as he groped for the right words. However, he got off so many bright cracks that he soon became the most quoted and quotable man in Washington. Before each press conference he was briefed on points that might come up. "I like these press conferences," he once remarked. "They make me find out what is going on around here." He brought subordinates in to help him answer questions. "It's kind of like I was quarterback," he said, "and can pass the ball to the other players."

Wilson got so good at his public relations that he even gave advice to subordinates on how to handle themselves before Congressional committees. Instructing his Deputy Defense Secretary, Reuben Robertson, to be a little vague when he testified before Congress, Wilson said, "Reuben, I suggest you give them more blue sky and not so much machinery."

One point on which Wilson was most ignorant of all when he entered the Defense Department was conflict of interest. He had no conception of the fact that businessmen in government must remain aloof from contracts affecting their own companies, and he had no inkling that he would be required to sell his stock in General Motors.

It came as a rude shock, therefore, when Senator Byrd of Virginia telephoned Senator Saltonstall of Massachusetts, chairman of the Armed Services Committee, to warn him of a law which might bar Wilson from becoming Secretary of Defense unless he sold his stock. At the Senate hearing which followed, Wilson at times acted as if he were doing the senators a favor by appearing before them. At times he was positively rude. He even preached a sermon on his own integrity and implied that he belonged to the ruling class. Senator Saltonstall, whose family dates back to the Pilgrim Fathers, is a mild-mannered, tolerant gentleman, but even he did not relish Wilson's behavior. Most surprising was Wilson's statement that he had planned to handle General Motors contracts as Secretary of Defense.

Wilson had no realization of the fact that the American soldier does not fight without using some piece of General Motors equipment—either trucks or tanks, half-tracks or airplanes, guns or refrigerators, AC spark plugs or locomotives; plus gas engines, Diesel engines, airplane engines. He had no realization of the fact that General Motors at that very moment was negotiating the largest tax refund in history, eventually resulting in a return of $206,000,000 to the General Motors treasury from the U.S. Treasury. Wilson did not know, or else had forgotten, that one of his subsidiaries, Allison Motors, in making jet fighters for use in the Korean War had pyramided its profits so that the total over-all profit was 39 per cent.

Most interesting of all, however, was the fact that H. R. Boyer, a General Motors man loaned to the government as chairman of the Aircraft Production Board, had urged that the Fisher Body Division of General Motors be awarded a contract for 757 vertical turret lathes despite the fact that Fisher Body had no experience in making lathes, and despite the fact that their cost was $52,600 more per lathe than the bid of the Bullard Company, an experienced concern. Total loss to the government on this order recommended by a General Motors executive was $68,000,000.

Swan E. Bergstrom, a machine-tool expert, when asked by Congressmen why General Motors was to be paid $90,600 for the same turret lathe which other companies were selling for $38,000, replied that it was perfectly normal for Fisher Division of GM to charge the government two and a half times as much, because Fisher was "inexperienced" in making machine tools. "Does that answer your question?" he asked.

"It's just as clear as mud," replied Congressman Hebert of Louisiana.

Such is the penalty to the American taxpayer when an official wears two hats. And such was the position in which Charlie Wilson wanted to put himself by also wearing two hats—one as Secretary of Defense, the other as a very large stockholder in General Motors.

Wilson's motto is "I co-operate with the inevitable."

In the end he sold his stock. One friend estimated that it cost him $4,000,000 to quit his $600,000 job to take a job for the government at $25,000.

Charles S. Thomas, Secretary of the Navy, confided that he once walked into Wilson's office to find him signing personal checks. He was looking glum. "My wife," remarked the Secretary of Defense, "must think I work for General Motors."

Even after the Senate Armed Services Committee hammered home upon him the fact that he must not discriminate in favor of his former company, the new Secretary of Defense had difficulties. As a production man he believed in efficiency. As Secretary of Defense he was supposed to believe in military safety. At first production efficiency got the better of military safety, and Wilson cracked down on several General Motors competitors.

He ruled that there were too many factories making tanks, artillery, and trucks. One company, he said, could make them more efficiently. In the past the Defense Department had deliberately parceled production contracts out among many factories in order to get geographic diversification in case of enemy attack. It did not want all tank production wiped out with a single A-bomb. Therefore, three automobile companies, Chrysler, Ford, and General Motors, were producing the Patton M-48 tank. Charlie Wilson arbitrarily declared Ford out of the running and left it up to Chrysler and General Motors to bid against each other. Likewise, Studebaker was ruled out of the bidding on the 2.5-ton truck and was ordered to wind up its production by September 1953. This left General Motors' Truck and Coach Division to bid against Reo Motors, Inc., for the truck contract. Chrysler and American Locomotive were ordered to stop production of the M-47 tank, though simultaneously production of the M-41 tank was continued full speed at General Motors' Cadillac plant in Cleveland. In addition, General Motors was ordered to take over the added production of antiaircraft guns hitherto manufactured by American Car & Foundry.

The order caused consternation in the automobile industry. Loss of these contracts might well put Chrysler out of business. Wilson's old competitors began to realize that he definitely meant it when he said he thought "what was good for the country was good for General Motors and vice versa."

The new Secretary of Defense, however, reckoned without the hand of God and the effect which God's hand had on his own company. During the summer of 1953, fire broke out in the General Motors plant producing hydromatic transmission drives at Lavonia, Michigan. The fire destroyed hydromatic production for Oldsmobile, Pontiac, Cadillac, all produced by General Motors, together with such non-GM cars as Nash, Kaiser, and Lincoln. Charlie Wilson, as head of General Motors, had concentrated most of his hydromatic production in this one plant, and as a result, General Motors' production came to a temporary halt.

So Charlie Wilson, by this time Secretary of Defense, took the hint. He revoked his previous order concentrating tank and truck production in one or two companies. The previous Pentagon policy of diversification was reinstated. Concentration of production, Wilson concluded, was not good for either General Motors or the United States.

In 1956, as Wilson was about to announce to his press conference the 100 top Defense Department contractors, he told aides: "I think I'll tell them that my former company and I both fared much better under the Democrats."

He was right. General Motors for the first time had become number-two contractor with the United States. Boeing Aircraft ranked first.

To the end of his days as Secretary of Defense, Wilson would never admit that a businessman in government could do wrong. When Robert Tripp Ross, his Assistant Secretary of Defense, was investigated by the Senate because his wife, as vice-president of a clothing firm, sold sporting goods to the Army with the benefit of her husband's intervention, Wilson stoutly defended him. "I think it is bad enough to make a man sell everything he owns," he said, "but if he has to divorce his wife too—that's going pretty far."

One of the men he brought into the Pentagon was W. W. White, vice-president of Esso Standard Oil, who, while working for that company, negotiated a $30,000,000 agreement to sell aviation gas to the Air Force overseas. White kept his stock in Standard Oil. Incidentally, he helped use an extra amount of the gas he was buying by flying in an Air Force plane to Iceland for the Fourth of July, 1955, to go fishing.

Wilson surrounded himself in the Defense Department with a

battery of businessmen of this type. At General Motors they were called vice-presidents. In the Pentagon they were called Assistant Secretaries of Defense. There were so many of them that not even newsmen who covered the Pentagon could keep track of them. And the career military men, as far as possible, ignored them. Once Wilson complained to the Secretaries of the Army, the Navy, and the Air Force: "You men are perfectly willing for my Assistant Secretaries to be my eyes and ears, but you don't want them to be my mouth."

When Wilson was head of General Motors he had a reputation for getting along with people. He even got along so well with labor that some of his executives referred to his initials, C.E., as meaning "Compromise Everything." And after he settled down as Secretary of Defense, everyone there also liked him. He took pride in his subordinates, listened to them sympathetically, seldom bawled them out. "It's like making your children behave," Wilson once confided. "You have a certain latitude of tolerance and you love them just the same." He tried to persuade them not to bring small problems up to the top of the Defense Department, but he listened to them patiently whenever they did. Sometimes he quoted from the Bible, Exodus 18:26, on how Moses handled the Children of Israel: "The hard causes they brought unto Moses, but every small matter they judged themselves."

Paraphrasing this advice to his staff, Wilson added, "But don't be afraid to kick a few up to Moses if you have to."

He once philosophized, "When a man asks for the authority of a czar, he's asking for power to do the wrong thing and make everybody suffer."

He didn't believe too much in trying to boss his subordinates. "It's like trying to tell a man how to suck an egg," he said. "You give him a job and let him go and suck it his own way."

But he also said, "The best fertilizer on the land is the master's footsteps."

At the end he told his subordinates, "You're my boys, my crowd. You're good fellows—stout fellows. A stout fellow is one who looks good from any angle, the reverse of a whistling s.o.b."

Once, after a Cabinet meeting at the President's Gettysburg farm, Wilson noted that Ike's personal secretary looked peaked. "Ann Whitman," he observed, "looks like one of our heifers after nursing two calves all summer."

Yes, it was evident that a great deal of the milk of human kindness flowed through Charlie Wilson's veins. However, warmth and kindliness do not necessarily make a great Secretary of Defense. Wilson had other qualities. He was both an engineer and an administrator, had the concentration of a scientist, was not easily jarred out of deep thought, kept two slide rules in his desk and pulled them out to compute problems. At any other time, and in any other administration, Charlie Wilson would have gone down in history as a great Secretary of Defense. That he failed as Secretary of Defense was due to the fact that he was caught on the horns of a dilemma. He was serving an Administration which was determined to cut the budget and yet which faced the most powerful potential enemy the United States has ever faced. Wilson was completely unequal to this dilemma. He did not take a strong stand behind his Joint Chiefs of Staff, who demanded more military preparedness, and he did not take a strong stand behind the Secretary of the Treasury, who wanted less.

He used to pad leisurely around the Pentagon, apparently unruffled by the controversy that whirled around his head. Only his constant chain-smoking and the slight shaking of his hands betrayed any nervousness. Sometimes he would look up at the portrait of Louis Johnson. "You're sometimes in the place where you have to take the heat regardless," he remarked, "just as Louis Johnson had to take it." Once he told George C. Marshall, another former Secretary of Defense, "I've got all my predecessors looking down on me. They're watching every move I make."

When he felt frustrated over budget-cutting, he would say: "I'm like a frog trying to jump out of a well."

"The only way to save money is to be smarter," he philosophized. "There's no cheap road to security, whether by heavy bombs or ballistic missiles, by carriers or submarines, by paratroopers or guided missiles."

"No one enjoys paying taxes," he warned his old business friends. "I thought my taxes too high for twenty-five years, but I haven't squawked about it. I could join the meat-ax boys who want to chop down the defense budget if I didn't know so much about it. Some of the attitudes in Washington remind me of an old purchasing agent I had to call on to sell parts for autos. His opening remark always was 'Your price is too high—what is it?' "

Wilson chided his old friends in the U.S. Chamber of Commerce for asking for defense cuts while "making more money than they ever had before," and he vigorously opposed cutting the budget "with a meat-ax, no matter whether it is the U.S. Chamber of Commerce or any other group of individuals who demand it."

Yet he never took a firm and forthright stand to make the military men inside the Pentagon revise their budget on a common-sense basis. He never knocked heads together among the Joint Chiefs of Staff; and finally, he never realized the ever growing strength of the Russian military establishment.

At a meeting of the National Security Council in late 1953 after the Joint Chiefs of Staff had brought in their "new look," Secretary of the Treasury Humphrey put his finger on the main military problem.

"All you've done is put some chromium plate on your bumper," Humphrey chided. "You've got the same old model shined up a little bit, but how are we going to fight atomic wars with the same old car plus a chromium bumper?"

He pointed to the fact that the military chiefs had merely split military spending three ways, with no regard to military need or strategy. The Navy took its usual share regardless of the fact that a whole task force can now be put out of commission by a single H-bomb. The Army took its usual share regardless of the dubious value of foot soldiers. And the Air Force took its usual share despite the fact that the airplane was becoming outmoded by ballistic missiles. The military chiefs had merely cut the budget three ways with no regard for the precipitous rush of new weapons on which Russia was concentrating.

Charlie Wilson, during all his days as Secretary of Defense, never cracked down on the military to make them scrap old weapons and concentrate on the new. He was too kindly, too considerate; too much of the milk of human kindness flowed in his veins. Also, he devoutly wanted peace. Perhaps this was why he refused to get alarmed over the intelligence reports that came across his desk, reporting new and terrible weapons in Russia.

Early in his administration of the Defense Department, Wilson insisted that Russia couldn't build a long-range jet bomber for years to come. On May Day, 1954, American military attachés stood in Red Square, reviewing the usual May Day exhibition of Russian military might. A giant jet thundered over Moscow housetops at an altitude of only 250 feet. The bomber was so tremendous that its shadow literally spanned Red Square. American observers quickly noted that its four intake vents seemed larger than any they had seen at home, that the heavy plane easily kept up with the swift jet fighter squadrons. When the shocked reaction was cabled back to

Washington, however, Secretary Wilson refused to be alarmed. He dismissed the bomber as a single, hand-built prototype, assembled by the Russians to scare the rest of the world into more defense spending. He noted that the plane had only four engines and pronounced it an underpowered showpiece. Air Force generals disagreed, but Wilson overruled them.

One year passed. Once again the Kremlin flew its bombers across the Russian skyline. By that time the lone bomber of the previous May Day had company—eighteen more big battle planes. Of these, thirteen bore routine Red Air Force markings. Six, with no markings, apparently were so fresh from the factory that they hadn't been assigned to combat units. Each sported a new underbelly bulge, an ominous modification that experts identified as extra room for the hydrogen bomb.

American intelligence went to work compiling technical data. All available facts on the monster bomber were secretly supplied to our own manufacturers, who were asked to figure how long it took the Russians to produce such a plane. The whole Soviet air build-up was re-examined, and the fantastic truth emerged.

In eleven short years the Russians had not only caught up with us in design but outstripped us in production of jet planes. Numerically the Soviet Union had the world's largest air force. American manufacturers concluded from their secret study that Russia's jet Bison had completed the cycle from drawing board to military service in four years—compared with the eight years which the United States spent developing the B-52. The first Bison appeared over Moscow two years before our intelligence thought it could be possible. When the Russians flew nineteen in formation one year later, the United States had only two complete B-52s.

Despite this, Charlie Wilson was unperturbed. "The Russians," he said, "are not nine feet tall."

Two things terminated Charlie Wilson's tenure as Secretary of Defense. One was his wife, who hated Washington. The other was his President, with whom he had some disagreements. The disagreements with Eisenhower could have been patched up. Mrs. Wilson's aversion for Washington, however, could not. Once a Westinghouse stenographer, she had come to be the biggest social frog in the Detroit automobile puddle. In Washington she was hardly a tadpole. In a city where Cabinet officers, Supreme Court justices, ambassadors, and senators are a dime a dozen, Mrs. Wilson didn't rate. She didn't like Washington and wanted to go back to Detroit.

It was not until after she had publicly berated the President of the United States that social Washington knew there was a Mrs. Charles E. Wilson. After that she did rate. After that she became a personage, the toast of Washington newspaper women and of the now fast-growing group which did not like Ike.

By this time, however, Jessie Wilson had talked so much about getting out of Washington that even though she had come to like it, she couldn't reverse herself. And what Jessie wanted, Charlie bowed to. They had met almost fifty years before, when he was getting $80 a month as an electrical engineer with Westinghouse and she was a perky stenographer. Charlie and Jessie had graduated from that $80 a month to a 4,000-acre plantation in Louisiana, a mansion outside Detroit, and a summer home at Walloon Lake, Michigan; plus three daughters, three sons, and eighteen grandchildren. There had been a lot of headaches and heartaches along the way, together with some victories. One of the victories was the design of a self-starter which really gave Wilson his first big boost up the automobile ladder. Then there was the more recent victory, when he became Secretary of Defense. Wilson used to come home from the strain of that dubious victory and pour himself a highball. He sat in front of the open fire, his slippers on, forgetting the bickering of the admirals and the generals. Then he would reach for another highball. "No, Charlie," remonstrated Jessie. He never took the second highball.

So when Jessie said, "Let's go back to Detroit," Charlie agreed to go back to Detroit.

This decision actually had been made before Wilson tangled with the President of the United States over the National Guard, and before Jessie in turn tangled with the President over her husband. It began when Wilson told the House Armed Services Committee in January 1957, "It was a sort of scandal during the Korean War—a boy seventeen and a half to eighteen could enlist in the National Guard and not be drafted to fight in Korea." He told Congressmen that Regular Army officers were right; the National Guard should be combined with the Army.

At his next press conference, Eisenhower, who by this time had heard from Senators Styles Bridges of New Hampshire, Lyndon Johnson of Texas, and other powerful champions of the National Guard, did something which he had never done before. He publicly rapped the knuckles of a Cabinet member, calling Wilson's statement "unwise," made "without stopping to think what it meant."

Whereupon Mrs. Wilson proceeded to slap the President's knuckles. In an interview with Rose McKee of International News Service, she called his statement "uncalled for. . . . I do not think that John Foster Dulles, who Mr. Eisenhower praised, has done any better job than a lot of other men," she said.

"I have stood back and listened to criticism until I am tired of it," said the irate lady from Detroit. "Up to now I have been very, very careful not to make any criticisms of any kind. But you reach a point sometimes—and this is it."

Secretary Wilson emerging from a call at the White House, was asked by newspapermen, "What did you discuss with the President?"

"This is not my dunghill," he replied. "If there is anything else to be announced here somebody else ought to announce it."

Actually, Wilson did not use the word "dunghill." Newspapermen cleaned up his language. He used a shorter, less quotable Anglo-Saxon word used to describe a small wooden house located behind farmhouses in the days before running water and modern bathrooms.

After that White House newspapermen formed the "SOD" society—"Sons of the Dunghill." After that the President, who hates trouble and nearly always appeases those who differ with him, invited Secretary and Mrs. Wilson to fly south in his private plane as he visited the Georgia plantation of another Cabinet member who differed, Secretary of the Treasury Humphrey.

At long last Mrs. Wilson had come into her own. Washington, which once ignored her, now acclaimed her. The Women's National Press Club, giving a dinner in her honor, named her "The Spunkiest Wife of the Year." At the dinner Wilson made a speech.

"I've always known that I couldn't be as smart or as competent as Jessie thought," he said, "but I didn't want to argue or disillusion her. I felt proud, but not surprised, when Jessie stood up for me."

Jessie and Charlie then sang a ditty which they had been singing at parties for years. It went:

"Some liquor was spilled on the barroom floor
As the guests were leaving for the night,
When a little mouse crept from his hole in the wall
To dance in the pale moonlight.

"He lapped up the liquor from the barroom floor,
And upon his haunches he sat,
And all through the night you could hear him shout,
'Bring on that gosh-darned cat.' "

Wilson's differences with Ike over the National Guard heightened rumors that he would resign, and he was badgered by the press. "The simple fact that I haven't made up my mind about what I am going to do seems to bother people," he replied. "I hate to make up my mind until I have to."

By the late summer of 1957, he had outlasted nine millionaires and one plumber in the Eisenhower Cabinet, and Mrs. Wilson, relaxing at Walloon Lake, said, "The news looks good. Mr. Wilson was a complete novelty in Washington. He spoke the simple truths in a place where politics is more generally the native tongue. He came as a great shock."

In many respects she was right. Her husband once said, "The price of progress is trouble—and I must be making a lot of progress."

Little did he realize how much trouble the Defense Department and the nation would be in shortly after he stepped out as Secretary of Defense. Nor did he realize that part of this trouble would be his fault.

"If Mr. Wilson had felt different about background research," said Dr. Clifford C. Furnas, his former Assistant Secretary of Defense for Research and Development, "I think we'd have gotten along much faster." Furnas revealed that in 1956 he had warned Wilson the United States would suffer a terrific propaganda defeat if it did not spend more money in launching a satellite. Wilson's reply, he said, was "So what?"

Charlie Wilson was never enthusiastic about an arms race which might lead to a war which nobody could win. He once said, "This military business is a funny thing. We hope it all goes down the drain." Once he took an indirect crack at John Foster Dulles, without naming him, for "brandishing the atom bomb."

He did not dislike the Russians. "It was too bad the Russians did away with the czars completely," he said. "If they only had a few czars left around, then the Russians would hate them and wouldn't be hating us so much." . . . "Every effort ought to be made to understand the Russians as best we can, even though we have to keep tongues in cheek and we don't trust them very well. I don't cheer over an all-out armaments race with the Russians. I don't think that is the answer either."

Wilson's farewell press conference was held October 2. Everybody joined in asking him pleasant, flattering questions. Wilson unbent as never before. Discussing segregation at the Georgia-Navy game at Norfolk, Virginia, he said, "I suspect it's been going on for many years, and I don't know why we should pay too much attention to it this year. I went to school sixty years ago with a little colored boy and it never hurt me any."

"Did it hurt the colored boy?"

"I don't think so, and he wasn't the dumbest boy in the class, either."

Wilson was even asked to explain that famous crack of five years before when he was being confirmed by the Senate, that "what was good for the country was good for General Motors and vice versa." He said he still believed in it, but the vice versa had been misinterpreted. What he really meant was "what's bad for the country is bad for General Motors. I'm not ashamed of the big-business tag," he added.

Asked if the cut in defense spending would eliminate permanent institutions, he replied: "In this world nothing is permanent."

Two days later Russia launched its first sputnik. The news caught Wilson just as he returned to his old home in Detroit. The paeans of praise sung at his departure suddenly turned to hymns of hate. Congress announced an investigation to see who was responsible for the missile-satellite defeat. Top Republicans held secret strategy meetings and decided to make Wilson the goat. He was hanged in effigy at the Army Missile Base at Huntsville, Alabama.

For several days after leaving Washington, Wilson sat around the house in Detroit as if in a state of shock. His former aide, Lieutenant Colonel James George, found him just sitting, staring out into space. Mrs. Wilson and Colonel George tried to stir him into activity. George finally persuaded Wilson to take him on a tour of the farm. Gradually Wilson snapped out of it.

"I don't know why they're mad at me," he said when he heard that he had been hanged in effigy in Huntsville. "I'm the one who put them in the Jupiter business. They must have me mixed up with the Ku Klux Klan. . . .

"It's only natural when things go wrong for Americans to look for a fall guy or a goat," he said. "If some of them want me to be the goat, that's all right. If I were a smart man I would never have taken the job in the first place."

As to whether his defense policies had been wrong, he told friends that he had done the best job he knew how. "It's futile to talk too much about the past," he said, "something like trying to make birth control retroactive."

viii

HE WHO GOT KICKED

It was about six weeks before President Eisenhower was taken ill at Denver that he received his bluntest warning the United States was falling behind Russia in developing the weapon of the future. He had, of course, received previous intelligence reports to this effect. But in the summer of 1955 Trevor Gardner, Assistant Secretary of the Air Force for Research and Development, finally got to see the President in a blunt-spoken attempt to get action. It was the first time Gardner had briefed the President of the United States and he was nervous. Because of this and because it was a warm day, he perspired so copiously that he had to go home and change his suit. However, he made more impression than he realized.

He took with him Dr. John von Neumann, the Hungarian-born refugee mathematician who was advising the armed services on missile development, as well as General Benjamin A. Schriever, the Air Force missile expert, together with Allen Dulles. The President listened without comment as Gardner pounded home the fact that Russia was far ahead of the United States in developing missiles and that a counterprogram to catch up would cost billions. Allen Dulles added his voice to the warning. All his intelligence, he said, indicated that Russia was far ahead of us in developing this new and deadly weapon.

Six weeks passed. One fateful night in September the President was stricken with a heart attack. During the next two months he was first under an oxygen tent, then confined to his bed, then relaxed in lounging robe around the hospital. Stunned by the tragic news, the American people found comfort in the belief that all was well with the world. At home the economy flourished. Affairs were being well handled abroad. The might of the American military left the nation in no danger. President Eisenhower, according to repeated announcements by members of his Cabinet, was keeping in touch with the world, had his fingers on the pulse of the nation. Trip after trip was made to Denver by Sherman Adams, Secretary of State Dulles, Secretary of the Treasury Humphrey, Secretary of Defense Wilson, after which each assured the public that all was well. President Eisenhower, they said, was making important decisions. From his bedside in Denver the machinery of government was being conducted just as efficiently as from the White House in Washington.

Secretary Wilson, after conferring with Mr. Eisenhower on October 17, emerged from the hospital to tell the American people that they were going to get "more bang for a buck." This was his way of describing the "new look" in national defense, whereby, he said, the Administration would reduce the numerical strength of our military but increase its retaliatory power by putting more stress on technological warfare—in other words, missiles. He had cut the military budget by $3,900,000,000, but he assured the public as he left the hospital in Denver that the United States would be even better prepared.

It was not until six weeks later, when a New York *Times* photographer overheard President Eisenhower remark to his Cabinet members at Camp David, Maryland, that he did not know the French had walked out of the United Nations over Algeria, that the press corps began to realize the steady stream of visitors which went to Denver did not fully inform the President. Henry Cabot Lodge, Ambassador to the UN, after calling upon Ike at Denver, had told the press that he had reported on the French-Algerian crisis at the United Nations. But later it developed he had not. It developed that the President had not been permitted to read a newspaper for five weeks, much less receive an intelligence report. The news brought to his hospital was carefully censored. Any word of controversy was stricken out.

But while the President lounged around the Denver hospital in red pajamas, the Soviet factories were busy turning out more Red missiles. And while Secretary Wilson was assuring the public that they were getting "more bang for a buck," Wilson was actually engaged in untangling himself from his own red tape. He had turned the missile program over to so many managers that it had become almost unmanageable. He had appointed administrators, advisers and co-ordinators with duplicating duties, overlapping authority, and divided service loyalties. Their conflicting claims and contradictory reports, processed through committees within committees all revolving in different directions, created near-chaos. It was not until November 8, 1955, three days before Eisenhower was released from the hospital, that this unwieldy administrative machinery finally gave a go-ahead signal for the manufacture of the first 1,200-mile American intermediate-range missile. Russia had probably given that go-ahead two years before.

It was not until November 22 that President Eisenhower was strong enough to get some idea of the tangled mess bogging down our missile program. This occurred at a special Cabinet briefing held in the Catoctin Mountains west of Washinton, at the Presidential retreat which Franklin D. Roosevelt had called Shangri La, but which Eisenhower renamed Camp David after his grandson. By helicopter and limousine the Cabinet officers had journeyed to the former Civilian Conservation Corps camp. They met at rustic Laurel Cottage part way up the mountainside. The Cabinet officers sat around a table; lesser officials scheduled to do the briefing took chairs in the rear. The full briefing on missiles was to last only forty-five minutes, and each participant was given strict instructions to limit his time. Because the Army and the Navy, as well as the Air Force, were scrambling for their part of the missile pie, each was allotted eight to twelve minutes. Deputy Defense Secretary Reuben Robertson, who opened the briefing, wasted eight precious minutes with a sales pitch punctuated with oratorical gestures. He knew little about missiles.

Ike took a sour view of the Balkanized missile organization which Robertson described. "That looks like the kind of organization that builds empires and won't get the job done in a hurry," he said. He warned that it would only generate interservice rivalry. He did not appear impressed when Secretary Wilson replied with great earnestness that such competition had built up the automobile industry.

Robertson was followed by Major General John B. Medaris for the Army. Since he had been in charge of the Army's ballistic-missile program for only nine days, he knew little about it. However, he was well coached and gave a standard Army briefing. Next came Secretary of the Navy Charles Thomas, a cloak-and-suit manufacturer from Los Angeles who, according to some of his colleagues, "wouldn't have recognized a missile if he had been run over by one." He flourished charts to illustrate his ten-minute lecture and spoke gravely of the threat of submarine-launched missiles. Ike, growing fidgety, broke in impatiently, "If these damn subs can only carry a few missiles, they will shoot them and have to go all the way back to base for more. Are you telling me that is a threat? I don't see it."

Summoned to tell the Air Force story was the Assistant Secretary in charge of research, Trevor Gardner, who had brought with him once again Dr. John von Neumann and General Schriever. By this time, the President was more restless than ever. Secretary Wilson, never a missile enthusiast, was smiling blandly. Atomic Energy Chairman Lewis Straus was drumming on the table.

Gardner explained that he wasn't as competent as his two backstops, von Neumann and Schriever, but that he would speak for them because he was supposed to be a better salesman. This broke the ice. Ike grinned and said, "Go right ahead." Gardner plunged into an urgent discussion of the Russian gain and the American lag in missile development. When he mentioned the fact that the Air Force hadn't started to build missiles of the 1,000- to 1,800-mile ranges while Russia was already testing them, the President looked irritated.

"Charlie," he rasped, turning to his Secretary of Defense, "along about four or five months ago we had a meeting on this, and I told you to get going on this program. What in the hell have you done on this?"

Wilson pulled his head down in his collar. "We are making progress, Mr. President," he said lamely.

Gardner also complained, somewhat bitterly, that the Air Force's intercontinental ballistic missile was being neglected. Admiral Arthur W. Radford, Chairman of the Joint Chiefs of Staff, interrupted to challenge this. The ICBM had a number-one national priority, he said, and he argued that this could scarcely be called neglect. Gardner retorted that eighty other projects had the same priority, which made it meaningless. The haphazard priority system, he charged, was breeding hideous waste and confusion.

The Cabinet briefing, prompt to its forty-five minutes, broke up with a demand from Eisenhower: "I want to be briefed on this every two weeks." Gardner, von Neumann and Schriever climbed aboard their helicopter for the bumpy trip back to Washington. They were a hopeful, but doubtful, trio. They knew that the President, though full of good intentions, did not always follow through. Dr. von Neumann, in particular, must have wondered whether his trip had been necessary. He had left Germany just ahead of Hitlerism to join Dr. Einstein in his scientific research at Princeton; later had devoted this great talent to pushing the armed forces ahead on missiles and nuclear weapons. But he was dying. He had cancer and wore a brace to protect his spine. The helicopter ride was rough and he suffered great pain. Probably he knew as he flew back to Washington that this was to be his last Presidential briefing.

Trevor Gardner did not know it, but he too had briefed the President for the last time. He was to be brought under all kinds of pressure—amiable and sinister—to stop making trouble over missiles. But he refused to give up the battle for his convictions and in the end went down in political flames. The story is one of the blackest in the record of our snarled-up missile mess.

Charlie Wilson is not the only man whose name must be placed in the historical record on the pages marked "guilty." Alongside his must be written the name of Donald A. Quarles, who served successively as Assistant Defense Secretary in charge of research, Secretary of the Air Force, and Deputy Secretary of Defense. Quarles is one of the most delightful gentlemen in Washington. His personality is so disarming that it's difficult to disagree with him, impossible to dislike him. Yet he has skirted every major decision it has been possible to skirt, and even after Sputnik I he was still putting economy ahead of the nation's desperate needs. Completely opposite in personality and mannerism, Quarles and Gardner clashed continually. It was a clash between energy and inertia; and as so often happens in government, inertia won.

Gardner came into the Air Force in 1953 in the forefront of the Eisenhower Crusade. His first big assignment from Wilson was to survey the missile milieu. Gardner's orders were to tie up—and where possible clip off—the loose ends of the missile program for the purpose of reducing costs.

He organized what came to be called the Teapot Committee, which made a searching investigation of both the Soviet and the American missile programs. After untangling the confusing and often conflicting reports from behind the Iron Curtain, the committee took the first clear look at what the Russians were doing. Its sobering conclusion was that the Russians were *at least two years* ahead of the United States in missile technology.

Under the ailing Dr. von Neumann, the committee also evaluated the technical feasibility of intercontinental missiles. Up to 1953 a practical intercontinental missile was out of the question. It would have required a warhead weighing half a million pounds and a guidance system with bull's-eye accuracy to make a long-distance missile across the ocean practical. The machinery for making hydrogen explosions was much too unwieldy in those days. In fact, the first hydrogen explosion, in November 1952, had not even been caused by a bomb, but by a device so huge that it was nicknamed the "H-House."

Then, in 1954, came a revolution in hydrogen weapons. Between March and May of that year, hydrogen tests in the Pacific proved that a small, compact, lightweight warhead could carry an explosive impact as deadly as all the explosive material unloosed in World War II. This suddenly made the intercontinental missile a dangerous threat to any nation. A hydrogen warhead could be delivered by rocket, and its enormous explosive power made exact accuracy of the rocket unimportant. For the vast explosive power of the warhead could destroy a target without a direct hit.

In the summer of 1954, Gardner understood the meaning of the giant mushrooms that were sprouting in the Pacific. Abandoning the instructions he had been given to curtail the missile program, he sought to increase rather than decrease the budget. He began what was to be an eighteen-months-long fight to smash through the White House ring and get his information to the President.

Finally, through two former Democrats on the National Security Council and the President's Scientific Advisory Committee, Gardner was able to get the ear of Robert Cutler, the powerful Secretary of the National Security Council. But even after Cutler had been acquainted with the missile facts, it took another three months before Gardner was permitted to brief the President. By now it was already the summer of 1955! There followed the session described earlier in which the nervous Gardner perspired so freely but after which the President took a definite interest in missiles. The President had made no comment following Gardner's impassioned plea, and the anxious Gardner wondered bleakly whether he had failed. But Ike apparently had been more impressed than his manner indicated, for not long afterward he made the ICBM the nation's top defense project.

This started more trouble than it solved. Jealous of Gardner's scoop for the Air Force, the Army and the Navy began demanding equal status for their own pet projects. To keep the peace, they were given their way. One priority demand led to another until, before Wilson knew what was happening, the Defense Department had eighty-four number-one-priority projects all competing with each other for money, men and materials. The word "priority" had lost all meaning. The Secretary of Defense, however, did not for a minute dream that this was the fact. After one fervent Gardner lecture on pushing ahead with missiles, Wilson said, "You have the highest priority."

"But eighty other projects have the same priority," Gardner complained.

"That's not true!" snapped Wilson.

Gardner insisted it was true and Wilson agreed to check for himself. He found there were eighty-four projects with number-one priority.

Gardner was also finding it increasingly difficult to get past Quarles, upon whom Wilson leaned heavily for scientific advice. Quarles held back not only on the ICBM but on other major programs. He avoided decisions by referring problems back to committees for further study—a technique for which he had good precedent, for it was practiced continually by the White House. Only by weaving through the ranks of assorted Assistant Secretaries whom Wilson had added to his staff was Gardner able to get to the Secretary's block-long office overlooking the Potomac. Then, oblivious of the difficulty of penetrating his inner sanctum, Wilson would say with a shrug, "Nobody has been in to see me about this."

On those occasions when Gardner persuaded Wilson to sign a directive, it usually became mired in administrative quicksand. An Assistant Secretary might ask for an interpretation of the Wilson order. On occasion this could take up to three months. Another three months might be necessary to get the comments of others who didn't understand the interpretation. A thick file would build up—all over a few paragraphs of Wilsonian prose. Wilson took this as a sign of activity and believed he was getting results. The unhappy truth was that his directives could be implemented swiftly or delayed interminably—depending on how subordinates wanted to interpret them. Ever since the Army and the Navy were "unified" into one sprawling, far-flung Defense Department, the Secretary of Defense has tended to be a prisoner of his admirals, his generals, and his Assistant Secretaries. To some extent it was the fault of the system, not the man. But because Charlie Wilson was schooled in private business, with more loyalties than bureaucratic business, he leaned too heavily on the labyrinth of aides around him.

From this labyrinth, one of the most self-effacing, charming gentlemen in Washington emerged as Gardner's chief opposition. It was not that Donald Quarles was opposed to missiles, but rather that he was opposed to stretching the budget for missiles. Quarles's greatest ambition was to become Secretary of Defense, and he has climbed the Pentagon ladder a long way toward that goal. But with every move up the ladder, he kicked further down the ladder appropriations for missiles and scientific research. This was understandable. For the political goal of the Administration has been to cut the budget; and he who achieves economy achieves favor in the eye of the White House.

Eisenhower had been in office less than a year when, on December 9, 1953, Quarles, then Assistant Secretary, wrote a memo to the research-and-development policy committee of the Defense Department opposing $1,300,000,000 sought for research and development for the fiscal year 1955. "It is incompatible with the over-all objective of reducing Department of Defense expenditure," Quarles wrote. If his advice had been the opposite, if that appropriation had passed, the United States would not be the second-class power it is today.

The man who has so consistently dragged his feet on missile research started work at the age of sixteen as a public-school teacher in Van Buren, Arkansas. He taught in the winter in order to study in the summer at the University of Missouri, worked his way through Yale by tutoring. When Wilson brought him into the Pentagon, Quarles was surrounded by the aura of a technical expert. He had come from the research environment of the Bell Telephone laboratories where, although he was largely an administrator, he had managed to soak up enough scientific knowledge to qualify as a scientist for industrial purposes. It has been said that he was retired by his Bell bosses for being too conservative.

In his first post as Assistant Secretary in charge of research, Quarles so ingratiated himself to the warmhearted Wilson that the Secretary of Defense came to regard him not only as the voice of science but as its last word. Even after leaving research to become Air Secretary, Quarles continued as Wilson's most trusted scientific adviser. It would be unfair to Quarles to suggest that, in pursuit of ambition, he deliberately engaged in a sort of scientific confidence game. It would not be unfair to say that he overvalued his own judgment.

When budget limitations came down from the White House, it was to Quarles that Wilson turned for reassurance that it would be safe to obey them. There is no record of Quarles's ever putting up a battle. He always seemed to agree that the armed forces could get along on less than whatever they were getting. In technical matters, he would become obsessed with details, was never willing to sanction those bold gambles which produce the scientific breakthroughs.

A patient listener, Quarles can sit politely through endless briefings. He can be presented with irrefutable evidence of Soviet progress and still refuse to believe. "I am not convinced," he will say, and then he will proceed to overrule Air Force experts without a qualm. The conferences in his office are interminable. But the end result is nearly always the same: a veto, postponement or slowdown for any project costing money.

Trevor Gardner's last showdown with the powers that be in the Pentagon came over the question of making an all-out push to catch up with Russia. He had prepared a very careful document on Air Force missile needs. It showed that the Air Force would need three to four billion dollars more for fiscal year 1957. The increase for research alone was $316,000,000. The United States had broken through the scientific barriers on new propulsion ideas and aerodynamic concepts that held tremendous promise; yet for economy reasons the Defense Department had held back. The report was approved by every expert in the Air Force from General Nathan F. Twining, then Air Force Chief of Staff, down.

Gardner marched into the office of cautious Donald Quarles, then Secretary of the Air Force, and laid it on his desk. Quarles shook his head solemnly. "I am glad you went through this exercise," he said. "It has cleared the air and cleared your mind." But he added sadly that because the Air Force was under strict budget limitations, it would be impossible to carry out the program.

Gardner begged Quarles to listen to a briefing. This would prove beyond doubt that the Russians were leaping ahead in the missile race. Quarles said he had already heard such briefings.

"But this is basic," pleaded Gardner.

Finally, with a sigh, Quarles agreed to listen again and did, in fact, spend most of a Saturday sitting through two long sessions. If Quarles was impressed, he was still unmoved.

"I am sorry, Trevor," he said, "there is nothing I can do. We have been dictated a budget ceiling."

Gardner set his jaw. "Let's go fight," he urged. "You are Secretary of the Air Force. You can fight. If you want to fight dirty, I'll help you. We can go to the Hill or we can go to the public."

Quarles recoiled at the suggestion.

"I wouldn't think of that," he replied. "Actually, in my judgment, the nation cannot afford that sort of research program."

"And what about the judgment of all these people?" demanded Gardner, waving under Quarles's nose the names of the Air Force's finest scientists, who had approved his recommendations.

"I'll mention it to Wilson," Quarles compromised.

"Mention it, hell!" exploded Gardner. "What we need to do is fight for the program, not try to fob it off."

Quarles invited him to go back over his proposals, cut out the waste, then bring them in again. Gardner stood firm. They had already been trimmed to the limit of safety, and if Quarles would not act upon them as they were, then Gardner threatened "for the sake of my conscience" to take them to Wilson direct. Faced with such resolution, Quarles gave his approval.

When Gardner reached Wilson's office, he put up such a battle that the Secretary swept him off on a calming trip to Florida. Gardner was given the "Kettering suite" in the Wilson home, reserved for Charles F. Kettering, Wilson's old associate in General Motors, and for several days they sat in a cabana at the Surf Club hashing out the missile situation. Gardner, who loves to swim, ignored the beach and devoted every minute to proselyting Wilson. When the little holiday was over, Wilson went home with a tan from exposure to the sun but with no mental mellowing from exposure to Gardner.

Gardner did get one message across to the Secretary of Defense, however. It was that he, Gardner, was prepared to risk his career over the missile issue and that he, Wilson, could expect the shrapnel to start flying. The unsubdued Gardner had hardly returned to Washington when a Wilson aide slipped quietly around to see him.

He sought to soothe Gardner's ruffled feelings, told him "the old man" was very fond of him and would like to put him in charge of the whole missile program. Such a promotion, of course, would require that Gardner behave and not be a thorn in the side of the Administration. The aide also pointed out that the British government was about to decorate Gardner for his missile work and that both the President and Wilson also wanted to honor him. Such laurels, he was reminded, could be awarded only if he stayed on the job. Gardner indicated he was less concerned about medals than about missiles, whereupon the pressure took a darker line.

Gardner was warned that he would have to be careful of what he said, or he might have his security clearance removed. He should also remember that one day he would be going back to his company, which had defense contracts. If he hoped to do business with the Pentagon, it would be better to leave friends, not enemies, behind.

"If I didn't know you so well," replied Gardner, "my reply would be a punch on the nose." He told the Wilson aide to go back and tell the Secretary of Defense that he, Gardner, was more determined than ever to make the missile mess an issue.

Shortly thereafter, Gardner's resignation was submitted and accepted. As he crossed the Pentagon threshold for the last time, Wilson and Quarles collected all his memos and locked them in a vault. They may not have known too much about missiles, but they certainly were not going to have any explosive missives lying around. This was not all. As Gardner was about to leave the Air Force he found himself under investigation by the Senate Government Operations Committee. Robert F. Kennedy, brother of the Senator from Massachusetts and counsel for the Senate Committee, queried Gardner regarding a subcontract given to his former firm, Hycon-Eastern, by an Air Force prime contractor in Boston. Kennedy suspected that Gardner, as an Air Force official, had helped place this Air Force contract with his old firm, and he subjected Gardner to a lengthy cross examination.

"Didn't you have a thirty-three-minute telephone conversation with General Schriever last August?" he asked, referring to Ben Schriever, the officer in charge of pushing the intercontinental ballistic missile.

"Yes," replied Gardner.

"Wasn't that all from your home?"

"Yes, it was."

"Did you collect from the government for it?" pursued the Senate probers.

"No, I run up a phone bill of two or three hundred dollars a month at home, some calls to my family, some for the government, and I never can remember which is which. So I don't charge the government."

"Now, didn't you talk to General Schriever about getting that contract for Hycon-Eastern?"

Senate prober Kennedy obviously was suspicious that Gardner had telephoned General Schriever from his home so that the call wouldn't show on the telephone records of the Pentagon. Gardner told the investigators he had not talked to General Schriever about the contract; and his past record indicates that he was telling the truth. He had sold his stock in Hycon before entering the government, making a clean break with the company. If he had kept it, he would have made a profit of $2,000,000.

There followed another significant development. After it became known that the Senate Government Operations Committee had checked on Gardner, William P. Rogers, then Deputy Attorney General, wrote a letter to the Senate committee asking for a copy of its file on Gardner. This was a most unusual step. Senate committees have turned up glaring conflicts of interest in the Eisenhower Administration, including that of Harold Talbott, the Air Force Secretary; Peter Strobel, the Public Buildings Commissioner; Carl O. Hanson of the Farm Home Administration; and Hugh W. Cross, the Interstate Commerce Commissioner; but in no case hitherto had the Justice Department shown the slightest interest. No request had been made for a record. In the case of the man who had resigned with a blast of criticism against Secretary Wilson and President Eisenhower, however, the Justice Department suddenly became active. It reviewed the testimony, but it did not act. There was no ground for action.

Gardner was summoned before various committees of Congress to explain his reasons for resigning and his reasons for believing the United States was in a dangerous position vis-à-vis Russia. Democratic Congressmen were friendly, Republicans generally hostile. He charged bluntly that our military planners "are underestimating the Russians," that intelligence reports from behind the Iron Curtain indicated Soviet scientists were progressing far faster on atomic- and guided-missile research than we had realized. "Our most precious asset is time," he warned.

When he reminded Congressmen that the previous year they themselves had "arbitrarily cut eighteen million dollars off our research and development budget," Congressman Scrivner of Kansas remarked, "Would you mind striking out the word 'arbitrarily'?"

"Yes, I would," Gardner replied.

That was the record of the blunt-spoken, uncompromising Assistant Secretary of the Air Force who did more than any other one man to try to goad the Eisenhower Administration into action, but who got rapped over the knuckles in return.

President Eisenhower's State of the Union message for the opening of Congress in 1956 was delivered just forty-five days after the Camp David briefing at which his own missile experts disturbed him with the warning that the United States was lagging dangerously behind Russia. Despite this warning, the President told the Congress and the American people on January 6, "We have improved the effectiveness and combat readiness of our forces by developing and making operational new weapons and by integrating the latest scientific developments, including new atomic weapons, into our military plans. We continue to push the production of the most modern military aircraft. The development of long-range missiles has been on an accelerated basis for some time."

The President knew, of course, that the development of long-range missiles was not on "an accelerated basis." It was badly bogged down. The public, however, had no way of knowing until after Trevor Gardner resigned. After that Eisenhower went before his press conference February 8, 1956, to reassure the American people that the United States was "doing everything that human science, brains and resources can do to keep our position in proper posture."

The exit of Trevor Gardner from the Defense Department left a double hole. For the man who had pushed the hardest for the development of missiles was, in effect, replaced by the man who had lagged most behind. For three years Donald Quarles sat through briefing after briefing by the Air Force in which it sought to build a reconnaissance satellite called the Pied Piper. It was to weigh 400 pounds, was to carry TV equipment, and was to be launched into the heavens to gather vital information about outer space. Quarles was still withholding his decision on October 4, 1957, when Sputnik I suddenly popped out of Siberia and passed him by. Air Force officers immediately urged a crash program to get the Pied Piper up there too. They warned that Russia was building even heavier satellites and rockets to reach the moon. But Donald Quarles sat through the long argument, politely, patiently, completely oblivious to the Soviet satellite which had hurtled twice around the world even during the course of his meeting. "You gentlemen," he complained, "want to move too fast."

ix

THE HIGH PRIEST OF ECONOMY

THE MOST IMPORTANT INFLUENCE on Dwight D. Eisenhower during his years in the White House has been not Mamie, not the whole Cabinet, not the Senate or Congressional leaders, but a small group of intimates known as the "Augusta Golfing Cabinet." Their influence has been economic. And it was they who started Ike down his pell-mell road to cut the budget no matter what the military consequences. To balance the budget was, of course, a wholly laudatory goal. But cutting the military budget must be done with a surgeon's scalpel, not a butcher knife. And those who launched Eisenhower on his budget-cutting path and hounded him to make sure he followed that path did not care whether the job was done by the surgeon's scalpel or not. They were interested only in lower taxes. They did not subscribe to the theory, now demonstrated to be a fact, that it is far better to cut some of the luxuries of life than to jeopardize the military security of the nation at a time when it faces the most serious threat since the Civil War.

What compounded the tragedy was the sweet talk fed to the American people that the national defense was being based on revolutionary, new and cheaper weapons, when in real fact those weapons existed only in embryo. Thus we found ourselves like the Emperor of Hans Christian Andersen's fairy tales, striding through the market places naked and unprepared, yet confident that we were well armed and ready to master the world.

The knives which slashed our military muscle were held by others; but the surgery had the five-star approval of Dwight D. Eisenhower. All the glamour and prestige of his position as Supreme Allied Commander during the war, as Chief of Staff after the war, as NATO

Commander in Europe, plus his forty-one years of military service, were behind the assurances to the American people that the national defense, though costing less, was now more sound and secure than ever. Without these assurances from a man who had given his life to military service, the American people would have raised question marks earlier than they did.

Explaining to the nation on April 30, 1953, that the huge $8,500,000,000 slice he was making in the defense budget would make no difference to the nation's safety, the President said, "These savings will not reduce the effective military strength we will deliver to ourselves and our allies during fiscal 1954."

Just four months before, as he entered the White House on January 20, 1953, America's military machine was the most powerful in the world. And as the President continued to sacrifice the national safety on the altar of fiscal policy, he continued to assure the American people that they were safe, the national defense was strong. On January 21, 1954, when he made further cuts in the military budget, he told Congress and the people, "With the shift in emphasis to the full exploitation of air power and modern weapons, we are in a position to support strong national security programs over an indefinite period with less of a drain on our manpower, material and financial resources."

During his election campaign Dwight D. Eisenhower had made many promises to the people. He had promised better schools, 100-per-cent-parity prices for farmers, the strengthening of the Civil Service, the end of corruption in government, end of the war in Korea, a reduced budget and the cutting of taxes. Of these he hastened to make good only two—the ending of the war in Korea and slashing the military budget. During his first term in office, no action was taken on schools, the Civil Service was disrupted, corruption increased, and farmers' prices decreased. But a little clique of businessmen around the newly elected President took his promise on tax reduction with deadly seriousness. For years, under Roosevelt and Truman, they had paid high corporation taxes and even higher personal income taxes. And they were determined, regardless of national security, to get these taxes lowered. They even placed one of their own men in the most strategic Cabinet spot to make sure this pledge was fulfilled.

This little group of fiscal influencers, later known as the Augusta Golfing Cabinet, appointed Cabinet members, dictated fiscal policy, determined the complexion of White House stag dinners. It, more than any other, decided that Ike must run for a second term. And to it belongs part of the blame for the downhill slide of American power and prestige.

How this group came into being is one of the most extraordinary untold stories of the Eisenhower era. Its nucleus was Sidney Weinberg, born in Russia, raised in Brooklyn, long considered a Democrat, who rose from office boy to be head of the giant investment firm of Goldman, Sachs, and who has placed more friends in the Eisenhower Cabinet than anyone in the nation. He also serves as director of more corporations than almost anyone else. The fact that he had his hand inside the government, no matter what the party in power, has not hurt either his pride or his position. During Roosevelt's New Deal he bobbed in and out of Washington as part of the ill-fated NRA. Came the war and he was part of the Office of Production Mobilization, then joined the War Production Board. He even maneuvered to appoint Donald Nelson, then head of Sears, Roebuck, to head the War Production Board, following which Weinberg became Nelson's assistant. Weinberg was a director of Sears, Roebuck, so it was a simple matter for him to switch Nelson from Chicago to Washington. While oscillating back and forth between his office in Wall Street and his office in Washington, Weinberg got to know General Lucius D. Clay, later deputy to Eisenhower in Germany and commander of the U.S. forces in Europe. Came the time when General Clay was to retire from the Army; Weinberg got him a job as head of giant Continental Can. Came the time when Eisenhower needed money for a cleverly devised system of blanketing the air waves with political spots just before Election Day in 1952; it was Sidney Weinberg who was instrumental in raising $2,000,000.

Thus was formed the nucleus of the Augusta Golfing Cabinet. Chief motive originally was to put Dwight D. Eisenhower in the White House. Both Clay and Weinberg were nominal Democrats. The next man to join was also a nominal Democrat—Robert Woodruff, head of Coca-Cola. Woodruff came from Columbus, Georgia, General Clay from Marietta, Georgia. All his life Eisenhower had been considered a Democrat, and these sometime Democrats rallied behind him. They added to the group William E. Robinson, business manager of the New York *Herald Tribune*, later president of Coca-Cola; Clifford Roberts of Reynolds & Company; and Alton B. Jones of Cities Service. This was the group which built at the Augusta Golf Club what has been called "Mamie's Cabin," which in actual fact is an eighteen-room, seven-bathroom example of the best that money can build tucked away in the foothills of Georgia. Featuring $160 door locks, air conditioning, radiant heating, indirect lighting, two stainless-steel electric ranges, a food freezer, an intercom system, two giant built-in television sets, free furniture flown by air from New York, and even a barber's chair for the President, this gift to Ike from his Wall Street friends cost, including the adjacent fish-pond, a total of $200,000.

This is the group which also picked Ike's Secretary of the Treasury and exercised more influence on fiscal policies than any other half-dozen men in the nation.

There was a time when it looked as if the Augusta Golfing Cabinet had picked the wrong man to carry out its goal of reducing taxes. Attending a dinner at the exclusive F Street Club in Washington, General Eisenhower, then president of Columbia University, had held forth in no uncertain terms on the importance of high taxes. He believed not only in high taxes, but in wartime confiscatory taxes. Republicans attending the dinner came away with grave doubts as to whether Eisenhower was the man they really wanted to elect President. Later, Russell Davenport, editor of *Life* magazine, General Edward Clark, John G. Bennett, the New York political leader, and James Russell Forgan of the Glore-Forgan brokerage firm called him on high taxes. When Eisenhower proposed that business make no profit from defense contracts, Bennett reminded him, "General, you pulled the furniture down on your head once before at the F Street Club when you proposed that idea. And you will do it again if you take that stand. It's contrary to the free-enterprise system."

Eisenhower frowned.

"Yes," interposed Forgan, "if John hadn't called you on that I would have."

Eisenhower argued that a man's life is more important than corporate profits, and that when you ask a boy to sacrifice his life in war it's only fair to ask a corporation to sacrifice its profit.

"You can't sell that to the Republican Party," his friends warned. Eisenhower finally agreed he would compromise by taking a stand for a "fair return on investment."

All of Dwight D. Eisenhower's background, dating back to his boyhood in Kansas, tended to support the theory he expressed at that exclusive dinner party in 1950—namely, that life is more important than property. His mother, a devout member of Jehovah's Witnesses, had certainly felt that way. His father, who worked for a meager salary in the Abilene Creamery, was a high-tax William Jennings Bryan Democrat. All his long career in the Army Eisenhower had favored adequate military expenditures and adequate taxes to pay for them. But also running through his life was a deep respect, sometimes bordering on worship, for business achievement. This was only natural. Never having had much of the world's worldly goods, Ike cherished a respect almost bordering on cupidity for worldly goods. That explains why he did not hesitate to receive such a deluge of gifts while Commander in Europe that an extra airplane was required to bring them home. It also explains why he accepted the luxuriously equipped cottage at Augusta without any thought that he might prejudice his future fiscal policies. That was why he accepted gifts for his Gettysburg house and farm, ranging from furniture to expensive landscaping. And that also explains why shortly after his statement that life is more important than property in the sacrifices of wartime, he completely reversed himself. He made it clear that he did not approve of confiscatory taxes in time of war, in fact he did not approve of high taxes, period.

All this, occurring as it did before Dwight D. Eisenhower became President of the United States, is necessary to any understanding of why a man who spent forty-one years as a soldier should lead the nation to its most disastrous slashing of the defense budget in all history.

As President-elect Eisenhower returned from Korea on the U.S.S. *Helena*, he scrawled in his own handwriting his notion of how his new administration was to approach reduced government expenditure. "Like a heavy truck racing down an icy hill," he wrote, "the brakes must be lightly and expertly applied to avoid a wreck and slowly come to a stop before turning off in the right direction."

But while the new President may have thought he was delicately applying the brakes, his new Secretary of the Treasury figuratively was pulling hard on the emergency. Humphrey, the man whom the Augusta Golfing Cabinet had picked as high priest of the economy cult, had laid down his own terms when he accepted appointment as Secretary of the Treasury. "Any place where money is concerned," he stipulated, "I want to be consulted." In accepting those terms, the new President made his first important surrender. This concession entitled his Secretary of the Treasury to poke his long and capable arm into every department of the government. And it later caused him to challenge the President of the United States, publicly and roughly, over the size of the budget—an act of defiance unprecedented since the day when Harold Ickes challenged President Truman's appointment of Ed Pauley as Under Secretary of the Navy and immediately got kicked out of the Cabinet for his pains. Humphrey was not kicked out. He not only escaped without rebuke but in the end forced the President to capitulate publicly.

Only a few days after George Humphrey moved into the gray stone mausoleum which has more gold buried beneath its front lawn than any place outside of Fort Knox, Kentucky, he issued his first ultimatum. It was to hack the Truman budget down to a size the taxpayers could digest. He was frank and honest in his belief that the nation could not continue indefinitely with an unbalanced budget. Furthermore it didn't take much scrutiny of the budget figures to see that any substantial saving would have to come out of the Defense Department and a memo was sent to Charles E. Wilson to that end. Wilson, however, was off inspecting his new armed-services domain, and the budget cuts fell to his Under Secretary, Roger Kyes, and to the Comptroller of the Defense Department, Wilfred J. McNeil, a former admiral, who sent a blunt, almost peremptory letter to Air Force Secretary Harold Talbott nominating that branch of the service to make the chief sacrifices. "It appears the possibilities of limiting obligations in the Air Force for the balance of this year may be greater than those indicated by your proposals," McNeil wrote.

The result was a drastic five-billion-dollar slash in new funds for the Air Force at a time when Eisenhower was already devising a new military policy which depended entirely upon the Air Force. The Air Force was to be America's main striking arm, or, as Eisenhower called it, "the new look." This turned out to be less a policy than a justification for military reduction. However, it was pounded home on the public as a great achievement. There was no mention of the fact that at the very time Administration propagandists were selling the new look, the Air Force was being slashed by five billion dollars.

The hit-or-miss manner in which the armed services were being meat-cleavered was exposed by Senator Margaret Chase Smith, the Maine Republican, who, as a member of the Senate Armed Services Committee, has a habit of asking penetrating and sometimes embarrassing questions. When she questioned Secretary of Defense Wilson regarding drastic Air Force cuts, he confessed, "After we got the things together we added them up. Much to Mr. Kyes's surprise and mine, most of the cuts seemed to show up in the Air Force program." Under Secretary Kyes, sitting beside Wilson, chimed in: "I did not realize it until Secretary Talbott called the statistical result to my attention."

Meanwhile, Secretary of State Dulles assured the American people at the American Legion convention in St. Louis, September 1953, that the United States had evolved a new and powerful policy—"massive retaliation." He did not explain to his applauding listeners or to the complacent American people how we could retaliate massively by delivering an atomic bomb while simultaneously we were drastically slashing the armed service entrusted with delivering the bomb. The Eisenhower-Dulles slogan seemed to outline a novel and almost moral concept, but close examination showed that the new look was merely the same old look in a small economy size.

But invoking all his military mystique, the new President was able to push the new look through Congress. The glitter of his five-star reputation outshone the military background of the few critics who rose to challenge him. So, although the armed forces were still fighting in Korea, and although Russia had just developed its first atomic bomb, the defense cuts were accepted.

True, the new President sometimes seemed worried about his campaign for military economy. There were times when he vacillated. When the high priest of economy, Secretary Humphrey, demanded further drastic economies beginning July 1, 1954, Secretary of Defense Wilson objected and Eisenhower impulsively sided with him. Humphrey wanted to cut the military budget to ten billion dollars less than the Truman figure; but the President got warmed up in a little speech to the Cabinet in which he wanted to know why national security should be sacrificed to balance the budget. Why should not some of this non-defense money such as veterans' benefits and farmers' price supports be sliced their fair share, too, Ike asked. In the end he lost. It was not that his voice carried little weight, but rather that he did not use his voice often or loudly enough. He did not bellow. And a President sometimes has to bellow—or cuss, as Harry Truman did—to get his ideas across in Washington. Payments to veterans and farmers veered upward, and spending on defense moved in the reverse direction, though not at the plunging pace urged by Secretary Humphrey. As Ike himself once said of his fiscal team, "I have given way on a number of personal opinions to this gang."

Significantly, it was Wilson, not Eisenhower, who came under fire for the new look. When aides pointed out to the President that Wilson was getting all the blame, he rapped out, "I don't feel neglected." That Ike escaped most of the barrage was again due to his five-star stature. Even the hardiest Democrat hesitated to lace into him directly. There were a few anxious voices on Capitol Hill, but not many. Senator Stuart Symington, Democrat of Missouri and former Secretary of the Air Force, complained, "I share the businessman's traditional dislike for deficits, but I am convinced that no loyal and informed American would knowingly consent to dangerous concessions in our security program in order to achieve some otherwise desirable fiscal objective."

In the inner Cabinet debates, Secretary of State Dulles' voice was generally on the side of adequate defense. Repeatedly he reminded his Cabinet colleagues of the potential danger of Soviet aggression. He particularly stressed the need for military assistance to friendly nations, including on one occasion modern weapons for Ethiopia. To Charles E. Wilson this was a waste of money. He did not regard Ethiopia's military potential as worth bothering about. The President, however, supported Dulles. "You win, Foster," yielded Wilson. "We'll send them some modern spears."

Wilson's closest friend outside the automobile industry was Arthur Godfrey, freckle-faced star of radio and television. As each new Eisenhower budget contained more bad news for the armed forces, Godfrey took a trip with bomber General Curtis LeMay and came back a special pleader for the Air Force. At one time, Wilson had tried to appoint Godfrey an Assistant Defense Secretary; but even without the title, the comedian freely offered Wilson his views on air power.

Before going under ether for a serious operation, Godfrey phoned Wilson from a Boston hospital and begged him not to injure the Air Force. "Go ahead with the operation and don't worry," Wilson assured him. But Godfrey remained uneasy about defense cuts, and when he recovered he invited Wilson and LeMay to spend a weekend at his farm in Virginia—a thinly disguised attempt to provide LeMay with a captive audience of one Defense Secretary. Wilson finally got fed up with the effort to high-pressure him, packed his bags and went home. That ended the famous Wilson-Godfrey friendship.

In July 1955 President Eisenhower came back from his Summit Conference with the Kremlin leaders, infused with the "Geneva spirit." He was quite sincere about this. He told his associates enthusiastically that he believed he had got through to the Soviet leaders, and for a time he genuinely believed the cold war was over. And as John Foster Dulles praised the President's God-given ability to reconcile differences between men, the President felt he could now concentrate more than ever on his Holy Grail. He summoned his Cabinet, pulled out a written statement and read: "A deficit of from 1.5 to 1.7 billion dollars is still likely for this fiscal year. This amounts to only three per cent of the federal spending planned for this year. . . . Surely in this giant government there are still programs, administrative costs or wasteful practices of one sort or another that we can rule out without danger to anything essential. I think we can at least find that three per cent and balance the budget this year . . ."

Ike acknowledged that the Soviet threat had not evaporated and cautioned against economy at the expense of security. Wilson pointed out that he was already slashing his budget by 5 per cent. An additional 3 per cent, he warned, would add up to a difficult economy goal. But the old soldier in the White House said he still thought the armed services could cut out more of the fluff. He barbed his argument with a little story about how, when he was an aide to General Douglas MacArthur in Washington, only MacArthur as Chief of Staff had an automobile; the rest of the General Staff were given streetcar tokens when called upon to testify on Capitol Hill.

Promising to do his best, Wilson issued a policy guide to his departmental chiefs calling for the new economies. He urged them to try to maintain the country's strength "within the limits of the national resources that are made available for military purposes." But obeying the President's instructions could be accomplished only by curtailing the rivalry between the armed forces, by chopping down on the outmoded weapons of defense. Instead, slashes were made in both jet-aircraft and guided-missile procurement.

During the welter of debate over reducing taxes by cutting the military, one man was unwavering—the high priest of economy, George Magoffin Humphrey. The Secretary of the Treasury was relentless in holding his chief's feet to the economy fire. He was also relentless in scorching the chiefs in the Pentagon. He did not hesitate to pick up the telephone and lecture the President of the Unitd States, and he did not hesitate to go over the head of the

Secretary of Defense and lecture the subchiefs in the Pentagon. When President Eisenhower went to Boston in September 1953 and told the American people that "no sacrifice, no tax" was too great for the defense of our freedom, Secretary Humphrey immediately put through an urgent phone call to the President. The newspapers had interpreted this sentence to mean that the excess-profits tax and high personal-income tax might not be dropped after December 31 as previously promised in Washington. Humphrey was aware of the President's private inclination to keep taxes high. He remembered the F Street Club dinner at which Ike had minimized the importance of a businessman's profits. So Humphrey called the President in Boston. The President reassured him. He had not meant to imply, he said, that these tax reductions were out the window.

Not once during his first four years in office did George Humphrey relax his vigil over the fiscal views of his chief in the White House. His influence was felt everywhere. His office became an informal clearinghouse for government policy. Other department heads learned that it paid to enlist Humphrey's support before they took a proposal across the street to the White House. As Ike himself once said of his Secretary of the Treasury, "When George speaks, we all listen." Eisenhower even invited Humphrey to sit on the National Security Council, which handles matters of military and foreign policy. Although Humphrey had no vote on the Council, his strong personality and his known influence with the President tended to dominate the Council just as they did the Cabinet.

Because Humphrey started almost immediately shrinking the Pentagon down to size, inevitably he came into conflict with another big-business man, Charles E. Wilson. Humphrey had been chairman of the M. A. Hanna Company, one of the biggest holding companies in the U.S.A., which sold steel to the automobile manufacturers. Wilson had been the head of the biggest manufacturing concern in the world, which purchased steel from Humphrey's firm. The Secretary of the Treasury found that Wilson gave him more opposition to budget cuts than anyone else inside the Cabinet. Humphrey had a way of wearing down opponents with arguments, then winning back their friendship with kind words. He used to belt Charlie Wilson around the head in a verbal encounter, then apply balm to the bruises. When Wilson was damn-blasted in Detroit for his famous remark comparing workers to dogs, Humphrey telephoned him. "Don't worry," he said, "we aren't going to throw you to the wolves. You are a great American and don't you forget it." Later he flew to Chicago and met Wilson before the latter's public apology. Placing a hand around his shoulder he asked, "Is everything all right, Charlie?" Then the busy Secretary of the Treasury hurried back to Washington on the next plane.

Humphrey never hesitated to pursue his fiscal objectives beyond Wilson to the men under him. He would call Wilson's deputy, Roger Kyes, or his comptroller, Wilfred McNeil. He regarded them as "practical men" who appreciated the military value of the dollar. Even Admiral Arthur Radford, Chairman of the Joint Chiefs of Staff, discovered that the shortest distance to the budget decision was a straight line between his office and that of Secretary Humphrey. Thus the purser on the Eisenhower ship of state began to take a hand in navigating the ship.

George Humphrey was one of the few people in Washington who not only realized but had the courage to hammer home the point that the military budget could not be cut merely by carving up the defense dollar into three equal parts among the Army, the Navy, and the Air Force. Humphrey made it clear to the military chiefs that the United States could not build atomic weapons on one hand and continue conventional weapons on the other. We could not afford both, he emphasized.

Nine months after Eisenhower took office, the normal gestation period for a budget, the military chiefs in the Pentagon still were haggling. They had not come to terms. Suddenly a mysterious newspaper story hit the headlines. Papers in New York and Washington simultaneously carried a dispatch that the Eisenhower administration would slash the budget by another six billion the next year, most of it to come out of the armed services. There was nothing in the newspaper account to indicate where this important announcement had come from. But news travels fast along the Potomac grapevine. It was only a few hours before the admirals and the generals knew that the "leak" regarding Eisenhower's budget plans had come from none other than the Secretary of the Treasury. It was his way of forcing their hand.

Thus did the high priest of economy dominate not merely the fiscal policies but the defense policies of the nation.

Basically, of course, George Humphrey was right. He was right that any real budget reduction would have to come out of the nation's largest spender—the military. He was also right that the military could not cut their budget by both keeping conventional weapons and developing modern weapons. He was right that the new look had to be more than mere chromium plate on the bumper. He was right in knocking together the heads of the defense chiefs. It was not his job to do this, but when a Cabinet officer sees that he has a weak President—and Humphrey knew better than anyone else that Ike was weak—he has an obligation to go beyond his own department. Humphrey did. But did he, could he, go far enough? Perhaps if George Humphrey had been Secretary of Defense instead of Secretary of the Treasury the economies he urged might have taken place without jeopardizing the national safety. As it was, that safety was put in grave peril.

There was another factor which hurt George Humphrey. People suspected he had a motive. They knew that as one of the nation's bigger taxpayers he had a personal reason for wanting to reduce taxes. They knew that during the twenty years of Democratic rule, the favorite topic of conversation among men in Humphrey's tax bracket was the burden of Democratic taxes. But, in addition, he had flouted a long-standing law of the United States which forbids the Secretary of the Treasury from conducting trade or commerce. When on January 19, 1953, he was before the Senate Finance Committee for confirmation, Senator Byrd of Virginia asked Humphrey, "The law says you shall not directly or indirectly be concerned or interested in carrying on the business of trade or commerce. . . . While you are Secretary of the Treasury will you engage in any business or trade or commerce personally, directly or indirectly?"

"I will engage in no business whatever, personally or indirect," Humphrey replied.

"You do not intend to influence any of these companies in any way in the conduct of their businesses while you are Secretary of the Treasury?" Byrd asked again.

"I will have no connection with the management of these businesses," Humphrey stated emphatically.

However, as time passed it became apparent to other members of the Administration, particularly those in the Pentagon whom Humphrey was batting over the head for budget cuts, that the Secretary of the Treasury was not carrying out his pledge to the Senate and that he, perhaps more than any other high official in the Administration, was profiting personally from the high position he occupied and the policies he espoused. The chairman of the Senate Finance Committee, Senator Byrd, who had treated Humphrey with such deference during his confirmation hearings, kept under lock and key the list of Humphrey's stock holdings. Neither the public nor fellow senators were allowed to see them. (Later it developed that Senator Byrd's son, Harry Byrd, Jr., had been given a lucrative position with one of Humphrey's subsidiary companies, Industrial Rayon, Inc., at Covington, Virginia.) It was known, however, that the holdings of the Secretary of the Treasury extended to seven big corporations of which he was chairman, three of which he was president, and thirty-four of which he was a director. Their total assets were $2,600,000,000—almost as much as the national budget prior to the Roosevelt Administration—and included Pittsburgh Consolidation Coal, the biggest coal company in the world; National Steel; Industrial Rayon; one of the biggest banks in Cleveland; a sugar company; a nickel company; vast ore deposits; and even a biscuit company. He was either chairman, president, or director of the M. A. Hanna Company, Hanna Furnace Company, Susquehanna Anthracite Corporation, Eastern Steamship Company, La Belle Steamship Company, Virginia Steamship Company, Jefferson Coal Company, Donner-Hanna Coke Corporation, the Great Lakes Steel Corporation, Weirton Steel, the National City Bank of Cleveland, Lake Erie Harbors, Inc., Phelps Dodge, Oak Hill Supply Company, Weirton Coal Company, Hanna Ore Mining Company, Hanna Exportation Company, Michigan Steel Corporation, Midwest Steel, Northwestern-Hanna Fuel Company, Tri-County Lands Company, the Dominion Sugar Company, Iron Ore Company of Canada, Ohio and Western Pennsylvania Dock Company, Lower Lake Dock Company, Morton Ore Company, Ozark Ore Company, Douglas Mining Company, Northern Iron Ore Mines, Limited, Western Copper and Mining, and the Western Ore Company.

From humble beginnings Humphrey had worked his way up the ladder of success in the traditional American fashion—though his spectacular rise was not handicapped by the strategic marriage of his son Gilbert to the daughter of a director of a Hanna corporation, nor by the marriage of his daughter into the Hanna family itself. Thus it was that George Humphrey took over the great economic empire begun by Mark Hanna, the Ohio politician who put William McKinley in the White House. It was not a sizable economic empire when Humphrey took it over in 1929. But Humphrey's stock holdings, which were eventually made public, showed that it had become one of the mightiest in the nation, thanks first to Humphrey's hard-driving business sagacity and later to the position he occupied as the Mark Hanna of the Eisenhower administration.

It was General Lucius Clay, one of the earliest members of the Augusta Golfing Cabinet, who picked Humphrey to be Secretary of the Treasury. Clay had come to know Humphrey when he, Clay, wanted to reverse the then Secretary of State, General George Marshall, regarding the dismantling of German industry. Marshall, as Secretary of State, had ruled that the dismantling of German industry would have to continue, under the terms of the Potsdam Agreement. But General Clay, then commander in Germany, disagreed and, after some maneuvering, got a committee of businessmen appointed to study the matter. George Humphrey, who went to Germany with that committee, was instrumental in reversing the Secretary of State and retaining the key factories of Germany. General Clay, grateful to Humphrey, later recommended him for the post of Secretary of the Treasury.

General Clay's brother officers in the Pentagon were by no means as enthusiastic about the man who became the most powerful in the Eisenhower Cabinet. Little by little, they found that even George Humphrey had clay feet. Little by little it leaked out that tremendous corporate advantages were being gained by the companies formerly controlled and still owned in part by the man who demanded budget cuts for the military and lower taxes for his companies.

The first little-noticed concession to the Hanna-Humphrey empire took place just four days before Eisenhower was inaugurated January 20, 1953. On January 16, Humphrey's son Gilbert had signed a contract with the government on "heads I win, tails you lose" terms which meant a minimum profit to the Humphrey empire of around $19,000,000. The government agreed to write off 85 per cent in taxes on $22,000,000 to build a nickel-smelting plant in Oregon; agreed to pay the Humphrey firm twenty cents a pound for 125,000,000 pounds of nickel, which meant a profit of sixteen cents a pound; agreed to loan Humphrey's company $25,000,000 under terms which meant the government in effect would pay the $25,000,000 back to itself. The Korean War was on, and the Defense Department desperately needed nickel. So the plant was a virtual gift to the Humphrey empire. In addition, the contract gave the Humphrey concern a $100,000 yearly fee to manage the smelting operations; and if production costs increased, the government was required by an escalator clause to pay more. Finally, if Humphrey's company found that the smelting process was not "technically feasible," it could abandon the whole operation, leaving the government stuck with the bill.

No wonder officials of the M. A. Hanna Company were anxious to sign the contract before the chairman of their board should become the Secretary of the Treasury. After January 20, such a contract would have been highly embarrassing. Signed as it was four days before the Eisenhower Administration took office amid paeans of praise such as the press has seldom showered on any other new President, the contract passed almost unnoticed by the public, though not by officers at the Pentagon who were taking the measure of the man they had to deal with on the budget.

Some of Secretary Humphrey's private interests ran parallel to the public interests. Some did not. For a quarter of a century, ever since Herbert Hoover was in the White House, Presidents of the United States have endeavored to put across the St. Lawrence Seaway. Always a little group of senators from the states at the mouth of the Mississippi and from Atlantic seaboard ports blocked it. For years also, George Humphrey was opposed to the seaway. He called it a "socialistic ditch." But when the M. A. Hanna Company, faced with dwindling iron-ore reserves in Minnesota, purchased a large deposit of iron ore in Labrador, Humphrey suddenly switched. And as Secretary of the Treasury he put his potent influence behind passage of the Seaway Act. Men like Congressman Harry McGregor of Ohio, who had fought and bled to oppose the seaway for years, suddenly found themselves voting for it. Senator George Bender of Ohio, whose chief financial support had come from Humphrey, complained a bit plaintively, "Why couldn't he have given us the signal a bit earlier? We didn't even have time to get our alibis ready." Humphrey was Secretary of the Treasury when, in July 1954, he took time off from his official duties to go to Canada and speak at the opening ceremonies of Northern Iron Ore Mines, Limited, of Canada, the Hanna subsidiary. Addressing the crowd, Humphrey declared: "It is a great day. It is the culmination of a dream of twelve years."

Iron Ore of Canada then began soliciting orders from British steel mills. Humphrey's son, Gilbert, was personally active in the negotiations to sell iron ore in England. When you have the prestige of the Secretary of the Treasury behind you, however, you don't have to be much of a salesman. When Charles Reginald Wheeler of the British Iron and Steel Federation and chairman of Guest, Keen Iron and Steel, Limited, arrived in the United States in October 1954, he had appointments with other ore companies including Premium Ore, owned by Cyrus Eaton. But after calling upon Humphrey in Washington, Wheeler canceled his appointments with other ore companies and signed a contract with Humphrey's Iron Ore of Canada. There was no evidence that Secretary Humphrey ever discussed an ore contract with Wheeler. But the power and the prestige of the Secretary of the Treasury is great. He can sway the policies of the Export-Import Bank, and he has influence with the International Bank. His good will is important to British industry when it comes to loans and credits.

The Secretary of the Treasury also is the chief executive of the taxing unit of the United States, the Internal Revenue Service. One of the Humphrey firms' chief competitors in Canada has been Premium Iron Ores, Limited, of Canada, owned by Cyrus Eaton, chairman of the Chesapeake and Ohio Railroad, and William R. Daly, president of the Cleveland baseball club. Although the Canadian government had ruled Premium Iron Ores tax exempt on the ground that it was developing strategic materials, and although under a tax treaty with Canada this ruling was considered binding upon the United States, nevertheless the Treasury Department assessed $1,572,240 back taxes against Eaton and $338,283 against Daly for the period of 1943–49. On April 23, 1957, eighteen judges of the U.S. Tax Court ruled these taxes could not be collected. Nevertheless, the U.S. Treasury continued to prosecute the case.

For ten years the Treasury had not attempted to collect taxes from Eaton or Daly or Premium Ores. Then in 1953, just after George M. Humphrey, chief competitor of Eaton and Daly, became Secretary of the Treasury, suddenly a demand was made for back taxes. Cyrus Eaton charged that this was personal discrimination by the Secretary of the Treasury himself. He demanded a Senate investigation. And although he reduced his charges to writing and conferred with some of the top leaders of the Senate, he was able to arouse no spark of courage in the Senate. Those who have tax problems, and many Senators do, don't like to tangle with the Treasury.

In the House of Representatives, there was more courage. Congressman James Roosevelt suggested that Humphrey be impeached. Representative Albert Thomas of Houston, calling on Humphrey in connection with the Treasury's refusal to grant a fast tax write-off to the Baytown Steel Company of Baytown, Texas, got into quite an argument. Humphrey explained that he was against fast tax write-offs. "They add to inflation and give favorite companies an unfair advantage over competitors," he said.

"But they weren't so bad when you got a $315,000,000 tax write-off for your National Steel Company," shot back Congressman Thomas. "Or when you got $111,000,000 for your Canadian ore company. If these tax write-offs are so bad, why don't you repeal them?" asked the Congressman from Texas.

That ended the interview.

It takes time for the facts about high government officials to leak out. When a Cabinet member can operate in complete secrecy, and when the press is not particularly alert, the public has little realization of how a subtle word here, a chance remark there, may influence the fiscal policies of nations. The public did know that early in the Eisenhower Administration Secretary Humphrey took a very dim view of loans to Latin America. He was so vigorous against loans that in November 1954, Merwin L. Bohan resigned as U.S. Ambassador to the Rio de Janeiro Economic Conference because he knew that conference would be dominated by Secretary Humphrey and his no-loan policy. A few weeks later, the President's own brother, Milton Eisenhower, also resigned from the American delegation to the same conference for the same reason. Both Milton Eisenhower and Ambassador Bohan knew that the conference would be a failure unless the United States followed a liberal loan policy. But suddenly Humphrey switched. He proceeded to open up American purse strings through the Export-Import Bank for sizable loans to Latin America. His switch was doubtless due in part to his trip to Rio and a better realization of Latin American problems. But almost simultaneously there was a switch of policy in Brazil which strongly favored the company over which George Humphrey had once ruled and in which he had not sold his stock.

In March 1953, Brazilian Ambassador Walter Moreira Salles had called on Under Secretary of the Treasury Randolph Burgess to discuss a $300,000,000 credit to Brazil.

"My boss doesn't like Brazil very much," Burgess stated bluntly, and he went on to tell how the M. A. Hanna Company, of which Secretary Humphrey was long president, had been negotiating for the manganese concession in the territory of Amapa north of the Amazon, when suddenly it found that Bethlehem Steel had got the concession instead.

With the Brazilians, a word to the wise was sufficient. Shortly thereafter Brazilian National Steel, 85 per cent owned by the Brazilian government, canceled a long-standing arrangement to buy coal through Eastern Fuel and Gas. It had been buying coal from this company for about ten years, and was entirely satisfied. But suddenly it switched and placed an order for 750,000 tons of coal with Pittsburgh Consolidation Coal Company, a Hanna subsidiary.

Shortly thereafter Brazilian National Steel received a $35,000,000 credit from the Export-Import Bank, of which Secretary Humphrey was the controlling member.

In January 1953, when Humphrey became Secretary of the Treasury, Pittsburgh Consolidation stock had a market value of $126,160,704. In the spring of 1957, as Humphrey prepared to leave the Treasury, it had a market value of $368,306,250. In other words, it had increased in value $242,145,546 during the period George M. Humphrey was Secretary of the Treasury.

These were some of the facts that began to leak out regarding the man who was demanding that the Defense Department curtail the budget for the purpose of cutting taxes. They were facts which increased the doubts of Pentagon planners regarding the motives of the Secretary of the Treasury.

There was another interesting loan to Brazil extended by the Export-Import Bank in 1956 for $151,400,000 for improving port facilities, building railroads, dredging harbors, and constructing electric-power projects. The loan had been turned down by the World Bank as a risk. It was approved July 19, 1956, by the Export-Import Bank, of which Secretary Humphrey was the guiding genius. The day after it was approved the president of the Export-Import Bank, Sam Waugh, had so few facts that he wrote Dr. Lucas Lopez, president of Brazil's National Development Bank, asking him to detail the purposes for which the loans were to be used. The details showed that the largest beneficiary was to be the St. John d'el Ray Mining Company, Limited, of London, which owned one of the richest iron deposits in the world in Minas Gerais, but which had been unable to develop the ore without new railroad and harbor facilities. The company had been unable to borrow the money to build the railroad, dredge a harbor, and construct more loading docks. But suddenly the St. John d'el Ray Mining Company, Limited, was purchased by Hanna Coal and Ore, 51 per cent owned by M. A. Hanna Company, and 49 per cent owned by Secretary Humphrey and his family. After this purchase there seemed to be no great difficulty in securing a loan from the Export-Import Bank.

Eventually, as George Humphrey made it clear that he was about to resign from the Treasury, investigating Senators got bolder. Simultaneously Mr. Humphrey got more brazen. Senator Matthew M. Neely of West Virginia disclosed the fact that Humphrey had given a very generous tax concession to the Arabian-American Oil Company, despite the fact that his M. A. Hanna Company owned common stock in Standard Oil of New Jersey, at that time a 30-per-cent owner of Aramco, valued at $26,885,722. With these disclosures the heat was too much for Humphrey's old friend, Senator Byrd of Virginia, whose son was still on the Humphrey-Hanna payroll. Byrd was forced to publish the list of Humphrey's stock.

For almost five years it had been kept in the secret files of Byrd's Senate Finance Committee, not even shown to his fellow senators. The list showed that Humphrey owned 67,555 shares of common stock in M. A. Hanna Company, which paid him a dividend of $202,665 in 1956 alone. It showed that the value of M. A. Hanna's stock had increased $119,018,592 in the period Humphrey had been Secretary of the Treasury; that National Steel had increased $110,-203,290; and that Hanna Coal and Iron had jumped from $46,741,500 when Humphrey became Secretary of the Treasury to $441,416,000 in 1957, the year he left. This was largely due to the development of the St. Lawrence Seaway and the sales that fell into his company's lap from foreign companies anxious to curry favor with the powerful Secretary of the Treasury. According to an estimate by Congressman Wright Patman of Texas, chairman of the Small Business Committee, the stocks held by Secretary Humphrey had increased from $7,000,000 in 1953 to $12,600,000 when he stepped out from the Treasury Department.

No wonder Pentagon officials, harassed by Humphrey over budget cuts, viewed his operations with a cynical eye and agreed with John L. Lewis when he said in a public speech in May 1957, "The grape yieldeth not, except to the foot. As one particular grape I always wanted to get under my foot George Humphrey. He has plenty of juice in him."

The year 1957 was a crucial one for the United States. As early as 1954 we had received intimations that Russia was working on secret missiles. By 1955 Central Intelligence had reported fairly concrete evidence that Russia was not only working on ballistic missiles but probably was ahead of us. But in January 1957 there occurred the bitterest battle of all over the budget. Intimations came from the Treasury Department, even before the budget message went to Congress, that trouble was brewing in the Eisenhower official family. Talking to a close friend, the Secretary of the Treasury growled, "The people across the street"—and he nodded toward the White House—"never had to meet a payroll. They've got to cut out all this welfare nonsense. We can cut off ten billion dollars more from the budget."

A little later he held his historic press conference in which he warned that if the Eisenhower budget was not reduced we would have a depression "that would curl your hair." Such a statement in any other recent administration would have meant the immediate resignation of the Cabinet officer who made it. Ever since Charles G. Dawes established the Bureau of the Budget under Warren G. Harding, it had been the unwritten rule of both Republican and Democratic administrations that no member of any administration criticized the budget once it was fixed. Arguments were staged in private, not in public. There must be a united front. Humphrey was the first to break this united front. Once when Henry Morgenthau, Jr., told Harry Truman that he would resign as Secretary of the Treasury if he was not included in the American delegation to Potsdam in 1945, Truman handed him a pad of paper and said, "Here, write out your resignation now." But in similar circumstances Eisenhower immediately retreated.

"If Congress can," he said publicly, "it is their duty to cut." The Democratic-controlled Congress immediately accepted his invitation and slashed the defense budget by a staggering $2,600,000,000. As if to emphasize his retreat further, the President then journeyed to Thomasville, Georgia, to relax on the plantation of the man who had literally slapped him in the face publicly regarding the budget. This was the signal for any member of the Administration or any member of Congress or any member of the Pentagon to engage in a free-for-all regarding any or every item in the budget, even including the weapons which Russia was known to be building—missiles.

In May 1957, Russia test-flew its first intercontinental ballistic missile from a base in the Arctic to the Sea of Okhotsk opposite Alaska. On May 21, 1957, Secretary of Defense Wilson signed a secret directive, number 7200.4. This clamped a flat fiscal ceiling on the Pentagon. Because the Defense Department had $70,800,000,000 in unspent funds, counting new appropriations and carry-overs; because the national debt was bumping up against the statutory $275,000,000,000 limit; and finally because the Administration wanted to promise the voters a tax cut during the 1958 elections, Secretary Wilson slapped a rigid $38,000,000,000 ceiling on defense spending.

Never has there been such economic chaos in the Defense Department. Vital contracts were chopped off right and left. Projects were held up or stretched out. Both bomber production and missile production were curtailed. Senator Symington of Missouri warned of trouble ahead. "There has been no evidence given the Congress that

Soviet menace has lessened," he said. "In fact, the contrary is true . . . but in order to attain a fiscal position, to keep the promise of a balanced budget, we have discovered that the promised defense strength is being broken by fiscal devices which, until these hearings, were secret."

In its first term, the Eisenhower Administration decreased military expenditures but at the same time increased non-security spending even more—the money going chiefly for farm price supports and the Soil Bank program to give political support to an area in which the Republican Party was losing votes. These expenditures were accompanied by a big boost in the interest rates, which Secretary Humphrey had increased from approximately 1½ per cent to 3¼ per cent. Thus what money was saved all came out of national security. Meanwhile, in August 1953, the Russians had developed the H-bomb. In 1954 Russia produced the Bison jet bomber and intercontinental plane, which meant that for the first time in history America became subject to direct enemy attack. Then followed the first test of the intercontinental ballistic missile in the spring of 1957.

The answer to this was slash after slash in the defense budget.

One of the President's promises was to level out spending peaks of military production. More orderly defense orders, it was promised, would save money. But in 1957 the giant B-52 jet bomber's production schedule jumped from 5 per month to 17 per month and up another notch to 20 per month and finally cut back to 15 per month. All the while the goal remained the same—603 of the monster planes—which the makers could have turned out steadily at the rate of 45 per month. But in order to carry out the promised fiscal ceiling on defense spending, production schedules were juggled. Result: These aircraft, which could have been produced for $6,000,000 each, actually cost $8,000,000 each. If this was economy, it is doubtful that its chief architect, George Humphrey, would have tolerated it in the Hanna empire to which he finally returned.

X

IKE PROVES ABE LINCOLN WRONG

IT IS THE UNWRITTEN RULE of American politics that the responsibility for the state of the Union rests upon the man in the White House. Dwight D. Eisenhower has been an exception to that rule. Our thirty-three previous presidents got acclaim when the nation prospered, abuse when the nation faltered. But with Dwight D. Eisenhower it has been a one-way street. When military mistakes were made, Charlie Wilson got the blame. When foreign policy alienated friends abroad, John Foster Dulles reaped abuse. When the nation's farmers writhed and raved against farm policies, Ezra Taft Benson was the scapegoat.

The President, aloof on his pedestal, got only praise.

Yet it is an ironic fact that the nation's military decline began under the leadership of one of its most illustrious generals. Of Dwight D. Eisenhower it must be said that he displayed his five-star reputation in the show window while he whittled away the nation's might in the back rooms of the Budget Bureau.

That he was able to do so without reaping the blame resulted from a combination of hero worship, public complacency, and canned Madison Avenue publicity which put the President on a pedestal beyond the reach of any who might dare criticize.

This was by no means accidental. It stemmed from a deliberate policy by the big newspaper publishers, the big owners of magazines, the owners of radio and television networks, and the advertising agencies of Madison Avenue. Together they proved that Abraham Lincoln was wrong and that it is possible to fool all of the people all of the time. It was they who deliberately and carefully created the Eisenhower myth and who must share some responsibility for the fact that the American people long remained blissfully ignorant of the fact that while Russia was pushing forward in arms, science, and education, we were rapidly falling back.

There is an amazing amount of anecdotage surrounding the Eisenhower myth, and it requires the closest study to strip it down to essentials. What emerges is a character that is at once simple and complex; highly moral in belief, not always so moral in deed; candid, yet secretive; firm to the point of an explosive temper, still strangely timid in the exercise of authority; opinionated, yet eager for compromise. All this is wrapped up in a personality of extraordinary charm—a charm that has sent Eisenhower to the White House twice with resounding public approval, the second time despite the handicap of a bad heart and a major abdominal operation.

Sick of the tribulations of war and the uncertainties of peace, the American public had lost confidence in the politicians. There was a deep, emotional demand for a father figure who could shoulder the nation's burdens. Ike fitted this wishful measurement. He was a victorious general, therefore qualified to cope with defense problems. He had welded the wrangling Allies into a military team which he had commanded in both hot and cold war. This suggested an understanding of international affairs. His open face, the blue eyes as clear and guileless as the sky above his native Kansas, compelled trust and confidence. He could be trusted to clean up corruption in government.

There is also an all-American quality about Dwight D. Eisenhower. It may be his easiness of manner, his engaging sincerity. Or perhaps it is the way his whole personality smiles every time his face lights up in a grin. He has a gift, too, for expressing himself movingly and for reducing great issues to simple moral principles. There is nothing suave or subtle about him; none of those sophisticated mannerisms which Americans are inclined to distrust.

In addition, Ike has a peculiar, mystical quality which Freeman Gosden, radio's Andy of the Amos 'n' Andy team and one of Ike's bridge cronies, describes as "a quality that almost brings tears to your eyes." The President's pastor, the Reverend Edward Elson, put it another way: "Just as the father and mother tend to symbolize a family's aspirations, President Eisenhower has become a symbol of the nation's aspirations."

Between these evaluations lies the answer to the Eisenhower equation: a people's idol who has all the warm attributes which allow him to sit comfortably on the cold pedestal of power.

The political ingredients were present; it remained for the press to weave them into a myth. From pages of friendly print arose a public image called Ike, whom few could fail to like. His warmth was projected like a spring thaw upon voters, for twenty years cold to the Republican ticket. His famous grin became a familiar sight on the front pages. For a long time few Eisenhower photos without that grin found their way into print. His virtues were magnified to hero dimensions. His faults were presented in a sympathetic light as evidence of his humanity. His light, never hidden under a bushel basket, was fanned by the press to a bright flame.

After his triumphant arrival at the White House, Ike continued to be pampered by the publishers who helped send him there. No President in history, not even George Washington, enjoyed a more favorable press. Criticism of Eisenhower was all but stifled in three fourths of the nation's publications. The same papers that once banner-lined Senator Joseph R. McCarthy's charges against President Truman ignored the press releases McCarthy ground out against Eisenhower. The papers that condemned the Trumans for accepting a deep freeze took no exception to several thousand dollars' worth of gifts to Ike, including twenty-five head of cattle, a $4,000 tractor, forty-eight tall Norway spruce, four hundred nut trees, $1,000 worth of shrubs, two thousand bulbs, a five-year-old pony, a sorrel mare, a black Arabian filly, antique furniture, one modern General Electric kitchen, a $3,000 putting green, a corn planter, a disk harrow, a side-delivery rake, plus the perpetual loan of a pickup truck by the U.S. Army. The papers that praised Ike for giving up the Presidential yacht Williamsburg as "a symbol of needless luxury" made little comment when he acquired a twin-engine plane, two helicopters, and a Navy yacht for golf commuting to Newport, Rhode Island. Seldom, in fact, was he called to account by the press for anything he deigned to do.

Gradually the President came to feel entitled to this immunity from unfavorable publicity. Upon one occasion the White House staged a televised Cabinet meeting, which press secretary Jim Hagerty promised would be the real thing, spontaneous and unrehearsed. When the Washington *Post* exploded this by revealing that the meeting had been secretly rehearsed and all present coached by the Madison Avenue advertising firm which manufactures White House slogans, Batten, Barton, Durstine and Osborn, the President was so furious that he threatened to deprive reporters of their half-century precedent of occupying a press room in the White House. He let it be known that if the press was going to accept free office space in the west wing, then correspondents should conduct themselves as guests and not report on "family matters." Again, when William McGaffin of the Chicago *Daily News* inquired at a press conference about the two expensive new helicopters, Ike flew into a tantrum and cut McGaffin off.

Many publishers and newspapermen deliberately bowed to this policy of intimidation. When Merriman Smith, crack reporter for the United Press, overheard Eisenhower remark to a friend in the White House, "I had to say yes because they didn't have time to build up another candidate," the United Press Washington bureau refused to distribute it. The remark was made in the winter of 1956, at a time when the American people vitally needed to know the circumstances under which the President decided to run for re-election. Despite this the United Press censored the story.

When on November 22, 1955, at Camp David, Maryland, the President held his first Cabinet meeting after his heart attack in Denver, a New York *Times* photographer heard him exclaim, "You mean to say the French just got up and walked out of the Assembly?" The photographer dutifully reported this to his newspaper. Remembering that Ambassador Henry Cabot Lodge had announced to newspapermen in October that he had informed the stricken President in Denver that the French had walked out of the UN over the Algerian crisis, this photographer thought it was significant that either the President had a failing memory or else was not really being kept informed. However, the New York *Times* fell in step with the Eisenhower myth. It did not report the revealing incident.

When the President, visiting at the Humphrey plantation in Georgia, lost his temper over failure to hit a golf ball and threw his club angrily at the side of his jeep, narrowly missing his caddy, there was only one newspaperman who reported the incident.

Andrew Tully of the Scripps-Howard newspapers, who did report it, later was asked whether other newspapermen were present. He replied in the affirmative. Asked why the others had not reported a burst of temper which not only was news but gave insight into a matter affecting the President's high blood pressure, Tully replied, "I guess they didn't want to get in wrong with Jim Hagerty."

Staying in right with Jim Hagerty is a problem for any newspaperman covering the White House. If he gets in wrong, he loses the chance to get autographed photographs of the President for his publisher, to obtain secret support for TV-license applications, and a hundred and one other favors which only the White House can extend. Even more important, he also risks real trouble for himself —trouble that can take the form of income-tax investigation.

When Ethel L. Payne of the Chicago *Defender*, only Negro daily newspaper in the United States, persisted in asking embarrassing questions at White House press conferences as to when Eisenhower was going to integrate restaurants in the District of Columbia, Hagerty finally called Miss Payne into his office. There he proceeded to cross-examine her as to why she had received $150 a month from the CIO Political Action Committee during the previous election campaign. Miss Payne had helped prepare literature to Negro voters, for which she was paid, and which is against Press Gallery rules. Hagerty threatened to take the matter up with the Press Gallery if Miss Payne persisted in asking embarrassing questions. Obviously he had had access to her income-tax returns.

When Milton Friedman of the Jewish Telegraph Agency persisted in asking questions of Eisenhower as to why he didn't push his own immigration bill, Friedman was called in by Max Rabb, Secretary of the Cabinet, and told that if he would play ball with the Administration he would be given inside news. When Friedman refused this "news bribe," his boss in New York got a call from Bernard Katzen, head of the Jewish division of the Republican National Committee, who protested that Friedman was embarrassing Eisenhower. He asked that Friedman be muzzled. The Jewish Telegraph Agency did not, however, discipline Friedman. It increased his salary.

No one would ever guess, watching President Eisenhower at his press conferences, that he hates them. But he does. He feels that they put him on the defensive and refers to them in private as "those weekly press rows." He postponed or canceled a total of 114 press conferences for reasons other than health during five years in office—more than any other President in history. Weeks have sometimes passed with no appearance before the press. This, in a country which does not have the parliamentary system, is important. In England, France, and most democracies of the West, a Prime Minister must appear periodically before the parliamentary opposition to answer questions. Under the American scheme of government, the White House press conference has come to be substituted for this parliamentary question period.

Though the President grouses at the necessity of holding press conferences, on the whole he has been amazingly effective. It was a daring, revolutionary step when Jim Hagerty persuaded the President to permit conferences to be televised. But Hagerty, as much showman as newsman, figured that the personality of the President would come through beautifully over the TV cameras. He was right. Ike's sincerity, even his fumbling for words, have had real appeal to TV viewers who do not know that the conferences have been filmed and that embarrassing questions are often edited out. They also do not know that televising conferences has the effect of discouraging hostile questions. For the newspaperman who asks hostile questions usually gets edited out of the film; so if he wants to be seen by his editor and readers back in El Paso or Little Rock he asks friendly questions. Thus the parliamentary function of the press conference is diminished.

When Dwight D. Eisenhower was first elected, but not yet inaugurated, he confided to Jim Hagerty, "When I walk through the lobby of the Commodore and see all those newspapermen with their legs stretched out, I feel as if they were trying to trip me." On that occasion they were not trying to trip him. At that time they probably would have been fired had they tried to trip him with an embarrassing question.

Since then, times have changed somewhat. Gradually, some publishers, notably Jack Knight of the Chicago *Daily News*, William Randolph Hearst, Jr., and the Chicago *Tribune* instructed their staffs to ask searching questions about the Great Crusade. And five years after Ike had taken office the New York *Times*, once tender in its news treatment, reported that the Eisenhower Administration had placed detectives on the trail of newsmen who broke exclusives. The technique had been employed since 1953, but it took the *Times* five years to get around to reporting it.

Those who give Jim Hagerty sole credit for building up the Eisenhower myth forget the help he has had from Madison Avenue and the advertising agencies whose tentacles reach into the highest board rooms of magazines, newspapers and television. When the Democratic National Committee wanted to find an advertising agency to handle its national publicity, it could discover only one, William H. Weintraub, Inc., which was Democratic. Most of the others were not only Republican, but their executives had contributed to the Republican Presidential campaign of 1956 as follows:

Batten, Barton, Durstine & Osborn	$ 5,000
Benton & Bowles	1,500

Biow-Beirn-Toigo (now Biow Co.)	2,000
Campbell-Ewald Co.	11,350
Dancer-Fitzgerald-Sample	1,000
D'Arcy Advertising Co.	1,500
Foote, Cone & Belding	500
Geyer Advertising	500
J. Walter Thompson Co.	12,600
Kenyon & Eckhardt	3,000
Kudner Agency	500
Lennen & Newell	2,000
Leo Burnett Co.	500
MacManus, John & Adams	500
Maxon, Inc.	500
McCann-Erickson	1,650
Ruthrauff & Ryan	500
Sullivan, Stauffer, Colwell & Bayles	1,000
William Esty Co.	3,000
Young & Rubicam	2,500

When Eisenhower appointed Jock Whitney as Ambassador to London, the American public did not know that, besides contributing with his wife $47,100 to Eisenhower's campaign fund, Whitney owned TV stations in Tulsa, Galveston, Houston, Indianapolis, and Fort Wayne, Indiana. Whitney could, and did, influence important segments of the American public. Or when Eisenhower appointed Clare Boothe Luce to be Ambassador to Italy, most people did not fully comprehend the fact that her husband's magazines, *Time, Life,* and *Fortune,* not only made subservient obeisance before the Eisenhower pedestal, but also owned television stations in Salt Lake City, Denver, Minneapolis, Indianapolis, and Grand Rapids, all of them influencing public opinion, and all of them contributing to the complacency of the American public regarding our missile-satellite defeat.

When Mrs. Fleur Cowles, then wife of the publisher of *Look* magazine, was appointed American Ambassador for the coronation of Queen Elizabeth, the public did not know that a deal had been arranged whereby Vice-President Nixon's picture would be on the cover of *Look*. Subsequently, the Cowles publications, already owning monopoly newspapers in Des Moines and Minneapolis, were awarded additional TV stations, thereby giving them tremendous impact on the mind of the Middle West through TV stations in Des Moines, Sioux City, Minneapolis, Hutchison, Kansas, and Huntington, West Virginia. They too contributed to the complacency of the American public.

One of the biggest aviation manufacturers in the United States is Victor Emanuel, whose Crosley Broadcasting Corporation also owns television stations in Cincinnati, Columbus, Dayton, Indianapolis, and Atlanta. His chief representative in Washington, George Allen, is the bridge-playing friend of the President and original copartner in the purchase of the Gettysburg farm. Naturally the Crosley network of stations could not be expected to report penetrating criticism of Eisenhower or his missile failures. How far some segments of the press leaned over backward to pervert the news was illustrated when the Associated Press described Allen as the "confidant" of Harry Truman and the "occasional golfing partner" of Eisenhower. Truman had banished Allen from the White House.

Another molder of public opinion is RKO Teleradio Pictures, Inc. It owns television stations in Boston, Los Angeles, San Francisco, New York, and Memphis. But few people who listen to its programs realize that it is owned and controlled by General Tire and Rubber, which also owns Aerojet, a company which seeks and gets important missile contracts from the Eisenhower Administration. Its news is by no means unbiased.

These are some of the important molders of public opinion who helped Jim Hagerty prove that Abe Lincoln was wrong.

When Abraham Lincoln told the nation, "You may fool all the people some of the time; you can even fool some of the people all the time; but you can't fool all of the people all the time," he was living in a day of free-thinking, hard-hitting country editors imbued with the down-with-the-crown traditions of Tom Paine. He lived in a day when the Chicago *Tribune*, which helped put him in the White House, did not hesitate to turn the whiplash of criticism against him, and when Lincoln himself used such earthy words as "a mush toad buzzard" in describing the Chief Justice of the United States. "Shall he be permitted," asked Lincoln, "to vomit the filthy contents of his stomach on every decent man in the country without having his neck twisted?"

Abe Lincoln never dreamed that his free-swinging, free-criticizing day would give way to an era when the concentration of radio, television, newspapers, and Madison Avenue advertising would combine to fool nearly all of the people for an awfully long time.

Of all the garments of infallibility which the press draped over Ike, none was more shatterproof than his military reputation.

Whether he was "unleashing" Chiang Kai-shek to attack the Chinese mainland or dismissing Sputnik I as having "not one iota" of military significance, his military judgments were treated as Scripture by an admiring press.

Ike's first order as Commander in Chief was to remove the Seventh Fleet as an obstacle to Chinese Nationalist attacks on the mainland. This was clearly a political stunt to appease the "Formosa first" wing of the Republican Party, but the press hailed it in headlines as a bold stroke. The hullabaloo of press comment didn't mention the fact that Nationalist armies, which had fled the mainland leaving most of their equipment behind them, couldn't possibly reinvade China unless American Marines cleared the way. Nor was it reported that the Seventh Fleet had not been hindering Chiang at all, but in fact had been protecting him from Communist raids against Formosa. Later, when Chiang threatened to send his armies against Red China, and the Red Chinese massed for retaliation, Ike shuddered at the risk and hastily clamped a control valve on Chiang's fuel supply. The press, which had acclaimed the move to unleash Chiang, was strangely silent when he was put back on the leash.

Down through the years of slash and save, the press rarely challenged Eisenhower's defense cuts. Like most soldiers of his generation, Dwight D. Eisenhower had been trained to think in terms of extravagance in war and parsimony in peace. As President, he was sincere in demanding that waste be cut. As President, his duty was no longer to the Army alone but to the American taxpayers. In his enthusiasm for economy, however, he overlooked a factor that had entered the military art since he had practiced it—the dawning of the space age, which could be entered only at great expense. The cost of that oversight is being measured today.

Although Ike had turned in his uniforms for civilian clothes, he never shed the aura of the military hero. This gave his military pronouncements the ring of infallibility. It took a brave critic to question the nation's foremost soldier on military matters. Those who did, like Senators Stuart Symington of Missouri and Henry M. Jackson of Washington, were voices crying in the wilderness. Their speeches were dutifully reported, but there was no campaign by the powerful publishers and opinion molders to make sure funds were appropriated and properly spent to keep ahead in the race for missiles. The press has waged some notable campaigns in recent years, for the end of price controls, for cleaner unions, for unleashing Chiang Kai-shek, for McCarthy, and later against him. But when the authors reported on May 31, 1956, that Russia was ahead of us on the ICBM and would launch a satellite ahead of us, and when both the authors and the Alsop brothers time after time called attention to our missile lag, it evoked little response. The public and most of the publishers were too deeply involved with the father complex. The man who knew best about military matters could do no wrong.

It took the shock of the sputniks to first shake seriously public faith in Ike's infallibility. Only then did question marks begin appearing on the editorial pages, though many accepted at face value Ike's assurance that the sputniks had "not one iota" of military significance. Every expert in the Pentagon above the rank of second lieutenant saw frightening implications in these celestial invaders, but the President saw it differently. It was only human, of course, for Ike to defend his military policies and cover his blunders with verbal camouflage. He did this in a series of chins-up speeches, which many newspapers swallowed whole. Others, however, began to gag on his confident claim that the United States was somehow still stronger than the Soviet Union.

For anyone who bothered to add up the military score, the totals were not comforting. But this side of the story was not advertised by the Eisenhower Administration. The disturbing facts were never hidden so deep the press couldn't find them, but a majority of newspapers preferred Ike's happier military outlook until the Gaither report leaked disturbing segments about the danger facing the nation and the Rockefeller report gave the facts with alarming bluntness. Even then, when the Explorer followed the Soviet sputniks into space, newspapers did not generally mention the sober fact that Sputnik II alone could have carried forty satellites the size of the Explorer.

Ike's shiny military armor was tarnished, but not greatly damaged, by the Soviet missile challenge. But what of the man inside the armor? Ike's character, like his reputation, was shaped by the military. Probably no other profession makes a more profound impact upon the characters of the men who serve it. It demands loyalty to country and to command. It demands devotion to duty and courage under fire. Military training puts backbone in a man's physical and moral posture.

But the very discipline that does all this can also have a stultifying effect. It does not encourage imagination. Loyalty to superiors and subordinates can be subverted into a shield for inefficiency. Military secrecy can be used as a screen to hide mistakes. The monotony of military life between wars can produce habits of mental sloth. The endless round of bridge and cocktail parties, cocktail parties and bridge, has its impact on any mind. Army politics, the art of getting the next promotion, can be played just as skillfully—and ruthlessly—as precinct politics in Brooklyn or the Bronx. For an art dedicated to conflict, compromise also plays an extraordinary role in military affairs.

When Dwight Eisenhower was called to the Presidency, he had forty-one years of Army life behind him. No man could shed this mold overnight. He brought to the White House a strong sense of duty and a fierce loyalty to American traditions. As one who understood war, he also came with a mission to achieve world peace.

But he found it difficult to make the policy decisions once made for him by Roosevelt, Churchill, and George Marshall. It was not too difficult to translate their decisions into military orders. It was another matter to make them himself. Time has now shown that Eisenhower the President is plagued with indecision. He has emerged as a man timid about taking political gambles; gingerly testing winds of public opinion, disliking to be in the middle of a squabble; hating to upset the status quo. These are the failings, not seen under the sheen of the military hero, which have become apparent in the civilian President.

The human impulse is deeply imbedded in the Eisenhower character. It has never been any secret among those close to him that he can best be won over to a cause by translating it in human terms. Instinctively he identifies himself with the human race. He meant every word when, in ringing tones, he told the Anti-Defamation League that every American has the right to face his accusers. Upon another occasion, after listening to Congressman Alvin M. Bentley of Michigan, a fellow Republican, rail against the Immigration Act, Ike said firmly, "Every one of us is either an immigrant or the son of an immigrant." He has also delivered many impassioned little speeches to the Cabinet and the National Security Council. "We must be unceasing in our efforts to educate and inform the people" has been one of his favorite themes.

But unfortunately there is a gap between Ike's human impulses and their fulfillment. The Eisenhower record shows a tendency to retreat from principle to platitude; to make lip service of the speeches that spring from his heart. Just as he meekly allowed defense funds to be hacked to the bone, his brave words about the rights of the accused did not change his Administration's attitude toward victims of Joe McCarthy.

Eisenhower went so far as to issue a high-sounding memorandum, marked "Personal and Confidential," to department heads, stressing the "need to protect subordinates . . . against attacks under which they otherwise might be helpless." But there is no evidence he enforced the principles so nobly enunciated. On the contrary, he failed to back Harold E. Stassen in a showdown with Senator McCarthy over strategic trade with Communist countries. When he made a rousing speech against bookburning, he refused to let it be broadcast on the Voice of America and even issued a statement that he meant no reflection on McCarthy—after the Senator had stormed down to the White House and demanded a retraction.

Throughout the McCarthy hysteria, Ike would blaze in private against the Wisconsin Senator but never mention him in public. He would shrug off questions at his press conferences with "I don't know what the term McCarthyism means." When C. D. Jackson wrote a blistering anti-McCarthy statement for the President, he tossed aside the typescript. "I won't get into the gutter with that guy," he said. Some observers insisted that Ike's refusal to deal with McCarthy was shrewd strategy. The truth was he had no strategy. He only had personal dislike for sailing into a political gale.

Again, the President's stirring defense of immigration to America didn't prevent him from appointing a McCarthy satellite, Scott McLeod, as State Department security chief and permitting him to sabotage the immigration program. Deliberately and carefully McLeod defied the President's announced objectives by throwing up technical barriers against the refugees the President decreed were to be admitted. For his obstructionism McLeod was not punished. He was promoted to be Ambassador to Ireland.

By nature frank and open, Ike has a passion for secrecy that is often as unaccountable as it is confused in motive. On the one hand, he is an ardent advocate of the virtues of a free press and full discussion. Yet he does not hesitate to withhold information that might cause controversy or embarrassment. A press "leak," especially one concerning routine military matters, can spark him into fury.

After the first Soviet sputnik was launched, Ike did everything possible to keep the public from learning about the missile lag. The very word "missile" in a headline was calculated to rouse the Presidential dander. When Assistant Air Force Secretary Trevor Gardner made a speech about the Falcon missile in 1955, he took the precaution of clearing it for security with the Pentagon's experts, then for policy with his boss, Secretary Harold Talbott. But even this meticulous observance of Pentagon protocol did not prevent Ike from snatching up a telephone and raising Cain with Secretary of Defense Charlie Wilson. Gardner said later, "Apparently the President felt that nothing should be released to the public concerning guided missiles."

Almost every time there was a reference to missiles either in the daily press or in the trade journals, orders would come from the White House to clamp the lid down tighter. Most of these complaints landed on Gardner's desk, since at the time he was in charge of Air Force missile research. He said, "It was represented to me in each case that the orders came from the President himself."

The studied campaign to shy away from admission of the missile failure results from a streak of timidity in the Eisenhower make-up. His indecisions, in public and in private, have caused Washington wits to invent a new dance step, the Eisenhower Waltz: "One step forward, hesitate; one step sideways, glide; one step back."

His Korean War settlement produced no real solution and left Chinese Communist armies free to advance on French Indochina. There the heroic tragedy of Dien Bien Phu left Ike unutterably depressed. For days he could not shake off his gloomy mood. But he did not give the French the aid for which they pleaded, and in the end Indochina too was divided and became another Korea, hopelessly split between Communism and the West. The Formosa crisis was "solved" in the same way—by drawing a cautious line through the straits between the island and the mainland, then warning the Chinese Reds not to cross one way and Chiang Kai-shek not to cross the other. Somewhat later the gallant freedom fighters of Hungary were to find the President's moral indignation in their behalf a poor substitute for the material help which he denied them—though they had been encouraged to dare, with pitiful weapons, the might of Russia by loose talk of "liberation" from Secretary of State Dulles.

Ike is good at handling people and has a remarkable gift for finding the middle ground between two points of view. He likes to deal with people face to face, rather than by telephone or memo or letter, so that he can turn on his charm. He enjoys drawing out those around him, getting their differences into the open, then finding some course that will satisfy all. This is a valuable skill, but it can also be a dangerous one. For it makes the art of compromise more tempting. It is easier than the harder task of tough decision.

Difficult decisions can, and do, make Ike physically ill. Though his personal physician and old friend, Dr. Howard M. Snyder, is always swift to deny that the President suffers from emotional hypertension, the fact is that Snyder also denied that Ike had heart trouble or ileitis before his attacks. Other White House insiders admit Ike knots up inside over crises and conflicts. As previously reported in these chapters, when Ike spoke up for pre-Korean War defense cuts in 1950 and clashed with his old comrades in arms, he became so upset that he had to go to Key West, Florida, to recuperate; while the afternoon before his ileitis attack he had experienced a disagreeable session with former Senator Harry Cain, a bitter Republican critic of the loyalty program.

Despite White House determination to convince the nation that Ike's three illnesses have not impaired his ability to rule, there can be no doubt that they have taken a heavy toll and have produced character changes by accentuating some traits over others.

As Dr. John W. Gofman of the University of California testified before the Senate Labor and Public Welfare Committee, "Arteriosclerosis of the brain, that is narrowing of the blood vessels of the brain, is definitely related to arteriosclerosis of the heart." It brings, he said, "loss of effectiveness due to diminishing blood supply to the brain in large numbers of crucial individuals in their most effective years."

Eisenhower has always been a man of swift mood; now his emotions are even closer to the surface. Ebullience is more rare, depression more frequent. Although Ike does not brood about his health, stoically placing his fate in the hands of a higher power, he does resent the restrictions imposed upon him. He feels criticism more keenly, and his quick temper is more easily aroused.

His doctors have decided that, within reason, he should be allowed to do what he likes. To deny his inclinations makes him low-spirited and restrains his remarkable gift for "self-therapy," the medical term for curing yourself by doing what you enjoy. They have also noted that public praise is his best tonic. They let him go to the NATO meeting in Paris only weeks after his November 1957 stroke, because they knew the plaudits of the multitude along the Champs-Elysées would bring back old memories, restore confidence, and do him a world of good.

It is a burden of the Presidential office that a great deal of work is not only inevitable but vitally necessary. Even in full health, Eisenhower disliked the drudgery, loathed plowing through long papers and preferred a crisp oral briefing. Following his illnesses, dislike for Presidential chores has amounted almost to an abhorrence. He is apt to fidget if a meeting runs too long or barge out of his chair if it gets too dull. Faced with a pile of papers to sign, he will grumble, "Why do I have to do this?" Aides are told, "Get to the point; keep it brief." And if a visitor takes too long explaining a problem, the President is likely to show his impatience and lack of interest by getting up and making practice swings with a golf club.

Although Ike is not a patient listener, he gets most of his information by ear. He prefers oral reports to written memos. In either case, he regards brevity as a sign of efficiency. Yet brevity is not one of his own strong points. He tends to be both long-winded and rambling. He likes to talk out his thoughts and will suddenly get up and say, "Let me think out loud a bit." Then he will pace the floor, putting ideas into words as they come to him.

A random reader, Ike will only skip and scan the newspapers, relying on Hagerty to give him an oral digest—brief, of course—of what the press is saying. But there is one type of literature to which the President is devoted: pulp Westerns. One of the chief duties of his Army aide, Lieutenant Colonel Robert L. Schultz, is to make sure he has a constant supply. On journeys the carefully locked Presidential brief case is often stuffed with as many Westerns as official papers. Ike has an attractive, almost boyish, enthusiasm for all things Western. The first of his mishaps at the White House was a nipped hand which resulted from showing Mamie how cowboys "fan" a .44 revolver.

It is this insistence on getting information in tablet form that often leaves the President fuzzy and confused on major issues. He has never fully understood, because he has not taken time to understand, the intricacies of budget problems, tax policies, or farm plans. It is impossible, therefore, not to wonder whether his grasp of defense problems has not also suffered from the same lack of homework. In purely civilian affairs he has relied almost completely on his advisers, being led instead of leading. In military affairs he has felt more competent to act on his own judgment. When civilian and military interests found themselves in conflict, however, as they did over the defense budget, the politicians usually won. They were able to present arguments which, for lack of full understanding, he was unable to refute.

When Eisenhower first considered running for President, he remarked to friends that he expected to handle the Presidency in a manner similar to the President of France. He would preside at meetings, attend functions, lay cornerstones, but he thought the detailed drudgery of the job could be handled by others. This was the technique he used as commander of the Allied armies in Europe. A subcommander was given an objective to take and so many troops with which to take it, and was responsible for doing the rest. Eisenhower has never given up the idea that he could handle the Presidency thus.

When he first entered the White House, therefore, one of his first steps was to build up a staff on military lines under a chief assistant, Sherman Adams, the craggy little former Governor of New Hampshire. Since the Presidency was loaded down with trivia, it seemed an eminently sensible approach. But staffs have a way of spawning. Ike kept adding new aides who, in turn, hired more clerks and more secretaries until they numbered over 1,200 people—the largest and costliest White House staff in history. Whereas the executive offices cost $8,166,000 during the last year under Truman, Eisenhower asked for $12,047,000 in 1958—and this did not include helicopters, which are charged to the Army, his private plane, which is charged to the Air Force, military aides and staffs, which are charged to the Pentagon, or the host of special committees working on the perimeter. What was designed as a system to safeguard the President from unnecessary chores soon put him in the position of a man in the middle of a maze, to whom fewer and fewer facts and visitors were allowed to penetrate.

Ike's illnesses have had a great deal to do with building up a protective curtain around him, though the curtain was becoming more opaque even before his heart attack. The staff had begun early to impose a virtual censorship on what persons the President could see and what could be placed before him. Adams bluntly ordered department heads to place their problems before him and not the President. He scolded visitors who dared to bring Ike bad news. This increased after each successive illness.

The desire to shield Eisenhower from unpleasant news is rationalized. The staff doesn't want to risk triggering his temper, which is so explosive it might affect his heart. In a flash the sunny grin can vanish, the jaw jut out, and the eyes become steel-hard. He may fly out of his chair with hot words bursting like shrapnel. During the spring of 1953 he was called off the golf course at Burning Tree by the National Security Conference to make a decision regarding an armistice in Korea. Returning to his office, he picked up a book from his desk, slammed it across the room, and exploded, "This God-damned Korean War has been with us two years and it's going to be with us two more years. I don't want to be bothered with this kind of thing any more." No one wants to endanger the President's health by raising his blood pressure, but getting bad news and doing something about bad news are part of the business of running any country.

Perhaps this was one reason why the Korean War reached a precarious armistice shortly thereafter under terms that could have been made almost any time before and which could burst into war at almost any time in the future.

Little things that fret the President are: the glare of the public spotlight ("I can't even have a bellyache in private"); the requirements of security ("all this confinement gets on my nerves"); struggling into starchy, formal clothes ("if men continue to wear tight collars, future generations will be born with grooves around their necks"); long airplane rides, which he lightens by constant visits to the cockpit. But most of all it is controversy and decision that jar him to the anger he seeks to avoid. In particular, pressure on him to make a decision causes him to sizzle.

Since his three illnesses the President finds it difficult to give full attention to a subject for more than an hour at a time. To duck controversy, he tends to push subordinates to the front. To minimize the strain of decision, he has farmed out more and more problems to special committees. He has also turned the Cabinet and the National Security Council from purely consultative into policy-making bodies—something quite new in American government—and increased his insistence that all staff differences must be reconciled before any issue is presented to him.

After Queen Elizabeth II had visited Washington in the fall of 1957, Dwight D. Eisenhower talked wistfully about her job of laying cornerstones, opening Parliament, attending receptions. He thought back to those early days in 1952 when he thought he might preside over the White House like the President of France. That dream had never borne fruit. But the President even today is inclined to think of himself as a sort of good fairy sitting serenely on top of an administrative Christmas tree, whose branches are loaded with problems that can be handed up to him for disbursement only when they have been suitably gift-wrapped. If the good fairy's complexion suddenly becomes more rubicund and he begins to fiddle with the cap on a front tooth (on at least two occasions he has dislodged it), then look out for the squalls; the gift wrapping has not been to his satisfaction.

It has become increasingly noticeable to those around the White House that Ike, who has never liked to mix work and play, is finding it harder to stay in the office he calls "the maelstrom." He itches to escape to his golf practice, to a Western, or to his painting. He can lose himself completely in his art, though his portraits of Lincoln and Washington, copies of which he presented to friends as Christmas gifts, were actually sketched by a professional artist; Ike simply added the coloring.

Relaxing activity is necessary for the President; it keeps the devil of despondency at bay. It might be said that it was despondency as much as anything else that persuaded him to run for a second term. He was at Gettysburg, the weather was cold, and the putting green frozen stiff. The depression that follows a heart attack was upon him, and there seemed to be nothing he could do to alleviate it. He even complained to friends that Mamie was babying him too much. As he stared out across the bleak landscape, the hurly-burly of world affairs seemed wonderfully attractive. Of such small circumstances—bad weather and a frozen putting green—are the destinies of men and nations guided.

Dwight D. Eisenhower told his doctors after his November 1957 stroke, "I'll do anything that the boys want me to do; I'll go anywhere the boys want me to go." This, in one sentence, epitomizes the policy of President Eisenhower today. He will do anything those around him tell him to do, but he will not tell them. He will not lead the way. If peace in the world is to be achieved, if the United States is to be restored to its old position as a first-class power, it will have to come from other leaders than Dwight D. Eisenhower. It is only tragic that this warm, human, lovable man with so many strengths should have elected to follow behind public opinion where he might have marched with renewed glory in the van.

xi

CHANGING ROCKETS IN MID-SPACE

On the last night of January 1958, a Jupiter-C missile, stamped with the number 29, was cut loose from its space dock at Cape Canaveral, Florida. Tiny figures swarmed around it, making last-minute adjustments, like worshipers performing a ritual at the feet of a great pagan god. At 9:42 P.M. a mournful horn sent the workers scampering for cover, and the metal monster stood alone in the bright eye of the spotlight. At precisely 10:48 P.M., the monster came to life with a sudden shudder, blew a volcanic cloud out of its tail, and, as if in a terrible rage, rose agonizingly off the ground.

On giddy legs of flame it sprang into the heavens, lighting up a cloud bank like an orange-red lantern. Then it disappeared like a retreating blowtorch into the night. High in space, the main hull dropped off and surrendered to gravity. Spinning clusters of smaller rockets pushed on. Not quite seven minutes after the launching, the Promethean tip was flung loose—an 80-inch space dart. Thus was born Explorer I.

At the missile center below, Dr. Charles A. Lundquist picked up the first flashes from the listening stations and quickly calculated that the satellite was in orbit. He reached for the phone to notify Army dignitaries waiting in the Pentagon, but the lines were tied up by reporters telephoning their papers. He hurried to a pay booth, scratched around in his pocket. No dime! He begged for telephone money from passers-by. Finally and triumphantly an Army aide produced the right change. In the Pentagon, Secretary of the Army Wilber M. Brucker, a veteran Michigan politician, cracked nervously, "This is like waiting for the precinct returns to come in." At last the call from Florida came through.

At 12:44 A.M., President Eisenhower was called away from a midnight bridge game in Augusta and notified that America's first satellite had started its roller-coaster ride around the world. If a twinge of regret crossed his mind when at 1 A.M. he issued a triumphal announcement, he had good cause to temper his jubilation with chagrin. For as the Explorer began piping its weird electronic music from outer space, he knew that it had been launched with rocket hardware that had been sitting in an Alabama warehouse for two years. If he had heeded his old Army comrades and used that hardware, he could have beaten the Russians into space by months.

With every sweep around the world, the American sputnik was spelling out an old aphorism in the new vernacular of the space age: Never change rockets in mid-space. Except for a handful of insiders, few remember the name of a project called Orbiter which in the summer of 1955 was scratched off the Pentagon books because of interservice rivalry. Yet the Jupiter-C which put the United States into outer space was only Orbiter revived.

Its history began in early 1954 at "Rocket City, U.S.A.," the name frequently given to the Army's missile base at Huntsville, Alabama. At Huntsville, Dr. Lundquist, a Ph.D. with the humble Army rank of private, developed a sudden passion for satellite research. He spent his spare time calculating orbital problems with the quiet encouragement of his civilian chief, Dr. Ernst Stuhlinger. Lundquist's calculations came to the attention of Dr. Wernher von Braun, technical director of the Army's missile arsenal, who assigned others to the project. Gerhard Heller studied the possible effects of extreme temperatures on a satellite; Josef Boehm designed the satellite itself; von Braun occupied himself with the propulsion problem.

From Huntsville, their work moved to Washington, where a historic, secret meeting was held on June 25, 1954, in Room 1803 of Tempo 3, a temporary building constructed during the World War II emergency and supposed to be torn down after the war. The ragtag remnants of government which didn't rate space in modern offices were relegated to these war-built firetraps. But the scientists in Room 1803 had their minds fixed far above the worn carpet and scuffed furniture of their neglected conference room. Their goal was outer space.

Around the table sat men whose names may go down in history as the Columbuses and Cortezes of the space age: Dr. von Braun, the German rocket pioneer turned U.S. Army expert; Fred Durant, president of the International Astronautical Federation; Dr. Fred L.

Whipple, famous Harvard astronomer; David Young, astronautical scientist for Aerojet-General Corporation; Dr. Fred Singer, brilliant young University of Maryland physicist and refugee from Hitler; Alexander Satin, naval air engineer; and Commander George Hoover of the Naval Research Office.

It was a curiously casual affair for a discussion that was to play such a part in American history. They spoke of technical advances which were steadily lifting man's ceiling beyond the limits of the earth's atmosphere. They needed to understand more about the strange hazards of space: the swift streams of meteorite dust that can perforate the toughest steel, the sudden cosmic storms, the mysterious magnetic tides, the terrible temperatures that range from extreme heat to extreme cold.

They had sought the answers with high-soaring research rockets, but each flight had been like a finger plunged into the ocean, then quickly withdrawn. The flights were too short for any more than the most superficial observation. What was needed, the group concluded, was a celestial laboratory that would soar through space for a prolonged period. They agreed that a man-made satellite, containing meteorological instruments and a radio transmitter, was no longer a scientific gimmick but a necessary tool if the frontiers of space were to be pushed back.

At the start, Dr. von Braun disposed of the biggest doubt. He described the research already started at Huntsville and calmly announced that his Army team could slam a satellite into space. For this purpose, he proposed souping up a Redstone battlefield missile with Loki antiaircraft rockets. Commander Hoover, speaking for the Navy, offered to supply the pay load: a five-pound satellite packed with precision instruments. Those who listened to von Braun's calm assurance and promised to co-operate with him had no idea that his plan would be canceled—with disastrous consequences—before it would eventually come to pass.

The project wasn't exactly launched on the spot. The experts—wise in the ways of government—first began clearing away the red tape. They presented their notes to Rear Admiral Fred Furth, naval research chief, who sent a delegation to Huntsville to confer with the commander of the Army's missile arsenal, Major General Holger Toftoy. He flew to Washington and put the case before Major General Leslie Simon, ordnance research chief.

Up through the layers of bureaucracy moved the proposal, accumulating endorsements, until it reached the desk of kindly, cau-

Space Flight Committee, was Milton Rosen, in charge of the Navy's Viking rocket program.

The Viking, designed by the Martin Company, already had an engine built by Reaction Motors. But Dr. Porter sold Rosen on the idea of developing an improved Viking with a GE motor. They talked of using it as a satellite launcher, a possibility which they pursued through the Rocket Society; and on November 24, 1954, Rosen summed up the arguments for an earth satellite in a technical report to the Society. Apparently he did not know that the Orbiter team had already presented blueprints to the Defense Department for a satellite project.

Dr. Porter, who shared Rosen's dream of sending a satellite into space aboard an improved Viking, powered by a GE engine, forwarded the report to the National Science Foundation, which was preparing for the International Geophysical Year. The IGY Committee, eager to exploit this great scientific occasion, was persuaded by the report to go ahead with a satellite program. So impressed was the committee, in fact, that it invited Porter to head the satellite panel.

The chief problem in launching a satellite is getting enough force to break through the crust of atmosphere surrounding the earth. To heave this sort of scientific shot-put into space, therefore, the IGY scientists needed rocket power that could be found only in the Defense establishment. Their appeal to the Pentagon resulted in the January 1955 decision to let the Army and Navy go ahead with Project Orbiter. Porter, Rosen and company, however, had other ideas about getting the rocket power to launch a satellite.

They became the storm center of a scientific uproar over using military weapons as satellite launchers. For the sake of pure science, they preferred building special research rockets. Disgruntled whispers were also heard regarding the Army's use of imported German scientists. There was talk of making the satellite an "all-American" project, thus ruling out Dr. von Braun's team.

The agitation against Project Orbiter reached such a pitch that Donald Quarles, as the Pentagon's research chief, formed a secret nine-man committee to review proposals from all three services. He selected as chairman Dr. Homer Stewart of the California Institute of Technology. Also named to the committee was none other than General Electric's Dr. Porter, who as IGY satellite chief was in a unique position to influence his colleagues.

The existence of the committee has never been officially acknowledged. Dr. Stewart refused to admit that he had anything to do with it, even though it came to be called by his name.

"I can't talk," he said, when queried by the authors.

"My instructions don't permit me to comment at all," he said when pressed further.

"You can't even comment as to whether you are chairman of the Stewart Committee?"

"No, I can't comment on whether I am chairman of the committee. All I can say is that I've served on several committees."

This locking of the stable door after the horse was stolen was to cover up error, not protect security. The satellite project, as emphasized by no less than President Eisenhower, was a scientific, not a military project. Regardless of this secrecy, here are the censored facts as to what happened inside the Stewart Committee.

Three alternatives were placed before its members. They were:

1. The Army proposed to continue with Project Orbiter. Dr. von Braun of the Army gave a flat promise that he could launch a 15-pound satellite in a year. This would have put the launching date in mid-1956, well ahead of the International Geophysical Year, which began July 1, 1957, and during which Russia was expected to launch a satellite.
2. The Navy supported Rosen's proposed new Viking, which, it claimed, would be a more sophisticated rocket and could launch a 40-pound satellite. The Navy later admitted that it could launch a satellite of only half that weight.
3. The Air Force proposed an ambitious plan to launch a super-satellite with equipment from its intercontinental-ballistic-missile program, even though that equipment was still undeveloped.

There is little doubt that Dr. Porter played a powerful part in working out the final decision, which adopted the Navy's Viking rocket with the General Electric motor, thereby scuppering the Army's Orbiter. He was supported by Dr. Joseph Kaplan, chairman of the IGY Committee, who admitted knowing little about guided missiles but who argued that more instruments could be packed in a 40-pound than a 15-pound satellite. Voting with them were Dr. Charles C. Lauritsen of Cal Tech; Professor John Rosser of Cornell; Gerald M. Clemence of the Naval Observatory; and Admiral Paul Smith, secretary of the committee.

Only three men voted for Orbiter: Dr. Stewart, the chairman; Dr. Robert McMath, University of Michigan; and Dr. Clifford Furnas,

University of Buffalo, who later succeeded Quarles as Assistant Defense Secretary in charge of research. They argued that speed was the most important consideration and that the Army project offered the best chance to beat Russia into space.

The arguments which sent Orbiter back to the shelf paid little attention to the harsh facts of Russian competition and the damage to national prestige of a Soviet first in the satellite race. The Army was fully conscious of this peril and wanted to get a satellite up ahead of Russia, even by rough-and-ready means. But the Stewart Committee seemed determined that Orbiter should never get off the ground. It not only voted for the Navy project but as a second alternative recommended going ahead with the Air Force proposal. Orbiter was kicked into a corner.

The day after the committee's decision, Dr. Stewart confided to von Braun, "We have pulled a great boner." It was not until January 31, 1958, three years later, as the United States finally put a 30-pound Orbiter satellite renamed the Explorer into space four months behind Russia, that Dr. Stewart was to see his prophecy fully confirmed.

Back in July 1955, it must have been gratifying to Porter when the Martin Company, obeying the Navy's specifications, switched from Reaction to GE engines to launch the new satellite. The name, too, was changed, from Viking to Vanguard. Friends claim that Dr. Porter did not realize the Vanguard would use GE motors and that he would never put his company's interest ahead of his country. When the authors asked Dr. Porter about the fact that his company benefited from the switch of motors, he replied, "I don't know anything about the contract."

In a subsequent conversation he was more candid. Apologizing for having been previously evasive, Dr. Porter said, "I knew the Vanguard would be using GE engines when I voted for it, but this did not influence my decision. Our recommendation was made strictly on the basis of technical factors."

In the framework of the Pentagon, in which servants of private manufacturers operate side by side with servants of the nation, it is almost impossible to ascertain when and where technical factors take precedence over national interest and vice versa. Probably it's more the system than the individual that's at fault.

Meanwhile, in 1955, the Army had received strict orders to abandon Project Orbiter and to forget all about satellite work. Dr. von Braun, however, did no such thing. He wangled authorization to develop a 1,500-mile missile which the Army called the Jupiter. To blaze the way for the Jupiter, von Braun insisted that he needed some test missiles, technically known as test vehicles. The request reached the desk of Reuben Robertson, then Deputy Secretary of Defense, who agreed to let the Army build twelve test vehicles but warned they must be used as part of the Jupiter program. In order to stay within the bounds of technical compliance, the Army obligingly called them Jupiter-Cs—the C meaning a "composite" missile. Actually the Jupiter-Cs were not Jupiters at all. They were the powerful souped-up Redstone missiles that von Braun had proposed as necessary to launch satellites through the earth's atmospheric crust. The Army, voted out of the space business by the Stewart Committee, was determined to stay in the race no matter what the name given to its missiles. This fact was not entirely unknown to those who ruled the Pentagon. Certainly if they did not know it firsthand, they had a chance to learn it secondhand when on May 31, 1956, the "Washington Merry-Go-Round" published the first news of these test missiles. "Army experts," it was reported, "claim privately they will shoot 3,000 miles with an uncanny accuracy varying only one yard for each mile." Again on July 22 came the prediction, "The first Jupiter-C will be fired in September 1956."

By September 20, two Jupiter-Cs were ready at Cape Canaveral for the predicted test. The second missile was on hand in case the first attempt failed. Also on hand was an elongated object which looked suspiciously like a satellite. In fact, it exactly resembled the Explorer which sailed into orbit sixteen months later. This caused considerable uneasiness in the Pentagon, where it was feared the enthusiastic Dr. von Braun might try to launch an "accidental" satellite ahead of the Navy, then say "Oops, I'm sorry" after it was safely in orbit. This, incidentally, was exactly what von Braun planned to do. But when the military grapevine carried this report to the Pentagon, Secretary of the Army Brucker warned Major General John Medaris, von Braun's superior, that the Army could not risk defying the ban against launching an Army satellite.

Medaris had no choice but to instruct von Braun, "I must put you under direct orders personally to inspect that satellite to make sure it is not live."

The first Jupiter-C, sans satellite, flew a distance record of 3,300 miles at a speed of nearly 16,000 miles an hour. It was not necessary to use the reserve missile stamped with the number 29. It was returned to a warehouse in Huntsville for sixteen months. By ironic coincidence, this same number 29 was trundled back to Cape Canaveral a year and four months later to launch the first Explorer. There is no reason to doubt that it could have done on September 20, 1956, what it was finally permitted to do on January 31, 1958.

Meanwhile, von Braun shot off two more Jupiter-Cs in order to test the guidance system and to return a nose cone at sizzling speed through the atmosphere without burning up. Another Jupiter-C was damaged during static tests on the ground. The remaining eight were kept in the Huntsville warehouse awaiting the day the Pentagon brass might change their minds about Army satellites.

To break the ban, Lieutenant General James M. Gavin, the Army's unquenchable research chief, argued, coaxed and pleaded with his superiors. He hoped a successful satellite would demonstrate the Army's rocket superiority and divorce it from the traditional role of foot-slogging infantry. "For two years," says Gavin, "we begged for authority to launch a satellite." He wrote endless memos documenting the Army's case. All told, the Army made ten official pleas to put the old Orbiter team back in business. But Assistant Secretary of Defense Wilfred McNeil, the Pentagon's Comptroller General, went so far as to send his budget detectives to Huntsville to make sure the Army didn't spend a dime on satellites.

The eight Army satellites continued to be in an Alabama warehouse, peaceful, undisturbed, unknown to the world. They were complete with Fiberglas, radio transmitters, and gyro mechanism. But instead of being projected into outer space ahead of the Russians, they lay in a warehouse gathering dust.

Von Braun's scientists grated their teeth with exasperation. Once they tried to help the Navy with its satellite by offering advice on a new approach to a particularly vexing Vanguard problem. But they "were literally thrown out of one office" for their trouble, the Army's representatives reported. Finally, one Navy expert consented to see them. If they could produce facts to show that the Navy was wrong, he said grudgingly, then their suggestions would be considered.

Like Orbiter, Vanguard was supposed to be put together as cheaply as possible with hardware off the shelf. But the project soon ran into serious snags. The cost, originally estimated at $22,000,000, began to soar at such a rate that it looked as if dollar signs would be circling the earth long before any satellite. In what seemed no time at all, $50,000,000 had been spent.

The harassed scientists tried to patch the Vanguard together with the cheapest material they could find. In one instance they even used ten-cent mousetraps. The original blueprints called for special springs that would permit the nose cone containing the satellite to open like a blossoming flower in space and cough out the shiny, round metal space ball. The springs, it was estimated, would have to be specially constructed at a cost of ten dollars each. But Paul Smith, manager of the Operations Planning Team, walked across the street to a local hardware store, bought several ten-cent mousetraps, removed the springs and fitted them into the Vanguard.

The project continued to lurch and wallow in a bureaucratic caldron, while all kinds of technical cooks spoiled the satellite broth. The project director, casual, pipe-smoking Dr. John Hagen, who likes to carry his lunch to work in a battered tin box, would be seen staring morosely at the funny-paper clippings that cover his office walls, as if hoping they would preserve his sense of humor. Milt Rosen, as technical director, was to discover that there were at least six other administrators either above him or equal to him in rank. As time went on, both Hagen and Rosen sneaked envious glances at the Army hardware previously brushed aside.

At the end of eight months, Project Vanguard was already eight months behind schedule. This led Trevor Gardner, chief of Air Force research, to remark acidly at a Pentagon meeting, "The project has slipped one month for each month it has been going." He urged an all-out spending program to get the satellite off the ground. But Secretary Quarles was not disturbed; he was satisfied to move along at an easy, economical pace. "What do you want to do," demanded Gardner, "slip two months?"

Shortly after this he resigned.

When Quarles moved from the third to the fourth floor of the Pentagon to become Air Force Secretary, he was replaced as the Defense Department's research chief by the same Dr. Clifford Furnas who had cast his vote for Project Orbiter and against Project Vanguard. Furnas is the blunt-spoken president of the University of Buffalo, and during the year he stayed in the Pentagon he raised a ruckus over the satellite lag and warned Secretary of Defense Wilson urgently that Russia would have a satellite in space ahead of the United States. "So what?" replied Wilson with an indifferent shrug.

Furnas finally gave up the losing battle. He too quit his post and returned to civilian life in February 1957.

By the following July, Rear Admiral Rawson Bennett, Chief of Naval Research, was on Capitol Hill with his gold-trimmed cap in hand asking Congress for $34,200,000 to add to the $62,000,000 already spent on Vanguard. Later the total cost was revised upward to $110,000,000. Bennett explained that Project Vanguard had to be built within a framework of time and performance over which the Navy had no control. Time was dictated by the International Geophysical Year and the performance by nature, he said, so "we have to use money to get out of trouble."

What was the trouble? One was the GE motor—a hopped-up version of the old Hermes engine designed by Dr. Porter, the man who had helped switch Project Orbiter to Project Vanguard. The GE engine is described by some technical experts as sensitive to weather and not always reliable. Other experts claim the difficulties were no more than any manufacturer might encounter and point out that it was delivered exactly on schedule. General Electric went to great pains to correct the faults, but this continued to be one of the greatest handicaps delaying Project Vanguard. The Vanguard structure also suffered from vibration and, though little time was lost putting it right, it cost money.

While the United States fussed, fumed, and delayed, Russian scientific journals indicated that Russia was pushing ahead with plans to launch its first sputnik. The most categoric warning came in June 1957 in the Russian magazine *Radio*, which predicted that a satellite would be launched on September 17, 1957, the one hundredth anniversary of the birth of the great Russian scientist, Konstantin Tsiolkovsky. But long before that, Dr. Hagen, in urging more funds and personnel, had warned the White House of the catastrophic repercussions if Russia won the race into outer space. Secretary Dulles pooh-poohed the idea. President Eisenhower didn't seem to care.

The President himself was present when an ominous warning was given to the National Security Council as early as May 26, 1955, regarding the world repercussions should Russia launch the first satellite; while, in the Pentagon, General Gavin sounded the same warning. "The thing that really worried a number of us," he said later, "was how serious Sputnik was going to be. We knew it would be very damaging; we predicted this in our memorandums to the Defense Department."

By an ironic twist of fate, Secretary of Defense Wilson's successor, Neil McElroy, happened to be dining at Huntsville with the Army missile men on October 4, 1957, as the first sputnik wobbled into space.

"You will discover that all hell has broken loose back in Washington," von Braun warned the new Secretary of Defense. "But remember that we can fire a satellite into orbit sixty days from the moment you give us the green light." McElroy appeared skeptical.

"Sixty days," repeated von Braun firmly. He knew what the new Secretary of Defense did not know, that eight Army satellites had lain for months in an Alabama warehouse gathering dust.

In Barcelona, Spain, where he was attending an astronautical conference, Major General Holger Toftoy, commander of the Redstone Arsenal, issued an angry statement. The Army, he said, could have launched a 15-pound moon in 1955. "The Army group thought it up, said we could do it, and by God, we could have done it," he snorted.

The silencer from the Pentagon was swift. On October 9, five days after Sputnik I hit the headlines, Washington issued this order to Army commands: "Addressees will take immediate steps to assure that personnel for whom they are responsible refrain from public statements or discussions bearing on the current missile or satellite situation." Similar instructions went out to the Navy and the Air Force. It was made clear that the order came from the Commander in Chief himself. "President desires that Air Force personnel refrain from making public comment on the satellite program of the U.S. and other countries," read the cryptic teletype from Air Research and Development Command.

Then suddenly in his press conference, President Eisenhower officially and formally announced to the world that the United States would lauch a satellite "in December of this year."

Eisenhower's announcement was couched in official gobbledygook to make it appear that the United States had never had any intention of launching a satellite ahead of Russia, and in fact was in no hurry whatsoever. He said:

"In May, 1957, those charged with the United States satellite program determined that small satellite spheres would be launched as test vehicles during 1957 to check the rocketry, instrumentation, and ground stations, and the first fully instrumented ground satellite vehicles would be launched in March of 1958. The first of these test vehicles is planned to be launched *in December of this year.*"

The President's announcement was made on October 9, exactly the same day his directive was being sent to all military personnel clamping down on public comment. And automatically his statement nullified the secrecy ban he himself had imposed. For the entire world immediately focused attention on Cape Canaveral, where the President said the first satellite was to be launched in December. There, on December 6, 1957, in full public gaze, the first miniature satellite was hurled barely 75 feet before it fell to the ground, bleating pathetically the electronic signals that were supposed to have come from outer space. Project Vanguard became Project Rearguard.

At this point Secretary of Defense McElroy remembered von Braun's sixty-day guarantee. In desperation the President turned to the Army, which late in the sultry Florida night of January 31, 1958, put the United States back in the race for control of outer space.

The whole world applauded. The jeers over the first "sputternik" were partially forgotten. But still the question remains: Why was Project Orbiter ever nudged aside in the first place? Why did we change rockets in mid-space?

xii

THE NICKERSON COURT-MARTIAL

THREE COURTS-MARTIAL in the last three decades have left their impact on the history of the United States. The court-martial of Brigadier General William Mitchell, U.S. Army, in 1925 woke up the nation to the importance of air power. The court-martial of Major General Smedley D. Butler, U.S. Marine Corps, in 1931 focused attention on a European dictatorship. The court-martial of Colonel John C. Nickerson, Jr., U.S. Army, in 1957 aroused the nation to the importance of ballistic missiles. All three courts-martial brought travail or punishment to those on trial, but all three did a service to the nation.

General Mitchell was stripped of his rank and banished from Washington when he insisted that his superiors were wrong in ignoring the potential ability of airplanes to make mincemeat out of modern cities, modern fortresses, and modern battleships. It took a long time, but history proved General Mitchell right. It has also taken a long time, but General Douglas MacArthur's friends have almost convinced the American people that he voted for the acquittal of Billy Mitchell, though he previously said he did not.

The court-martial of General Smedley Butler was ordered by President Herbert Hoover after Butler made a speech in which he reported that Benito Mussolini, dictator of Italy, had run over a child and ordered his car not to stop. The court-martial was abruptly dropped after the American public put Mussolini, not General Butler, on trial for hit-and-run driving. Seldom has the head of a foreign government been so excoriated.

The Nickerson court-martial came at a time when the great majority of the American people either did not or could not distinguish a ballistic missile from a dart which a small boy finds in his stocking at Christmastime. It came at a time when the public had no realization that the missile makers of the Kremlin were working night and day to forge ahead of the United States. It came at a time when the American people were serenely confident that their leader in the White House was keeping the United States fully armed and completely competent to withstand all enemies. It was precipitated by the fact that leaders of the U.S. Army, better informed than the public, saw themselves with the cavalry disbanded, artillery outmoded, airplanes transferred to the Air Force, with all the glitter and glamour of a once proud service evaporated except for sixteen gray horses still retained to haul funeral caissons at Fort Myer, Virginia. They saw themselves commanding an army of caretakers and barrack orderlies, cooks and kitchen police.

The young officer who precipitated this court-martial never dreamed he would become famous. He had no idea his court-martial might speed the launching of an American satellite in the race with Russia to explore outer space. But the fact is that his court-martial and the writing of a confidential memo which precipitated the court-martial helped to arrest the downward skid of the United States.

Johnny Nickerson was reared in the placid little tobacco town of Paris, Kentucky, wangled an appointment to West Point in 1934, and was catapulted into World War II, where he served as an artillery officer, collected a breastful of ribbons for gallantry in action, and got the reputation of being a "soldier's soldier." He balanced his own mess kit in the chow line with his men, and his battalion got credit for firing more rounds at the enemy than any other in its area.

With the end of the war, Nickerson saw that the day of the foot soldier was over. He turned to missiles and turned early. In the last year of the war, 1945, he got himself appointed liaison officer to the California Institute of Technology and was so eager to soak up technical knowledge that he paid his own tuition. There followed three years at the top-secret Special Weapons Project at Albuquerque, New Mexico; then a five-year hitch in the Pentagon as chief of the Army's rockets branch.

Nickerson was due for overseas assignment when General John B. Medaris, a man who was to loom large in his life, asked him to help organize the new Army Ballistic Missile Agency at Huntsville, Alabama, in 1955. There Nickerson became the number-three man on Army ballistic missiles. Ahead of him ranked General Medaris and Dr. Wernher von Braun, the former V-2 rocket expert for Adolf

Hitler. The three were a team. Leading the team was the dashing, debonair General Medaris of the quick strut and the swagger stick. He had come up the hard way, earning his expenses through high school by driving a cab, fudging on his age when only twelve years old in order to take flying lessons, and enlisting in the Marines on his sixteenth birthday as the quickest way to get into World War I. After the war he took a degree in mechanical engineering at Ohio State University, won a commission through the R.O.T.C., served six years in the Army, then got bored and gave it up. When Hitler invaded Poland in 1939, Medaris returned to the Army, and the second peace saw him climbing the brass rungs of the promotion ladder with speed and agility. He had become Assistant Chief of Army Ordnance when, in November 1955, he was given the missile command at Huntsville.

By that time the Army, the Navy, and the Air Force already were maneuvering against each other to develop the weapon of the future, and General Medaris was well equipped to continue the maneuver. As Chief of Army Ordnance, Industrial Division, he had refused to adopt the Navy's proven system of moth-balling unneeded military equipment at one-tenth the cost. When the Navy showed that a tank could be preserved from rust at a cost of $1,500 a year simply by keeping it in a cheap dehumidified steel building, Army Ordnance under General Medaris insisted on rolling tanks out periodically for "exercise" at a cost of $15,000 per tank per year. Medaris was the type of military stickler who, in escorting the Argentine Minister of Defense around the United States, telegraphed to Fortress Monroe, Virginia, to be sure to have Argentine wine at a dinner in honor of the Minister, together with silver bearing the crest of the fortress. Monroe's officers could find no Argentine wine, found that crested silver would cost them one thousand dollars. The Argentine Defense Minister dined without Argentine wine or crested silver.

To spearhead the Army's battle to stay in the missile race, Medaris picked Nickerson as his liaison officer between the Army Ballistic Arsenal in Alabama and the Pentagon in Washington. Nickerson virtually commuted between Huntsville and Washington. A brilliantly articulate officer, hiding an aggressive energy behind a scholarly appearance, he put the Army's case before Secretary of the Army Wilber Brucker, General Maxwell D. Taylor, Chief of Staff; and General James Gavin, Chief of Army Research. No colonel of forty-two could have been more effective or could have looked forward to a brighter future.

Shortly after the 1956 election, disturbing news seeped from the Pentagon to the Huntsville Arsenal. The word was out that "Charlie" would side with the Air Force in the battle over the 1,500-mile missile and limit the Army to missiles of only 200-mile range. "Charlie," of course, meant the Secretary of Defense. Limiting the Army to a 200-mile missile meant that the Army, despite its initiative in bringing the von Braun team of German scientists to this country, would be cut back almost to its old foot-slogging role. In any new war it would be low man on the military totem pole. In peace it would be the Orphan Annie of the military budget. It would go back to kitchen police and those horses pulling the funeral caissons at Fort Myer.

On November 9, 1956, Medaris called a few aides behind closed doors at Huntsville and put together the Army's arguments for continuing to produce its 1,500-mile intermediate-range missile, the Jupiter. When this material was assembled, he classified it "Top Secret" and had only four copies made. One remained in his personal file; the other three were hand-delivered by secret courier to Secretary Brucker, Army Chief Taylor, and General Gavin. The intent was that Brucker should use this material to persuade Secretary Wilson to change his mind.

Colonel Nickerson, of course, knew about this document. He urged Medaris to allow him to wage a campaign against the Wilson order through Congress and the press. Medaris did not give his approval, although Nickerson and other officers got the impression he would not be unhappy to have an undercover campaign without his official knowledge.

Nickerson set off to Washington to scout the interservice battlefield. There he learned that the Wilson order against the Army and in favor of the Air Force was about to be put in writing. He even managed to squeeze in on a lunch with Brucker on November 24, just before the Army-Navy football game, where he pleaded the Army's case. When he asked the Secretary whether Wilson really appreciated the Army's need for a 1,500-mile missile and whether the whole case had been explained to him, Brucker shook his head.

Two days after Nickerson returned to Huntsville with this bad news, the formal Wilson decision was published, November 26. It put the Air Force in charge of both the 5,000-mile intercontinental ballistic missile, the ICBM, and the 1,500-mile intermediate-range missile, the IRBM. The Army, as the Pentagon grapevine had previously reported, was to be confined to missiles of 200-mile range. This meant the Army was virtually cut back to long-range artillery. The town of Huntsville promptly went into economic collapse. Dr. von Braun and his German scientists were deluged with lucrative private offers. It looked as if the entire Army missile agency was about to disintegrate.

It was at this particular moment that Colonel Nickerson shut himself up in his bedroom and drafted a memorandum which was to get him court-martialed and which was to send the Pentagon's hitherto backstage missile dispute flaring across the headlines of the nation.

Before Nickerson wrote the memo, his assistant, Lieutenant Colonel Lee James, had dropped into the outer office of General Medaris to chat with Lieutenant Henry Magill, Medaris' aide. As luck would have it, Medaris barged out of his inner office and asked James what was on his mind.

"Well, sir," James replied, "I suppose I should take this up with your aide first, but I'll ask you about it. We've had a telephone call from some people in RCA with respect to the impact of this directive." He referred, of course, to the Wilson directive cutting the Army out of missile development. "And the question on my mind," Colonel James continued, "is whether we should make any effort to tie General Sarnoff into this. We know that RCA is interested in the continuation of our mission here."

General Medaris responded in clipped, brusque language, "Yes, by every right you could have and should have taken this up with Magill, but since I'm here I'll answer it. I see no reason why you should not tie him into it."

Medaris' remark left no possible doubt that he would like to see the powerful Radio Corporation of America and its persuasive chairman, General David Sarnoff, bring pressure to change the Wilson order. But Medaris' insistence that James should have taken the matter up with his aide, Lieutenant Magill, not with him, also indicated that Medaris wanted to keep safely and officially in the background.

A less impulsive man than Nickerson would have taken Medaris' coyness as a signal for caution. But Nickerson had the bit between his teeth—or, more accurately, a pencil which he chewed nervously for the next three days, November 30 to December 3, drafting a detailed attack on the Wilson decision. He drew most of his arguments from the document that Medaris himself had sent to Secretary Brucker. He took his finished thesis to his secretary, Jane Nelson, to type and instructed her to make copies without any secret markings. Then he had about three dozen sets of the material mimeographed.

On December 5, the security-control officer at the missile agency, Lieutenant Colonel Daniel Shepherd, saw the document and warned Nickerson that it contained classified information. Nickerson said he would take full responsibility and Shepherd should forget the matter. Later Nickerson was to explain, "I understood this was what General Medaris wanted me to do."

Nickerson and his assistant, Lieutenant Colonel James, then set about distributing the documents where they thought they would do the most good: to RCA, to certain key members of Congress, and one copy to the authors of this book.

At that time we had neither met nor talked with Colonel Nickerson. Furthermore, there was nothing on the memorandum to indicate that he had written it or who had written it. It was not stamped "secret" or "confidential." One look at it, however, was enough to convince anyone with a slight knowledge of the defense of the United States that it was packed with as much explosive power as is packed in the warhead of a ballistic missile. It accused the Secretary of Defense of favoring his own former company rather than the best interests of the nation. It charged the Chairman of the Joint Chiefs of Staff with being prejudiced against the Army. It charged the Secretary of the Air Force with being ambitious to become Secretary of Defense. It charged some of the nation's top industrialists with lobbying for missile contracts for profit rather than the welfare of the nation.

"Admiral Radford," said the memorandum, referring to the Chairman of the Joint Chiefs of Staff, "is a rather bitter enemy of the U.S. Army and has made a long series of recommendations to Mr. Wilson which are hostile to legitimate Army interests. . . .

"The aircraft industry, and particularly the Douglas Aircraft Co., openly oppose the development of any missile by a government agency," charged Nickerson. "It is suspected that the Wilson memorandum has been heavily influenced by lobbying by this company and by the Bell Telephone Co." Bell Telephone was the former company of Secretary of the Air Force Quarles.

Nickerson also pointed out that the AC Spark Plug Division of General Motors was contractor for the vertical-guidance system of the Air Force's rival Thor; and then he proceeded to make a charge which is almost never made publicly by a career military man, that big business was lobbying for contracts. "Discontinuance of Jupiter," said Nickerson, referring to the Army's Jupiter missile, "favors commercially the AC Spark Plug Division of the General Motors Corporation." This was pointing the finger directly at the former head of General Motors, Charles E. Wilson. . .

The Nickerson memo contained much information that the American people had a right to know. It has long been the policy of the United States government, though one not always followed by its officials, that the American people have a right to know about every penny spent. Since they put up the money for government orders, they have a right to know whether that money goes to certain favored firms, whether it goes to the companies of executives inside the government, whether it is spent efficiently and wisely. Therefore, the Nickerson charge against such giants of industry as General Motors, Douglas Aircraft, and Sperry Gyroscope was extremely important and something the public had a right to know. This is discussed elsewhere in these pages.

It has also been an American tradition that the people have a right to know about their safety, and the Nickerson memo raised some red flags regarding the concentration of industry on the California coast, more readily available than inland sites to Russian bombing. It also pointed to the danger of concentrating missile production in a few companies.

"Discontinuance of the Army missile," wrote Nickerson, "will result in the concentration of the following programs in the Bell-Douglas combination: Nike and Nike I and Nike B, Nike II, IRBM, and ICBM. This is too much missile concentration in one combination. Should one add the Sage and Cesar program at Bell, and the Navy and Air Force contracts at Douglas, the over-concentration is obviously serious.

"Furthermore, discontinuance of the Army IRBM [at Huntsville] would result in an even greater concentration of development in southern California. This concentration is already the source of considerable worry from a defense standpoint. The southeastern United States, on the other hand," said Nickerson, referring to Alabama, "is strategically a sound location for a missile program."

Another point which Colonel Nickerson emphasized was the long research, the long experimentation, the long travail by the Army which was now bearing fruit.

"Eleven years," he said, "have elapsed since the start of this program. During this time many Army officers, enlisted men, and employees have gained a wealth of experience in the development, production, storage, maintenance, and operational employment of these weapons.

It takes six or seven years and about $500,000,000 to develop a large guided missile. It is obvious that major policy reversals will delay the availability date of the weapon and waste large amounts of money. The government must know what it wants before it starts such a program; it must adhere steadfastly to the objectives throughout the long period required to do the work." Here Nickerson put his finger on one of the most tragic delays in missile development.

He also touched upon the bitter rivalry between the Army and the Air Force over the weapons of modern warfare. During the Korean War, and ever since, the Army has contended that the Air Force let troops on the ground fight their own battles without tactical support from the air. The Air Force, the Army has charged, was more interested tallyhoing off on more glamorous and sometimes safer bombing missions.

"The U.S. Air Force gives top priority to strategic bombardment and air defense," Colonel Nickerson said of this controversy. "The Tactical Air Command is a poor relation kept because the Air Force does not want the Army to have any high performance aircraft. Let's face it: Most Air Force officers think there is no need to have an Army; consequently a command based on the existence of an Army gets little but lip service in the U.S. Air Force. When the Korean War broke out, there was no Tactical Air Command—not even a headquarters.

"To assume that the Air Force can furnish the needed artillery fire with its missiles is to erase the memory of the deaths of General McNair and our soldiers at Saint-Lô, who were killed by the then virtually independent Air Corps." Nickerson referred to the tragic death of General Leslie McNair, accidentally killed by U.S. airmen shortly after the Normandy invasion.

"To trust the devastating future nuclear artillery weapons to the erratic hands of another service," criticized Nickerson, "is to forget that only a few months ago one of the best trained air crews missed a nuclear test target by over five miles in clear weather under daylight conditions with no enemy opposition."

Most of the above was information which the American public had a right to know. While secret, it was also information which the Russians already knew. They knew, for instance, that American defense industry was concentrated in southern California. They also knew, from reading the American technical journals, practically all of the history of ballistic-missile development. And they knew about the controversy between the Army, the Navy and the Air Force. They knew, but the American public did not fully know.

As the authors read over this bristling memo, filled with charge and countercharge, we noted that it also contained highly secret information which a potential enemy did not, and should not, know. It contained, for instance, the date upon which the next intermediate-range missiles of both the Army and the Air Force were going to be tested.

"The first Thor flight test," read the Nickerson memo, referring to the Air Force's IRBM, "is scheduled for 10 December 1956 and the first Jupiter for February 1957."

Nickerson's memo came into the authors' hands in early December 1956; so publication of the above paragraph would have given Russian submarines a chance to lie off the Florida Capes and observe the December 10 Thor tests.

The Nickerson memo also contained references to the performance of various types of missiles. The Army's Redstone Arsenal, Nickerson wrote, had:

> —Brought altitude record to U.S. in 1949 by firing a two-stage rocket consisting of the V-2 and Corporal to an altitude of 250 miles.
>
> —Fired a Jupiter-C missile to a range of 3,300 miles on 20 September 1956. This raised the range record to beyond 1,000 miles for the first time. It also set a speed record of about 19,000 feet per second or MACH 19. An altitude record of 600 miles was also set.
>
> —Designed and constructed the first missile capable of placing an artificial satellite in an orbit around the earth. This missile is in the missile assembly shop at the Army Ballistic Missile Agency awaiting Defense Department permission to fire.

Nickerson referred to the Jupiter C-3, which those who ruled the Pentagon had kept under wraps, but which the Army was finally permitted to use for the launching of the first American satellite. The launching partially helped atone for the stinging defeat of the Soviet sputnik. But it did not take place until January 31, 1958. The Nickerson warning was written November 30–December 3, 1956.

Such were the highlights of the sensational memorandum, bearing no name or identification, which came into the hands of the authors.

During many years of Washington reporting, we have established a policy of consulting competent agencies of the government regarding news affecting the national defense, especially news which might contain security information prejudicial to the nation. This system, which was required in wartime under voluntary censorship, has been followed by the authors in peacetime. The Army, the

Navy and the Air Force have always been delighted to co-operate in advising whether certain information might be detrimental to the nation's security. In accordance with this policy, we showed the memo to Brigadier General Andrew Kinney, the Air Force press-relations chief, both for security guidance and for the point of view of the Air Force. General Kinney gulped hard and rushed to the office of Air Force Secretary Quarles, who made equally good time taking the memo to Secretary of Defense Wilson. Without further ceremony, Wilson confiscated the document. He turned it over to his deputy, Reuben Robertson, for investigation.

It lay in Robertson's safe for ten days before the head of the Army got wind of it. Then Secretary of the Army Brucker stormed into Robertson's office and demanded to know why he had not been consulted. Angrily, he accused the Deputy Secretary of Defense of conspiring secretly with the Air Force. He also cussed out Drew Pearson. Before Brucker departed, still breathing fire and fury, he took custody of the document for the Army itself to investigate.

Meanwhile, we demanded the return of the memo. It had not been marked secret, contained no mark of identification, was not an official document; yet we had submitted it to the Defense Department in good faith for security guidance. In reply, the Defense Department took out the "secret" stamp and stamped it on the Nickerson memo. No government official, we were told, could now return it without risking a $10,000 fine and a sentence of one year in jail. Even Air Secretary Quarles, who seemed genuinely distressed by the confiscation, claimed he could do nothing without incurring criminal penalties. We suggested that the Pentagon censor out all security matters, then return the memo. This was agreed to, then reneged on. After an inconclusive, fruitless exchange of correspondence, we finally went to the Pentagon with blood in our eyes to see Wilson himself. Our conversation follows:

PEARSON: I should like some guidance on what should or should not be classified. Would you say that a statement that your guided-missile program 'favors commercially the AC Spark Plug Division of General Motors'—should that or should that not be classified?

WILSON: Well, of course it is a misstatement, but there is no reason why it should be classified unless it is hung on to a part of a document that in itself was classified.

PEARSON: Then why did you not return that document to me with such portions Xd out that should have been classified?

WILSON: Didn't we release some official correspondence with you about it?

PEARSON: You did. The correspondence was not very edifying.

WILSON: We appreciated your bringing it to us in the first place, and obviously it had certain things in it which you thought should have been classified, or you would not have brought it to us. We like that kind of co-operation. I don't know whether I have made myself clear, but I have tried to.

PEARSON: You make yourself very clear, and I appreciate that explanation. But it is just a little difficult for a newspaperman who is in the habit of trying to check things that might be classified and who is worried about it—it is a little difficult to continue that custom, which I think is a good custom.

WILSON: You will sleep well with yourself as long as you do the right thing.

It's difficult to argue with a man as frank and charming as Charlie Wilson. We lost the argument. But while it was going on, the net had been fast closing around Colonel Nickerson. It required no great detective genius to spot Huntsville, Alabama, as the geographical source of the document. The Inspector General, rough, tough Lieutenant General David Ogden, personally flew to Huntsville to unearth the culprit. He threatened and bullied until Nickerson was named as the author. But Ogden used such roughshod methods that he violated Nickerson's legal rights—with the result that the court-martial almost blew up before it got off the ground. Grilled by the Inspector General on January 2, Nickerson did not at first admit writing the document. After the interview, he hurried to his quarters and, with his wife's help, burned all copies still in his possession.

But the military police were not far behind. At 3:30 the same afternoon they barged into his bedroom, arrested him at his desk, and marched him to General Medaris' quarters. Other officers searched the Nickerson home, found the incriminating ashes and a brief case containing secret papers. The house was put under armed guard.

Inspector General Ogden, in his haste to investigate what he thought was a simple news leak, failed to take formal statements and to advise witnesses of their rights. As a result, the Third Army took jurisdiction, which put Nickerson in the hands of stern General Thomas F. Hickey, a man who goes strictly by the book.

In the thorough investigation which followed, two colonels took General Medaris' secret deposition on January 12. His cautious answers are still secret. However, they abetted the impression, already held by Nickerson, that he had given Nickerson encouragement. Medaris was asked if it might have been possible "to infer that while you did not want to have any official knowledge to oppose the Wilson order, that if someone took some action without your knowledge you would have no objection?"

"In a general sense it could be interpreted that way," the General replied, "but without placing it in the framework of our decision and what we were to do regarding the Wilson directive . . . I did not desire to be informed of each separate action that was being taken, [but] at no time did I intend to infer that they should take any actions that were either improper or illegal."

As time passed General Medaris became panicky. He started telephoning the Pentagon in Washington from his office in Huntsville to protect himself. His superiors had picked up the impression that General Medaris had secretly encouraged Nickerson. "Are you sure," they demanded, "that you did not feed these people too much raw meat?" It looked for a time as if Medaris' career might be in danger, and the General anxiously sought to convince the Pentagon brass that he served nothing but regulation meat. General Hickey soon put a stop to Medaris' telephone calls. He threatened to court-martial Medaris if he did not cease meddling in the Nickerson case.

On March 4, 1957, Nickerson was ordered court-martialed. The charge: "divulging secret documents relating to the national defense of the United States and containing information which he had reason to believe could be used to the injury of the United States or to the advantage of a foreign nation." The charges were based on Articles 92 and 134 of the Uniform Code of Military Justice.

Nickerson retained as his attorneys Ray Jenkins of Knoxville, Tennessee, famous as the counsel for the Senate committee during the Army-McCarthy hearings, and Robert K. Bell of Huntsville, former law partner of Senator John J. Sparkman of Alabama. It soon became apparent that his attorneys planned to substitute Secretary of Defense Wilson for Nickerson as the real defendant. They called on Secretary of the Army Brucker and demanded a long list of top-secret documents which, under the rules governing courts-martial, they were entitled to get. "We intend to defend Jack Nickerson to the limit," they said. "For that reason we feel honor bound to point out to the Army what that will involve. If the Army wants to pursue this matter, that is a decision it will have to make."

Publication of certain documents having to bear on General Motors, it was insinuated, might be highly embarrassing to Secretary Wilson. For a time Mr. Wilson became suspicious that his old friend from Michigan, the former Governor of that state whom he had appointed Secretary of the Army, might possibly be double-crossing him. He suspected that Brucker might be more loyal to the Army than to him. This was not the case. However, Brucker too was worried. He became so concerned that he summoned General Hickey from Atlanta to report on the preparation of the court-martial. A court-martial is not supposed to be the subject of political discussion or pressure from the Pentagon, and General Hickey marched into Brucker's office to deliver an ultimatum. "I am not here to receive instructions," he said stiffly. "I am here to report progress."

Brucker was so flabbergasted that he sat back meekly and listened. All he ever asked was whether Hickey needed legal advice. Hickey did telephone the Judge Advocate General, Major General George Hickman, but confined his questions to points of law. When he got his answers he banged down the receiver. In fact, General Hickey told his superiors in the Pentagon so little that their best source of information was the newspapers. Privately, General Maxwell Taylor, Chief of Staff, favored soft-pedaling the court-martial because he feared Secretary Wilson, in effect, would be placed on trial. He feared this would only antagonize the Secretary of Defense and further hurt the Army's cause. However, General Taylor also kept out of the case and so did Wilson himself.

The trial began on June 24 before a court of five generals and five colonels, Major General Crump Garvin presiding. The prosecution dropped the Army's charges involving espionage and perjury, while Colonel Nickerson in turn pleaded guilty to fifteen charges of violating security regulations by failing to safeguard secret information and divulging it to unauthorized persons. This narrowed the issues and saved Charlie Wilson and General Motors the embarrassment of being placed on trial *in absentia* in the crowded courtroom at Huntsville.

When Colonel Nickerson took the stand in his own defense, he repeated serious charges that the Air Force is influenced in its missile program by business firms and the airplane lobbies of Washington.

He charged that the aircraft industry had no intention of letting government contractors working under Civil Service, such as those at Redstone Arsenal, get the big missile money.

"They realized that contracts for aircraft were going down and those for missiles were going up," he testified; and he told how the struggles inside the Pentagon over missile appropriations were decided in favor of the Air Force, due in part to pressure from the big aircraft manufacturers.

On cross-examination Captain Charles H. Taylor, assistant trial counsel, asked Nickerson why he had testified that the Air Force would develop its own "inferior" Thor missile rather than accept the Army's Jupiter.

"A private firm doing missile work for the Air Force can come up with facts and figures that will make everything look all right," Nickerson replied. He cited Major General Benjamin A. Schriever, commander of the Air Force's ballistic-missiles division, as being unable to get a true picture of the situation because of the pressures around him.

"General Schriever came here and had a long talk with General Medaris and was very much impressed," Nickerson testified. "He realized he had been considerably misled by his advisers on the West Coast.

"When an Air Force team was invited here to inspect the Jupiter work," he said, "one of the names on the list was that of Sam Ramo, executive vice-president of the Ramo-Wooldridge Company." Ramo-Wooldridge is a private scientific firm hired by contract to advise the Air Force.

Captain Taylor asked Nickerson if other men high in the Pentagon did not agree with Wilson's decision to take the Jupiter IRBM away from the Army.

"They've got to agree or leave," Nickerson replied. "You can see who's still there and figure out who agrees."

Two witnesses who supported Nickerson on the witness stand were Dr. Wernher von Braun and Dr. Ernest Stuhlinger of the German missile team brought to the United States by the Army.

"He was a kind of quarterback, telling us what to do, which move to make, and what meeting to attend to present our case," testified von Braun. "I think that there would have been no Jupiter had it not been for him. It was Colonel Nickerson who enabled us to sell the Jupiter program to the Department of Defense."

Of General Medaris, Dr. von Braun said, "He felt it would be wiser not to fight back."

Dr. Stuhlinger echoed von Braun. He said, "I know that Colonel Nickerson's participation was not only helpful; it was even decisive.

Really, I am convinced that without his activity, particularly in the fall of 1955, without his action, activity, and his dedication, we would never have had the assignment at Redstone."

The court by its questioning betrayed sympathy for Nickerson. On occasion, General Garvin, presiding officer, interrupted the prosecuting attorney impatiently. Mrs. Nickerson and two of the children, Jeanne Carol, fifteen, and John Charles III, sitting in the front row, were confident the Colonel would be acquitted. So were the spectators. As the court was about to suspend the taking of evidence and proceed with the final argument, it decided to hear from one more witness: Nickerson's commander, General Medaris. This was the man who had requested his assignment at Huntsville, had called him his "Secretary of State," had described him as a "hard-driving, imaginative individual" with an ability to grasp, reason, and expound technical problems "in a fashion that approaches brilliance." Nickerson's impulsiveness he had dismissed as "superficial."

But on the witness stand that fateful day at Huntsville, General Medaris had forgotten all the praise he once heaped on the man whom he had sent to Washington to battle it out for the Army's Jupiter.

"It is my opinion," testified Medaris, "that Colonel Nickerson has violated the fundamental military code, and I do not think he has any further potential value to the service."

"If he is allowed to remain in the service, would you be willing to have him back in your command?" Medaris was asked.

"I would not," he snapped.

"I tried to temper his impulsiveness but failed," he continued. "I question today whether his judgment can be tempered. I have no idea how much he has learned that the end does not justify the means."

A ripple of astonishment went through the courtroom. Fellow officers who knew how close Nickerson had been to Medaris could not believe their ears. And for weeks afterward they refused to speak to Medaris except in line of duty.

Ray Jenkins, Nickerson's trial attorney, gave Medaris one more chance.

"Will you tell the court," he asked, "that in your opinion, while Colonel Nickerson acted improvidently and that the means he used to attain the end were wrong, nevertheless the end in view was right?"

Medaris declined to yield even on that.

"I can't say that, Mr. Jenkins," he replied.

The ten-man court spent only forty minutes in secret session. General Garvin wrote out the sentence in his own handwriting: "Suspended from rank for one year; to forfeit $100 per month for 15 months, and to be reprimanded."

Nickerson could have been sentenced to thirty years in prison and discharged from the Army.

From grateful superiors in Washington, General Medaris got his reward. He was given over-all command of the Army's missile effort, the promise of a third star, and all the bows before the television cameras when the Army finally pulled the shamefaced Eisenhower Administration out of its hole after the Russian sputniks, by belatedly launching the first American satellite.

With that launching, newspapermen tried to reach Colonel Nickerson, then serving in the Panama Canal Zone, far removed from the missiles which he had made his life work and whose problems he had championed. He would not come to the telephone. But Mrs. Nickerson said, "He has orders not to comment on missiles. But I have no orders not to talk. And I think it's wonderful that the Army has lived up to all the things it promised."

Various attempts were made by members of Congress after that to get Colonel Nickerson reinstated. When Senator Neuberger of Oregon tried to get him transferred back to missile work in the United States, the White House issued a curt statement that there would be no review of the Nickerson case. After serving his year in limbo, he was given security clearance and restored to command authority, though not directly to missile work.

But while remaining in semiexile, Nickerson watched two of his dreams come true. Not only did the missile he had worked on carry the first American satellite into outer space, but the new Secretary of Defense, Neil McElroy, completely reversed Wilson and ruled that the Jupiter would remain in the hands of the U.S. Army.

There are those at Huntsville who will tell you today that an Army which believes in loyalty will never forget the manner in which Major General John B. Medaris went back on a friend. But, far more important, there are those in the Army, the Navy, and the Air Force who will tell you that we would be even further behind Russia in regard to missiles and satellites if it had not been for the impulsive, courageous indiscretion of Johnny Nickerson.

xiii

PROFITS VS. PATRIOTISM

WARFARE HAS BEEN a profitable business since it first became professional. Behind the soldier has stood the supplier, behind the patriot the profiteer. When Julius Caesar invaded Gaul, it cost only 50 cents to kill an enemy. But the Roman contractors who supplied the swords, shields, spears and provisions raked in the riches. Today it costs $197,000,000 to equip one infantry division with "conventional weapons" and $55,000 for every enemy laid low by these already-obsolete means. As the missile age advances, costs continue to soar like the missiles themselves. So does everything else that goes with them, from pencils, of which the armed forces buy one million a year, to stationery, of which they buy $75,000,000 worth a year, to armor plate and electronics equipment, for which the bill runs into billions.

What the Pentagon buys affects the economy of the nation. It can mean life or death to a corporation. The corporate scramble for defense dollars is so vital that companies pay big salaries to affable gentlemen who know the right people in Washington. They can afford to rent the swankiest homes in Washington on a year-round basis to entertain the admirals and the generals and to dangle tempting salaries before key military men even before they doff the uniform. The board of directors and executive staff of almost every airplane company, every electronics company, and every oil company feature one or two retired admirals and generals who are on a first-name basis with the top brass of the Pentagon. Usually the new top brass served under the retired brass and owe their promotions to them. It's all tax deductible, and in the end the United States government pays the cost of having high-powered lobbyists tell the government what it should buy instead of having the salaried officials of the government, who are paid to make decisions, decide what it should buy.

There are exceptions to this rule. The Ford Motor Company does not go in for hiring retired military men. Nor does General Motors. General Motors puts its own men inside government.

But when Colonel John Nickerson, in his secret memo on guided missiles, charged that Washington's biggest lobby operates not on Capitol Hill but in the cocktail lounges of Sixteenth Street and Connecticut Avenue where personable people from Detroit and Los Angeles seek to ingratiate themselves with the Pentagon brass, he was telling the truth. He elaborated in detail how the biggest corporations in the United States were hurting the defense of the United States by their battle over missiles; and he named the former corporation executives, now inside the Pentagon, who lined up with their former corporations for and against certain types of missiles.

When Colonel Nickerson was cross-examined on the witness stand regarding these charges, he did not retreat. The Pentagon did retreat, but not Nickerson.

"High-ranking officers of the Air Force, including general officers," he said, "get to thinking about retirement and the job as head of missile research with Lockheed or some other firm.

"Sales officers of aircraft companies in Washington are 'primarily lobbyists,'" he charged. "Eighty-five per cent of the aircraft sales are with the government. These firms put pressure on Secretary Wilson through the Joint Chiefs of Staff, through Congress, and through direct contacts by representatives of the aircraft industry with all levels of the Pentagon."

He even charged that a private firm could put across an inferior weapon with the Air Force and that the Air Force would accept that inferior weapon because of influence. Exactly one day after Nickerson started enumerating these charges from the witness stand, his court-martial was abruptly halted. He was let off with a slap on the wrist.

Before examining this indictment in detail, let it be said that some big corporations have performed valiantly and patriotically for their country. When the Air Force ran out of funds for Operation Farside, Ford put up the money. When the Air Force was scraping the bottom of its appropriations barrel for the intercontinental missile, Convair continued to research at its own expense. Holmes and Narver, which built the facilities for the Eniwetok atomic proving ground and the first ICBM base near Cheyenne, offered to furnish the benefit of its experience to rival companies to build future ICBM bases. But the big corporations have also made money. And after wars, they have usually inherited—for a pittance—the factories in which they did their producing, factories built at the taxpayers' expense. What should be a two-way street between business and government has become an alley running one way and a broad boulevard running the other—with all the traffic signals, all the policemen speeding the flow of defense dollars toward industry.

The trend in defense buying has made big corporations bigger, and small corporations smaller. Scores of struggling firms have been ruthlessly squeezed out of business altogether. In time of war—with the big factories easy targets for enemy bombers—the small plants might be the saviors of the country. Yet of the $30,000,000,000 a year the Defense Department spends on new procurement, only a meager trickle goes to small business. Even this is steadily drying up. In the Eisenhower Administration's first fiscal year, beginning July 1, 1953, small business received 25.3 per cent of defense spending. In fiscal year 1955 this was cut to 21.5 per cent, then it dropped to 19.6 per cent in fiscal 1956 and remained at this level in fiscal 1957. Since the Pentagon is the nation's biggest buyer, its policies are largely to blame for the fact that under Eisenhower more firms have merged or gone out of business than at any time since the great depression of the 1930s.

On the other hand, ten giant firms received one third of all military contracts—worth a staggering $38,500,000,000—during the five years between 1951–1956. One hundred big companies also got 75 per cent of all prime defense contracts. General Motors topped the list with orders worth $6,874,000,000—more than all the nation's farmers collected in price supports for the same five years. The men who ran the Defense Department seem to have followed the advice of Secretary Wilson that what was good for General Motors was good for the United States. Other members of the Big Ten: Boeing Aircraft $4,537,800,000; United Aircraft $4,198,800,000; General Electric $4,003,200,000; Douglas Aircraft $3,906,600,000; North American Aviation $3,486,200,000; General Dynamics $3,109,600,000; Lockheed Aircraft $3,109,000,000; Curtiss-Wright $2,221,400,000; Republic Aviation $2,209,100,000.

Just as these huge sums were concentrated in a few pockets, so was the power to disburse them. With one lone exception, the nation's Defense Secretaries have been picked from the ranks of big business. The exception was General George Marshall, though even he served as a director of Pan American Airways. The others were James Forrestal, first Secretary of Defense, former head of the giant investment firm of Dillon, Read with directors placed on the boards of various manufacturing concerns; Louis Johnson, an attorney for the Pennsylvania Railroad and Pan American Airways; Robert A. Lovett, head of Brown Brothers, Harriman and Company, which has financed many firms doing defense work; Charles Wilson, presiding genius of General Motors; and Neil McElroy, whose company, Procter and Gamble, is one of the biggest soap manufacturers in the world. In appointing Wilson and McElroy, President Eisenhower merely followed in the path of his predecessors. Almost always have representatives of big business been picked to run the armed services. The public is not fully acquainted with the manner in which some corporations have put profits ahead of patriotism partly because the record has been glossed over by Congress and the press. The same Big Ten which get the break of the defense contracts also dominate national advertising. The big national magazines could not exist without them. Newspaper editors are tougher disciples of the truth. But the radio and TV executives and most of the magazine publishers will throw up their hands in horror at publication of any news critical of General Motors, U.S. Steel, Lockheed, Boeing and members of the Big Ten.

In October 1955, the Defense Department even tried to slip one over on the public by omitting the name of General Motors from the published list of big war contractors. General Motors was the biggest contractor; and Secretary Wilson was the former head of General Motors. But its name was omitted from the annual list of contractors given to the public.

Another reason the public does not know the facts is that most Congressional investigators have no desire to tangle with the biggest political contributors to their campaigns. The Senate Armed Services watchdog committee had a heaven-sent opportunity to air Colonel Nickerson's sensational charges during the much publicized—and therefore politically profitable—investigation which was started after the first Russian sputnik soared into space. Nickerson had pointed an accusing finger at General Motors, Bell Telephone, and Douglas Aircraft—had accused them of putting profits ahead of patriotism.

The Armed Services watchdog committee is supposed to keep an eye on national defense and should have investigated Nickerson's allegations as its first order of business. Yet, despite the array of

TV cameras which would have carried the facts to the American public, it ignored Nickerson altogether. Of the diverse assortment of witnesses which streamed through the spacious Senate Caucus Room, it asked not one question which might reflect on Big Business.

This was not the first time the Senators had shown a coy reluctance to investigate the business barons. When the committee examined the shortcomings of Air Force planes in the Korean War, it deliberately hushed up the 30-per-cent profit made by a General Motors subsidiary, Allison Motors, in the manufacture of the F-86 jet fighter. It also suppressed the manner in which Allison executives Daniel Babcock, Edward B. McNeil, and I. E. Settle, while lagging far behind in Sabre-Jet production, had time to get barns and homes for themselves built at cost by a construction company, Hunt and Nichols, doing business for the government. Senators knew in detail what had happened. Their investigators gave them the evidence in proven, admitted testimony. But they did not let the public know about it.

Not since Thurman Arnold, former head of the Justice Department's Antitrust Division, dug out the secret agreements between Nazi Germany and certain American corporations has the public been told the extent to which business has pulled wires and profited from the defense program. On more than one occasion the pursuit of profits has come shockingly near to treason.

The record goes back to 1929, when Standard Oil of New Jersey and I. G. Farben Industries of Germany agreed to divide up new patents for synthetic rubber and synthetic gasoline, thus forcing the American people, after Pearl Harbor, to walk; to the day when the Aluminum Company of America agreed to produce only 2,000 tons of magnesium a year while Hitler's companies produced 10,000 tons, thus permitting Hitler the biggest air force in the world when the blitzkrieg struck; to the day when Bausch and Lomb, given contracts to make periscopes for American submarines, turned blueprints over to its co-operating partner in Germany, Karl Zeiss, then engaged in the same work for the Nazi Navy.

Earlier, the Electric Boat Company of New London, Connecticut, indirectly helped Kaiser Wilhelm launch his murderous undersea warfare which eventually brought the United States into the war, by selling the Germans and Japanese the blueprints of America's first submarine. Yet Electric Boat is now enjoying a big bite of the billions going for atomic submarines, while the government must pay the huge overhead cost of keeping its own submarine yards idle at Portsmouth, New Hampshire.

Other defense contractors have not hestitated to meddle with our national defense in order to keep their hands in the government gravy bowl. In 1927 William Baldwin Shearer, a well-known Navy enthusiast, was paid $40,000 by Bethlehem Steel, New York Shipbuilding, Newport News Ship, and Fall River Shipbuilding companies to go to the Geneva Naval Conference and scuttle President Coolidge's attempt to further naval disarmament.

When Gerhard Westrick, Hitler's personal envoy, came to this country in 1940, he got surprising support from big-business leaders in his campaign to keep the United States neutral. Westrick's report, seized at the end of the war, is startling. He stated: "Among those I saw in the United States were Torkild Rieber of the Texas Company, Eberhard Faber of the Faber Company, James Mooney of General Motors, and Edsel and Henry Ford. I first saw Edsel Ford when I got to New York. I got a phone call from the secretary of Henry Ford asking me to come again to see Henry Ford. I paid Mooney a visit. One day he came to visit me in the Waldorf-Astoria, and on his own initiative he told me that he and a group of other people had the intention of seeing the President and trying to convince the President that he should insist on normal political relations between the United States and Germany." This was after Germany had invaded Poland, Holland, Belgium, France, Denmark, and Norway!

Lobbying to grab the thirty billion dollars in defense contracts which the Pentagon ladles out to American industry every year falls into four general categories:

The brazen wirepullers are Congressmen or defense officials who let contracts for politics' sake or in return for campaign contributions.

The inside wirepullers are dollar-a-year men or corporation executives inside the Pentagon who help out their own companies.

The old-school-tie wirepullers are the retired officers who go to work for private industry and get favored by fellow officers.

Big business wirepullers are a conglomeration of officials who, working in a department whose chief is a representative of big business and whose military officers have a natural awe of big business, go out of their way, sometimes quite honestly, to favor big business.

The combination is one which would justify the following inscription over the stately river entrance of the Pentagon: "To him that hath, more shall be given."

President Eisenhower, who spent forty-one years in the Army, could not have been unaware of the military's shameful record of putting profits ahead of patriotism. In fact, there is evidence that he rebelled against it. However, early in his administration it became apparent that businessmen who had contributed to the party had the inside track at the Pentagon.

After the Air Force had awarded a contract to the American Hydrotherm Company to heat bases at Mountain Home, Idaho, McGuire Field, New Jersey, and Dover, Delaware, Calvin Boggs, brother of the Republican Governor of Delaware, organized a brand-new company, Plant Management, Inc. And after Senators Butler of Maryland and Williams of Delaware, Republicans, wrote letters to the Defense Department, the Air Force suddenly canceled its contract with American Hydrotherm and awarded the contract to Governor Boggs's brother. The contract was canceled with suspicious abruptness shortly before midnight on June 30, thus permitting a company which had no experience and no personnel, and which was organized only on May 18, to jump in and hire the personnel of the canceled company. Calvin Boggs had never heated an air base before in his life. But he did have a brother who was a close friend of a family which had contributed $200,000 to Eisenhower—the duPonts—part of it through Secretary of the Air Force Talbott.

There was also the case, previously noted, where Secretary Talbott awarded a contract to Pan American Airways, whose executives had been faithful contributors to the party, to operate the vital Cape Canaveral missile base in Florida—an award which set the free world back many months in launching a satellite. The Air Force called for no competitive bids, merely handed the missile base over to Pan American Airways. And though Brown and Root of Texas had wantonly flouted the labor laws and had used powerful political influence to settle a criminal tax case against it, nevertheless Brown and Root was picked by the Defense Department to handle part of the construction of American bases in Spain. George R. Brown, powerful partner in Brown and Root, operates a year-round home at Warrenton, Virginia, where senators and Administration leaders are his weekend guests. He finds that influence has paid dividends. George and Herman Brown are listed among the seventy-six wealthiest men in the United States.

Generous contributors to the Eisenhower campaign fund in 1952 were officials of the Harvey Aluminum Company, which in the past had made Democratic contributions. But with Eisenhower a sure winner in 1952, Harvey took out some political insurance with the Republicans. After the campaign Harvey sought to collect. It cast a covetous eye on the heavy-press aluminum-extrusion plant at Halethorpe, Maryland, which Kaiser Aluminum operated for the Air Force. Secretary Talbott, former chairman of the Republican Finance Committee, was ever grateful for campaign funds. He first sought to cancel Kaiser's five-year lease, but his lawyers would not concur. Then he ordered the Air Force to take "competitive" bids for a new lease. Harvey Aluminum, Reynolds Metals, and Kaiser Aluminum all submitted bids. But Kaiser Aluminum, having received word that its telephone wires were tapped and its files surreptitiously scrutinized, carefully mimeographed and ostentatiously distributed a "trap" bid, guaranteeing to pay the Air Force a minimum annual rental of $250,000 on the Halethorpe aluminum press. This bid was never actually submitted to the Air Force. A few hours prior to the closing of the bids at one o'clock April 21, 1955, Kaiser delivered its bona fide bid by courier to Wright Field. The bids, however, were not opened. Wright Field officers put them in a package and announced they would be sent to Washington.

Politics being politics, Kaiser Aluminum executives were suspicious. They knew how contracts were sometimes let in the Pentagon. They also knew that long-established custom required bids to be opened immediately. So they protested. Whereupon Roger Lewis, Assistant Secretary of the Air Force, later to take a high-salaried job with Pan American Airways, called a meeting in his office in Washington at 4 P.M. April 25. Chad Calhoun, Ward Humphreys and Lloyd Cutler, representing Kaiser; Keith Linden, representing Harvey; and Maxwell Caskie, representing Reynolds Metals, were present. The Assistant Secretary of the Air Force announced sarcastically that in order to remove all suspicion he would have the bids opened publicly. Lewis' aide then proceeded to slit open the envelopes. But he did not read the bids.

"Aren't you going to make them public?" asked Calhoun.

"No," replied Lewis. "You wanted them opened so we've opened them. They'll now be taken back to Wright Field by Colonel Toomey and evaluated in the usual manner."

The Air Force officers present looked embarrassed. The representatives of industry looked incredulous.

"You are forcing me to make a formal protest against the manner in which the bids are now being handled and to protest that they are not being read to us at this time," stated Calhoun.

The Assistant Secretary of the Air Force, however, was adamant. "We've conformed to your request," he said. "We've opened the bids."

"It is utterly meaningless to have brought us over here to merely witness the slitting open of some sealed envelopes," protested Calhoun.

Mr. Cutler, attorney for Kaiser, asked Lewis if he would ask the other industry representatives if they would agree to have the bids read.

"That is no function of mine," replied Lewis. In the end, the bids were bundled up and sent back to Wright Field, opened but unread.

Kaiser, however, had submitted a bid so high that the Air Force could not reject it. Harvey Aluminum had bid a rental of $300,000 per year, just over Kaiser's "trap" bid of $250,000. Kaiser's real bid was $500,000. It retained the operation of the heavy-press aluminum-extrusion plant at Halethorpe, Maryland.

Thus operate the brazen wirepullers.

It pays to have a man working inside the Defense Department. How much it pays the public doesn't realize, and the Congress, though making many attempts to ascertain this cost, still has no idea. One inside wirepuller was Robert Tripp Ross, who as Assistant Secretary of Defense under Eisenhower did not hesitate to help his wife and his brother-in-law, executives of Wynn Enterprises, Inc., and Southern Athletic Company, both of Knoxville, Tennessee, regarding their contracts for athletic equipment for American troops. Southern Athletic Company had repeatedly violated the federal labor laws and was blacklisted by the Labor Department. Nevertheless, the Assistant Secretary of Defense, strategically placed inside the Pentagon, conveniently arranged a meeting between his brother-in-law, Herman D. Wynn, and a Marine general to iron out a dispute over the quality of baseball uniforms sold to the Marines. During a Senate investigation of this inside influence, Assistant Secretary Ross, piously professing innocence, resigned.

Another of Charles E. Wilson's "vice-presidents" was Robert Carr Lamphier, Jr., Deputy Assistant Secretary of Defense in charge of supply and logistics. His company, the Sangamo Electric Supply Company of Springfield, Illinois, is one of the important manufacturers of sonar listening equipment by which submarines detect approaching vessels. When it was discovered that Lamphier had retained his vice-presidency of Sangamo Electric and his financial interest in companies which were supplying highly important electronics equipment to the same Defense Department in which Lamphier was in charge of supplies, he quietly resigned. When the facts leaked out, Secretary of Defense Wilson issued a vigorous statement defending Lamphier. To him, defense of a comrade-in-business was sometimes more important than respect for the law.

In 1955 the House Government Operations Committee investigated the old-school-tie wirepullers who retire from government to draw lush salaries in private business. "We see generals retire from active duty one day," said Congressman Mollohan of West Virginia, "only to become heads of civilian agencies next. Even more disconcerting is the list of retired generals and admirals who as of December 31, 1954, or later, are employed by a goodly percentage of the 100 principal firms doing business with the Department of Defense. In every instance these high-ranking officers serve their firms in such capacities as chairman of the board, director or vice-president of the corporation. Their firms fill more than fifty per cent of all the contracts entered into by the Defense Department.

"Let me remind the members of Congress that Section 281, Title 18 of the U.S. Code specifically prohibits any retired officers from representing any person in the sale of anything to the government through the department in whose service he holds retired status."

When a lawyer retires from the Treasury Department he is required by law to wait two years before he represents a client whose tax case he handled in the Treasury. Other civilian branches of the government restrict their officials from immediately cashing in on the inside information they obtain and friends they make while working for the government. An admiral or a general retires on a pension far more generous than that of a civilian. If he has a physical disability he even gets a concession on paying income taxes. Despite this, officer after officer has jumped into the outstretched arms of corporations having contracts with the government. If the American taxpayer is to save money on the defense budget, one of the most important steps the Congress could take is to forbid any officer to accept employment with a company doing business with the government until two years after his retirement and further specify that if he accepts such employment he automatically forfeits his pension.

It is difficult, if not impossible, to trace the favoritism granted to generals retired from the Pentagon by generals still inside the Pentagon. There are seldom such clear-cut cases as that of General Ingalls, who, when Chief of the Signal Corps, favored the prosecution of the Radio Corporation of America, but who, when hired by the Radio Corporation of America, was delighted to have the Signal Corps suddenly drop RCA's prosecution.

One company which seems to lead a charmed life when it comes to airplane-engine contracts is Curtiss-Wright, one of the Big Ten, which between 1951 and 1956 got $2,583,700,000 in orders from the government. It got them despite the fact that during the Korean War Curtiss-Wright built an engine for the F-84 fighter escort which was so full of mechanical bugs that at one time a big backlog of sorely needed F-84 planes was stacked up waiting for bugless engines. The Curtiss-Wright engine for the experimental X-2 rocket plane also caused trouble and delayed a vital program. Yet Curtiss has the remarkable knack of snaring contracts. Before Pearl Harbor, its executives flatly refused to build new airplane factories for the hard-pressed government despite a special RFC loan, until the Treasury had given Curtiss an agreement that it could write off the cost of the new aviation plant in five years. Very bluntly Curtiss-Wright told the Treasury that they did not want the planes, it was the government which wanted them, and intimated that if a favorable tax agreement was not worked out they would not feel obligated to accept the airplane contract. This was the beginning of the tax-write-off plan later extended to other companies.

In those days one of the fair-haired boys with the Army Air Corps was Burdette Wright, executive vice-president of Curtiss-Wright and son-in-law of former Congressman Philip Campbell, the Kansas Republican and powerful chairman of the House Rules Committee, later lobbyist for Standard Oil. More recently Curtiss-Wright has followed the practice of hiring potent retired officers. On its board of directors is Levin H. Campbell, Jr., former Chief of Ordnance, while the general manager of its aeronautical division is Major General Edward M. Power, once of the Air Force.

Another aviation company which can do no wrong as far as the Air Force is concerned is Fairchild Aircraft. Its "flying boxcar," the

C-119, has suffered more crack-ups than any other Air Force plane. During the Korean War Kaiser Aircraft was given a supplemental contract to manufacture this plane in order to speed up production, but after the war Fairchild wanted all C-119 production in its hands. Working through the new Secretary of the Air Force, Harold Talbott, and his close friend Grover Loening, a big stockholder in Fairchild, it succeeded in having the Kaiser contract canceled.

The night after the cancellation Richard S. Boutelle, president of Fairchild, entertained at a victory party on the terrace of the Shoreham Hotel in Washington. Everybody of importance in the Air Force was present: General Hoyt S. Vandenberg, Chief of Staff; General N. F. Twining, Vice-Chief of Staff; Lieutenant General C. B. Stone III, Comptroller, Deputy Chief of Staff; Lieutenant General J. E. Briggs, Assistant Deputy Chief of Staff for Development; Major General W. D. Eckert, Assistant Deputy Chief of Staff, Materiel; Major General R. W. Burns, Assistant Deputy Chief of Staff, Personnel; Brigadier General H. Harris, Jr., War Plans Division; Major General Don Putt, Vice-Commander, Air Research and Development Command; Brigadier General Sory Smith, Chief of Information; Assistant Secretary of Defense McNeil; Senator Glenn Beall of Maryland; and Congressman Dewey Short of Missouri, chairman of the House Armed Services Committee.

Air Force Regulation 30-30 states that no officer shall "accept any favor or gratuity . . . where such favor or gratuity might influence" a contract. General Jacob Loucks Devers, retired, is technical adviser to the president of Fairchild Engine and Airplane Corporation.

When the Army faced the problem of moth-balling valuable equipment after the war it contracted with International Harvester for a research program costing $750,000 to decide what should be done with this equipment. The Army Ordnance did not turn to the Navy, which had conducted research for five years and which had evolved a practical and efficient means of moth-balling equipment. General Levin Campbell was Chief of Army Ordnance in 1945 when the contract was given International Harvester. In 1946 he became vice-president of International Harvester. International Harvester, though paid $750,000, did not do the job itself. It farmed the job to Arthur D. Little, Inc., of Boston, and Arthur D. Little, in turn, asked the Davison Chemical Company to take over. The handsome fee of $750,000 paid to International Harvester could have been saved completely merely by consulting the Navy. But things are not done that way in the armed services.

International Harvester, incidentally, has done extremely well since General Campbell became its executive vice-president in 1946. It got the huge total of $687,400,000 in Defense Department orders from 1950 to 1956.

Perhaps no industry has danced more of its executives in and out of government than the oil companies. President Eisenhower's first guided missile adviser, Eger V. Murphree of Standard Oil of New Jersey, was one of the Standard officials who helped negotiate the secret agreement with Germany by which Standard and I. G. Farben withheld synthetic rubber and synthetic oil from the United States. He was succeeded by another oil man, W. T. Holliday, former research director of Socony-Mobil Oil Company. And though the Air Force had a fully qualified regular officer, Colonel Roger W. Moore, West Point '31, trained to handle oil purchases, Secretary of Defense Wilson insisted on going to Standard Oil of New Jersey and appointing one of its vice-presidents, W. W. White, to handle oil and gas purchases. This put White in the position of doing business with his own firm. Congressmen investigating the long roll call of generals in private industry and industry executives in the Pentagon were flabbergasted when they cross-examined Brigadier General White. Here is their cross-examination:

> CONGRESSMAN HEBERT OF LOUISIANA: You are not on the payroll of Standard Oil at this time.
>
> GENERAL WHITE: No, sir.
>
> HEBERT: And you are not paid any money at all from Standard Oil?
>
> WHITE: Yes, sir.
>
> HEBERT: You are?
>
> WHITE: I am collecting.
>
> HEBERT: You are collecting?
>
> WHITE: Yes, sir.
>
> HEBERT: Then you are on the payroll?
>
> WHITE: No, I am not on the payroll.
>
> HEBERT: Well, is it through stockholdings or salary?
>
> WHITE: I receive the amount of money which is the difference between my normal salary and my present salary.

Standard Oil of New Jersey got $684,000,000 in orders from the

Defense Department in 1950–56, during two years of which time General White was in charge of purchasing oil and gasoline.

Seldom do the retired admirals and generals bring any real skill to the companies which dangle the fancy salaries before them. Their value lies in knowing the right people. If a general is not able to influence the right people, he moves on to other fields of endeavor. Lieutenant General K. B. Wolfe was one of the most important procurement men in the Air Corps during the war. After the war he became the president of Oerlikin Tool and Arms, a Swiss company manufacturing an antiaircraft gun. But Oerlikin, despite General Wolfe's potent aid, was not able to get orders from the United States. It was feared the Swiss had connections in too many international places. So General Wolfe moved on to become vice-president of the Garrett Corporation of Los Angeles, which is gradually building up its business with the Pentagon. It got $188,400,000 in orders in 1950–56.

One company which is doing better is General Precision Equipment Corporation, which snagged $355,000,000 worth of defense business during 1950–56. Its far-flung ramifications extend from Askania Regulator to Link Aviation to Graflex to the Society for Visual Education. It has placed Admiral Malcolm F. Schoeffel in charge of weapons planning.

Another company which has done well both in defense orders and in hiring old-school-tie men is American Machine and Foundry. It has hired Eisenhower's former Chief of Staff, General W. Bedell Smith, Lieutenant General Laurence C. Craigie of the Air Force, and General Russell Maxwell of the Army. Its defense orders totaled $201,000,000 in 1950–56.

Thus does the old school tie influence the economic life of the nation.

One general, leaving the Pentagon, did not go in for a plush salary from private industry. General Omar Bradley, stepping out as Chairman of the Joint Chiefs of Staff, accepted a position as adviser to the Bulova Watch Company for $10,000 a year. He was offered more. "That's all I'm worth," he said, declining the increase.

Government planners long ago decided that two of the best ways to discourage attack were to spread defense production geographically around the United States so no one industry could be bombed out of commission; and second, not to concentrate too much production in big companies. Politically, small industry has been the backbone of the capitalist system. Big industry can be taken over too easily by a fascist or communist regime. The plan to organize industry for future war needs is called the Production Allocation Program, known more informally as PAP. This is exactly what the program has boiled down to under Eisenhower—pap.

When George C. Marshall was Secretary of Defense, planning contracts were awarded to many small firms. He followed a policy inaugurated by Louis Johnson even before Pearl Harbor. Production was located all over the United States. In some cases small companies were given "educational" orders so they could learn wartime jobs in the comparative leisure of peace. Marshall understood the peril of keeping too many military eggs in too few baskets. He split up defense contracts among several suppliers, kept vital plants operating at low levels of production rather than let them close down. The more plants he could save from rust and ruin, the more would be ready for war production if needed. A dispersal of production sources multiplied the targets an enemy would have to destroy.

Charles E. Wilson was hardly installed in the Pentagon before he started pulling down Marshall's structure. He decreed, as described elsewhere in these pages, that he would save money by concentrating defense work in larger, more efficient factories. It mattered not that this immediately increased the defense orders and dividends of General Motors. It mattered not that some of its chief competitors —Chrysler, American Locomotive, Mack Truck, and Reo Motors— got canceled out. Eventually, Wilson was forced by Congressional outcry, plus the advice of his own military experts, to abandon this plan. But favoritism toward big companies continued.

It is difficult for a small company to afford a full-time lobbyist in Washington to take procurement officers out to dinner, or find out what contracts are going to be let in the Pentagon. It is also difficult for a small company to afford the cost of constructing a prototype or sample of a proposed Pentagon product. Some small firms have taken this gamble at great cost, only to be rewarded with the runaround. Heyer Products of Belleville, New Jersey, once went to great cost to build prototypes or samples of power units for aircraft which required only thirty to forty-five minutes of testing by the Air Force. Yet it took two and a half years to persuade the Air Force to get these prototypes on the qualified list for purchase.

Just the opposite treatment was given to a big company, Chatham Electronics. It had designed a lightweight power unit for converting AC to DC power in B-52 jet bombers. The prototype pleased the generals and they promptly made it the only such unit on the qualified list. They wrote specifications to fit the Chatham model, then gave other companies only thirty days to build rival units and submit their bids. Although any real competition was ruled out, the Air Force went through the face-saving rigmarole of sending out 100 bid sets, comprising 150,000 pieces of paper. At the last minute the generals got nervous and relaxed the specifications. But this was a meaningless gesture made on the twenty-ninth day of a thirty-day offering. By that time it was too late for anyone else to bid.

Big companies frequently do not have to pay for the cost of building a prototype or sample. When the Army wanted a lighter-weight jeep developed it authorized the Ford Motor Company to do the work—at the expense of the Army. Total cost for Ford's experimentation and development was $6,747,460. Meanwhile, the Willys-Overland Company, Inc., original inventor of the jeep, had gone to work on its own, without expense to the Army, and developed a lightweight jeep. When its officials telephoned Frank Higgins, Assistant Secretary of the Army, however, asking for a chance to demonstrate, he refused. He would not even allow the new jeep to be parked at the Pentagon.

"You are not going to bring that thing down here," groused Higgins. "We have no space for it."

Willys-Overland officials then took their jeep up to the House Armed Services Committee. It weighed one thousand pounds less than the wartime jeep, had a platform which could be folded to one side and was adapted for landing by parachute. It had been developed at no cost to the Army, whereas Ford was paid $6,747,460 by the Army. But when Assistant Secretary Higgins learned the Congressmen were looking at the new jeep, he complained. "The Willys-Overland people are pulling an end run," he told Congressmen Harry Sheppard of California and George Mahon of Texas.

"On the contrary," exploded Congressman Sheppard, "I understand that you have been given every opportunity to see this new jeep and that you won't allow it a parking place at the Pentagon."

The Defense Department would much rather not bother with small companies but leave it up to the prime contractors to choose their own subcontractors. The natural inclination of any prime contractor, however, is to make the profitable parts himself or to turn over subcontracts to another large company on a scratch-my-back-and-I'll-scratch-yours basis.

Take the case of National Die Casting, a small Chicago firm, which had been doing a healthy business with the Air Force until the advent of Charles E. Wilson. At that point, its contracts dropped from $1,380,000 in 1953 to a mere $20,000 in 1956, then skidded to a flat zero in 1957. When National Die Casting complained to the Air Force, it received a bleak reply that the parts it had been manufacturing were no longer being purchased by the Air Force but by the prime contractors. The company was advised not to bother the Air Force, which it had served so well, but to offer its wares directly to the large airframe makers. It sent out sixty-three letters to prime contractors and got back eleven replies, all indicating no interest.

Obviously, a prime contractor is not anxious to build up a small company when he can enlarge his own plant and get the benefit of a fast tax write-off in the bargain. The great Bendix Aviation Corporation, for example, built a new plant at Davenport, Iowa, to manufacture oxygen regulators, previously made by three or four small companies. Having been given authority to select its own subcontractors, Bendix decided to make the parts itself, share the gravy with no one. In the case of the B-58 supersonic bomber, Convair, the prime contractor, handed out all the subcontracts to big firms. Not a crumb was left over for small companies.

One sinister means of keeping small firms outside the golden door wherein lie defense profits is the simple matter of security clearance. This is rightly required. But by a process as baffling as the old conundrum about the chicken and the egg, security clearance is usually available only to companies which *already* have defense contracts. This clearly favors the big companies. The small manufacturer with a new idea finds it almost impossible to secure the classified information he needs to make a proposal.

This makes him easy prey for the big contractors, who will buy his know-how, then take over the profitable production work after gaining all his information. The small producer cannot protect his idea, because Uncle Sam requires contractors to waive proprietary interest in any technical developments resulting from government work. The purpose is sound—to prevent companies from exploiting ideas developed at national expense for the good of all. But this injures the small companies which have nothing to sell except know-how, then must waive all rights to their ideas.

Another advantage the Pentagon has arbitrarily given to many big companies is the use of government-owned tools and plants. The list of firms occupying government plants reads like Who's Who in Big Business and includes most of the top aviation, metal and machine companies. These government plants, owned by the taxpayers, are made available to contractors on the most favorable terms. A company can move in without risking a cent in capital, then pay a reasonable rental out of its profits. Boeing, for instance, produces most of its big bombers in government-owned plants. Boeing even had the gall to ask the Air Force to build a new plant at Richmond, California, so it could produce Bomarc antiaircraft missiles without putting up a penny.

Few small companies, of course, can afford to offer fancy salaries to the generals and admirals as they are about to retire from the Pentagon.

Where big companies are concerned there's usually no competitive bidding. Sometimes competitive bids are taken; but afterward pampered contractors have been allowed to match the low bids of competitors. Other low proposals have been thrown out on the grounds that the small manufacturer was not "qualified." Western Electric was given the $2,400,000,000 job of installing the radar warning network in the Far North without even going through the motion of a bid. New York Shipbuilding at Camden, New Jersey, was authorized to build an aircraft carrier without competitive bidding—despite the fact that the jigs, dies and molds were already in existence both in the Brooklyn Navy Yard and at the Newport News Shipbuilding Company. The taxpayers pay for fully equipped Navy yards at Norfolk, Brooklyn, Portsmouth, New Hampshire and on the West Coast, but the prize contracts are given to the private shipbuilding companies. What this means is that the taxpayer pays the overhead upkeep of the government shipyard while the private shipyards get the profit.

By far the biggest lobby inside the Defense Department is the worship of Pentagon officials for bigness. They have set themselves up as the unpaid, full-time, day-in-and-day-out wirepullers for big industry, even when that industry is being opposed by other branches of the government. They work hard, even though unpaid. In 1948, when the American Telephone and Telegraph Company faced an antitrust suit brought by the Justice Department, the then Secretary of Defense, Robert Lovett, a Republican appointee in a Democratic administration, made personal representations to the Justice Department that the case be dropped. He acted, in effect, as the private unpaid attorney for American Tel and Tel. The Justice Department refused.

Came the end of the Truman Administration and the new Secretary of Defense, Charles E. Wilson, emulated his predecessor and also became, in effect, the personal attorney for American Tel and Tel. He had the help in this case of M. J. Kelly, president of Bell Telephone Laboratories, who had quietly gone to work inside the Pentagon "without compensation," supposedly out of patriotism. During his six months as an unpaid public servant, however, Kelly seemed more interested in serving his company's stockholders than the taxpayers. He dropped persuasive words into the ear of Secretary Wilson, who then wrote a letter to Attorney General Herbert Brownell, urging that the case against AT&T be dropped. Wilson even used the exact words drafted for him by the patriotic Mr. Kelly.

Brownell received Wilson's ghostwritten letter on July 16, 1953. Delivered by hand by a full colonel as befits so important a missive, it was almost lyrical in tone. It listed the massive contracts awarded to the Bell system, ranging from the production of guided missiles to the humble field telephone, and "respectfully urged that the Department of Justice review this situation with a view of making suggestions as to how this potential hazard to national security can be removed or alleviated."

Brownell then arranged a secret chat with AT&T Vice-President T. Brooke Price at White Sulphur Springs, West Virginia, but subsequently couldn't get his own subordinates in the Justice Department to okay a compromise.

Summer faded into fall and fall into winter. By May 1954, AT&T representatives were getting restless. Once again they enlisted the help of their unpaid attorneys in the Pentagon. (A total of twenty-nine former AT&T officials have held policy-making jobs under Eisenhower, most of them in the Pentagon.) This time it was Wilber Brucker, then general counsel, later to become Secretary of the Army, who went to bat for AT&T. He fairly glowed as he wrote another letter to Brownell, enumerating the great virtues of the telephone company. Again the Justice Department was urged to make a compromise "short of actual trial."

The Justice Department yielded. The telephone company made minor concessions. The trial was dropped. The Defense Department, unofficial attorney for the biggest utility in the United States, had knocked a home run.

Washington has seen a lot of lobbying battles, but push-button warfare has developed the fiercest struggles to date. Never has the battle for contracts been so frenzied; never the lobbying so frantic. For the first time in years entrenched airplane manufacturers with well-oiled entrees at the Pentagon saw their position challenged. They saw young upstarts in the industrial world, such as Ramo-Wooldridge, challenging their supremacy. They realized that the new sleek missiles of the push-button age represented just as radical an industrial change as the departure of the old Studebaker wagon from the farms of America and its replacement with tractors and trucks. They saw in the new unmanned missiles a weapon which did not need an army of workmen to bolt sheets of aluminum together, a weapon which might make useless their vast hangars and assembly plants. So the airplane manufacturers became frantic. They had powerful friends at the Pentagon and they used them to keep newcomers out. They also used them to keep government itself out of the missile business.

Just how influential the airplane manufacturers can be in the struggle to influence friends and win contracts is indicated by the case history of Douglas Aircraft.

"It should be noted that the aircraft industry and particularly the Douglas Aircraft Company," wrote Colonel John Nickerson in the confidential memo for which he was court-martialed, "openly oppose the development of any missile by a government agency.

"High officials of the Douglas Company have stated that Douglas is paying particular attention to the possibilities of calling off the operation at Huntsville, Alabama," continued Nickerson, referring to the Army's development of its own highly successful missiles, the Jupiter and the Redstone.

For the Army, which hitherto had specialized in foot soldiers, to manufacture anything that flew, was, in the eyes of Donald Douglas, president of Douglas Aircraft, nothing less than sacrilegious. For years Douglas had enjoyed such an inside pull with the Air Force that before Pearl Harbor he was able to sell Japan the blueprints of the DC-4 and get away with it. Development of the DC-4 had been largely financed by Uncle Sam, but Douglas sold it, for $706,720. After Pearl Harbor the DC-4 became one of the most potent planes in the Japanese Air Force. When news of the deal leaked to the press before Pearl Harbor, Douglas issued a self-righteous denial saying he would never, never under any circumstances sell blueprints to Japan. The news was suppressed.

After the war, however, Japanese documents were captured which showed that Douglas had lied. The documents showed how anxious both the Japanese and Douglas were to camouflage the sale so the American public would not know that the biggest supplier of aircraft to the United States was simultaneously supplying aircraft blueprints to Japan. Here is the letter written by the Japanese, August 14, 1939, just after Douglas finally decided that, with the obtaining of an export license, the news must be discreetly leaked.

> Major V. E. Bertrandias
> Douglas Aircraft Company
> Santa Monica, California
> Dear Mr. Bertrandias:
>
> Looking over the Saturday edition of the New York Times, I could not help but write this letter to compliment you for the most excellent way of disclosing the sale. Those "in the know" will not object to the transaction as they are limited to those in our trade, while laymen possibly don't know what the ship is anyway when mentioned singly by your designation as in the paper. . . .
>
> It was an excellent way of handling the difficult matter in a delicate situation and I wish to share the feeling of relief, if you ever felt one. Hope you had similar luck with your local papers!
>
> Sincerely yours,
>
> S. Akabane
>
> Nakajima Aircraft Company

Douglas' alibi, after this leaked out, was that he had received permission from the Army Air Corps to sell the blueprints. This may have been true. Donald Douglas, Jr., married the daughter of General Hap Arnold, wartime Chief of the Air Corps, and for years Douglas Senior has had inside influence with the Air Force.

Today Donald Douglas still pulls strings at the Air Force and those strings have won for him the highly prized contract to manufacture the intermediate-range ballistic missile, the Thor. It is being turned out at the Douglas plant at Sacramento even though this adds to the already heavy concentration of important defense factories on the West Coast. Not satisfied with his contract to manufacture the Thor, Douglas wanted to keep the United States government out of the missile-building business altogether.

Not merely the aircraft manufacturers but the cities in which they were located suffered a case of the jitters as the result of push-button warfare. Wichita, Seattle, the areas around Los Angeles saw the big bombers which had helped make them prosperous replaced by missiles manufactured in other cities. They, too, joined in the lobbying.

When North American Aviation lost its contract to manufacture the winged Navajo missile and fired 12,000 employees, the people of Los Angeles were up in arms. First, North American's lobbyists swarmed into Washington like a high-school senior class at cherry-blossom time. Then they mobilized the Congressmen from California.

Actually the Navajo should have been canceled long before. It is an old-fashioned missile traveling only 3,000 miles an hour compared with the modern 19,000-mile-an-hour ballistic missile. At a White House meeting in December 1957, Senator Clinton P. Anderson, Democrat of New Mexico, scolded President Eisenhower and Secretary of Defense McElroy for wasting three quarters of a billion dollars on the Navajo.

"The Navajo was started in 1946," Anderson reminded the White House group, "and terminated in 1956. It was an air-breathing missile, yet it went above sixty-five thousand feet where there isn't any air to breathe. North American Aviation, which was manufacturing it, knew this. Yet North American continued making the Navajo until 1956 at a cost to the taxpayers of seven hundred million dollars. Why?"

"Well, we stopped it," replied Deputy Defense Secretary Donald Quarles. "Was that a good job or not?"

"It sure was," replied the Senator from New Mexico, proceeding immediately to other duplications in the missile program.

"You've got the Little John and the Honest John," he pointed out. "They're both about the same. The Little John has a range of fifteen miles, the Honest John a range of twenty miles. They're both classified as artillery weapons. They both use solid fuel, both are produced for the Army, one by Emerson Electric and Douglas, the other by Douglas and Hercules Powder.

"Why this duplication? Are we just trying to help the aviation companies pay dividends?

"Then there are the Sergeant and the Corporal. Both are artillery weapons, both produced for the Army, the Sergeant with a range of fifty miles, the Corporal with a range of seventy-five miles. Can anyone tell me the real difference in the mission of the two?" Anderson demanded that there be a central office on missile control.

Despite the prolonged production of the Navajo at North American, the Congressmen from Southern California demanded that North American keep operating. They demanded new missile orders, though not even they had the gall to demand that the Air Force reinstate the Navajo contract. They wanted North American to manufacture the new B-70 supersonic intercontinental bomber. They were so harsh in their demands that Senator Thomas Kuchel later wrote a letter of apology to James H. Douglas, Secretary of the Air Force.

Bids for the B-70 were submitted by Convair, Boeing and North American. Convair had built the huge B-36, long the backbone of the Bomber Command. Boeing had built a whole line of operational bombers from the B-17 Flying Fortress, and the B-29 Super Fortress of World War II, to the raked-wing B-47 and B-52 jet bombers of recent day. Of the three, many experts considered North American least qualified for a bomber contract, although it had more experience in supersonic flight. North American won the right to build the B-70.

This may well have been good economics; it was certainly good politics. It did not, however, alleviate the concentration of vital defense plants on the West Coast. As Russian missiles have become more deadly in their power and more accurate in their aim, American defense production has conveniently given them an easier, more concentrated target nearer to the bristling bases of Siberia.

The automobile industry also got into the push-button warfare lobbying act. Chrysler, hardest hit of the big auto makers, had managed to get in on the ground floor with the Army and secured a contract to manufacture the Jupiter missile. It had the blessing, incidentally, of Dr. Wernher von Braun's brother, who worked for Chrysler. Later, both Secretary of Defense Wilson and his successor, Neil McElroy, proposed cancellation of the contract, but each time Chrysler lobbyists were too active and too potent. Each time they set up such a din on Capitol Hill that the contract was reprieved. Cheering Chrysler behind the scenes was Wilber Brucker, Secretary of the Army, who, as a former Governor of Michigan, is a great friend of the auto autocrats. Chrysler offered as its main argument the fact that the automobile industry was in a serious slump and that unemployment in Michigan was dangerous—an argument that was hard to answer. But the Air Force was hell-bent to get the Army out of the missile business. It had nothing against Chrysler as a company, but it did not want Chrysler making missiles for the Army. So at a secret Pentagon meeting the Air Force top brass decided to offer the industrialists of Michigan economic compensation. General Thomas White, Chief of Staff of the Air Force, and General Curtis LeMay, Vice-Chief of Staff, sent word to the automobile industry that three quarters of the Air Force missile money goes for ground-support equipment. From that moment, they promised, a larger share of these juicy contracts would go to Detroit.

Thus are defense contracts sometimes let.

What the lobbyists who battled for Chrysler did not publicize, and what probably some of them did not know, was that Chrysler had murdered the defense dollar when it came to the cost of producing the Jupiter. It was guaranteed a fixed fee to be added to the total production cost. Thus there was no incentive to Chrysler to keep costs down. The result was a subcontracting program that barely managed to stay within the bounds of sanity. Chrysler set nominal ceiling prices on what a subcontractor could charge for missile parts; but if the subcontractor sang the blues, Chrysler seemed happy to raise the ceiling. Prices were cheerfully doubled and trebled, almost at the subcontractors' whim. After all, it didn't cost Chrysler a single penny.

One missile part, MB-55742, a little hand-made metal clamp, illustrated the devil-may-care characteristics of the cost-plus-fee system. Between November 30, 1954, and October 24, 1955, Chrysler bought 395 of the clamps at prices ranging recklessly from $20.68 to $47.78 apiece. Finally, after inexcusable delay, Chrysler got around to asking for competitive bids on the little clamp. Winning bid: $2.52.

Of this haphazard system of buying, the General Accounting Office took a very dim view. Reporting on Chrysler's contract for building the Jupiter missile, the watchdog over the government's books stated: "Our review of Chrysler's procurement of 27 parts used in missile production disclosed that unreasonably high costs, ultimately borne by the government, resulted. . . . The prime contractor [Chrysler] has little incentive to strive for economy in his subcontracting where, as in these cases, the prime contract is of the cost-plus-a-fixed-fee type under which the prime contractor does not share in cost reduction."

The old-line companies are still doing all right at the Defense Department. Newcomers have barged into the missile business, but the friends and lobbyists in the know—Douglas, Boeing, Convair, North American and Chrysler—are tough to dislodge overnight. Some newcomers have come a long way in the missile field, have cashed in handsomely on push-button warfare. But others who have tried to storm the barricades of the entrenched companies have failed.

One which has been successful is the Ramo-Wooldridge Company, formed by Simon Ramon and Dean Wooldridge, who helped to build up the electronics orders for Hughes Aircraft to $200,000,000 a year, but who, in September 1953, went into business for themselves. They now form a sort of electronic brain for the Air Force, having convinced the air generals that one master company should manage the technological side of the missile program. This made sense. However, the scientific twins soon went further and convinced the Air Force they should not only serve as the brain factory on missiles, but should also produce them. The Air Force balked at this. It knew something of the uproar which might take place on Capitol Hill should it be revealed that one company had a monopoly of both missile design and missile production. That company could then design the type of missiles it wanted to produce. However, Ramo-Wooldridge got a foot in the production door. It split Air Force business into two parts and called the second part "space technology laboratories." This half of the company planned the missiles, and a second half of the company produced some of the electronics necessary for the missiles. This meant that Ramo-Wooldridge was drawing up specifications with one hand while its other hand was scratching for contracts based on the same specifications. Result: In 1957 Ramo-Wooldridge did a business of $43,000,000, of which all but $8,000,000 was for brain-trusting the Air Force missile program. The two young scientists have made money; they have also done a good job.

Doing a good job, however, does not necessarily land a contract with the Defense Department. It also depends on who you are. Take the case of Reaction Motors, the first company to get into the business. Founded in 1941 by four early members of the American Rocket Society, the late James Wyld, Lovell Lawrence, Jr., John Shesta and Franklin Pierce, they pioneered the first rocket engine ever built in the United States. Reaction also designed the engine that propelled the Air Force's X-1, the first American aircraft to crash the sound barrier. It also helped develop the MX-774, forerunner of the intercontinental ballistic missile. Finally, it was a Reaction motor which powered the Navy's Vanguard rocket engine until Richard Porter moved in and won the contract for General Electric.

One of the heavy investors in Reaction Motors has been Laurance S. Rockefeller, who is long on money, short on political know-how. In fact, no company ever wielded less political influence in Washington. With no defense orders coming in, Reaction was finally forced to merge with the Thiokol Chemical Corporation, a larger firm which developed solid propellants for missiles. Thiokol had invented the technique of mixing solid propellants with an elastic substance so that the propellant has the consistency of rubber. This was the most important breakthrough in developing a solid fuel for long-range missiles; and it was just what the armed forces had been looking for—especially the Navy. Liquid fuels are dangerous to stow aboard a submarine. In addition, liquid fuels require the long, laborious count-down as the crew of technicians check every single valve, every single gadget to make sure the rocket engine is in perfect working order. These count-downs take so long that an enemy could blast most of the defense factories of Europe before an American missile is launched.

Thiokol's development of a new solid fuel for rocket engines, therefore, looked like a heaven-sent opportunity for the armed forces, especially for the Navy's new Polaris. Thiokol bid for the contract. So did Aerojet. Aerojet had no experience in solid propellants beyond building Jato boosters to give planes jet-assisted take-offs. Aerojet had also built one small solid-propellant rocket called the Spero. This is about the size of a super Fourth of July rocket and equally useful. It was a long way from having the power to propel a giant 1,200-mile missile such as the Navy's Polaris. In fact, only one company had solid-propellant engines large enough to be used—the Thiokol Chemical Corporation which had merged with the most experienced rocket-motor company in the nation, Reaction Motors.

Aerojet, however, had other assets. Its president is gruff, likable

Dan A. Kimball, former Secretary of the Navy, who commutes back and forth between Washington, where he talks to Defense officials, and Sacramento, where he manufactures missiles. Dan Kimball was in the missile business even while he held the job of Secretary of the Navy under Truman, and he was accused at that time of failing to divest himself of his financial interest in Aerojet. The fact that he has gone back to Aerojet to become its chief salesman in Washington would seem to bear out that accusation. Dan Kimball is a Democrat. In the Eisenhower Administration, however, he has important friends on the Republican side of the street. The executives of his parent company, General Tire and Rubber, are the O'Neills—staunch Republican supporters of the late Joe McCarthy. They reign over a combined and diverse industrial empire which includes not only Aerojet but the Buyers Company, Pennsylvania Rubber Company, RKO Teleradio Pictures—doing a total of $442,000,000 in business with the Defense Department in 1950–56. Up until recently the O'Neill family owned the Mutual Broadcasting Company, and they still own four key television stations which help mold public opinion in the nation. Aerojet also has some friends in the Defense Department. It hired General Richard W. Hayward of the Marine Corps and Admiral R. S. Hatcher of the Navy to join its staff in California. With the former Secretary of the Navy at the head of the firm, this makes a formidable line-up when it come to getting Navy contracts.

Result: The Navy awarded the Polaris contract to Aerojet. It was not a competitive bid. The contract was negotiated.

But here is the real irony. When the Navy wanted to start preliminary tests of the Polaris it needed six solid-propellant engines. Aerojet was still struggling to develop its first Polaris engine. It could not come up with anything. So the Navy went begging to the company which it had turned down, but which had a solid-fuel propellant ready. Thiokol loaned the Navy the six test engines which Aerojet had not been able to produce.

Pull and politics sometimes pay off in the battle of profits vs. patriotism.

xiv

CIVIL WAR ON THE POTOMAC

BICKERING BETWEEN the armed services costs the people of the United States more than any other American extravagance. It costs more in lives, and it costs more in dollars.

When four hundred U.S. Army paratroopers were shot down over Sicily by American naval vessels, it was due to lack of teamwork resulting from bickering. When General Leslie McNair was killed by American airplanes during the battle of Saint-Lô, when American Navy men had to wait in shark-infested waters for Army pilots to correlate orders to pick them up off Guadalcanal, again it was caused by lack of teamwork resulting from bickering.

The waste in dollars is less precious than that in lives, but more frequent. Eighty-four cents out of the tax dollar goes to pay for past or future war. Sixty of these cents pay for current preparations for war. If the national budget is to be balanced, if there is to be any real saving in the economy, it must come from elimination of military waste. Congress can debate for four years—as it did—a school-construction bill calling for $400,000,000 a year and then fail to pass it. But it will vote in record time $1,300,000,000 to construct a carrier task force, then authorize an additional $2,000,000,000 to outfit it for combat. Yet there is grave doubt in the minds of strategists that the big carrier is not completely outmoded by missiles and atomic-hydrogen warfare.

The expense of running the Labor Department, the Interior Department, the State Department, the Commerce Department, is peanuts compared with the military budget. Yet because of bickering between the armed services, because of pride in weapons which may be completely outmoded but give prestige, the tremendous flow of tax dollars into the military budget continues. As modern weapons become more intricate and more expensive, the expense of bickering becomes greater. American military strength can come only from American economic strength. And if we sap our economy we undermine our military strength. Yet the battle between Army, Navy, and Air Force continues. It continues over such trivia as the bust measurements of WAVES and glockenspiels in Armed Service bands.

When the Navy band, forced to economize, asked its glockenspiel player to double up in brass and play a second instrument, his pride was deeply hurt and a smooth-talking Air Force officer had no trouble persuading him to desert the Navy and join the Air Force band. Many years ago, after the Army band went to the Seville Exposition, it boosted its charge for private concerts 25 per cent over that of the Navy band. It had played before a king.

And there was the rivalry between the WAVES and the WAFS which became so heated that General Hoyt Vandenberg, then the Air Force Chief of Staff, recruited the glamorous pilot and beauty specialist Jacqueline Cochran, wife of financial tycoon Floyd Odlum, as special consultant to improve WAF standards. She reported that the Air Force ladies were "tattered, bedraggled," and even cross-eyed. "I personally came across a WAF who was approximately four feet, nine inches tall and who admittedly weighed 134 pounds," reported Miss Cochran. "This is far too much weight for the height, but what is even worse, she is very much out of proportion as to bodily profile and in addition she is cross-eyed . . . I am informed that this type of error has been duplicated many times." General Vandenberg hastened to add a four-week course in WAF grooming in order to bring the ladies of the Air Force up to the ladies of the Navy.

At one time rivalry between the Army and the Navy became so bitter that eleven men from West Point and eleven men from Annapolis were not permitted to line up against each other on a muddy football field to satisfy an ancient rivalry between the two branches of the service. For four years the annual football classic was called off. The issue: The three-year eligibility rule for intercollegiate athletics which the Army refused to follow.

If armed-services rivalry were confined to football, glockenspiels, and the bust measurement of WAVES, it would make good copy for the newspapers but would affect neither the economy nor the safety of the nation. Such is not the case. Rivalry in the high command is bitter, deep-rooted, and mixed up with a certain amount of civilian insubordination. It dates back to the days when the U.S. Navy hanged the son of the U.S. Secretary of War "at the yardarm of the brig *Somers* for insubordination and attempted mutiny." It flared in the early part of this century when General Arthur Murray, Chief of Artillery, demanded that submarines become a part of the Army because the Army was charged with protecting the coasts of the United States, and the submarine in those days was not considered capable of traveling more than a few miles from shore. The armed services have been squabbling continually as to who is charged with protecting the United States. At one time Brigadier General William Mitchell, stormy petrel of the Air Corps, later ousted for his storminess, endeavored to head off any aviation ambitions by the Navy by asking Congress to limit the Navy's aviation duties entirely to the sea. Later the Army suddenly woke up to find that Admiral William A. Moffett had quietly built a three-purpose plane adapted not only to scouting at sea, but also to torpedoing and bombing. The Army claimed this was a clear violation of the historic responsibility of the Army to operate on the shores of the United States and demanded that the Navy use pontoons, not wheels, on its planes. This would make sure that the Navy kept at sea. The dispute became so bitter that the Navy reminded the Army that the latter had been unable to prevent the British from burning the city of Washington in 1814, despite its vaunted responsibility for coastal defense. The Army retorted that it was Army guns at Fort McHenry, Baltimore, not the Navy, which hurled back the British fleet while Francis Scott Key was composing "The Star-Spangled Banner."

As the years have passed, the dispute has become more diverse because there are now three services, instead of two, battling against each other for the biggest slice of the taxpayer's dollar. As the battle has intensified and as duplication has increased, it has cost the taxpayers more money.

The techniques of waging war between the armed services have become so refined that each service has built up its camp followers, its legislative weapons, its arsenals of propaganda. The Navy and the Air Force have called back to duty reserve officers, newspapermen, and radio commentators who are to wage the battle of the airplane carrier and the long-range bomber. The Navy at one time actually established a secret propaganda office, unknown to its civilian Secretary, to wage war against the Air Force. The Air Force relies heavily on the airplane manufacturer. The Navy relies heavily on the steel industry. The Navy is the biggest user of steel armor plate in the world. And it was no accident that the Navy League was founded, for the purpose of promoting a bigger and better Navy, by such metallurgical magnates as Charles M. Schwab, Bethlehem Steel Corporation; J. Pierpont Morgan, U.S. Steel Corporation, and controlling investor in Carnegie Steel; Colonel R. N. Thompson, International Nickel; B. F. Tracy, attorney for Carnegie Steel and Harvey Steel, director of Tennessee Coal and Iron; George Westinghouse of Westinghouse Electric; Clement A. Griscom, director of Cramp Ship and Engine, Electric Boat, and U.S. Steel; S. S. Palmer, director of Lackawanna Steel; and eighteen members of Midvale Steel.

It was the Navy League which officially accused President Herbert Hoover of "abysmal ignorance" when he proposed replacing 10,000-ton cruisers with fast, maneuverable 6,000-ton cruisers. It was the big steel manufacturers who had elected Hoover but later "impugned his intelligence" when he spiked their armor-plate contracts. He was so irate that he summoned his Secretary of the Navy, Charles Francis Adams, and demanded that the Navy issue an official statement that the President of the United States was not "abysmally ignorant." The Navy did so. The admirals made it a matter of official record that the President was not ignorant. They had to. And subsequently the sinking of the 10,000-ton German cruiser *Graf Spee* off Montevideo in World War II by two light British cruisers indicated that Mr. Hoover was not so ignorant after all.

Not all the bickering is between branches of the armed services. Some of it is with the State Department, some with the White House, some with the civilian chiefs of the services. The man who first saw the wastefulness of the battleship and tried to relegate it to the scrap heap was Charles Edison, Secretary of the Navy under Roosevelt. The admirals were furious. He lost the battle. Later he argued that if the battleship were to be retained it must be revamped —that the warfare of the future would be in the air, that battleships would have to fire straight up, not broadside; therefore, their superstructures would have to come down. They couldn't be in a position of firing at their own crow's nests.

The admirals went to F.D.R., who loved everything and anything about the Navy. Shortly thereafter Charles Edison was advised to run for Governor of New Jersey. This was before Pearl Harbor. During World War II not one battleship got close enough to any enemy vessel to fire one shot. Had Edison's advice been followed, the American people would have been saved millions.

Today all American battleships are in moth balls. They were retained far beyond their time, chiefly because of the prestige that goes with a battleship command. When an admiral commands a battleship he has power and prestige, finer quarters, more perquisites, the command of 3,000 men. A submarine is cramped, uncomfortable, unglamorous. But Russia today has built 600 submarines; the United States only 110. The U.S.S. *Nautilus*, first atomic-powered submarine, dove under and all around the fleet during its first maneuvers. It bobbed up six or seven times right in the middle of the fleet and could have demolished practically every ship. Yet for years the admirals resisted the building of an atomic submarine, just as the generals opposed dismantling our old Indian forts, and just as Major General Harry Bishop, Chief of Field Artillery, was made to pay for the tires when he replaced horse-drawn caissons with rubber-tired wheels to haul the field artillery. It is human nature to oppose change. But not to make change is expensive.

By far the most effective friends of the armed services are members of Congress, and the Army, the Navy and the Air Force have gone to extreme lengths to woo them. They have developed lists of key constituents in the home district of every important Congressman, and they resort to a temptation which is hard for any Congressman to resist—free travel. There was a time when the Navy had the inside track over every other service when it came to travel. It had ships. It would ready an airplane carrier at Norfolk, bring Congressmen from Washington for a cool weekend cruise on the Atlantic while officers whispered sweet arguments about the fighting powers of these great ships. Their cost was seldom mentioned. The Navy at one time even transferred the entire scouting fleet from Newport, Rhode Island, to Montauk, Long Island, in order to please Congressman Fred Britten, Republican of Illinois, then chairman of the House Naval Affairs Committee and a heavy stockholder in a real-estate group which sought to boost Montauk as a summer resort.

Of late, however, the Air Force has had the edge over the Navy when it comes to free travel. In these days when some three hundred Congressmen are itching to tour the world immediately after Congress adjourns, the Air Force finds its transport planes almost monopolized by Congressional junketeers. Sometimes it causes an extra drain on pilots and airplanes, but it pays dividends when the time comes for appropriating defense dollars. This is how defense appropriations are frequently made—not on the basis of the most effective weapons for the United States, but on the basis of which Congressmen love which branch of the service.

The man who is most powerful in swaying Congress and who is the pampered captive of the Navy is Representative Carl Vinson of Milledgeville, Georgia. Congressman Vinson loves the Navy and the Navy loves him. There isn't anything the admirals wouldn't do for the crusty, crotchety chairman of the House Armed Services Committee, and he in turn has probably cost the American taxpayers six hundred million dollars for large airplane carriers which the nation doesn't really need, plus twelve to eighteen billion for accompanying task forces which the nation only partially needs. Some people have wondered why the state of Georgia has more military and naval installations than any other state save Texas. The answer is very simple. The chairman of the House Armed Services Committee comes from Milledgeville, Georgia, and the chairman of the Senate Armed Services Committee, Richard B. Russell, comes from Winder, Georgia. What they want from the Army, the Navy and the Air Force they usually get. There are few men in the United States outside the President who could have rescued the funeral horses of the U.S. Army at Fort Myer, Virginia, when economy-minded Secretary of Defense Wilson decided they were to go. Congressman Vinson, however, rescued them. There were few men in the United States who could have rescued the Army Veterinarian Corps when Secretary Wilson decided also that it should be curtailed. There are only 116 horses in the entire U.S. Army, plus 314 mules and 950 dogs, so Wilson decided veterinaries must be curtailed. Congressman Vinson, however, decided they must be retained and Vinson won. These are small items. Airplane carriers are more expensive. It would take a corps of accountants to figure up what the cantankerous Congressman from Georgia has cost the American people.

Into this melee of charge and countercharge, of snoop and countersnoop came Dwight D. Eisenhower. He knew, as few others, that if there was one lesson which World War II should have engraved upon the hard shell of the military mind, it was that victory had been a triumph of teamwork. It took great combined operations—a triple thrust of land, sea, and air forces to defeat the enemy. Even the humblest serviceman recognized that warfare had to be conducted in three dimensions and that soldiers, sailors and airmen must fight together on the same team. No sooner did the admirals and the generals lay down their weapons of war, however, than they picked up the cudgels of politics. They spied on each other, tapped each other's telephones, and conducted massive campaigns of personal and political vilification. Dwight D. Eisenhower watched this bickering and played a small and belated part in two big battles to cut out bickering. They were:

> The campaign to pass the Unification Act in 1947 and thereby make sure that the Army, the Navy and the Air Force played on the same team. Eisenhower was Chief of Staff at this time. He favored unification but did not take off his gloves to fight for it.
>
> Eisenhower's own drive to streamline the Pentagon—a drive which he launched in 1958 only after the bickering between the armed forces under him as President had reached a white-hot fury.

It was a National Guardsman from Missouri, then President of the United States, who first saw the importance of unifying the armed forces. He was supported by the former Secretary of War, Henry L. Stimson, by the then Secretary of War, Robert P. Patterson, by General Eisenhower, then Chief of Staff, and at first by Admiral William F. Halsey and Admiral Chester Nimitz, the top wartime commanders in the Pacific. But after Admiral Ernest King, Chief of Naval Operations, buttonholed Halsey and Nimitz, they switched. The big-business lobbies, which always support the Navy, threw their full force into the lobbying battle, and the Secretary of the Navy, James Forrestal, lined up against his President, Mr. Truman. Knowing that they could not defeat some kind of unification, the Navy argued that the new Secretary of Defense should be a co-ordinator, not an administrator. He should not have absolute powers to knock the admirals' and the generals' heads together; he should merely be a co-ordinator.

The Air Force was fighting hard to win a divorce from the Army. Its officers wanted rapid promotion, chafed at being held back by the slow promotion pace of the Army. General Carl Spaatz called on President Truman to thank him for the third service. "What I want," replied Mr. Truman, "is one service."

What he got was one service in name but three services in fact. The man who had fought unification hardest, James Forrestal, was made the first Secretary of Defense. Having worked hard to make the new unification plan unwieldy, Forrestal was given the job of making it wieldy. Having worked to make the Secretary of Defense a co-ordinator, not an administrator, he was given the job of co-ordination. He did not handle it well. Its problems contributed to his mental pain, upset his equilibrium, and drove him to suicide.

Even before he left office there was brewing a battle between the

Navy and the new Air Force over the relative merits of the aircraft carrier and the long-range bomber. The battle was to break with full fury over the head of Forrestal's successor, Louis Johnson. The man who masterminded the battle was Admiral Arthur Radford, a powerfully persuasive personality with a politician's instinct for in-fighting. Brilliant, dramatic, aloof, he was sometimes called the Navy's General MacArthur, though he was without MacArthur's arrogance. He had risked his career before—once over an affair of the heart which almost led to his court-martial, again when he supported naval aviation against the battleship admirals. And now he risked it the third time in the battle against the long-range bomber.

In his youth Radford had married Dorothy Hume, to whom he had been so attached that he gave her name to a glacier and a lake which he discovered on a survey of Alaska. On the map of Alaska today there are still to be found Dorothy Glacier and Lake Dorothy. But time and women can change all men, including admirals, and later in life Radford fell in love with Marian McMichael, the wife of his commanding officer. He fought for her with the same verve and daring that he has fought for the Navy, with the result that he came out of the mix-up with Marian as his wife. For this romantic insubordination he was almost booted out of the Navy. But somehow he weathered the storm. "He didn't smile for three years," said his first wife afterward.

Such a crisis might have chastened the spirit of another man, but not Radford. Never one to soft-pedal his views, he had fought the unification bill down to the last legislative ditch. He had sailed so close to the wind on Capitol Hill, had become so adroit at priming Congressmen, that he earned the enmity of a spokesman for the other side—Dwight D. Eisenhower, then Chief of Staff of the Army. Ike became so angry that he once threatened not to attend another meeting if "that so-and-so Radford" were present. Radford was not impressed. "I didn't know they expected everybody to sit around and kiss each other," he said. For this reckless campaign, Radford was hailed as a hero within the Navy. It was only a skirmish for fiercer battles to come.

In 1949 the Navy launched its most vitriolic attack of all against the new Air Force, against its new Secretary, Stuart Symington, and against the new Secretary of Defense, Louis Johnson. What started the attack was Johnson's realistic approach to carving up the taxpayer's dollar. He knew that not even a country as wealthy as the United States could continue the luxury of two duplicating services,

Navy air power and Air Force air power. So he ruled against the Navy's proposed big new airplane carrier. Out of sentiment for the late Secretary of the Navy, and because they knew the campaign would have human appeal, the admirals had proposed naming their new carrier, then only on blueprints, the U.S.S. *James V. Forrestal.* Johnson, however, ruled that the long-range bomber, at that time the B-36, was more practicable, cheaper, and more effective as a military weapon.

The admirals planned their campaign against the Air Force just as carefully as if they were preparing General Jimmy Doolittle's surprise bomber raid on Tokyo during the war. They set up a secret publicity bureau inside the Navy, named Operation 23, and placed it under the command of one of their shrewdest officers, Captain Arleigh Burke. They also used Captain John Crommelin, a daredevil officer where public relations were concerned, who did not care whether he got caught or not. To do this they had to bury the hatchet with Crommelin, who had once spilled the beans on the secret Green Bowl Annapolis fraternity, which he claimed was a clique by which the admirals helped each other get promoted. And when a young naval lieutenant, Sam Ingram, wrote a letter to the Washington *Post* castigating the Air Force, he was immediately asked to stop in to see Admiral Radford. He remained with Radford—a supposedly busy man—for two hours and left with an assignment to turn out charts against the Air Force.

The Navy campaign was conducted in the best cloak-and-dagger tradition, and naval investigators even checked on a visit which Secretary of the Air Force Symington had paid to Floyd Odlum at his ranch in southern California. Odlum was then head of Consolidated-Vultee, manufacturer of the B-36. The Air Force, in turn, managed to plant a spy inside the Navy's Operation 23. The Navy, despite its care, had failed to check the background of one of its civilian specialists on propaganda working inside Operation 23 and did not know he was an Air Force Reserve officer. He made regular reports to his first love, the Air Force, on everything this underground naval unit was doing.

This was how unification operated one year and a half after it was approved by the Congress of the United States and signed into law by the President. It also indicated how wantonly the admirals were willing to waste the taxpayers' money.

The start of the Navy campaign against the long-range bomber was a strictly secret memorandum for Navy eyes only written earlier by Admiral Dan Gallery, in which he said: "The time is right now for the Navy to start an aggressive campaign aimed at proving that the Navy can deliver an atomic bomb more effectively than the Air Force. The Air Force will never be able to match the performance of our A-bomb carriers with the trans-oceanic bomber."

Admiral Gallery made only six copies of his memo and distributed them among his most trusted colleagues. He took the precaution of changing the key word in each copy so he could trace the source of any leak. His precautions were justified, but unavailing. Embarrassing passages from the memo turned up in the "Washington Merry-Go-Round." Gallery, however, was never able to discover which copy had been smuggled out of the Navy, for the paragraph containing the key word which he had changed was not published.

It was Admiral Radford who masterminded the strategy of the Navy. He fought the Air Force with the same determination that he once fought for his commanding officer's wife. It was one of the most notorious of all interservice feuds, conducted with a ruthlessness and savagery that have left scars to this day. It was to be equaled only by the subsequent feud over the control of missiles and rockets. At one time the feud became so bitter that Congressman Van Zandt of Pennsylvania, Republican, aired on the floor of Congress (where he enjoyed immunity from libel) a charge given to him by the Navy that Secretary of the Air Force Symington had a financial interest in Consolidated-Vultee and this was the reason he sought to build the B-36.

Officially, Admiral Radford's hand was not supposed to be seen. Officially, he was commander of the Pacific Fleet. Actually, he was running back and forth between the Navy Department and Capitol Hill instructing the Congressmen on what to say and what witnesses to call. But this wasn't supposed to be known. Then Congressman Vinson of Georgia, faithful champion of the Navy, let the cat out of the bag.

"I have not got Captain Crommelin on this list of witnesses," blurted Congressman Vinson, "because his name was not handed to me by Admiral Radford."

Crommelin's activities were so flagrant that he was finally dropped from the Navy at White House insistence, though not until after the admirals had given him the honorary rank of admiral. "Admiral" Crommelin went back to Alabama later to run for governor on a platform of exposing "the Satanic plot to mix the blood of the white Christian people of the South with Negroes . . . as directed and financed by the Communist-Jewish conspiracy." The people of Alabama seemed to think less of him than the Navy. In a race of fourteen candidates he came in twelfth.

Finally Admiral Radford himself, unabashed and unembarrassed, took the witness stand. He had been circulating a secret statement criticizing his chief, Secretary of Defense Johnson. A succession of Radford-coached admirals had testified that the big bombers were both ineffective and immoral. Now Radford publicly called the B-36 a "billion-dollar blunder." His challenge to civilian authority was so reckless that the mild-mannered Chairman of the Joint Chiefs of Staff, General Omar Bradley, who had been sitting on the sidelines, silent but writhing over the vituperative feuding of his brother officers, followed him as a witness. General Bradley prepared his statement one week in advance. He did not deliver it impromptu. His voice was shrill and his tone was angry, but he had considered his words carefully when he flung the charge "Fancy Dan Admirals" at the Navy rebels. Later in Tokyo General Douglas MacArthur told Bradley that this was one of the finest statements he had ever read. Ironically, it was only a short time afterward that MacArthur himself bucked civilian authority and was fired. Had President Truman given as drastic punishment to the Navy rebels who conspired against his Secretary of the Air Force and his Secretary of the Navy, the need for drastic action against MacArthur might have been avoided. In addition, continuing feuds in the armed services might have been stopped.

Truman did discipline the admirals, thanks in large part to the man he had appointed as Secretary of the Navy, Francis Matthews. Later, however, he dulled the force of the discipline. Matthews was a dry-land lawyer from the Nebraska prairies who the admirals figured would be a pushover. Admiral William Blandy walked into his office after Matthews first became Secretary of the Navy and blandly informed him that he, Blandy, was to be the new Chief of Naval Operations. Then and there Matthews decided he would have to run the Navy his own way or become a failure, so he crossed Blandy off the promotion list. Later, when his Chief of Naval Operations, Admiral Louis Denfeld, testified that he believed Truman, Johnson, and Matthews were planning to scuttle the Navy, Matthews promptly fired him. Seldom has the Pentagon been in such a furor. There had been civil war before in the massive many-sided building which looks out over the placid Potomac. At one time during World War II, highhanded Admiral King restricted his civilian chief, Secretary of the Navy Frank Knox, from one wing of the Navy Department. Knox took it philosophically. But not Secretary Matthews. Never was there anything to equal the cries of "persecution, censorship and brass curtain" which the admirals hurled against Matthews.

Matthews was the nation's most distinguished Catholic layman. Pope Pius XII had named him Secret Papal Chamberlain with Cloak and Sword. He was a quiet, gentle soul, but his gentleness was only the moss on a character of granite. Discovering this, the admirals secretly ordered his Marine receptionist to keep a complete list of people who went to see the Secretary of the Navy and the exact number of minutes they remained. Not knowing this, Secretary Matthews complained to the authors, "My office must be tapped. The admirals seem to know everything I do." The admirals almost broke his heart. Not only did Admiral Denfeld insinuate to the House Armed Services Committee that Matthews was incompetent and inexperienced, but the admirals even brought pressure on the Secretary of the Navy through his church. The spearhead of this pressure was Monsignor Maurice Sheehy, delightful, busybody professor of religion at Catholic University and a reserve chaplain in the Navy. Sheehy pressured Matthews personally, then denounced him by telegram. A telegram was also received from Francis Cardinal Spellman. Sadly, Matthews pulled the telegrams from a drawer of his desk and showed them to the authors. One telegram urged him to get down on his knees and pray for forgiveness for opposing the admirals.

Francis Matthews did not pray for forgiveness. Nor did he bow either his knees or his head. He stood his ground. He continued to be just as devout a Catholic, and during the height of the attack on him he attended a reception at Catholic University. Awaiting him at the door stood Monsignor Sheehy, proffering a cocktail. "I prefer to get my own cocktail," said the Secretary of the Navy quietly, and he passed by the Monsignor.

The aftermath of the battle between the aircraft carrier and the B-36 was:

1. Francis Matthews when he died left not a penny of his ample fortune to the Catholic Church.
2. With Admiral Denfeld fired, Captain Crommelin retired, and Admiral Radford sent back to the Pacific, the admirals began to realize that they had taken a licking—though not quite. Theirs was only a semidefeat, because after Matthews refused

to okay the promotion of Captain Arleigh Burke, Truman went over his head and promoted Burke anyway; and later Truman transferred his courageous Secretary of the Navy to Ireland as Ambassador.

3. The taxpayer did not win. Behind the scenes the battle over the division of the tax dollar continued. It was less blatant, but it continued.

From this point on, the admirals watched the generals like hawks waiting to pounce. The Navy staged a carrier-force simulated attack on Alaska, at that time under joint command headed by the Air Force. Jubilantly the Navy announced that its carrier force had caught the Air Force completely by surprise and had destroyed, in theory, all of Alaska's military targets. But what the Navy did not know was that the Air Force had taken some photographs. The Air Force waited until the Navy's boast had hit the front pages too late to be withdrawn, then it quietly released pictures taken by high-flying bombers, showing the Navy carrier force spread out below like ducks on a pond. Obviously a couple of A-bombs could have destroyed the entire fleet.

The man who eventually brought peace between the Navy and the Air Force was not the Secretary of the Navy or the Secretary of the Air Force, or any man in military uniform, or the President of the United States. He was the unnamed scientist who finally developed a small atomic warhead. With an atomic bomb and a hydrogen bomb small enough to be carried in a carrier-based plane, the Navy quit battling. It had won its point. It could now participate in dropping the bomb.

The first strategy of the Navy back when James Forrestal was Secretary of Defense was to get for the Navy the right to participate in atomic bombing. When this failed, the admirals then argued against mass bombing. They played right into the hands of Russian propagandists by reminding the world of the tragedy of Hiroshima, and later spreading the identical stories about the Air Force that the Communists spread about the United States, namely that U.S. airplanes had been killing North Korean women and children.

"I think the B-36 is not a good weapon for doing bombing in a war," Admiral Radford told the House Armed Services Committee, "unless you are in favor of mass bombing."

When Congressman Melvin Price, Democrat of Illinois, challenged this, Radford snapped back, "Mr. Price, if you are in favor of the B-36 you are in favor of mass bombing."

Once a small warhead was developed, however, and airplane carriers could stockpile hydrogen and atomic bombs, the admirals dropped their argument against mass bombing like a hot potato.

Their change in propaganda tactics, however, did not change the fact that the American military budget was 'way out of balance. In fact, their change made it even more out of balance, because by that time they had not only won over Congressman Vinson to building the new carrier *Forrestal* but had come back for more and more carrier appropriations. The Air Force pointed out that a carrier force costs seven times more money, takes nine times more manpower, and uses thirteen times more fuel than an equivalent group of Air Force bombers. They pointed out that a carrier task force includes four carriers mounting about 450 planes, thirty destroyers, six cruisers, four scouting submarines, and a mine-sweeping force; and that this must be supplied by a mobile replenishment force of at least eight fleet oilers, an ammunition ship, a storeship, a destroyer tender, a refrigerator ship, and a fleet tug. This floating supply center, in turn, also needs protection, so the Navy assigns another carrier, five destroyers, four destroyer escorts, and three frigates as a screen. Then these ships must be resupplied and the ships supplying them must be protected in turn. Out of the carrier's 450 planes, at least half must stay behind and circle overhead to guard the task force against enemy raids. Even the 225 planes that finally can hit the enemy, the Air Force argued, can't reach the major target area since the Navy's farthest-flying bombers can't get to the industrial heartland deep inside Russia except on one-way suicide missions. Such a task force with full regalia costs roughly two and a half billion dollars. In comparison, a long-range bomber group complete with air base, fighter protection, antiaircraft defense, and full supplies costs less than one billion.

These are facts the taxpayer doesn't know when he reads the headlines of interservice bickering or when he sees pictures of a mighty carrier launching planes from its deck with precisionlike regularity. Like a spanking team of horses, the super aircraft carrier is beautiful to look upon. But like the four-horse team at the country fair, manes curried and harness polished, it is a visual adornment to the prestige of the United States, not a significant addition to her military power. The small carrier is important for escort-vessel purposes. The big carrier is important for decorative purposes. It has given us prestige in the Mediterranean, where Admiral Charles Brown, commander of the Sixth Fleet, has won friends for the U.S.A. as well as covering Marine landings in the troubled Near East. Russia, which has been building a fleet of its own in the Black Sea, has not wasted money on huge, old-fashioned, expensive carriers to carry bombs which its new, up-to-date intermediate-range missiles can carry instead. But thanks to the power of the Navy lobby, the indefatigable persistence of the irascible Congressman from Georgia, Carl Vinson, and the timidity of our civilian leaders, a preponderant amount of America's defense budget still goes to pay for these mighty dinosaurs of the deep.

No President in the history of the nation has better understood the waste and inefficiency, the loss of lives and the loss of money that result from armed-service bickering than has Dwight D. Eisenhower. For forty-one years he had watched it as a member of the Army. He watched close up as Chief of Staff under Truman. He highly disapproved of the tactics of Admiral Radford and the other admirals, but he did not speak out as did General Omar Bradley. When he became President it was expected that Eisenhower would be his own Secretary of Defense, that he at long last would knock brass hats together when they staged civil wars in the Pentagon.

The new President, however, took two steps which practically guaranteed that dissension among the armed services would increase.

The history of the United States sometimes turns on small incidents. If President-elect Eisenhower's plane had not stopped to fuel on Iwo Jima en route to Korea, military bickering might not have reached the crescendo it did during Ike's first five years in the White House. Or if Emmett Hughes, his ghost writer, had not prepared a speech promising that he would go to Korea, or if Admiral Radford had not decided to go to Iwo Jima, history might have been different. But far away in his tropic exile at Pearl Harbor, Admiral Radford, recalling his old clashes with Eisenhower over unification, confided to friends, "Maybe I should retire. I'm getting too political."

This is what Radford said, but not what he did. The Admiral could no more have kept out of the Administration's military policies than he could have kept himself aloof from his commanding officer's wife. He flew to Iwo Jima. The new President-elect, stopping at Iwo Jima to refuel and stretch his legs, had dinner with Radford. During dinner Ike fired questions about the Pacific, found the Admiral's snappy, off-the-cuff answers so articulate that he turned to those at dinner and announced, "If there's anything you want to know about the Pacific, ask Radford." Later Eisenhower took Major General Robert Ramey, the Air Force officer in charge of travel arrangements, to one side and asked, "Can't we make room for the Admiral?" So Radford was taken along to shiver in tropical khakis as the party landed in Korea on a bitterly cold December night. He was still on hand when the Presidential party made its leisurely way back aboard the U.S.S. *Helena*. Eisenhower was not scheduled to stop in Hawaii, but Radford persuaded him to stay over for a little golf. When Ike finally left Hawaii he told the man whom Truman and Secretary Matthews had put in the doghouse, "We may be sending for you."

But if Radford had impressed Eisenhower, he had doubly sold himself to the new Secretary of Defense, Charles E. Wilson, who was also aboard the *Helena*. Radford became Chairman of the Joint Chiefs of Staff. This was a signal to every officer in the armed services that civil war between the services could begin again. Air Force partisans immediately ground out a twenty-four-page attack on Radford and circulated it secretly to their friends in the press. "It will be recalled," said the memo, "that one year ago the Navy was opposing the appointment of General LeMay as Chief of Staff for the Air Force for the simple reason that General LeMay is a strategic bombardment commander and the Navy does not like strategic bombardment. General LeMay has never been charged with conducting a public or private campaign against the Navy. Admiral Radford, on the other hand, is widely credited with having conducted public and private campaigns against the Air Force."

Eisenhower followed up by appointing Admiral Arleigh Burke, commander of the notorious Operation 23, to be Chief of Naval Operations, jumping him ahead of several senior admirals. Five years later Eisenhower was to regret this decision, for Burke had to be reprimanded for opposing the new unification plan. Even at the time of his appointment, the moral seemed clear: The rebels had been received back with high honor; therefore rebellion paid off. With the new missiles as the prizes to be won, the top brass brought out their cloaks and daggers for another round of guerrilla warfare.

When President Eisenhower crossed from the other bank of the Potomac River to enter the White House he sought to divorce himself from his love of the Army and become completely impartial as Commander in Chief. He even refused to attend an Army-Navy football game because he was afraid he could not hide his pro-Army sympathies. In order to backslap the admirals and generals into burying their tomahawks, he invited them to a three-day frolic at Quantico, Va., where he dressed them in sweaters with "Varsity" lettered across the back to emphasize the team spirit. But almost immediately at Quantico Ike instructed the Joint Chiefs to send him only unanimous decisions. These were forwarded to him on bright-green paper stamped with a red seal, known in the Pentagon as the "final green form." The red stamp of approval meant there were no dissenting views, as the President had ordered. But this, instead of producing unity, had precisely the opposite effect. The fact that no differences appeared in the final green form did not mean an absence of disagreement but only that it had not been expressed. Those officers with minority opinions simply leaked their opinions to Congressmen and newspapermen.

The resultant rash of news stories infuriated the President, who had a military commander's aversion to seeing his subordinates airing their arguments in public. The red tide of his anger would rise up his neck and color his bald scalp. Sometimes he would soar out of his chair like a rocket, exploding with the un-Presidential expletives inherited from his barracks days. More than once he got Secretary of Defense Wilson on the telephone and demanded that the culprits be punished. These ultimatums produced frequent Pentagon probes which more often than not simply petered out. One Army partisan, Major General L. C. Metheny, however, was finally fingered by Wilson's detectives as the source of Tony Leviero's scoop in the New York *Times* about a proposed 800,000 cut in Army manpower —a story which favored the Army. The unhappy general was given his choice of retiring or being banished to some unpleasant outpost. He retired.

Ike's Army Chief of Staff, General Matthew B. Ridgway, led the rebellion against manpower cuts. At one point, Secretary of Defense Wilson warned Ridgway to go along with the President's wishes or expect a "directed verdict" forcing him to comply. Ridgway was not abashed; he angrily accused his superiors of whittling away the Army for political rather than military reasons. His defiance was more moderate and reasoned than that displayed by Radford and Burke in defending Navy carriers, but, unlike the admirals who defied Truman, he was not promoted. Instead, Ridgway was hustled into retirement. In backstage conferences, Ike accused him of being "parochial" in his military outlook and of failing to see beyond the limited horizon of his own service. "I get a little bit tired," the President once snapped, "of having to defend myself against the charge of being out to wreck the Army."

Thus, in the ceaseless tug-of-war between the Army and the Air Force for funds, Eisenhower sided with the Air Force, whose nuclear weapons offered, as Secretary Wilson so aptly put it, "more bang for a buck." Eisenhower agreed with the air generals not so much because he accepted their military philosophy, but because it offered the best argument for reducing the budget. At the same time, he argued against putting all military eggs into one basket and advocated blending the many ingredients of military power into a complementary defense system.

What this was to boil down to, in practice, was an attempt to check interservice rivalry by distributing a limited amount of money among the three services. But once more the feuds and furies were only intensified. Officers with obsolete ideas, or vested interest in obsolete weapons, were encouraged to wrangle for a "fairer share" of the defense dollar. The taxpayers didn't realize it, but they were financing three independent military forces, each capable of waging nuclear war on its own. In the vital missile field, each service duplicated efforts and squandered resources in separate pursuit of the frightening new weapons. Behind the Iron Curtain, meanwhile, the Russians were concentrating their total efforts on a "crash program." Their sputniks and ballistic missiles carried no label of either the Red Army or the Red Navy. They were simply marked with the hammer and sickle of Soviet Russia.

In the sprawling Pentagon on the banks of the Potomac, the Navy-Air Force battle over the B-36 has now been replaced by the Army-Air Force feud over ballistic missiles. The Army contended that the big missiles are really oversized artillery shells, hence they belong to the Army arsenal. The Air Force argued that missiles are merely flying bombs, therefore they belong to the Air Force. The two services were also savage in their controversy over which should handle antimissile missiles, the Army claiming these are an extension of the antiaircraft gun and the Air Force declaring they are pilotless interceptors. From the sidelines, the Navy occasionally reminded the public that its ships and submarines are the best missile bases of all.

While it is against the rules for officers to insult their sister services openly, behind the scenes it is another matter. There, concealed blackjacks and bowie knives have been the order of the day. The Army's case at first was peddled by a clique of colonels under the direction of General James Gavin. The Army even assigned colonel-lobbyists, usually from a Congressman's home state, to sell the Army's views to Congress.

It was at this point that General Nathan Twining, Chief of Staff of the Air Force, stopped speaking to General Gavin, his next-door neighbor. Twining is a gruff-spoken officer who bites his words out between puffs on a long cigar. Once a press officer brought Twining an editorial attacking the Air Force. The total ensuing discussion was limited to these words:

"Boss, you mad about this?"

"Yeh."

"How mad?"

"Damn mad!"

After Gavin resigned in a blaze of publicity, Twining, who became Chairman of the Joint Chiefs, was asked by investigating senators about his proposed relations with the White House. "The rules are that you should go along with the decision of the President or turn your suit in," said Twining, and he has followed that rule.

Others have not. The Army's antiaircraft commander, Lieutenant General Stanley Mickelson, loaded his guns with a devastating antiaircraft speech which revived the old Navy suggestion that the Air Force believed in "mass destruction of civilian populations." But the tough and unsmiling deputy chief of the Air Force, General Curtis LeMay, intercepted the speech and, with an advance copy in his hand and blood in his eye, marched in to see Secretary of the Air Force James Douglas. This speech had better be canceled, he growled, or he would make one of his own in reply.

Douglas fired a blistering memo to the new Secretary of Defense, Neil McElroy, declaring that the Air Force would not tolerate such a speech. McElroy, a soap tycoon before he stepped into Charlie Wilson's hot shoes, agreed that Mickelson's mouth ought to be washed out. The antiaircraft commander alibied he was not responsible for the crack about mass destruction. It had been written without his knowledge, he said, by subordinates. Finally the Army canceled the speech.

Meanwhile the rivalry over rockets became part of the Pentagon routine. It was the heyday of the calculated leak to eager reporters, the whispered word in the ear of a Congressman hungry for a political cause. If a story appeared in the papers praising one service, it was cause for anxious huddles on the opposite side of the Pentagon.

Typical was the reaction to a news story giving production figures for the Air Force's medium-range Thor missile. This inspired a hurried memo rushed from the office of Major General Henry Storke, the Army's press chief, to Colonel William T. Ryder, a missile-research expert. "General Storke is somewhat upset," the memo said, "about a story appearing in this morning's papers in which it was stated that Thor was in 'mass production.' The story continued to give production figures as an indication that the Air Force was producing the Thor missile. General Storke is convinced that the story was leaked from an Air Force source. He wants information relative to our most *optimistic* production schedule on Jupiter. I would like—so that it can be on the 2:30 messenger run—a short piece or collection of ideas . . ."

Even before the Army could fire its barrage of counterstatistics, however, the memo had fallen into the hands of Air Force officers, who were already preparing their counter-countermoves.

It is a common practice in the Pentagon in these days of internecine warfare to stamp documents "Army Eyes Only" or "USAF Eyes Only." But even these have a way of slipping into the wrong hands. The Army, for instance, once got hold of an embarrassing Air Force document in which Brigadier General Robert Scott gave directions to his public-relations staff for a massive campaign to swing public opinion in favor of the Air Force. "We must take the public past the point of uncertainty," wrote Scott. "We must convince them that investment in the Air Force will net a superlative payoff in continued freedom and safety."

When his secret memo fell into Army hands, Scott was furious. To retaliate he dressed an Air Force officer in Army uniform and sent him on a mission into the Army's secret sanctuaries to see what tidbits he could pick up.

All this time President Eisenhower remained aloof. For five long years, while the armed services of which he was once a part threw mud at each other, the President took no step to stamp out bickering. Came October 4, 1957, and the Russian sputnik. There followed a crescendo of editorials demanding that the military services pull together against Russia, not apart against the United States. By this time the secret memo of Colonel John C. Nickerson and his deliberate leak to Congress and the press had demonstrated in conclusive detail that the armed services considered themselves completely free to appeal to the public as their real commander in chief. Finally on January 8, 1958, in his State of the Union message, President Eisenhower stepped in. He warned his old comrades-at-arms that their bickerings were confusing and alarming the nation. "America wants them stopped," he declared. Firm words. But a few days later at a press conference the President took the stiffening out of them by explaining somewhat laboriously that no matter what ideas he might have about adjusting the services to the space age, he would be Commander in Chief for only another three years. Besides, he added, his recommendations required the full approval of his Cabinet and Congress.

Finally in the spring of 1958 the President faced reality. The Rockefeller report gave him a concrete plan for streamlining the Defense Department, making the Secretary of Defense an administrator, not a mere co-ordinator. His own Secretary of the Treasury, Robert B. Anderson, showed him that either we reorganized our defenses or we as a nation went broke. So five years after he became President and twelve years after Harry Truman began the first battle for reunification of the armed services, Dwight D. Eisenhower finally faced reality. He sent a plan to Congress for streamlining the Pentagon. It was a plan that would not have been necessary under strong civilian rule at the Pentagon, but there has been no strong civilian rule since the days of Louis Johnson, Francis Matthews, and Stuart Symington, one of whom was fired, while the other two were eased into other jobs.

What Eisenhower proposed was to give the Secretary of Defense full authority to determine the roles and missions of each of the armed services and to give him direct command over all military forces without going through the separate Secretaries of the Army, the Navy, and the Air Force. The Army and the Air Force as usual agreed. But the Navy as usual, while agreeing that the Defense Department needed streamlining, vigorously objected to curbing the autonomy of the three services, meaning, of course, the authority of the Secretary of the Navy.

Once again the admirals organized backstage for guerrilla war. Once again they ground out the propaganda. Once again they enlisted newspapermen who were reserve officers, or even recruited new newspapermen and made them reserves. They warned ominously that too much centralized authority would lead to a Prussianized military organization. They spread word that the President's reorganization would permit the Secretary of Defense to abolish the Marine Corps. Once again the Navy League and the Naval Advisory Council sprang into action. Retired Admiral J. W. Reeves, Jr., chairman of the Advisory Council, called on his members to pressure Congressmen to defeat the reorganization plan. In a confidential letter he warned: "Do not—repeat do not—speak as a member of the Advisory Council or the Navy League, but as an individual citizen. This personal contact is most important at this time either by telephone, wire, or person-to-person approach."

Reeves even arranged for ten airplanes, through his friend and successor, Vice-Admiral Robert Goldthwaite, Commander of the Naval Air Training Station at Pensacola, Florida, to carry members of the Advisory Council to a meeting at San Francisco. Thus the Navy, which was supposed to carry out the orders of the President of the United States, put itself in the position of helping defeat the orders of the President—and using the taxpayers' money to do it.

Best friend of the Navy, as usual, and chief enemy of the White House, as usual, was Georgia's crusty, crafty Congressman Carl Vinson, chairman of the House Armed Services Committee. Even before the President had prepared a reorganization plan, the Congressman from Georgia prepared a speech blasting Eisenhower for talking about reorganization but not sending Congress the formal recommendation. White House sleuths on Capitol Hill got advance wind of the speech and in order to thwart Vinson, Eisenhower rushed a proposed bill to the press just two hours before Vinson took the floor of the House to speak.

When emissaries from the White House called on Vinson to suggest that the White House would like to write the final version of the bill, the old gentleman replied, "I appreciate the President's interest, but Congress is going to write the reorganization bill." Vinson knew what he was talking about. He knew he had such a firm grip on his committee that he could—and did—snort at the White House. He knew that he could crack the whip over nineteen Democratic members of his committee who would vote with him on any kind of reorganization bill he chose to write. Furthermore, Congressman Leslie C. Arends of Illinois, the ranking Republican who was supposed to support the head of the Republican Party, President Eisenhower, had pledged to Vinson that thirteen of the sixteen Republicans would vote not with the head of the Republican Party but with the Democratic Congressman from Georgia.

It was at this point that Secretary of Defense McElroy, appearing before Vinson's committee, virtually threw in the sponge and indicated publicly that he would accept all the compromises Vinson proposed. Eisenhower was in Augusta playing golf at the time. Reading McElroy's statement in the New York *Times,* he got on the telephone, and for the first time the President appeared to be adamant.

"This is one I'm going to see through," he told his Secretary of Defense. He added that he was sick and tired of interservice bickering and he proposed to stop it.

Civilian aides in the Pentagon took heart. Friends of the White House also rallied to his support. William Foster, the former Under Secretary of Defense, Nelson Rockefeller, General Carl Spaatz, Harold Coolidge, General Twining, Senator Stuart Symington put their heads together to support the President. Some of them lunched with McElroy at his request. They agreed that there was no chance to fight Communism if the armed services were to spend their time and energy fighting each other. "Either we reorganize or we go under economically," warned Symington, the former Secretary of the Air Force who, though a Democrat, proved to be Eisenhower's best supporter on this question on Capitol Hill.

Eisenhower himself got on the telephone to talk to key Congressmen. He even phoned old man Vinson. The campaign did not dent Vinson's control over his own Armed Services Committee, but it did shake him in the Congress, and he finally agreed to a compromise which contained the essential features of the Eisenhower plan. To save face for himself, however, the compromise defended the autonomy of the Army, the Navy, and the Air Force and prohibited the Secretary of Defense from merging them. The result was a bill which would help a weak Secretary of Defense to rule the Pentagon. A strong Secretary of Defense would not have needed it. A strong Secretary of Defense long ago would have cleared away the twenty-nine deputy and assistant secretaries similar to vice-presidents of General Motors with whom Charlie Wilson surrounded himself. They had authority to say no but seldom yes. A strong Secretary of Defense could have cleared away the gigantic, unwieldy staff of 2,400 employees divided into empires within empires, who kept adding more employees on the theory that the more Indians they command, the bigger chief they become. The result has been to impede and obstruct decisions. A new idea must pass through stifling layers of bureaucracy. By the time it has run the gamut of assistants it is weighed down with so many comments that the Secretary of Defense has difficulty wading through the accumulated memos. The Chief of Staff of the Army, General Maxwell Taylor, complained that he had to pass through nineteen civilian officials between him and the Commander in Chief. All nineteen had authority to advise how the Army should be run.

It was not necessary to pass a reorganization bill to clear away this labyrinth of bureaucracy. Most of it did not exist prior to the Eisenhower Administration. General Motors is able to exist with a conglomeration of vice-presidents because each is in charge of a separate department competing against the others. Bureaucracy does not operate that way. And when the Army and the Navy compete against each other, their internecine warfare serves mainly the Kremlin's purpose. While the brass and the braid have been busy knifing each other, other knives have been whittling down America's once commanding position as a world power. If the Soviets are to be overtaken in time to save the free world from tyranny, then the cliques of colonels must be disbanded and the plotting of admirals and generals ended.

In the middle of the debate on the Eisenhower reorganization plan, the President received word from Caracas, Venezuela, that Vice-President Nixon was in serious danger from a rioting mob. He telephoned the Secretary of Defense and ordered troops to be rushed to the Caribbean. Secretary McElroy called in the Joint Chiefs of Staff and transmitted the Presidential decree. For several minutes the Joint Chiefs argued over which service should be sent to the Vice-President's rescue. It was finally agreed that Army paratroopers would be flown to the Caribbean in Air Force planes.

However, Admiral Arleigh Burke, Chief of Naval Operations and the man who had masterminded Operation 23, the secret propaganda bureau against the Air Force, slipped out of the meeting for fifteen minutes. While he was out, he ordered two squadrons of Marines flown to the trouble zone. When he returned to the meeting he blandly informed the other Chiefs of Staff that the Marines had scheduled maneuvers in the Caribbean anyway. Thus did the military carry out the spirit of the President's order for harmony between the armed services.

XV

THE MAN THE ADMIRALS DIDN'T LIKE

PRESIDENT EISENHOWER picked up the newspaper early one morning in January 1954 and almost spilled his breakfast coffee. What he read was a news report, apparently from authentic Pentagon sources, that the new atomic-powered submarine, the U.S.S. *Nautilus*, shortly to be launched, was not battleworthy, was merely a test, and, in effect, was not an important naval vessel at all.

The President was furious. In the first place he considered the story false. Second, Mrs. Eisenhower was going to launch the *Nautilus*. Third, being experienced in the battle of Pentagon politics, he smelled a Navy-inspired news leak. So he telephoned his Secretary of Defense.

Charles E. Wilson was not the early riser that his chief in the White House is, and the President routed him out of bed. Though sleepy when summoned to the telephone, the Secretary of Defense had no trouble understanding that the President was nettled; that he didn't like the Navy belittling its own submarine; finally, that the President seriously doubted that the Navy's "leak" had been cleared with the Atomic Energy Commission.

As an afterthought the President recalled, "Why, the Navy even asked Mamie to christen her!"

Admiral Lewis Strauss, Chairman of the Atomic Energy Commission, also read the news story at the breakfast table and was fit to be tied. He was required to pass on all statements by any branch of the government pertaining to atomic energy, and he too phoned Secretary Wilson.

With two phone calls under his belt, one even before breakfast, the Secretary of Defense arrived at his office in a bad humor. He immediately asked Under Secretary of the Navy Thomas Gates to have lunch with him, Secretary of the Navy Anderson being out of town. Under Secretary of Defense Roger Kyes joined the luncheon, and after lunch a roomful of admirals and Assistant Secretaries filed in respectfully, including Admiral Lewis Parks, Chief of Navy Press Relations. The meeting, including the luncheon, lasted more than three hours.

Wilson first asked why the news story had not been cleared with the Atomic Energy Commission. The admirals had no explanation. Furthermore, not one of them would admit to leaking the story. Technically they were correct. Several of them knew, but would not tell the Secretary of Defense, that the story had been leaked orally by a junior officer in Navy Press Relations. They did, however, produce a memorandum prepared first by Commander Slade Cutter and later signed by Admiral Parks, stating that the *Nautilus* wasn't battleworthy, that her torpedo tubes were added only as an afterthought, and that her delicate equipment would not work at high speeds.

The memo was supposed to be confidential. But Charles E. Wilson, though new in the Pentagon, had been around long enough to strongly suspect that it had been shown to the press. He kept reading it aloud to the admirals like a schoolteacher who has discovered two identical examination papers and wants to find out who is cheating.

"It's a strange coincidence," he said, "that the language of this memo and the quotations used in this newspaper story are so much alike."

At another point he asked, "Why belittle the *Nautilus*?"

There was no explanation.

Wilson had good reason to be puzzled. He knew that the *Nautilus* would be able to cruise around the world under water without coming up for air; that she could surpass the speed of most destroyers and run circles around a battleship; that she could probably catch up with and sink the vessels supposed to sink her. He knew the *Nautilus* could move faster, dive deeper, and stay under water longer than any other vessel ever built; that it would produce a revolution at sea; that fifty surface vessels were to be moth-balled immediately following the launching of the *Nautilus*.

But why the opposition of the admirals to this revolutionary new weapon? Why did they deliberately plant a report that the *Nautilus* was not battleworthy and was not an important naval vessel? The answer was threefold: First, the *Nautilus* was revolutionary. Second, it was built by the wrong man. Third, the Navy wanted to get into air power, not develop power under water.

It is only human to resist change. And the admirals were beginning to realize that the *Nautilus*, pioneered by an out-of-step, unorthodox naval captain named Hyman Rickover, was likely to bring a total realignment not only of the Navy but of naval strategy. The launching of this monster of the deep would probably mean the junking of all non-atomic-powered surface ships in the future. The great mammoths of the Fleet, the battleships, were already on their way out, and now cruisers and carriers might follow. The battleship and the cruiser have been the badge of naval distinction, fortresses afloat in time of war, luxurious accommodations in time of peace. They have been the pride of the Navy. The lowly submarine has been cramped, dirty, unheralded, unsung. Its method of fighting, sneaking silently upon its prey, lacked the noble grandeur of attack by battle fleet. The battle fleet, steaming majestically across the horizon, easy target for enemy airplanes, has been like the British regulars whom King George sent to fight the thirteen colonies—easy targets in red uniforms, plumed hats, and full regalia. Submarines have been like the colonial fighters of that day, unseen in the forests, outnumbered but effective.

The admirals also were beginning to have some inkling of the fact that this great, gray mechanical whale, built by a man they didn't particularly like, would be able to spout missiles into space; that it could strike from the ocean bottom at targets as far inland as 1,200 miles; that it could prowl under the waves, a dinosaur of the deep, without showing itself for months. Plans were to develop later to give this new sea monster a deadly bite with a set of missile teeth about 50 feet long and about 50 inches in diameter. These new Polaris missiles, using solid fuel rather than the liquid fuels which have caused such inefficiency at Cape Canaveral, could be fired instantaneously. Each missile packs enough explosive power to destroy a city, and each sub carrying sixteen Polaris missiles would have approximately the same firepower as the bases we are building in Europe and Asia for our 1,500-mile Thor and Jupiter missiles. Lurking under the polar icecap off the Russian coast, they can be the greatest deterrent to nuclear war. Yet the Polaris subs will be much cheaper and far less vulnerable than fixed bases located on foreign soil.

The admirals who met with Secretary Wilson did not know specifically at that time that the *Nautilus* would be capable of all these missile exploits, but they had some inkling of it. Specifically they knew that the Navy's great hope and ambition was to take to the air, not go under water. Their sights at that time were set on more aircraft carriers and they saw the *Nautilus* as a threat to those carriers. She could travel so fast that no protecting vessel could keep up with her; and a carrier is not supposed to move without a convoy of destroyers and light cruisers. This was why the atomic-powered aircraft carrier was temporarily scrapped; no convoy of destroyers and light cruisers then built or contemplated could keep pace.

Charles E. Wilson is a warm-blooded person who likes people and likes to be liked in turn. He did not realize all the subterranean jealousies and rivalries in the vast labyrinth of military offices over which he was supposed to rule. He kept reading the memorandum aloud. He read it over perhaps a half-dozen times. At one point in the discussion the name of Admiral Hyman Rickover came up. The entire group of officers meeting with Wilson expressed nothing but praise for Rickover, but the fact was that, only one year before, a selection board composed of their fellow admirals had passed him over and slated him for compulsory retirement. And despite the outward esteem of the admirals gathered before Wilson, the real fact was that only a few liked the critical, sometimes cantankerous son of a Polish pants presser who had hounded, haggled, and cut red tape until he had finally built an atomic submarine.

When Hyman Rickover began to urge that atomic energy could be harnessed to power a sub and that this would be the naval weapon of the future, the gold-braid brigade whispered that he was "balmy." That he was of Jewish faith did not escape mention in this whispering campaign. As a mark of naval esteem he was given a reconditioned ladies' rest room for an office in which to work. It was literally in a ladies' toilet that the *Nautilus* was born. Most of the Navy proceeded to ignore him. Only a few had faith. When he refused to be squelched, the gold braid closed ranks and tried to ease him out of the service. If the promotion board of nine admirals had been given its way, Rickover would have been handed a soft hat in place of his brass hat well before the first atomic sub was completed. It required repeated blasts published in the "Washington Merry-Go-Round," plus the intervention of Senator Henry Jackson of Washington and a command by Secretary of the Navy Robert Anderson, to secure Rickover's promotion.

Yet against the dark pages of our postwar military decline, the revolution at sea caused by the atomic submarine has offered the sole reassuring entry. In atomic submarines, at least, we are leading the Russians. Acutely aware of this, the Russian Navy is working feverishly to produce its own nuclear-powered submarine and to convert its great undersea fleet to the use of guided missiles. But as of now, the United States has the edge in quality, if not quantity. It was in spite of the Navy that this was accomplished.

This poses another puzzle. Why have the chief advances in nuclear power and modern weapons been achieved of late by immigrants to the United States and Americans of recent foreign descent? Why did the atomic bomb come from Fermi, Szilard, and Einstein, refugees from Italy, Hungary and Germany respectively? Why did the development of the hydrogen bomb come from a Hungarian, Dr. Edward Teller? Why was the first American Army missile chiefly pioneered by a German, Dr. Wernher von Braun? Why did the son of an immigrant from Poland, Hyman Rickover, pioneer the *Nautilus*? It is true that Dr. Edward Condon, a native of New Mexico, helped pioneer the hydrogen bomb, but he was purged from the government. Dr. J. Robert Oppenheimer, son of immigrants from Germany, helped to build the first atomic bomb, but he too was purged. Could it be that if Hitler and Mussolini had not made refugees of Fermi, Szilard, and Einstein, some other nation, not the United States, might have developed the first atomic bomb and used it against us? Why is it that native Americans of native stock have not pioneered these weapons? Could it be that modern Americans are too complacent, too satisfied, that they have lost their initiative except in the field of economic gain? Could it be that suffering, poverty, the philosophical and political worries that keep some men awake at night spawn the brilliance, the mental acquisitiveness, the thirst for research which have made this country great, but which the achievement of material gain has begun to dull?

We do not know the answer. But over Admiral Rickover's desk in his book-crammed office there is a framed quotation from Proverbs which may give part of the answer. It reads: "Where there is no vision, the people perish."

We also know that Edwin Weisl, counsel of the Senate Preparedness Subcommittee, tried to get part of the answer. At least he tried to get the answer as to how Rickover had built the atomic submarine. Here are Rickover's answers:

RICKOVER: We just said, here is a job to be done, and we are not bound by any rules that people have written in books on research and development.

WEISL: Did you follow the usual procedure that is followed in the military in getting this job done?

RICKOVER: No, sir. No usual procedure will accomplish unusual jobs. No, sir.

WEISL: How were you able to avoid following the usual procedures?

RICKOVER: One of the main reasons was that so many people were certain the project would fail and they did not want to be associated with it. That was one of the most wonderful and fortuitous things that happened to our program. It is quite different today. But at that time, everybody knew it was going to fail, so they let us completely alone. Almost completely.

WEISL: Did you get the job done ahead of schedule?

RICKOVER: We had no schedule. We decided to do it as fast as possible . . . Incidentally, no one ever assigned me my responsibility. But I assumed responsibility. And by responsibility I mean this: Who is going to be responsible when something goes wrong? There are always lots of people who are willing to have their pictures taken and say they are responsible when everything is going all right. But as soon as somethings goes wrong, it is always somebody else. Finally they go up to the President, and I think the reason they don't go beyond him is they are not certain they have a sure channel of communication.

Rickover's answers were not too enlightening. They gave no real hint of his months of struggle, his persistence, or the roadblocks placed in the path of what was to be the most important naval vessel in modern times. Even if you talk with Rickover privately in his office, he will tell you little about himself. You get some idea of the Gandhi life of the man, his dedication to work, his frugality. Luncheon in his office consists of a cup of consommé, one hard-boiled egg, soda crackers, and an apple, served on a battered tin tray by his secretary. He chafes at questions, is as crisp in his answers as the crackers, has a slight chip on his shoulder and an inferiority complex. He genuinely resents publicity, and this is not merely because it arouses the resentment of other officers in the Navy—though it does. Rickover just doesn't want to waste precious time on such frivolous things as photographs or newspaper men. He doesn't like to waste too much time on sleep, for that matter. When Clay Blair, Jr., whose book, *The Atomic Submarine*, gives a masterful presentation of Rickover's problems, asked that the Admiral pose for a photograph, Rickover refused. The Navy's press-relations office had to order the Admiral to pose. On another occasion Rickover had to be kidnaped from his office so the Secretary of the Navy could pin a medal on him; and as a young ensign aboard the U.S.S. *Nevada*, he refused his captain's invitation to dinner because he was too busy with his work. Captain C. S. Kempff rather admired the young ensign's enthusiasm, and instead of dressing him down he fixed another date at the ensign's convenience. Years later, after Kempff had become an admiral, he was one of the minority who did not look at Rickover with a fishy eye. When Rickover put in for submarine service and was turned down as "too old," Admiral Kempff pulled his rank and got Rickover the transfer.

Back somewhere in the life of Hyman Rickover is the answer to why he, among all other officers of the Navy, had the vision and the persistence to develop a naval vessel which has scored the one decisive triumph over Russian weapon-planning since V-J Day. Perhaps it was his childhood. At five Rickover was just another little immigrant mite tossed into Chicago's slum land. His father was a tailor. He was a good tailor, but there was little beyond the barest livelihood to be made in pressing pants, sewing on buttons, and making an occasional suit for a wedding. Young Hyman worked as a Western Union boy and part of his wages went to support his family; part he saved. When he graduated from high school he had hoarded about three hundred dollars. Another immigrant, Congressman Adolph J. Sabath, born in Czechoslovakia, was responsible for the next important step in Rickover's life. Sabath gave the boy an appointment to the Naval Academy at Annapolis.

All during his four years at the Naval Academy, young Rickover was out of step. He was out of step on the drill field, and out of step on the dance floor. His spending allowance of two dollars per month did not afford him much social life. His classmates did not warm up to the awkward immigrant from Chicago. He threw himself into his studies, working late, against the rules. Though low on deportment and naval bearing, he managed to graduate in the top bracket of his class—because of his scholarship.

There followed a lackluster career in the Navy: routine assignments on the destroyer *Valette*, the battleship *Nevada*, a postgraduate course in electrical engineering at Annapolis, more study at Columbia, a hitch on the battleship *California;* then submarine training, where he rescued a sailor from drowning, though Rickover could scarcely swim himself, and on another occasion went below to put out a battery fire while other officers huddled on deck fearful the ship would blow up. From submarines he was sent to the battleship *New Mexico*, then transferred to China as skipper of the mine sweeper *Finch*, the dirtiest, rustiest, most banged-up ship of the Navy; then to the Cavite Naval Yard in the Philippines. In each assignment he made his mark, but he also made enemies for his refusal to conform. While other officers spent their off-duty time at cocktail parties, he cleaned up the *Finch*. On the *New Mexico* he almost tore the ship apart to find out why it was consuming more oil than it should. At Cavite he converted organized waste into organized thrift.

On one occasion Rickover had to be ordered to "get into proper uniform" and attend a party aboard an admiral's flagship. He obeyed the order, but in his own way. As his boat delivered him at the gangway, he whispered instructions to the bo'sun, then mounted to the deck, paid his respects to the Admiral, hurried through the guests to the opposite gangway, and descended into his own boat again. It had quietly cruised around the flagship's stern to pick him up.

By now Rickover was a captain, recognized for his engineering ability, disliked for his refusal to conform.

After Pearl Harbor he commanded a group of engineers who were given the job of cleaning up the terrible debacle left by the Japanese. It was the most stupendous salvage and reconstruction job in naval history. When he arrived at Pearl Harbor he stopped a plan to tow the battleships *California* and *West Virginia* to the West Coast for repairs. "I can do the job here and save time," he rasped. Washington was harassed and desperate for ships. It let him try. Rickover kept his word and saved a year.

Back in the Bureau of Ships, Rickover gave the Navy an answer to the magnetic mine by "borrowing" a device from the British, despite patent rights and a maze of red tape. He seized on an infrared signaling device, which no one would take seriously, and got U.S. warships to use it to talk to each other visually at night unseen by the enemy. Anxious for action, he finally got a transfer to Okinawa, but was asked first to straighten out the Navy's vast supply depot at Mechanicsburg, Pennsylvania. Before he reached Okinawa in July 1945 the war was almost over.

Came V-J Day. Many top naval officers left for the lush opportunities which beckoned in civilian life. Rickover stayed on, was given the job of moth-balling the fleet on the West Coast. Again naval dignities were shattered. He crawled through ships from bridge to bilge, would pass nothing that he had not personally inspected.

It was at about this time that Rickover became fascinated by the prospects of atomic energy. He saw the day when steam would vanish from the seas just as sailing ships had vanished, and he decided to study the mystery of the atom. The Navy was assigning five officers to Oak Ridge, Tennessee, where the Monsanto Chemical Company was constructing the world's first atomic reactor. Rickover asked for the assignment. He was passed over and might never have been heard of again, but by this time Rickover had learned the advantages of friends, especially influential friends. Admiral Earle Mills, for whom he worked in the Bureau of Ships, intervened and got Rickover the Oak Ridge assignment.

The truth is that Hyman Rickover did not have to have a chip on his shoulder. He did not have to have an inferiority complex. The Navy, while guilty of some bigotry, is not nearly as bigoted as he thought it was. He had then, and still has, more friends than he has ever suspected. The primary dictum which has motivated the Navy for years is to fight hard—and relax hard. The great tradition of Annapolis is courage. Along with it goes a combination of qualities which Madison Avenue would call salesmanship, which the politicians would call the ability to pull for one's promotion, and which the stylists might call male pulchritude. The American naval officer can whip his destroyer or cruiser alongside a tanker in rough weather at breakneck speed and at great risk, with precisionlike accuracy and without batting an eye. He can organize his carrier so that jet fighters swoop down on his flight deck with the nonchalant regularity of bees lighting on a sugar bowl. He can get unswerving loyalty from a crew of 3,000 men under cramped, hazardous conditions, and he can man the bridge of his ship with the decks aflame and little hope of rescue. But he is not built for academic study. When he goes ashore he relaxes. He is much more at home off duty on the golf course, on the tennis court, or at a cocktail party than at his desk. He is not a dreamer.

So it was lucky for the American people that Hyman Rickover carried in his make-up a feeling of ostracism and spent his time off duty studying and dreaming. Had this not been so, the atomic submarine *Nautilus* might have been born ten years later.

At Oak Ridge, Hyman Rickover continued his dreaming. He also continued the chip on the shoulder. Assigned to Oak Ridge with him were four young officers, Lieutenant Commanders Louis Roddis, James Dunford, and Miles Libbey, and Lieutenant Ray Dick, who eyed him suspiciously. It was obvious that they were not going to get along. Rickover, however, had not learned the way of the brass for nothing. He called on the Army commander at Oak Ridge and got himself designated as "Senior Naval Officer Present" with authority to fill out the semiannual fitness reports on his junior officers. Once the four learned that Rickover had the power to influence their promotions, they forgot any advice they may have received in Washington and co-operated. In fact they became, as time went on, great friends and boosters of the rasping-voiced captain.

Suspicion continued, however, in the Bureau of Ships, and there appeared one day in Oak Ridge Captains Albert Mumma and Harry Burris, who informed Rickover that he must consider them his superiors. Mumma had been appointed in charge of the Navy's nuclear-power work, while Burris was liaison officer to the General Electric Company for work on the Navy's "atomic pile." Mumma promptly ordered that all future reports from Oak Ridge to Washington must go to him personally, not, as previously, to Admiral Mills. Once again Rickover invoked the technique of the brass hats. He told Captain Mumma bluntly that he could not accept the order unless it came through proper channels. This meant that Mumma would have to get the Chief of the Bureau of Ships to ask the Secretary of the Navy to ask the Secretary of the Army to direct the Chief of the Manhattan Project at Oak Ridge, Tennessee, to order Rickover to report to Mumma. Mumma retired, defeated. The Rickover team carried on.

Rickover continued his dreaming. It was during his studies of nuclear physics at Oak Ridge that he dreamed of building a nuclear submarine; and after completing the studies in the midsummer of 1947 he crystallized his dream by submitting a formal report to the Bureau of Ships in September for a nuclear-powered submarine. Rickover had previously submitted a report in the fall of 1946 forecasting that in less than two decades the Navy would be using atomic power on every major combat ship. By now Albert Mumma, the captain Rickover had torpedoed at Oak Ridge, had become a rear admiral and occupied a strategic position in the Bureau of Ships. Mumma persuaded Admiral Mills not only to pigeonhole Rickover's plan for a nuclear-powered submarine, but to scuttle the Rickover team of visionaries. The four junior officers were dispersed, and it was only after Rickover made a personal plea to his friend Mills that he was kept on in Washington as a special assistant on nuclear power and given as an office the former rest room used by the WAVES during the war. It looked as if Rickover's dream ship had suffered a torpedo strike at the waterline.

Rickover, however, refused to consider it sunk. And it's quite possible that this setback was, in actual fact, another milestone in pioneering the nuclear-powered submarine. Banishment to the ladies' washroom gave Rickover a chance to roam around the United States studying atomic development. At that time, approximately two years after the war, the government had experimented gingerly with the development of industrial atomic energy by putting it in the hands of two big companies—Monsanto Chemical at Oak Ridge and General Electric at Schenectady. With both, the experiment was a stepchild. The Daniels Pile, the name given to the Monsanto experiment at Oak Ridge, was about to peter out. Rickover had complained that the company had spent too much time on scientific theory, not enough on practical engineering. He went up to Schenectady, where the Bureau of Ships had proposed that General Electric build an experimental atomic-powered ship, a destroyer. This looked more encouraging, but again Rickover criticized the fact that General Electric was concentrating on research rather than on engineering. Rickover oscillated back and forth between Schenectady and Oak Ridge and his ladies' rest room in Washington. He was a catalytic agent trying to spur others on, but he was getting nowhere. He had no authority, other than the authority to harass. He used his nuisance value for all it was worth. His old rival, Albert Mumma, had been given complete control of the nuclear-power branch of the Bureau of Ships as of January 1, 1947, and Captain Rickover was on his own.

Finally he corralled a handful of scientists still remaining at Oak Ridge and persuaded them to go to work building a naval-type reactor. They were supposed to be winding up their work for Monsanto Chemical, but part of the money appropriated for Monsanto remained unspent and, without any authority from Washington whatsoever, Rickover started work on a water-cooled, slow-neutron type of reactor which could be placed in a submarine. He discussed carefully the problems of isolating the dangerous radioactivity thrown off by the reactor from the crew. He worked on the question of weight and pressure at great depths. Thus was begun, without authority, the first atomic-powered mechanism for a submarine.

Rickover was not so visionary that he did not realize that he could not continue this work at Oak Ridge without authority. He had the secret approval of Admiral Mills in the Bureau of Ships. And he then proceeded to spend three months getting authority from the Secretary of the Navy to build an atomic sub. It was not easy. He first approached Admiral Nimitz, drafted several letters for Nimitz to sign, finally got his okay. After that he got the okay of the Secretary of the Navy, but he never did get the approval of the Atomic Energy Commission. By this time Admiral Mills, supported by the power and prestige of Admiral Nimitz' endorsement, had become enthusiastic over an atomic submarine and the stanchest supporter of the irascible captain who had bulldozed and bothered his superiors until even the highest in the Navy were committed to his ideas.

Finally in the spring of 1948 the Navy announced that it would proceed with the development of an atomic submarine, and Admiral Mills, forced to choose between Mumma, the administrator, and Rickover, the man who always seemed to achieve the impossible, put Rickover in charge of the project.

To celebrate, Rickover moved out of the ladies' room to slightly better quarters in a war-built temporary building—T-3.

On June 14, 1952, President Truman arrived at Groton, Connecticut, to lay the keel of the *Nautilus*. Rickover sat in the back row of the grandstand, impatient to get back to his work. Admirals who had had little to do with the new submarine clustered around the President. A few weeks before, nine admirals, headed by Vice-Admiral John L. Hall, had plowed through the list of captains due for promotion and had passed him over. Rickover had been given the Legion of Merit; had received a Gold Star personally from the Secretary of the Navy; had pioneered one of the most revolutionary naval vessels since the Civil War. But the admirals passed him over.

In a column appearing August 3, 1952, the authors reported what had happened and accused the Navy of discriminating against Rickover, partly because of his religion. There was immediate public reaction. Nevertheless, the Bureau of Ships *Journal* printed a series of articles on the nuclear program which omitted all mention of Rickover and his associates. The new Chief of the Bureau of Ships, Rear Admiral Homer Wallin, wrote an article for a national magazine on the atomic sub, again failing to mention the Rickover team. The Admiral himself appeared on a nationwide TV program and gave the impression that he was the man who deserved chief credit.

Even Navy Secretary Dan Kimball seemed to be siding with the admirals regarding his promotion. They argued that a man's whole record had to be considered, implying that Rickover, brilliant though he might be in his narrow field, was not really admiral material.

Rickover refused to speak in his own defense. But the Senate Armed Services Committee summoned Vice-Admiral James Holloway, chief of naval personnel, together with Rear Admiral Wallin, for an explanation. Wallin delivered a long, woolly statement which gave perfunctory praise to Rickover but insinuated that the Navy's nuclear program was mainly the work of other men. "The nuclear billet in the Bureau of Ships," said Wallin, "is mainly a captain's billet. We now have a number of engineering-duty captains who are well qualified to assume this post. Several of them have participated in the nuclear-power program since its inception."

Senators, convinced that he was attempting to mislead them, were infuriated. Senator Jackson led the fight. In blistering language he declared: "Effective scientists and engineers do not behave like puppets. Original minds, men with imagination, men with the driving genius to get things done, must be able to find a place in the armed services. They must be able to bring forward and advocate their fresh ideas without fear of reprisal. Today I believe the case of Captain Rickover is a prime example of how not to treat splendid creative technical officers in the armed services. . . . The whole project has been treated as an orphan. The truth of the matter is that the Navy atomic-power program only began to move when Rickover and the charter members of what became the Rickover team went to Oak Ridge in 1946. He has led the atomic-power program ever since."

The new Secretary of the Navy, Robert Anderson, promptly cracked down on the admirals. He approved a special board to retain Rickover for one more year's active service until another gaggle of admirals could meet. Under what amounted to direct orders, they promoted Rickover to rear admiral. Wallin, though he had still two years to run as Chief of the Bureau of Ships, was stripped of the post and ordered to duty at Bremerton, Washington.

Gradually, the name of Rickover vanished from the headlines. As it did, the admirals came out from cover and began to put the screws on Rickover, but ever so gently. They did not want to cause the kind of screams that would attract the attention of the press and Congress again. They quietly stripped him of his authority over the atomic-submarine program, but they left him in charge of developing atomic reactors for new subs. He was not permitted to direct the construction, as he had done with the *Nautilus,* but was limited to tinkering with prototypes. As their final revenge, the admirals placed Rickover's old nemesis, Admiral Mumma, in authority over him as new Chief of the Bureau of Ships.

Members of the Senate Preparedness Subcommittee were flabbergasted when they heard their counsel, Edwin Weisl, develop this fact in cross-examination of Admiral Rickover.

WEISL: We have heard considerable testimony concerning the Polaris missile. Are you familiar with that?

RICKOVER: I know there is a Polaris missile, but I am not involved in that at all, sir.

WEISL: Do you mean to say you were not involved in developing the nuclear submarine that would launch the Polaris?

RICKOVER: No, sir. I am only involved in supplying components for that submarine. I have nothing to do with that, sir, the submarine itself.

WEISL: Does it not appear from the record that you are the most qualified man to develop a nuclear submarine?

RICKOVER: I think other people will have to answer that, sir.

WEISL: Were you consulted about the submarine by anyone?

RICKOVER: Not generally. The last time I talked with him (Raborn) was for a few minutes about two weeks ago when he happened to be in the office of the Chief of the Bureau of Ships. The time before that was about two and one half years ago when he first got on the job. I may have seen him twice on social occasions, but not— He has never come to me for any help.

WEISL: Do you know who is conducting the development of that submarine?

RICKOVER: I know in general. I know what I read in the newspapers and I know that certain work is going on.

WEISL: Is your organization able to perform this work?

RICKOVER: Oh yes, my organization is capable of doing large-scale development work.

WEISL: You did supply the power plant for the other nuclear submarine?

RICKOVER: For the first of each type, I not only supplied the entire power plant; I was responsible for the design, development and installation—every part of it.

WEISL: Do you know of any reason why you were not put in charge of this important job?

RICKOVER: That is something that you should ask other people—not me.

Rickover had not wasted time chafing over his restrictions. At first, the Navy had teamed up with the Army to build the 1,200-mile intermediate-range Jupiter, but in 1956 the Navy concluded it would be impractical to handle cumbersome, liquid-propellant missiles aboard ship, and it split off from the Army project to develop its own Polaris as a solid-propellant rocket.

Rickover visualized an undersea missile carrier as the most effective means of delivering the new rocket. He pleaded with the Navy to marry the Polaris missile to the atomic sub. "Do you realize what it will mean to have a fleet of submarines under the polar icecaps with missiles ready to retaliate at Moscow and Leningrad if they ever launch atomic war against us?" Rickover argued. "This can be the greatest deterrent to war of all." His ideas, however, were not welcome in the best naval circles. Not until 1957 was the first Polaris sub authorized as a leisurely project which would be finished sometime in 1963.

The shock of the sputniks jolted the admirals out of their lethargy. They suddenly realized the military advantage of ringing Russia with mobile missile bases that could hide in the deep, dark crevices of the ocean bottom. Rickover also pointed out the political, as well as military, impact of Polaris submarines. "Missile-carrying atomic submarines could make England a great power again," he said. "Such a fleet would give Britain the power to destroy Russia; hence would increase her influence around the international conference table."

Admiral William Raborn, head of the Navy's Special Projects Section, slashed away the red tape and won the Navy's highest possible priority for Polaris submarines. But the Electric Boat Company, a division of General Dynamics, had not waited for the Navy's go-ahead. Realizing the urgency of the project, the company had started construction without authorization and had switched girders intended for another submarine to the Polaris project. Twin subs began taking shape at the Groton shipyard. Construction was started on a third at the Navy's own Mare Island, California, yard. The launching date for the first Polaris sub was moved up from 1963 to early 1960.

That the missiles would be available ahead of the submarines was a matter for belated regret. The Navy urgently requested funds to build six more Polaris subs. The anguished budget balancers persuaded Secretary of Defense McElroy to limit the authorization to an additional two. But Congress threatened to build the Polaris fleet Rickover wanted whether the Defense Department liked it or not.

Outwardly Admiral Rickover has shown no concern that the Polaris project was put in other hands. "Whenever there is motion, there is friction," he says. But privately Rickover is sensitive. Privately he has some vigorous ideas about our military system. "You can't change the military," he says, "and you just bat your head against a stone wall if you try to change it.

"The Defense Department is already too large," he told the House Committee studying space exploration, "and if you let it grow on as it is, it will soon be controlling the entire country.

"The most pressing problem facing the nation is not space exploration, but better education of the nation's youth. If you people weren't concerned about political implications, instead of organizing a committee of this type you'd probably have a committee investigate what goes on in education today.

"You people set up laws on what is to go in people's mouths," the Admiral lectured, "but you won't even set up recommendations on what goes into their minds."

He urged Congressmen to sponsor a survey of how much more students learned in European schools. "It would only cost about fifty thousand dollars," he said. "But I know you people don't fool around with peanuts like that."

When Congressman McCormack of Massachusetts interrupted to observe that one of his subcommittees had recommended more stability in the technical services, the Admiral pointed an accusing finger at the gentleman from Massachusetts.

"I indict you," he said. "You wrote a report and then did nothing to put it into effect."

Let it never be said that Hyman Rickover was guilty of similar neglect. He dreamed a dream of harnessing warships with nuclear power and he did not rest until he had made that dream come true.

xvi

OUR "NAZI" SCIENTISTS

PRESIDENT EISENHOWER, trying to explain away Russia's missile achievements in 1957, told a press conference that "the Russians captured all of the German scientists in Peenemünde." Either Ike did not know, or he did not remember, what went on under his own command. His troops, acting on secret orders with the code name Operation Paper Clip, rounded up Germany's ablest rocket scientists. The real brains of Germany's rocket program, almost to a man, fell into American hands. While the Russians got a few technicians and engineers, none compared with the brains of the German rocket group.

Two years before that, in the black war year of 1943, Allen Dulles, then America's spy master in Geneva, picked up the first ominous reports that Germany was about to launch a mysterious and revolutionary new weapon. The Allied reaction was to send six hundred heavy bombers to pound a reported secret German rocket base at Peenemünde for three hours on August 17, 1943. Dulles' intelligence reports mentioned a young German count who appeared to be in charge of the rocket scientists. His name: Wernher von Braun.

The world in subsequent years was to hear a great deal about von Braun. In fact, he was to change the history of the world—though not until his outpost of the future had fallen victim to the forces of the present. He was to be criticized as a Nazi, an ardent devotee of Hitler. He was to chafe and rebel at the red tape and inactivity of the American military. After delay and frustration, he was to launch the first American satellite into outer space. And he was to receive help from both dreamers and doers in the U.S. Army, especially an officer named James Gavin who was killing Germans in the Battle of the Bulge when Wernher von Braun was a lieutenant in Hitler's black-shirted SS corps. These two, once on opposite sides in a bloody battle for survival, later became partners in attempting the American conquest of outer space.

Their story is much more than the story of two men. It is the story of the modern missile: its birth at Peenemünde on the bleak Baltic coast; its migration to America in crates of unsorted bolts, springs and parts; and its struggle for a place in the Army weapons system.

Wernher von Braun is the son of a wealthy Prussian baron, Magnus von Braun, who had served as pre-Hitler Minister of Agriculture and who from behind a white walrus mustache viewed his son's space ideas with wonderment. "My father thought I was crazy going to the moon," von Braun now says.

Wernher has been unshaken in his determination to reach the moon since his early boyhood when he first looked at the heavens through a telescope given him by his more sympathetic mother. She was an amateur astronomer and chose this gift instead of the traditional watch and long pants given to most German Lutheran boys on their confirmation.

Von Braun's first appearance in the missile field was as a space-struck schoolboy, full of the science fiction then being published in Germany under the pen name of Dominik. When he was barely seventeen, he became a devoted disciple of the German space pioneer Hermann Oberth, who had produced the theory of the rocket motor and who today is working with von Braun at Huntsville, Alabama. The scientific staff venerate him as "the old gentleman" and the real father of the rocket.

It was early in 1930 that Oberth developed the first modern rocket motor. His workshop was in a rickety shed on the shores of a tiny lake at Reineckendorf, a picturesque village on the outskirts of Berlin. His assistants were Rudolf Nebel, a World War I fighter pilot with a pitchman's talent for casting unenlightened businessmen under the spell of space long enough to pluck their pockets for needed finances; Klaus Riedel, a huge man who would gallop across open fields to catch spent rockets in his bare hands as they drifted down by parachute; and the teen-age von Braun, who quickly graduated from menial to technical chores.

The revolutionary but crude Oberth rocket motor could be started only by direct flame. The task of launching it fell to the heavy-footed Riedel, who had to dash up to the rocket with a flaming gas-soaked rag, fling it over the motor, then run for his life.

During school months von Braun studied engineering at the Zurich Institute of Technology, where he continued his experiments with space flight. He teamed up with an American medical student, Constantine Generales, to build a homemade contraption that would spin a mouse in simulation of rocket take-offs. They correctly concluded, from dissecting whirled mice, that high acceleration could cause cerebral hemorrhage. But their scientific quest was rudely halted by von Braun's indignant landlady, who objected to the splattering of mouse blood on her furniture.

Meanwhile, the rocket team moved from their work shed to an abandoned ammunition dump which Nebel had promoted for their free use in the Berlin suburbs. They hoisted a sign over their new headquarters proclaiming it to be the *Raketenflugplatz*, the world's first rocket airdrome. In 1932—one year before Hitler—von Braun brought a German Army team, headed by Colonel Karl Becker, chief of ballistics, to the *Raketenflugplatz* to inspect their work. Von Braun knew that the Army, its artillery limited by the Treaty of Versailles, was looking for a weapon that would get around treaty restrictions. He hoped to convince them that a long-range rocket, carrying a big warhead, was the answer, though his real objective was to get financial backing for his space dream.

His fellow rocketeers Nebel and Riedel, however, would have nothing to do with the German Army. Professor Oberth had already gone back to teaching, and the irrepressible Nebel claimed he could not work under stifling military restrictions. Riedel preferred to look to commercial firms for financing, on the belief that guided rockets could have a commercial use in delivering mail from city to city faster than air mail.

So the rocket team broke up. Von Braun, now nineteen, joined the German Ordnance Corps as top civilian specialist at its Kimmersdorf secret rocket works, hidden in a pine forest south of Berlin. "At this moment," he recalls, "I had exactly one mechanic."

That the youthful von Braun sold himself and his ideas to the German Army has led critics to charge that he was an opportunist space salesman, lacking technical qualifications and background. They point to his record: the fact that he never held still long enough to graduate from the Zurich Institute; the fact that his Doctor of Science degree from Berlin's Freidrich-Wilhelm University was arranged by Colonel Becker, ballistics expert for both the Army and the university, on the basis of a paper von Braun had written about the work in Oberth's shanty at Reineckendorf.

Regardless of his scientific background—or lack of it—the record from there on led steadily to war and Peenemünde. Von Braun worked under the direction of Dr. Walter Dornberger, who advanced rapidly from captain to general as the rocket center expanded and moved to new quarters at desolate, isolated Peenemünde. Von Braun's corresponding rise to the position of technical director of the V-2 project, over scientists twice his age, caused inevitable jealousies. There were those who claimed he dealt ruthlessly, arrogantly, ungratefully with more experienced men who tried to correct his blunders.

There has also been criticism from another quarter. It is charged that the atomic and space inventions of the United States have all come from foreigners; that few Americans have contributed materially to pioneering the vital inventions of the space age; that the ease of American living, the softness of American education may have slowed up American inventive genius, removed the sense of compulsion which has inspired the great scientists of other lands.

The leader of the rocket revolution was both a German and a Nazi. Now he is an American citizen with stanch convictions about democracy. "The prime mover of technological progress," says von Braun, "is man himself; man with his hopes, dreams and imaginations; man with his enthusiasm and pride of accomplishment; but man also with his personal ambition, greediness and thirst for pleasure. We believe in a free society where man can pursue his own dreams, follow his own ambitions and form his own life." Von Braun gave Hitler a terrible weapon that, had it been available a year earlier, might have won the war for the Nazis. Yet he now warns with intense feeling, "If the world's ethical standards fail to rise with the advances of our technological revolution, we shall all perish." He believes as devoutly in religion as in science. "While technology controls the forces of nature around us," he says, "ethics control the forces of nature within us. Only with God reinstated in the heart of the world will He furnish mankind and its leaders the ethical guidance through the dangers and pitfalls of the technological revolution."

Dr. Wernher von Braun, in the strict sense, is not a scientist. His critics call him a pusher, a promotor, a salesman of space, a picker of the brains of better men. Regardless of these detractors, it was he who dreamed of being the first man to reach the moon and who has been reaching for the moon ever since.

One vigorous von Braun critic is Dr. Paul Schroeder, a former Peenemünde scientist now in this country, who deeply resents the

American newspaper label given von Braun—"father of the V-2." Schroeder believes the title rightly belongs—if the work of many men can be attributed to anyone—to Walter Dornberger.

Dr. Schroeder's criticism reveals that just as there has been bickering in the development of American missiles, so there was friction among the Nazis. Producing the first V-2 rocket that terrorized London was not a matter of smooth German efficiency. There were many failures and mistakes, and Dr. Schroeder blames them largely upon von Braun's arrogance, his lack of scientific experience and his refusal to accept wiser men's ideas. Schroeder relates this experience: "Dr. von Braun sent a promise to Dr. Dornberger, based on ballistic calculations of his own make, he would throw one ton over 900 kilometers. The effect was a wire from Dr. Dornberger to me personally, asking how far we would be able to throw one ton by means of the propulsion system as prepared by Dr. von Braun. My answer went to Berlin the evening of the same day. It read laconically: '180 kilometers.' When it had gone, I had made an unreconcilable enemy."

The authors submitted this and other criticism to von Braun. Here is his reply: "I hired Dr. Schroeder myself, and he served about two years as head of our Mathematical Bureau under me. We had continuous collisions. It finally came to a break, and I told General Dornberger that I had no further use for Schroeder. In order to patch things up, Dornberger then placed Schroeder directly under himself."

The first great missiles of the future were already taking shape when von Braun's fellow rocket pioneer, Klaus Riedel, joined the Peenemünde team. Von Braun greeted him joyously, but here again there was friction inside the German rocket team. The words of welcome, according to Schroeder, soon turned to sour grapes. Riedel made the mistake, Schroeder claims, of improving some rocket boosters von Braun had designed for the Luftwaffe. "Riedel got his award, a charge of insubordination," Schroeder's account goes. "He lost his position as chief of the testing department and was expected to be grateful that he was not fired out of Peenemünde. Henceforward, Dr. von Braun used him as a kind of errand boy. Whenever a contractor with Peenemünde violated the deadline for the delivery of his product, Riedel had to go on the road and had to speed up those lazy folks. He complained often and bitterly to me about it."

Von Braun confirms that Riedel was removed as testing chief but claims he was transferred to other important duties developing the ground-equipment system. "Fact is," answers von Braun, "that

Riedel, who was a real close friend of mine, had often spoken to me about Schroeder's difficult character and his inferiority complex."

Whether Schroeder or von Braun is correct will never be known. The only man who could answer was killed in 1944 as the first V-2 rockets were terrorizing London. Driving home from a party at the Peenemünde Officers' Club, Riedel smashed his car into a tree.

In brief, Schroeder charges that the staff at Peenemünde found it easier to let von Braun make mistakes than try to check them. Even Dornberger, he claims, sometimes spoke disparagingly of von Braun, saying, "Let the child play." If this is so, then Dornberger has since reversed his opinion. Dornberger would hardly be human if he did not feel some slight twinge of jealousy over the publicity his protégé has been getting. Nevertheless, he described von Braun to the authors as "a man of outstanding ability" and a "brilliant co-ordinator who speaks the language of scientists and technicians."

Another question mark hangs over von Braun's past. Why did he accept a commission in Hitler's elite SS corps? We asked von Braun this question and here is his explanation: "About 1941, the SS tried to poke their fingers into the rocket pie by making me a synthetic lieutenant. It was the kind of thing nobody could refuse without getting shot." The commission, he added, was only an "honorary job comparable with a Kentucky colonel."

That von Braun was in less than good standing with the SS seems evident from a charge of treason brought against him in February 1944. Three Gestapo agents burst into his quarters at 2 A.M. and hauled him off to jail in Stettin. They had picked up an indiscreet remark he had made in a railroad-train compartment that his real purpose in developing a missile was not as a weapon but as a space vehicle. A Gestapo agent had been in the train compartment and reported what von Braun had said. He was jailed.

Dornberger has a different explanation of von Braun's trouble with the Gestapo. He believes von Braun was imprisoned because he had refused to go along with SS chief Heinrich Himmler in his attempt to grab the V-2 program away from the Army. Whatever the reason, von Braun says he was almost beginning to enjoy his enforced confinement, because it gave him "plenty of time to think," when Dornberger barged into Hitler's headquarters to warn the Fuehrer that without von Braun the V-2 project would collapse. Von Braun was released on direct orders from Hitler himself. Simultaneously, Hitler made him an honorary "professor" in the Third Reich.

Regardless of his relations with Hitler, it seems clear that von

Braun's mind was less on the conquests of Hitler and more on the conquest of outer space. When the first successful V-2 soared sixty miles over the Peenemünde marshes in 1938, Dornberger turned to von Braun and said, "Do you realize, Wernher, what we have accomplished? Today the spaceship was born." And as they continued to shoot their rockets higher and higher like steppingstones into space, von Braun continued to be the space-struck boy thinking in terms of Dominik's science fiction he had read in school. Once, while watching a great rocket poised for a test shot over the Bay of Danzig, von Braun remarked to a colleague, "Doesn't it look like a scene out of Dominik?" When the report came back that the first V-2 had smashed into London June 16, 1944, von Braun commented, "It's a success except that it has landed on the wrong planet."

As the advancing Allied armies closed in on Nazi Germany, von Braun was given conflicting orders, some commanding him to defend Peenemünde to the end, others ordering him to leave. Nevertheless, when the Russian armies finally overran Peenemünde they found it deserted. The missile makers had moved en masse to a new location in the Harz Mountains of central Germany.

At one point, the top scientists were in more danger from their own SS than from the invaders. The SS actually planned to massacre five hundred leading missile scientists to prevent their capture by the Allies. They never had time to carry out the plot.

By now von Braun was convinced that his future lay with the West, and he took most of his trusted, tested rocket team with him. Lacking gasoline, they filled up their trucks with rocket alcohol and headed for Bavaria to surrender to the Americans. On their way, von Braun's driver fell asleep at the wheel; von Braun emerged from the crash with a broken arm. They took refuge in a Bavarian mountain chalet, and von Braun's brother, Magnus, departed on bicycle to invite the Americans to capture the waiting rocket scientists. The U.S. Army cheerfully accepted the invitation. Thus began the second chapter in the life of Wernher von Braun.

It was von Braun himself who helped select 102 of his key scientists to go to America under Army contract to build rockets. They spent weary months, lonely and frustrated, hanging around Fort Bliss, Texas. In a world at peace, Congress could not be induced to spend money on long-range missiles, much less space vehicles. There followed lean years of mistaken judgment, budget-slashing, and contempt in high places. Von Braun was no stranger to the weird convolutions of high military policy. He had been through it in Germany, where he had learned the art of flimflamming the brass and the bureaucrats. What he had experienced in Hitler's Germany ran an uncomfortable parallel with what he went through in the free United States. It could have soured him; instead it steeled him.

The Army had the foresight to collect all the scattered V-2 parts it could find in Germany and ship them to the United States. These were loaded on three hundred freight cars and hauled across the country to the Army's desert proving ground at White Sands, New Mexico. A conglomeration of screws, springs, valves, and other rocket components were dumped off in the desert with no instructions for assembling them. This gigantic jigsaw project occupied the German engineers for several months. They were able to put together sixty-eight V-2 rockets for test-firing. Because some of the parts had been damaged, twenty-three of the missiles either exploded or went haywire. One zoomed out of control into a cemetery across the Mexican border and almost caused an international incident. From the forty-five successful launchings, the Army discovered that the V-2 could lift a 2,230-pound warhead into space at the incredible speed of 3,600 miles an hour and deliver it a distance of 190 miles in less than four minutes.

Not until the Korean War, however, were the German rocketeers permitted to do much more than tinker with their old V-2s. Then suddenly they became important. Suddenly money became available. Nothing was too good for them. They were transplanted to Huntsville, Alabama, and ordered to build the Army an atomic missile. Out of this finally came the 500-mile Redstone missile successfully tested in 1953.

But the way to space was still strewn with headaches and heartaches. Came the end of the Korean War, and with it came more economy. There also came intensified feuding over missile roles and the celebrated vacillation of Defense Secretary Charles Wilson. The Army was forced to fight for every penny it spent on missiles. Even the short-range Corporal and the Honest John were almost canceled for lack of funds. The Nike antiaircraft missile was even struck out of the budget twice before finally approved.

"I don't know of any missile program that the Army has got that hasn't been canceled at least twice," testified Colonel John Nickerson. He had acted as trouble shooter for the von Braun team until court-martialed for his efforts. "Quite often the orders have appeared in black and white under signatures. . . . When you have hurdled one cancellation, then you are halfway on the way to operational level."

During the missile controversy von Braun got support from at least one quarter—the Women's National Press Club, which he addressed in November 1954. Its members were electrified at his warning that the country which launched the first satellite would be able to photograph military bases, would have a tremendous propaganda weapon, and could probably reach the moon. "The nation which gets into space first will rule the world," von Braun told the ladies of the press.

At his next press conference Secretary Wilson was asked whether the United States would spend money on von Braun's recommendations. He replied, "No, I would rather keep my feet on the ground figuratively as well as physically speaking. I don't know that anyone knows how you would rule the world with a spaceship. It's a little dreamy, I think. I'm almost tempted to tell a story."

He then told the story of a man who was changing a tire in front of an insane asylum. Carefully, he put the lugs in one hub cap, then accidentally stepped on the rim, shooting all the lugs into a culvert. Dismayed as to how to fasten on the wheel, he looked up to see an inmate watching him over the fence. "Why don't you take one lug from each of the other wheels?" the inmate suggested. "That will give you enough lugs to put on the spare until you get to a garage."

"What is a guy with ideas like yours doing in the place you're in?" asked the admiring motorist.

"I may be crazy," replied the inmate, "but at least I'm not stupid."

This was Wilson's answer to the man who, three years later, was to put the first American satellite into orbit and repair some of the appalling damage done to American prestige by the success of the Russian sputniks.

No two men could be more dissimilar than Lieutenant General James Gavin and Dr. Wernher von Braun. Yet no two men formed a closer alliance for the American conquest of outer space. Von Braun is the son of a Prussian nobleman, a member of the Junker class which ruled Prussia for centuries and whose young men did not "belong" unless they bore a dueling scar across the cheek. Gavin was born into poverty in Brooklyn, was adopted by a Pennsylvania coal miner, sold shoes for a company which would give him only single shoes as samples for fear he might, if given a pair, wear them. At sixteen he enlisted in the U.S. Army. Gavin is a Catholic, von Braun a former Lutheran, now Episcopalian, from a part of Germany which frowns on, even dislikes, Catholics. Von Braun spent a carefree youth, never went through the rigors of German military training; Gavin is remembered by West Point classmates as a starchy, stiff second lieutenant who "sleeps at attention and eats with his sword." And while von Braun was manufacturing missiles which came near knocking out London, Gavin was whipping his paratroopers into battle in daring landings on Sicily, behind the lines in Salerno, and later at the Battle of the Bulge.

Yet these two ex-enemies formed an alliance. Gavin's passion was to keep the Army which he loved from being relegated to guardhouse duty and kitchen police. Putting the Army in the space business was his way of doing this. It was during the occupation of Berlin, when von Braun was on his way to White Sands, New Mexico, and Gavin was trying to restore order to beleaguered Berlin, that the young general first gave his thoughts to atomic warfare. Only a few months after the first atomic bomb was dropped on Hiroshima he prepared a war game on paper called Battle Mace which was to provide the basic, tactical concepts for the nuclear army of today. Britain's Field Marshal Montgomery called Gavin to Paris to get the benefit of his views, and later Gavin was called back to Washington and placed in charge of Army research. In the Pentagon, Gavin became the leader of the "young Turks," the aggressive, progressive officers who sought to hack away red tape and sweep away the cobwebs of obsolete military thinking. They wanted to build a modern, streamlined Army, equipped with the most advanced weapons of the atomic age; and they seethed inwardly, sometimes complaining openly as they saw the Army budget being hacked to pieces.

In the interservice battle for the control of the weapons of outer space, von Braun came up with the dreams and Gavin translated the dreams into a missile program. Von Braun was the brains in the laboratory, Gavin the battler in the Pentagon. Gavin fashioned von Braun's technical information into a political campaign inside the Pentagon for missile money. Gavin fought vigorously, impatiently, sometimes ruthlessly. Sometimes he fought the Air Force and the Navy almost with more vehemence than he had battled the enemy in the Ardennes Forest in the winter of 1944. In the Air Force his name was usually mentioned with a prefix of curses. He contended that ballistic missiles were simply an extension of Army artillery and bore no resemblance to Air Force planes. And he argued this with such vigor that although he lived next door to General Nathan Twining,

Chief of Staff of the Air Force, Twining refused to speak to him.

Again when Gavin checked over the huge appropriations going to the Navy, he snorted, "Who are we preparing to fight? Great Britain? Russia is not regarded as a naval power." The Navy, Gavin argued, is not confined to ships to carry out its sea missions, but has missiles, planes, tanks, marine infantry, as well as surface and undersea vessels. Therefore, the Army needed a similar variety of weapons, especially missiles to carry out its missions on the land.

Thus raged the battle over the appropriation dollar. It is the same battle that has always disrupted the American military services; and despite the new alleged unification in the Pentagon, it raged more than ever under Eisenhower.

General Gavin has been described by his best friends as something of a cross between General Douglas MacArthur and General Charles de Gaulle. He combs his hair crosswise over his balding head after the manner of MacArthur, and he has the same scorn for those who disagree as the general who dictated his own terms for taking over the French government. This kind of officer, mixing politics with military strategy, was bound to arouse antipathy in high places. Even before the end of the war General Dwight D. Eisenhower had come to look with some skepticism at the driving young paratrooper in Berlin. In Berlin also General Maxwell Taylor had come to understand what it was to cross swords with Gavin. Both were rivals for command positions. Both were paratroopers. Gavin was commander of the 82nd Airborne Division, an old infantry outfit with a great history, streamlined for airborne operations. General Taylor was commander of the 101st Airborne, a new division with no history prior to World War II. But General Taylor, back in Washington a few months after V-E Day, ordered the 82nd Division disbanded and his own 101st Division continued. Gavin bristled with anger. In Berlin he first learned how to use the press and mold public opinion as he later did in Washington. Newspapermen in Berlin cabled such a drumbeat of protests back to the American press that Taylor's order was countermanded. The 82nd Airborne Division commanded by General Gavin continued. The 101st Division was disbanded, later to be reactivated for the Korean War.

This rivalry, begun in Berlin, did not diminish later in Washington. General Taylor, as Chief of Staff of the Army, tried to be a part of the Pentagon team. "Before I go into a meeting of the Joint Chiefs of Staff," he once confided privately, "I pray I may be tolerant of the other services' views." General Gavin, on the other hand, believed so fiercely in a strong, streamlined Army that he didn't give a whoop for Air Force or Navy views, much less a prayer.

Between Gavin and Taylor there was patched up a live-and-let-live truce. Between Gavin and Eisenhower, on the other hand, there was bitter, open animosity. Eisenhower considered Gavin too smart, too politically minded. He hated Gavin with a passion. Gavin, he knew, belonged to the Omar Bradley-Matt Ridgway school which believed the Army should stay out of national politics and which had advised Eisenhower not to run for President.

All of this would have been no more important than the usual run of petty jealousy and bickering inside the armed forces if it had not been for its effect upon the status of the United States of America and the nation's gradual skid down the runway of military strength. Gavin, whether right or wrong in his methods, whether diplomat or non-diplomat, was genuinely worried that if the U.S. Army fell below twenty-eight divisions it stood in great danger of being attacked, even occupied, by Soviet Russia. "They'll move in on us and take all of North America. And what will we do with fourteen straggling divisions against a hundred and seventy-five modern, well-equipped divisions of the Red Army?" he asked.

After the Russian sputnik was launched on October 4, 1957, Gavin's demand for action by the United States became more intensified, the resistance of his superiors more bitter. His testimony before committees of Congress did not help his position in the White House, though it may have jolted the American public regarding the dangers facing them. When Gavin, testifying before the Senate Armed Services Committee, was questioned by Senator Stuart Symington as to the danger to neutral nations from radioactive fall-out, the general replied, "Current planning estimates run on the order of several hundred million deaths." John Foster Dulles grabbed a telephone. He protested that it was impossible for his diplomats to make friends with the neutrals if Pentagon officers were going to frighten neutrals out of their wits with the specter of hundreds of millions of people dying from fallout. General Gavin got a tongue-lashing but continued to testify. He told Senator Lyndon Johnson's special Armed Services Subcommittee on January 4, 1958, that the Army could have beaten the Russians into space had it been given a chance. He complained that civilian superiors had downgraded the Army's mission in modern war. And he bluntly criticized the organization of the Joint Chiefs of Staff. After that, and especially after Senator Johnson had published Gavin's supposedly off-the-record remarks, it became almost impossible for him to remain in the Eisenhower Administration. Previously, on December 23, he had told General Taylor he planned to retire; so after a lot of political legerdemain by Secretary of the Army Wilber Brucker which made it appear that Gavin was retiring because he had not been offered a promotion, the soldier who "slept at attention and ate with his sword," and who had done more than anyone else in uniform to put the Army in the missile business, finally took off the uniform.

Wernher von Braun and James Gavin, the two ex-enemies who had so little in common but worked so well together, never demonstrated their teamwork better than in beating the Air Force to the launching pads with a 1,500-mile missile. They presented the Pentagon with a bastard missile, the Jupiter, which their superiors never really wanted but permitted to be built as a monument to indecision. Gavin first won authority to go ahead with the project for five months, then wangled extensions for various periods—once for only forty-five days.

In 1954, the Air Force was concentrating on a 5,000-mile missile and the Army was preoccupied with short-range missiles. It was von Braun's suggestion not to neglect the targets in between. He offered to build an intermediate missile, and Gavin peddled the offer around the Pentagon. He presented it, in March 1955, to his friend General Matthew Ridgway, then Army Chief of Staff. Ridgway had the practiced eye of a man who looks first at the price side of the menu. When he learned the Jupiter would cost $25,000,000, he dropped the paper studies as if they were radioactive.

A few weeks later, an event occurred on the lonely steppes of Siberia that changed his mind. Our detection system picked up the startling intelligence that Russia had successfully tested an 1,800-mile missile. Yet we had not even started to build one.

This ominous news was combined with a secret report remarkable for its foresight, from a defense advisory committee headed by Dr. James Killian, president of the Massachusetts Institute of Technology, later to become President Eisenhower's chief scientific adviser. The Killian report argued that intermediate missiles of 1,500-mile range would be as effective from overseas bases as 5,000-mile intercontinental missiles from home bases. It also correctly estimated that a medium-range missile could be developed before the Air Force could perfect its ocean-spanning, 5,000-mile missile. (Another passage in the report, unhappily ignored, warned of the psychological importance of launching an earth satellite ahead of the Russians.)

With the Killian report in one hand and the Jupiter studies in the other, General Gavin once again marched around the Pentagon's outer ring, sometimes called the "brass ring" because the big brass have offices around that circle. This time he found his superiors more willing to listen, although it still took all summer to budge the budget.

The Air Force, fearing the Army would get into the bombardment business with a 1,500-mile missile, hastily came up with a rival proposal. From its intercontinental Atlas project, it offered to split off an Atlas Junior that would hit targets 1,500 miles away. This shrunken version of the Atlas was to become known as the Thor. And thus began the celebrated feud between the Jupiter and the Thor.

At a meeting of the Joint Chiefs of Staff on November 2, 1955, the Army's sister services formally staked out their rival claims for a medium-range missile. By a two-to-one vote, the Joint Chiefs decreed that the Navy and the Air Force had a "valid requirement" for a ship-based and land-based intermediate missile respectively. Six days later, Secretary of Defense Wilson authorized work to begin.

The rival missiles were started within six weeks of each other, the Army's Jupiter on November 8, 1955, and the Air Force's Thor the following December 24. It is all very nice to have twins, but they cost more in military life than in private life, and when they come at a cost of hundreds of millions of dollars the taxpayers can be excused for wondering. If duplication is wasteful now, surely it was wasteful when it began and should never have been permitted. Instead of racing the Russians, the Army and Air Force concentrated more on racing each other. There cannot be the slightest doubt that if all the energy, cash and talent had been pooled into developing a single intermediate missile, it would have gone into production much sooner.

From the first, the Pentagon policy makers favored the Air Force Thor. Admiral Arthur Radford, the Joint Chiefs' Chairman, and Donald Quarles, the civilian research chief, threw their tremendous influence behind the Air Force. And no other pair in the Pentagon had better range on Wilson's ear. Despite them, Wilson hesitated over Gavin's angry arguments and continued to grant extensions of life to the Jupiter.

Gavin claimed that a 1,500-mile missile would enable the Army to hit battlefield targets from safe distances. He visualized hidden, mobile launching sites which at 1,500 miles would be difficult for the enemy to locate and put out of action. Gavin consulted with von Braun in Huntsville for technical arguments to back up his memos. Colonel John Nickerson, who later got court-martialed for his pains, was the liaison officer between them. Von Braun was the more philosophical and patient. He had fought for missile money in two countries and had learned to be patient. Once Gavin told him, "I don't see how you can be so patient. I guess I'm too much of a paratrooper."

At Huntsville, von Braun and his scientists worked day and night. Eighteen months were estimated as necessary to build the Jupiter. But by cutting every possible corner, von Braun reduced the time to fourteen months. He was shrewd enough to realize that an Air Force contractor, North American Aviation, had developed a superior engine. Without the slightest hesitation, he ordered it for his Jupiter. "We bootlegged work," Dr. von Braun recalled afterward. "Night after night men like Dr. Ernest Geissler and many others put in needless hours at work. We had no authority and we had little money, but we decided to go ahead anyway."

Early in 1957, Wilson finally made up his mind to discontinue the Jupiter program. He struck it out of his budget request for the 1958 fiscal year, which was to start July 1, 1957. But the undaunted Gavin dipped into other inadequate research funds to keep the project going. Finally, after a schedule that had been authorized in spurts and had just been given a death sentence, the first Jupiter, glistening in the Florida sun, showed up at Cape Canaveral for testing on March 1, 1957.

After two failures, the Jupiter was fired successfully on May 31, 1957. It wasn't until November that the rival Thor caught up in performance. Air Force Secretary James Douglas admitted sheepishly to the House Armed Services Committee: "Some of the early testing of the Jupiter was more encouraging than some of the earlier Thor testing, and it is particularly since the end of November [1957] that we have had excellent Thor tests." The Air Force had stolen the march on the Army, however, by tooling up for production first. Technical experts still disagree over which missile is the best.

While the Jupiter-vs.-Thor battle occupied the main Pentagon arena, Wernher von Braun and James Gavin co-operated on two other ventures. One was a proposed rocket to the moon; the other was the first American satellite to be launched into the heavens. The two went hand in hand, for it takes a powerful missile to launch a satellite and an even more powerful missile to launch a rocket to the moon. To reach the moon is von Braun's greatest passion. He would even cheerfully man the first spaceship, despite the fact that he has a beautiful wife and two attractive daughters. As early as the spring of 1955 he proposed a four-stage rocket which would deliver a 150-pound research cone all the way to the moon. Von Braun worked out the project to the last detail and proposed a joint Army-Air Force effort because the Air Force had more cash available than the Army. The Air Force rocket experts in this case were all in favor of backing the Army; but Charlie Wilson's anti-moon obsession was too strong for the visionaries. The project never got beyond the study phase.

While General Gavin fought vigorously inside the Pentagon to support von Braun, von Braun and his scientists worked feverishly in Huntsville. They proposed a daring plan, which they called Project Adam, to send a man aloft in the nose cone of a Jupiter-C rocket. Von Braun tried to convince the Pentagon that man must be sent on preliminary hops into space, each hop higher than the last, before he can reach the moon. His scientific team adapted the Jupiter-C to carry a passenger 150 miles into space, then return him by parachute to earth. The rocket would fly straight and stable as an arrow, von Braun promised. Major David Simons, Air Force space researcher, designed a passenger cone and volunteered to ride in it for von Braun's experiment. The Navy and Air Force indicated interest in the project, then the Air Force backed out.

Meanwhile, the Army officer who had battled hardest for missiles, General James Gavin, had already announced his retirement from the Army he loved. He left behind his ex-enemy, a former Nazi, now an American citizen, who had retrieved in part America's tarnished reputation.

xvii

THE GALILEOS OF THE 1950s

IN THE SPRING of 1946 a group of senators met with Dr. Harold C. Urey of the University of Chicago at a private dinner in the Wardman Park Hotel in Washington which was to affect the future control of atomic energy.

The war in Japan had been over six months. The bombing of Hiroshima was still fresh in the minds of the nation. Congress and the country were debating what to do with this new and terrible weapon of war unleashed over Hiroshima. Could it be harnessed for peaceful, industrial purposes? Was it to be controlled by the military? Would it be allowed to run berserk and eventually bring the end of civilization?

With these worries especially haunting the scientists who had developed the atomic bomb, some of them asked one of the authors to arrange a dinner at which members of the Senate could get the views of Dr. Urey on the future of the atom. Invited were such Republican senators as Owen Brewster of Maine, Charles W. Tobey of New Hampshire, Alexander Wiley of Wisconsin, and Kenneth S. Wherry of Nebraska; also Senator Brien McMahon of Connecticut, a Democrat, and Stuart Symington, then Assistant Secretary of War, later to become Senator from Missouri. The emphasis was placed on Republicans because they then ruled Congress and because the Democrats already leaned toward civilian control of the atom.

Dr. Urey, a Nobel Prize winner and discoverer of the hydrogen atom of atomic weight 2, was one of the original developers of the atom bomb and had been in charge of the government's wartime project on atomic energy at Columbia University. He gave a fascinating description of the birth of the bomb and the problems of scientists working under the military.

The atomic bomb was born when Dr. Leo Szilard, the Hungarian refugee, wrote a paper on the possibilities of atomic energy. This Dr. Albert Einstein incorporated into a letter, delivered to President Roosevelt by Alexander Sachs of Lehman Brothers. Einstein reported that he had learned via the underground that the Germans were working on atomic energy and that he believed refugee scientists in the United States could develop it first. Following Einstein's letter, Roosevelt appointed Henry A. Wallace, then Vice-President, as chairman of a supersecret government board to ascertain whether the highly speculative goal of atomic energy was worth the expense. Wallace finally reported back to the President that atomic energy was definitely worth the enormous expense in dollars and manpower. Thus the Manhattan Project was born.

U.S. military leaders, however, were less than enthusiastic. They faced tremendous shortages of materiel and wanted nothing to detract from the immediate goal of winning the war. So there were times when the military referred to the atom bomb as "Roosevelt's two-billion-dollar boondoggle."

Dr. Urey told the senators in graphic detail the difficulties of working under a military regime.

"Scientists are individualists," he said. "They are considered queer people. They can't work by themselves in isolated cubicles. They have to exchange ideas. If they can't exchange ideas and communicate with each other, they can't be effective, and eventually they quit. They took a certain amount of military supervision during the war, but now that the war is over I find a strong tendency on the part of the scientists to drift back to ordinary civilian work. Atomic energy can go forward or it can stop in its tracks, all depending on whether the scientists are going to be regimented or whether they can work as human beings."

As an example of hampering regimentation, there was the amusing incident experienced by Dr. Szilard when he found that the bookcases in his office had been turned around to face the wall.

"There was a vial of uranium in your bookcase," explained the Army officer in charge, "and orders are that nothing shall be revealed or exposed. So we turned the bookcases to the wall."

The Republican senators seemed impressed. Subsequently they threw their weight behind the McMahon bill for civilian control of atomic energy. It passed.

Thus began a long battle between civilian science and the military, between freedom of thought and restricted thought, between atoms for peace and control of the atom solely for war. Though the first skirmish was won by the scientists in 1946 with passage of the McMahon bill and establishment of the civilian Atomic Energy Commission, the next skirmish was won by the military in 1953 when a Naval Reserve officer and investment banker, Admiral Lewis L. Strauss, was put in charge of the AEC.

The same battle raged over missiles. This time the military won. If they had not won, if the development of missiles had been placed under civilians in a new Manhattan Project, the United States might not have become a second-class power. Control of missiles by the military and the terrorist campaign waged against scientists by the McCarthyites were among the greatest factors influencing our missile defeat.

Just as the first traces of cancer can scarcely be detected, so the cancer of fear that drove scientists out of government was not detected in an obscure Congressional race in California in 1946. Few people who participated in that race realized that it was to launch a new type of political campaigning called "McCarthyism" and launch the career of a young naval lieutenant toward the White House. That naval lieutenant, Richard M. Nixon, devised the technique of pinning the Communist label on Congressman Jerry Voorhis without actually calling him a Communist. Voorhis was one of the wealthiest young men in Congress. His father had spent millions to educate underprivileged children; had founded and endowed the Voorhis School for Boys at San Dimas. Young Voorhis, a product of Hotchkiss School and Yale, had worked with the YMCA in Germany and in an automobile assembly plant in Charlotte, North Carolina. He later became a vigorously anti-Communist, liberal member of Congress.

In 1946, he found thousands of dollars poured into his district to brand him a Communist. Batteries of telephone operators were hired to phone voters and mysteriously ask, "Did you know that Congressman Voorhis was a Communist?" With Soviet Russia just emerging as a threat to the United States, the technique was unbeatable. Young Nixon won. And four years later he used the same tactics against Congresswoman Helen Gahagan Douglas, Democrat, to get himself elected to the Senate.

It happened that Nixon had voted against aid to Korea just before the Communists attacked Korea. It happened that he had voted to cut aid to Western Europe at the very time Western Europe was most under the shadow of the hammer and sickle. But to the voters of California it was Mrs. Douglas, not Nixon, who had befriended the Communists. For Nixon devised a pink sheet alleging that because Mrs. Douglas had voted with Congressman Vito Marcantonio of New York on slum clearance, public housing, aid to education, and price control, she was a very dangerous woman. Up and down the length and breadth of California Nixon campaigned to make the voters believe Mrs. Douglas consorted with Communists, voted with Communists, lived with Communists, and probably was a Communist. It was one of the most relentless, ruthless, fiendishly clever campaigns in modern American history. When Nixon finished that campaign, Mrs. Douglas didn't have a chance.

These tactics have been repeated many times since then, but in 1950 they were new in American politics. A young senator from Wisconsin earlier in that same year had helped initiate the same strategy—a strategy which was to drive scores of scientists out of government.

Two factors inspired Joe McCarthy's campaign. One was his desire to become Vice-President, perhaps even President, of the United States. The other was the advice of Father Edmund A. Walsh, head of the Foreign Service School of Georgetown University. Walsh was the nation's number-one advocate of preventive war with Soviet Russia. He had openly advocated preventive war in a speech before the Air War College at Maxwell Field, Alabama, and also influenced his close friend Francis Matthews, Secretary of the Navy, to make a public statement advocating preventive war. Matthews was cracked over the knuckles publicly by the White House; while General Orvil A. Anderson, commander at Maxwell Field, who, taking the cue from Father Walsh, had advocated preventive war in a speech before the Kiwanis Club in Montgomery, Alabama, was transferred and reprimanded by Secretary of the Air Force Thomas K. Finletter. There was nothing the White House or the Air Force could do about Father Walsh, however, nor about his undercover vendetta against Dean Acheson and the State Department. Up until the time Acheson became Secretary of State, Father Walsh's friends and graduates had occupied places of high influence in the State Department. His close friend, Robert F. Kelley, had been chief of the Eastern Europe Division, where he dictated policy toward Russia. For many years almost any graduate of Father Walsh's Foreign Service School at Georgetown was guaranteed a diplomatic post in the State Department—until the advent of Dean Acheson. He upset the Georgetown apple cart. This was probably not because his father had been the Episcopalian Bishop of Connecticut, but rather because Acheson entered the State Department with the belief that the peace of the world depended upon co-operation between Russia and the United States; also because he favored a liberal American foreign policy.

Whatever his motives, it was Father Walsh who, in the fall of 1950, advised Senator Joseph R. McCarthy that the man who campaigned against Communists in the State Department would be hailed throughout the land. Colonel William A. Roberts and Professor Charles Kraus of Georgetown University were present when this conversation took place. It was on February 9, 1951, that McCarthy first accepted Father Walsh's advice by stating in a speech at Wheeling, West Virginia, that there were 205 "card-carrying Communists" in the State Department "known to the Secretary of State." Next day at Salt Lake City he changed this figure to 57, and a day or so later in the Senate he changed the figure once again to 81. Later Nixon helped supply him with a list of names previously scrutinized by the Un-American Activities Committee but unproved as Communists.

When all the smoke of charge and countercharge had been cleared away by the Tydings Committee, when all the debris of broken reputations and smeared characters had been swept up, a confused public finally realized—belatedly—that only one man in the State Department had even been indicted as the result of the McCarthy investigation. He was Val Lorwin, indicted for perjury by the Truman Administration for denying that he was a Communist. Later it was the unhappy fate of Herbert Brownell, Attorney General under Eisenhower, to order dismissal of the indictment with an apology to the court because there was no evidence to sustain prosecution.

This was two years and many heartaches later. In the interim a Democratic Administration had been defeated largely on the issue of Communists in government; relations with Russia had reached the most tense and dangerous period in history; and an atmosphere pervaded much of the United States, and certainly Washington, in which it was highly dangerous, if not suicidal, to say anything favorable about Russia or the Russian people. It was an atmosphere highly conducive to preventive war—an atmosphere which did not displease Father Walsh at all.

It did not displease Joe McCarthy either. He had dropped the issue of Communists in the State Department and started flailing away at almost any target, in government or out of it, if that target stood for liberalism. In the fall of 1953, following a historic wedding ceremony at St. Matthew's Cathedral and a special blessing from the Pope, McCarthy left for a honeymoon in the Caribbean. While he was away on that honeymoon his right-hand man, Roy Cohn, stumbled across a preliminary investigation being made by the United States Army of its Signal Corps at Fort Monmouth, New Jersey. McCarthy had so terrorized the Eisenhower Administration that it had agreed to give him carbon copies of every personnel probe it was conducting, no matter how superficial. So as a routine matter the Army notified McCarthy's office that it was investigating Fort Monmouth, and Roy Cohn promptly made it anything but routine. He advised the Senator, in the Caribbean, to drop matrimony and rush back to the headlines. McCarthy did.

Therewith began the investigation which was to put McCarthy at cross-purposes with General Ralph Zwicker, was to win for McCarthy the undying opposition of the Army, and, most important of all, was to drive many key scientists from government.

Actually, the terror campaign against scientists was begun long before by Richard M. Nixon when he was a member of the House Un-American Activities Committee. Nixon and his friend, Congressman J. Parnell Thomas of New Jersey, later jailed for taking kickbacks, had ridden roughshod over a half-dozen young scientists who showed great promise but who had made political mistakes. In most cases their mistakes were those of association. Whether security risks or not, the effect on the scientific world was to terrorize and stultify the laboratories of the nation.

"It isn't necessarily the world-famous scientists who count," said Dr. Urey at the University of Chicago, "it's the little scientists. You never can tell when some young, struggling scientist the world has never heard of will come up with a substantial contribution. These are the men who are being scared out of working for the government."

But the terror atmosphere surrounding scientists even extended to the world-renowned scientists. It reached such lengths that Dr. Urey, traveling through Europe in 1954, three years before Russia launched its sputnik, found himself trailed by State Department agents. Wherever he went he was shadowed. Dr. Urey had been one of the original builders of the atom bomb. He had done vitally important research on heavy water and on uranium 235. He is one of the most eminent chemists in the world. Yet he was trailed by State Department agents all over Europe.

The persecution of scientists became such that Professor Linus C. Pauling of the California Institute of Technology, a Nobel Prize winner and one of the most brilliant chemists in the United States, was singled out for retaliation by Oveta Culp Hobby, then Secretary of Health, Education and Welfare. He had been doing important research on anemia for her department, but he also had signed a petition to stop nuclear tests because of their effect on future generations. Mrs. Hobby promptly canceled her research contract with Cal Tech. Then because the research was vital she tried to maneuver with Cal Tech to have the work continued without Dr. Pauling—all because he exercised his freedom as a citizen in supporting the same position as that taken by Adlai Stevenson regarding tests of the atomic bomb. The National Science Foundation, however, backed Dr. Pauling, not Mrs. Hobby, and the new Secretary of Health, Education and Welfare, Marion Folsom, reinstated Dr. Pauling's research.

Such were the handicaps under which American scientists labored at the same time the Kremlin was elevating Russian scientists to the highest pinnacle.

It remained for Senator McCarthy to deal the final, and perhaps most discouraging, blow against American scientific research. For weeks headlines flared throughout the United States over stories date-lined "Fort Monmouth." For weeks scientists working on projects vital to the national defense were yanked off their jobs, placed before the glare of the television cameras, and brainwashed regarding every detail of their intellectual and physical association. Two brothers were accused of associating with each other. Another man was accused of associating with his father. One scientist was investigated because he read a book by Max Lerner.

A total of thirty-six persons were suspended during the McCarthy investigation; of these, fourteen were among the top men at Fort Monmouth. Many of them had completed research projects at considerable government expense but, as a result of the McCarthy probe, were forbidden to write their reports. Many had waived patent rights to their discoveries and out of patriotism had given them to the government, cost-free, for the defense of the nation. No Fort Monmouth employee took the Fifth Amendment. Twenty-eight were reinstated a few hours after Senator McCarthy left. Eight were dismissed. All have now been vindicated by the upper courts.

When all the smoke of the investigation had cleared, it was found that twenty vital defense projects had been delayed. McCarthy had singled out the Evans Laboratory, handling special electronic devices, vacuum tubes, instruments for determining radioactivity, and other vital component parts to guided missiles. The job of perfecting the Nike guided missile had been set back six months. A project to supply radar defense equipment to Army troops was totally upset. A major antiaircraft-research project involving guided missiles and rockets was robbed of its leadership temporarily. Laboratories were demoralized. The actual loss could not be counted in dollars. Twelve top men not involved in the security clamor in any way whatsoever quit in disgust. If government scientists were going to be terrorized by the government they served, then they wanted to get out. They did.

According to the New York *Herald Tribune*, "This really vital and sensitive military installation has been wrecked more thoroughly than any Soviet saboteur could have dreamed of doing."

The security chief at Fort Monmouth who had started the original investigation, a copy of whose report went to McCarthy's office, was Andrew J. Reid. He first went to work at Fort Monmouth in 1941 as a chauffeur.

The first guided missile produced in the United States was built, not by the Army or the Air Force, but by the Bureau of Standards, a civilian agency of the Department of Commerce. This was a short-range missile called the Bat, used toward the end of the war against the Japanese. Dr. Edward U. Condon, then chief of the Bureau of Standards, had contrived with his scientists to put a radar set in the nose of a missile, and when launched from a plane the radar guided it direct to the target.

During the Korean War, the Navy supported the Bureau of Standards, and its work on missiles was stepped up. Dr. Condon moved the Bureau's missile work to Corona, California, to a surplus Navy hospital in the summer of 1951 and there produced the Kingfisher missile. This was tied in with one of the most important developments by the Bureau of Standards in World War II, namely the proximity fuse, a little radio set built into antiaircraft artillery and rockets which explode the shell or rocket if they come within proximate distance of the target. All during the war, the Bureau of Standards had conducted experiments of this kind vital to the nation.

But after the war, and while the Bureau was continuing its work on missiles, Richard Nixon and the House Un-American Activities Committee started an investigation of Dr. Condon. The chief fault they found with him was his wife. Mrs. Condon had made the fatal mistake of attending a cocktail party given by the Yugoslav Embassy. A loquacious lady, she gossiped freely about some of the things that went on in Washington; even dared criticize the highhanded tactics of the House Un-American Activities Committee. Her husband was promptly threatened with an investigation by that committee. The investigation was kept dangling over his head for two years until he was finally hauled up for a series of heckling cross-examinations which failed to establish any evidence reflecting on his loyalty.

Dr. Condon will probably be rated as one of the most effective heads of the Bureau of Standards. Dr. Edward Teller, father of the H-bomb, credits him with having shortened the development of the H-bomb by one year. W. Averell Harriman, then Secretary of Commerce and over-all executive of the Bureau of Standards, supported Dr. Condon one hundred per cent. Harriman flew back from a winter vacation at Sun Valley, Idaho, to defend Condon as Nixon and Parnell Thomas intensified their campaign against him. But finally Dr. Condon got tired and quit. He went to work for the Corning Glass Company at a salary three times what he was getting from the government. Scientists of Dr. Condon's experience are rare, and Corning Glass—a stanch Republican company, whose former president, Alanson B. Houghton, was appointed Ambassador to the Court of St. James's by Calvin Coolidge and whose present president, Amory Houghton, has been made Ambassador to France by Eisenhower—was delighted to hire him. Since Corning Glass handles government contracts, Dr. Condon had to go before the Defense Department's Eastern Regional Security Board, which cleared him as a security risk. The Board did not act precipitously. It spent one year, from July 1953 to July 1954, studying the record. His clearance was not actually published officially until October 19, 1954.

On that particular day Vice-President Nixon was in the Far West urging voters to defeat Senators Murray of Montana and O'Mahoney of Wyoming and former Congressman John A. Carroll of Colorado because their party had harbored Communists and because they were pro-Communists. Just at this particular moment Vice-President Nixon learned that Dr. Condon, the man he had hounded when a member of the Un-American Activities Committee and had tried to drive out of government, had been cleared. It was officially held that the man Nixon had tried to prove a security risk was not a security risk.

Immediately the Vice-President of the United States communicated with Washington. And the Attorney General of the United States, Mr. Herbert Brownell, at the instance of the Vice-President, telephoned to the Secretary of the Navy, Charles Thomas. He gave instructions that the security cloud over Dr. Condon's head be put back where it had been before. Secretary of the Navy Thomas knew very little about Dr. Condon. He did not even know that Dr. Condon had been cleared, that any charges had been made against him, or even that Corning Glass had asked that Dr. Condon have access to classified material. All he knew was that he had received a call from the Attorney General and that the Eisenhower Administration was determined to elect a Republican Senate in November.

The file on Dr. Condon is so voluminous that it weighs about ten pounds. It goes into every phase of his life. That was one reason the Eastern Regional Security Board took one year to act. However, the Secretary of the Navy acted in a little over twenty-four hours. In that short period he supposedly was able to review thousands of pages of testimony. Secretary Thomas had spent his life as a clothing manufacturer. He was a cloak-and-suit expert, not an expert on security problems. Yet in the brief period of twenty-four hours he reversed what a security board had taken one year to study. He declared Dr. Condon a security risk.

Vice-President Nixon, speaking in Helena, Montana, was able to announce publicly that he had once again protected the American people from a dangerous man.

By an ironic twist of fate, Dr. Condon a few weeks earlier had been asked by the Navy to devise a nose cone for a guided missile which would be able to withstand the tremendous pressure of the air as the missile hurtled through space. Dr. Condon went to work. But by the time he had finished the nose cone he had been declared a security risk, and when he drove the nose cone to Washington in his station wagon, the Navy refused to accept it from him. It could no longer speak to him.

The unwanted Dr. Condon drove his station wagon with the Navy's nose cone back to Corning, New York. Finally the Navy called him up; said they would take the nose cone. It was a refinement of Dr. Condon's product which President Eisenhower proudly displayed on television when, in November 1957, he boasted that the United States was not too far behind Russia.

But Dr. Condon, unable to work on government contracts, lost his job with Corning Glass. All other industrial plants were closed to him. He could find no work. He had devised a vitally needed nose cone for guided missiles, yet he was considered a security risk. Finally Washington University in St. Louis took him in.

All of this made a profound impression upon the scientific world. Here was a man who had helped to pioneer the first missile used in World War II. Here was a man who had shortened by one year the time in which the United States developed the H-bomb. Yet here was a man who, because of charges made by the Vice-President of the United States, was out of work. The reluctance of scientists to toil for the government became more acute.

There had been other developments which increased that passive resistance of the American scientific world. One was Secretary of Commerce Sinclair Weeks's attempt to place politics above science in the Bureau of Standards. Another was the purge of Dr. Robert Oppenheimer.

It was only a few weeks after President Eisenhower moved into the White House that his Secretary of Defense, Charles E. Wilson, moved to take research on guided missiles out of the Bureau of Standards. "Why should we have bureaucrats working on missiles?" asked Wilson. "That should be in the hands of private industry."

Simultaneously, Craig R. Sheaffer of Fort Madison, Iowa, head of the W. A. Sheaffer fountain-pen company, became Assistant Secretary of Commerce. Mr. Sheaffer had contributed $1,000 to Senator McCarthy, $1,300 to Merwin K. Hart; had sponsored radio commentator Upton Close. He had also had trouble with the Bureau of Standards in the testing of his famous ball-point pens. In March 1953 he was to have more trouble. The trouble would have been unimportant had it not affected the morale of scientists and the missile race between the United States and Russia.

Jess M. Ritchie, president of Pioneers, Inc., of Oakland, California, had developed an automobile-battery additive called AD-X2, supposed to prolong the life of a battery. Other battery manufacturers claimed this was not the case, and when the matter was submitted to the Bureau of Standards for a test, its scientists ruled that AD-X2 had no appreciable booster effect upon a worn-out battery. Thereupon Mr. Ritchie's California political friends, including the Vice-President of the United States, threw their weight against the Bureau of Standards which had ruled against AD-X2.

The Bureau of Standards operates under the Department of Commerce. Assistant Secretary of Commerce Sheaffer called in the Director of the Bureau of Standards, Dr. A. V. Astin, and asked him to submit his resignation within three days. Dr. Astin's scientists were merely doing what they had been doing for years—making an official finding at the request of the Post Office Department. His bureau had always been under the direction of scientists, not politicians. Every President had respected the importance of keeping politics out of this scientific bureau. Nevertheless, Dr. Astin was fired.

The ensuing wave of protest from the scientific world and the threatened strike of scientists inside the Bureau of Standards was so vigorous and so overwhelming that Secretary of Commerce Sinclair Weeks reversed his Assistant Secretary of Commerce. He did not do so, however, until scores of scientists had threatened to leave the bureau and until Congress had begun an indignant investigation. In the end Dr. Astin was rehired; Assistant Secretary of Commerce Sheaffer went back to Iowa.

But the damage to the scientific world had already been done. It had been done earlier by Nixon and McCarthy in their campaign of terror. Now it was cemented and solidified. Perhaps even more important, research work on guided missiles, pioneered in the Bureau of Standards, was removed from the bureau to private industry and the Pentagon. Thereafter it became a spoil of war. The Army, the Navy, the Air Force, the airplane companies, all were competing against each other to get their cut of the guided-missile pie. Instead of having this vital project under one body, as the development of the atomic bomb was under the Manhattan Project, missiles were spread out all over the defense lot.

The crowning discouragement to scientists came with the purge of Dr. Robert Oppenheimer, the man in charge of the Los Alamos project which built the atomic bomb. His purge resulted chiefly from a clash of ideas and ideals with Admiral Lewis Strauss, appointed by Truman to be a member of the Atomic Energy Commission, later appointed by Eisenhower to be its chairman. Both are Jews. Oppenheimer is a Jew who, when he saw pictures of his fellow Jews in Hitler's concentration camps and read of their destruction in Hitler's soap factories, threw the full weight of his scientific genius into developing the most deadly, awesome weapon of World War II. He was among those who believed his handiwork should be dropped on Hiroshima, even though he, more than others, appreciated the consequences. But when the photographs of seared flesh and the medical reports from Hiroshima came back, Oppenheimer was among the scientists who went through the tortures of the damned. Their souls were on fire, and they started a burning, private crusade against a proposed new hydrogen bomb which would have more impact in one unit than all the explosives fired in World War II together.

"Many times we scientists thought the war might end before we had a bomb," Dr. Oppenheimer told a Congressional committee. "But some of us did not stop, because we wanted the world to see the atomic bomb. It was to us the greatest argument for world peace."

But with the atomic bomb achieved, Oppenheimer, then chairman of the General Scientific Advisory Committee, argued inside his committee against developing the hydrogen bomb. Russia, he said, would merely build a bigger bomb. And Russia could hurt the United States more than we could hurt her because American cities are more concentrated, more industrial, more vulnerable to attack.

Oppenheimer was not alone. Other members of the General Scientific Advisory Committee—James B. Conant, president of Harvard, Isidor I. Rabi of Columbia, Lee A. DuBridge of Cal Tech—all expressed the same view. They argued that the United States had to do something to stop man's crazy race toward destruction. If we didn't stop the race, they feared, Russia would bring in a new weapon that would involve genocide, not warfare. They proposed, therefore, that the United States take a unilateral position against developing the hydrogen bomb. If Russia did not concur, if the Kremlin proceeded with its H-bomb, then, it was argued, the United States would know quickly enough from its intricate monitoring system how far Russia had progressed.

This was not Oppenheimer's idea alone. But he alone was singled out for attack, perhaps because he alone had tangled with the most military-minded man on the Atomic Energy Commission—Admiral Strauss. When the Republicans, under Senator Hickenlooper of Iowa, were investigating the Atomic Energy Commission, among other reasons for sending isotopes to Norway, Oppenheimer had taken the witness stand and made mincemeat out of Admiral Strauss.

Admiral Strauss is a Jew who requests that his name be pronounced "straws"; who once served as private secretary to President Hoover; whose family had guaranteed his security in the powerful investment-banking firm of Kuhn, Loeb & Company; and who likes to consider himself, not a Wall Street banker, but a Virginia gentleman on his 2,000-acre estate below the Potomac.

Admiral Strauss finally took his argument over the head of the Atomic Energy Commission, of which he was then only one of five members, to Louis Johnson, then Secretary of Defense. Johnson, in turn, took it direct to Truman. Senator Brien McMahon of Connecticut also took it to Truman. There followed further debate in the Cabinet. Truman finally ruled that a study of the hydrogen bomb should be made to see how and when it should be built.

On July 2, 1953, Eisenhower appointed Strauss Chairman of the Atomic Energy Commission. One of his first acts, five days later, was to ask for the file on Oppenheimer. Shortly thereafter he began a full-scale investigation. Calling Oppenheimer in to see him on December 21, 1953, Admiral Strauss said, "Someone has revived these old charges against you." He did not reveal that it was he himself who had pulled out the Oppenheimer file.

Strauss thereupon urged Oppenheimer to resign as an AEC consultant. Somewhat as Cardinal Bellarmine warned Galileo never to discuss his views that the sun, not the earth, was the center of our planetary system, so Strauss tried to persuade Oppenheimer to resign because he had once opposed building the hydrogen bomb. It mattered not that Oppenheimer had been the man most responsible for the actual construction of the atom bomb, nor that his views on the H-bomb might have changed. Strauss was determined to run him out of government. Two days later, December 23, Oppenheimer returned, handed Chairman Strauss a letter stating that he could not possibly resign in the face of the absurd charges made against him. He intended, he said, to fight. Admiral Strauss, in reply, handed Oppenheimer a letter suspending him.

The events that followed are history. Strauss appointed as one of the judges to try Oppenheimer Thomas A. Morgan, head of the Sperry Gyroscope Company. A judge must be beyond reproach. However, Tom Morgan had been guilty of somewhat the same offense charged against Oppenheimer—he once had an open mind regarding the possibility of friendship with Russia. On November 23, 1934, Morgan had been the chief speaker at a dinner honoring Peter Bogdanov, head of Amtorg, the Russian trading corporation. Standing under the red flag of Soviet Russia, Morgan had paid tribute to Bogdanov, urged more trade between the U.S.A. and the U.S.S.R. Even more important, Morgan was head of the Sperry Gyroscope Company when it faced a triple antitrust charge by the Justice Department September 1, 1942, for exchanging patents with German, Italian, and Japanese firms on strategic instruments such as automatic pilots, artificial horizons and directional gyroscopes, all of great value to our potential enemies. He personally was a defendant in this suit. Despite this, Tom Morgan sat in judgment.

Strauss himself also sat in judgment on Robert Oppenheimer. The Congress had debated for weeks the question of whether to put atomic energy under military or under civilian control and finally decided against the military. Yet Lewis L. Strauss, Reserve Admiral and martinet, was now in control. And like Pope Urban VIII, who in 1633 was determined to break the arrogance of a scientific mind which wanted to explore outer space, Strauss was determined to break his fellow Jew of the arrogance of a scientific mind which wanted to explore the world's hopes for peace.

The verdict was two to one. Morgan, who had given secrets to our potential enemies, voted with Strauss that Oppenheimer was a security risk.

Oppenheimer left Washington and returned to Princeton, his great brain denied to the government of the United States in the future.

At Princeton, Albert Einstein, godfather of atomic energy, had watched the crackdown on American scientists with a sickened heart. He had watched Frank Oppenheimer, brother of Robert, purged by Nixon, unable to get a scientific job, go to work on a small cattle ranch in Colorado. He had watched Bernard Peters go to Bombay to teach in the Tata Institute for Fundamental Research. He had watched David Bohm leave the University of California to teach in Israel. He had seen Joseph Weinberg hounded out of scientific work to become an employee of an optical company in Chicago. They had made political mistakes, but they had contributed to the development of atomic energy.

The old man, watching these things from his gray and weather-beaten home on a residential street in Princeton, was sick at heart. To cheer life up he had his house painted. But his house was like the state of scientific research in America. One post of the porch was eaten away, and there were signs of termites. The house of Einstein, like the house of science, needed more than paint.

His long white hair reached down over his shoulders and his brown eyes were still bright, especially when he encountered a fresh idea. For comfort he always had his violin where he improvised tunes of his own.

Later, as he weakened, he lay in bed, still worried over the fate of the world.

"I am sick," the father of the atom bomb told a caller, "and that does not matter. But the world is sick, and that does matter."

xviii

RUSSIAN SCIENCE AND AMERICAN FOOTBALL

THINGS MOVE FAST in the House of Representatives. They move so fast that experts can hardly keep up with them. In split seconds a motion is gaveled down. In a couple of seconds a voice vote is ruled on. The hubbub, the whispered conversation, the rattling of newspapers, the visiting along the aisle, are so loud that Congressmen can hardly hear the speaker.

It was during this fast-moving welter of debate, just two months before Russia launched its first sputnik in 1957, that a vote was taken which meant that American education started slipping dangerously behind Russia. For one hundred years the United States has been well ahead of Russia. For some fifty years American education has been considered the finest in the world. In most respects it deserved that reputation. Russian illiteracy under the last Czar had been 75 per cent. But as the House of Representatives voted on the school bill on July 25, 1957, Russia was beginning to catch up with the United States in education. We had been marking time. And with the repeated refusal of Congress to recognize the need for aid to schools, education started downgrade with an acceleration which will take many years to stop. It was a vote which pushed the United States a bit further toward the category of a second-class power.

The vote was very simple. It was on the question of whether the United States should spend $400,000,000 a year helping local communities build new schools.

Just a few weeks before, the President of the United States had pulled every political trick out of the White House bag to kill the resolution of Representative Wright Patman of Texas to investigate Eisenhower fiscal policies. The White House lobby was successful.

The resolution was defeated. However, when it came to passing a bill to better the education of American children, not one phone call came from the White House; no Cabinet members buttonholed members of Congress; no members of the White House staff were on hand to promise reward.

The school bill was defeated. The man who defeated it was none other than the President's own floor leader, Representative Charles A. Halleck of Indiana.

Its defeat climaxed a five-year period of unkept promises by an Administration which had repeatedly pledged aid-to-education but repeatedly moved behind the scenes to block fulfillment of that pledge.

The inside story of this betrayal of American education is one of the most revealing in the record of Dwight D. Eisenhower. It is also one of the most tragic.

The story goes back to the closing days of the previous Administration when, on September 6, 1952, John R. Steelman, Director of Defense Mobilization, issued a directive to encourage the training of American scientists.

"There is no limit in principle to the advances which can be made in science and technology," Steelman decreed. "One of the most far-reaching effects of the defense program is an acceleration of research and industrial technology. Industrial and scientific development, which normally would have been spread over a decade, must now be telescoped into less than half that time."

There followed a long and detailed instruction to encourage scientific education.

Four months later President Eisenhower took office. Of him the educational world expected big things. He was the former president of a great university, a man dedicated to the improvement and enlightenment of his country.

One of his first acts was to abolish the Defense Manpower Administration of the Labor Department, entrusted in part with carrying out the directive. Dr. Bernard B. Watson, the actual author of Steelman's warning that the United States must telescope ten years of scientific training into five, had to look for another job. One by one the government scientists and educators who realized the importance of the scientific crisis in education were relieved.

The Eisenhower Administration not only let the Steelman order urging scientific education gather dust, but simultaneously Mrs. Oveta Culp Hobby, first Secretary of Health, Education, and Welfare, proceeded to undercut the aid-to-education bill introduced in 1953 by Senator John S. Cooper of Kentucky, Republican, and pushed by Senator Lister Hill of Alabama, Democrat. Mrs. Hobby's opposition was discreet, but none the less effective. In the spring of 1953, as Senator Hill prepared to hold hearings on the bill, Sam Brownell, Commissioner of Education, prepared to testify. He never did. He stayed up until 3 A.M. preparing the testimony to be given before the Senate Labor and Public Welfare Committee at 10 A.M. But he never gave it.

Commissioner Brownell, brother of the Attorney General, a Cabinet member close to Eisenhower, carried more weight than the average bureaucrat. But he was stopped dead in his tracks when it came to any support of legislation for new school buildings. His carefully prepared statement is still gathering dust in H.E.W. files.

The reason which Mrs. Hobby gave to senators for the sudden censorship of her own Commissioner of Education was that she wanted a further survey of educational needs prior to passage of legislation. She wanted each of the forty-eight states to hold an education conference, followed by a final conference at the White House in Washington. Following this fanfare, the President was to put across the school bill just before the 1956 elections when it would do him the most political good.

Unfortunately, the Kremlin did not wait either for Mrs. Hobby or for the 1956 elections. Senators Cooper and Hill, sensing the urgency, pushed on with their education bill.

"There have already been seven national conferences on this question," said Senator Hill. "The conferences even began with the Hoover Administration. Seven million dollars have already been spent on school surveys. We know what the need is. Mrs. Hobby knows the need; so does President Eisenhower. They made a specific pledge to help the schools, and this is the time to do it. It is a time for action, not more surveys."

Even without the support of the Administration, Senators Cooper and Hill managed to get the school bill before the full Senate of the United States. It was during the closing days of Congress in the late summer of 1954 that it finally came up for a vote. The bill was on the consent calendar, however, where one vote could kill it. That one vote was cast by Senator Richard Russell of Georgia. Senator Russell had voted for tax concessions for Georgia Power and for Coca-Cola. He had managed to wangle out of the armed services proportionately more military installations for the state of Georgia than for any other state except Texas. He had never been backward in asking that money be spent on his section of the country. But when it came to the children of the country, Senator Russell, a bachelor, protested that the education bill carried too big an appropriation—half a billion dollars—to be on the consent calendar for action without proper debate. Technically he was right. But technicalities did not lessen the handicaps faced by the children who went back to overcrowded schoolrooms that September.

During that same summer, President Eisenhower invited to a White House luncheon certain key governors for the purpose of pushing a fifty-billion-dollar program for new highways. He urged them to make sure a highway bill was passed. He said nothing about passing a school bill which would cost the taxpayers one one-hundredth as much.

Meanwhile Russia, unfettered by Mrs. Hobby, the complacency of President Eisenhower, or the anti-aid-to-education campaign of the U.S. Chamber of Commerce, was pushing ahead, and news of its education program gradually began to leak back to the American people. At first they could not believe it.

It was William Benton, former Democratic Senator from Connecticut, defeated by the Irish of his state after he dared ask for an investigation of Senator McCarthy, who first came back from Russia with alarming reports of Russia's advance in education.

"Russian education is a bigger threat than the hydrogen bomb," warned Senator Benton in 1956.

His warning was echoed by John A. Kennedy, publisher of the Sioux Falls, South Dakota, *Argus-Leader*, who, after two trips through Russia, told Congressmen, "The battlefield of Waterloo was won on the playing fields of Eton. The battle of survival for the West is being lost in the high schools of America."

In speech after speech, editorial after editorial, these two tried to shake the American people out of their lethargy. Some of the facts they reported:

The average American high-school student spends 900 hours in class a year, the average Russian 1,200 hours.

The Russian teacher in a primary school has about seventeen students in her class, an American teacher has twenty-seven.

While America emphasizes more and better buildings, Russia emphasizes more and better teachers.

Seventy per cent of the advanced degrees given by Soviet universities are in scientific and technological fields.

Once admitted to a university, the Russian youngster doesn't have to register for the military draft.

An elaborate system of extracurricular activities is planned after school, partly to keep children off the streets, partly to develop their hidden abilities. Children work after hours building equipment for classrooms, repairing worn books and furniture.

Some of the Pioneer Palaces, run by the Communist Party for after school activity, are fabulous. One of them is housed in the former palace of the Czar at Leningrad. It has workshops for every conceivable type of activity.

There are children's railways and children's fleets where youngsters can learn to operate trains and ships.

Children under sixteen are barred from adult movies, but they have attractive theaters of their own.

Russian radio is loaded with education and culture. Good music occupies 50 per cent of the time on Radio Moscow, drama 30 per cent, news and education 20 per cent. Television features live plays, operas and ballets, with performances often lasting as long as three hours. There are no cowboy movies, no Westerns, no murder mysteries. Strangely, there is little communist propaganda on radio and TV within Russia, though there is plenty of it in schools and colleges. One of the Communist Party leaders' major headaches is that students don't pay enough attention to it.

"Russia's ten-year, primary-high school educational system has become perhaps the toughest secondary scholastic system in the world today," reported John Kennedy following his second trip to Russia.

Mr. Kennedy is a hard-boiled Hearst-trained newspaperman who developed a chain of radio stations in West Virginia and California, now publishes the leading newspaper in South Dakota. And while President Eisenhower was assuring Congress that all was right with the world, publisher Kennedy was warning Congress:

> Hard work and hard education in Russia are comparable to the philosophy of America in the pioneer days when students worked long hours on homework and thought nothing of walking four or five miles to school.
>
> In contrast I fear that Americans' desire for ease, luxury, and shorter hours is producing a condition which historically has told the story of the decadence of once proud nations.
>
> The Russian atheistic, scientific-trained brain being turned out in huge quantities by its ten-year schools today is by far the

> greatest threat of any weapon Russia has up to now produced. . . . The Russians have established a lead over the United States that's going to take almost superhuman effort for us to overcome.

Meanwhile six hundred students were discharged from New York schools for stabbings, rape, and criminal conduct. Meanwhile the American public-school system lacked almost half a million classrooms. Meanwhile three schoolhouse firetraps in North Carolina burned to the ground; one student was killed, one teacher died of burns. Meanwhile the average schoolteacher's average salary in the United States was less than that of a truck driver in Chicago. Meanwhile an American student can graduate from high school with only penmanship, physical education, typing, and English, while Russian students in central Asia are required to take either French, English or German, plus a six-year course in Hindi, Chinese or Arabic, plus six years of biology, five years of physics, four years of chemistry, together with mathematics through trigonometry, and one year of astronomy. The American schoolhouse, once the temple of every community, had given way to stadiums, high-salaried football coaches, and drum majorettes; with a steady trek of teachers leaving the profession to seek more lucrative though more menial jobs. No wonder Nikita Khrushchev, speaking at Rangoon, Burma, in December 1955, boasted, "The capitalists always regard our people as being backward. But today we have more engineers and more supporting technical personnel than any capitalistic country. Every year the Soviet Union's higher educational institutions train more engineers, agronomists, doctors, and other specialists, than does the United States of America."

It was not an idle boast. Said Nicholas DeWitt, leading American authority on Russian scientific education, "Training of specialized manpower in Soviet Russia exceeds not only that of the United States but all the NATO countries combined."

Time passed. The highway bill, with the backing of the Teamsters Union, passed Congress, adding an extra tax on the gasoline bill of every motorist. The natural-gas bill, to increase the bill of every housewife, was gaveled through the House of Representatives by Speaker Sam Rayburn. An aid-to-education bill did not pass. Mrs. Hobby got her much-vaunted conference on education, but she was not around to enjoy it. She was unceremoniously fired as Secretary of Health, Education, and Welfare. She was fired not because she had delayed aid to education, but because she had hopelessly balled up the distribution of Salk polio vaccine. Her White House conference on education, held in the autumn of 1955, found just exactly what Senator Hill of Alabama predicted it would find—a serious need for more schools, more teachers, and higher salaries for teachers. By that time, however, two precious years had been lost—two years during which it began to seep in on the American public that Russian education was catching up with the United States.

During those two years something had happened which was to make passage of the school bill doubly difficult. Previously the Catholic College of Bishops had opposed aid for education unless parochial schools shared in the benefits. This raised the issue of division between Church and State and caused opposition from some Congressmen in Catholic areas. But this was counterbalanced in part by the fact that some Southern Congressmen, vigorous defenders of separation of Church and State, pushed the school bill.

But in 1954, after the Supreme Court of the United States voted to integrate the public schools of the United States, Southern Congressmen, with a few exceptions, became unanimous, bitter-end opponents of a school bill. They reasoned that federal aid would not be granted to schools which delayed in carrying out the Supreme Court's edict; and their fears were promptly justified by the amendment to this effect introduced by Adam Clayton Powell, the Congressman from Harlem. His amendment, in fact the mere fear of his amendment, drove such hitherto stanch champions of aid-to-education as Senator Lister Hill of Alabama into a cold sweat. As chairman of the Senate Labor and Public Welfare Committee, Hill had previously pushed the school bill. Now he blocked it. He bottled it up in his committee and flatly refused to let it come out for a vote.

In the House of Representatives, Graham A. Barden of North Carolina, chairman of the equally potent Labor and Education Committee, also staged a sit-down strike. Many years before, Mr. Barden had been a schoolteacher. When Cardinal Spellman blasted Mrs. Eleanor Roosevelt for urging passage of an education bill, Mr. Barden had rushed to her defense. He had done his best to promote the passage of the bill. But with the specter of aid-to-education promoting, perhaps even hastening, integration of Southern schools, Barden in 1955 refused to let the school bill out of his committee. It took a rebellion engineered by Jimmy Roosevelt of California, Lee Metcalf of Montana, Mrs. Edith Green of Oregon, and Stewart L. Udall of Arizona, to finally bulldoze the bill out from under Barden and onto the floor of the House of Representatives. But this occurred only after more months of valuable time were lost.

The most tragic aspect of the battle over aid to education, following the Supreme Court's decision, was the fact that Southern opposition could have been prevented had it not been for the selfish political gyrations of one Negro—Adam Clayton Powell. Mr. Powell is married to Hazel Scott, the Negro singer. His greatest affinities are beautiful women, foreign sports cars, and the headlined imprint of his own name. He has probably done greater disservice to his own race than any other Negro of modern times. He has done equal disservice to the children of the white and Negro races.

In the summer of 1956 Congressman Powell found himself in serious legal difficulties. Three of his secretaries were under income-tax investigation for giving kickbacks, while he was also under tax investigation. Two of his secretaries, Acy Lennon and Hattie Dodson, were convicted. Another secretary, William Hampton, was indicted. About this time Congressman Powell got in touch with Vice-President Nixon, indicated that he, Powell, a Democrat, would support President Eisenhower for re-election, would even endeavor to woo the Negro vote over to the Republican column in November. Shortly thereafter the income-tax investigation of Congressman Powell was eased up. The grand jury considering his case was told to go slow. The Assistant U.S. Attorney in charge, Thomas Bolan, was told to put the case on ice. And it was not until over a year later, May 1958, when Bolan published this fact, that the grand jury ignored instructions from the politically minded Justice Department and indicted Powell.

During the year that intervened, the Eisenhower Administration seemed to have an invisible but quite definite hold over the political activities of Adam Clayton Powell. When they wanted him to be absent during a crucial vote on the Hells Canyon dam, they had no difficulty whatsoever in making sure that he was absent. Even though A. Philip Randolph, head of the Brotherhood of Sleeping Car Porters, and Clarence Mitchell of the National Association for the Advancement of Colored People urged Powell to be present for the Hells Canyon vote; even though Mrs. Green of Oregon, who had championed Powell in heated controversy with Southern Congressmen, went to New York to beg him to come back to Washington and vote, nevertheless Mr. Powell did not vote. He obeyed the Eisenhower Administration which had eased up its investigation of his income taxes and did not vote for Hells Canyon.

If the Eisenhower Administration had exercised similar influence over the Congressman from Harlem when it came to amending the school bill, the children of America would be enjoying better school buildings today. Congressman Powell had in his hands the question of whether or not a school bill would be passed. He was urged by such sincere champions of the Negro as Mrs. Roosevelt, her son James, and leaders of his own race, to drop his amendment withholding funds from schools which did not enforce integration. He knew, and they knew, it would bring the united opposition of the South, would probably defeat the school bill. Congressman Powell is a friend of the Republican leader of the House of Representatives, former Speaker Joseph W. Martin of Massachusetts. Though Powell is a Democrat, he and Martin frequently work together. Joe Martin has been consistently opposed to the school bill. He has followed the line of the U.S. Chamber of Commerce and the National Association of Manufacturers, which so deluged Congressmen with antieducation propaganda.

So Congressman Powell, pastor of the biggest Baptist church in the world, looked up to by millions of Negroes as their champion, one of three Negro Congressmen in the House of Representatives, put political headlines ahead of the welfare of the nation and, during the school debate of 1956, introduced his integration amendment.

That ended the school battle for 1956. Southern Democrats teamed up with conservative Republicans in the House of Representatives to kill the bill, 224 to 194. That September, children once again went back to crowded schoolhouses. Another year passed during which the Kremlin pushed ahead with more buildings, more teachers, more science training.

Came 1957. Once again, President Eisenhower paid mere lip service to aid-to-education. Fresh from one of the greatest electoral victories ever scored by any President, he could have demanded and got almost any type of school bill. His timid proposal of $1,300,000,000 to be spent over a four-year period on the basis of need was so inadequate that Representative Augustine B. Kelley of Pennsylvania, Democrat, introduced a substitute calling for $3,000,000,000 to be spent over four years based on population.

This time, Adam Clayton Powell, irked at Senator Wayne L. Morse of Oregon and the civil-rights compromise, had used this as an excuse to take a free vacation. He went to Rome, withdrew a fistful of counterpart funds from the American Embassy, rented a villa along the Adriatic, and sat out much of the 1957 summer Congressional session. It cost the American taxpayers something, but those who wanted a school bill considered it well worth the cost.

In Powell's absence, however, Representative Stuyvesant Wainwright II, Long Island Republican, cousin of the late General Jonathan Wainwright, scion of one of the oldest New York families, introduced the Powell amendment to withhold federal funds from schools failing to integrate under the Supreme Court ruling. The amendment was adopted by the House of Representatives, some Northern Republicans voting for it because they knew it was one of the best ways to mobilize Southern opposition to aid-to-education.

Even with this handicap, however, the school bill would have passed the House of Representatives had it received even mild support from the Administration. After all, only five votes were needed. Had Sherman Adams exerted himself to even a fraction of the degree that he pulled wires to block the Hells Canyon bill, had the President publicly endorsed the bill at a press conference just before the vote, the children of America would be attending better schools today.

Instead, the President postponed his regularly scheduled press conference which was to have been held the day before the vote. The postponement was deliberate—to avoid any embarrassing questions on Ike's stand on aid-to-education.

One week before, Mrs. Hobby's successor as Secretary of Health, Education, and Welfare, Marion B. Folsom, former executive of Eastman Kodak and a sincere believer in aid-to-education, had informed a press conference that he was confident President Eisenhower would throw his weight behind the school bill. He was wrong. Folsom was actually summoned to the White House afterward and reprimanded for making the statement. He was told that he was not to put the President on the spot for education. And to make sure no newspaperman put the President on the spot, the White House press conference was postponed.

These were the events leading up to the hectic welter of debate in the House of Representatives on July 25. Democratic Congressmen, realizing they could not pass their more ambitious school bill introduced by Representative Kelley, had previously agreed in committee to substitute practically all of the more modest Eisenhower school bill which had the official though not the actual blessing of the White House. And as debate opened on the floor of the House they agreed to accept the Eisenhower bill *in toto*, with no reservation whatsoever.

At this point, up jumped "Two-Cadillac" Charlie Halleck, Eisenhower's floor leader. Charlie Halleck had come to Washington a poor country lawyer from northern Indiana. Now wealthy, he was able to sport two Cadillacs immediately after the war when cars were difficult to get. He sent his children to private, not public, schools.

"Now this is the bill the President really wants," he declared. "I could support this amendment."

Later, Halleck had his remarks expunged from the *Congressional Record*—for reasons readily understandable.

Northern Democrats held a hurried huddle on the floor with Congressman Samuel K. McConnell, Jr., of Pennsylvania, Republican supporter of aid-to-education, in order to push the Eisenhower bill to victory. But Halleck was too quick for them. He walked over to the Democratic side of the chamber to Congressman Howard W. Smith of northern Virginia, leader of the conservative Dixie-Republican coalition. Halleck and Smith knew that the tide was going against them. They knew a school bill might be passed if the McConnell-backed Eisenhower bill was substituted for the Democrats' more ambitious bill. Smith rose, caught the eye of the Speaker, moved to strike the enacting clause of the original bill. It was a neat parliamentary tactic, and it worked. Speaker Rayburn gaveled the House to order; called the roll. Two-Cadillac Charlie voted with the Dixie-Republican coalition to kill the bill he had previously supported. That was why he expunged his remarks from the record.

Aid to education lost by only five votes. One telephone call from the White House could have changed those votes.

The U.S. Chamber of Commerce boasted publicly that it had killed the school bill. There was justification for that boast. Thomas A. Ballantine of Louisville, chairman of the Chamber's committee on education, had testified before Congress, "Such proposals as HR 1 [the Kelley bill] seem to us the most dangerous of all federal-aid proposals. Our investigation indicates that no national shortage in classrooms has been, or can be, demonstrated to exist. The pessimistic outlook reported was more the result of wishful thinking on the part of local school administrators than of any valid evidence of classroom conditions." These words were relayed by intensive campaign to every local chamber of commerce and almost every businessman in the United States.

Two months later, as the children of America returned to rundown, cramped and crowded schoolhouses, Russia launched its first sputnik, a triumph of Soviet scientific education. The U.S. Chamber of Commerce was mute.

Before that, however, President Eisenhower announced at a press conference that he had done his best to pass a school bill, which caused Congressman Cleveland M. Bailey, West Virginia Democrat, to explode, "He's a lousy liar."

Bailey knew the heartaches and headaches of those who had tried to pass the education bill. He knew how hard they had tried to get White House support. He also knew that on July 21, the Sunday before the House was scheduled to vote on school construction, the President's Committee on Education Beyond the High School had prepared for release a painstaking report on the need for better education. The committee was chaired by a conservative Republican and J. P. Morgan director, Devereux C. Josephs, chairman of the New York Life Insurance Company. He and his committee had prepared alarming statements about our lagging education. Publication of those statements would have had a profound impact on the Congress. So publication of the report was deliberately postponed until August 11—after the crucial vote in the House of Representatives.

That was why Congressman Bailey called the President of the United States a "lousy liar."

Six months after the Russian sputnik gave public proof of Soviet scientific advances, the United States Bureau of Education sent ten prominent educators to Russia to study firsthand the progress of Russian education. The group was headed by Dr. Lawrence G. Derthick, U.S. Commissioner of Education appointed by Eisenhower. Upon his return, Commissioner Derthick reported, June 13, 1958:

"What we have seen has amazed us in one outstanding particular; we were simply not prepared for the degree to which the U.S.S.R. as a nation is committed to education as a means of national advancement. Everywhere we went we saw indication after indication of what we could only conclude amounted to a total commitment to education. Our major reaction therefore is one of astonishment—and I choose the word carefully—at the extent to which this seems to have been accomplished. For what it is worth, ten American educators came away sobered by what they saw."

Commissioner Derthick then proceeded to itemize point by point the amazing advance of Russian education—no shortage of teachers, no overcrowded classrooms, abundant staff assistants to teachers—including doctors, nurses, curriculum experts—ample school funds, participation of parents in school affairs, continuation of educational work during the summer and after school hours.

"We came back convinced," concluded Dr. Derthick, "that we cannot as a nation afford to disregard the challenge imposed upon us by the Russian race for knowledge."

That, however, was exactly what Commissioner Derthick's chief in the White House and Republican members of Congress proceeded to do. When Democratic Congressmen proposed 22,000 scientific scholarships a year in an aid-to-scientific-education bill, President Eisenhower personally wrote a letter urging only 10,000. His leaders in Congress further disregarded the Russian race for knowledge by killing again the Eisenhower school construction bill, introduced the preceding year but sidetracked by Republican leaders in Congress. In a final attempt to pass the Eisenhower bill, Democratic members of the House Education and Labor Committee proposed in May 1958 that the Eisenhower bill be taken *in toto*, without the change of a single word, and reported out to the full Congress for a vote. Whereupon every Republican member of the Education Committee voted against the President's own education bill. This included such hitherto strong advocates of education as Congressman Carroll D. Kearns of Pennsylvania, a former schoolteacher, and Congressman Harry G. Haskell, Jr., of Delaware, who admitted that as a member of the Department of Health, Education and Welfare, serving under Eisenhower, he had personally helped to draft the school bill which he now voted against. Squirming uneasily in his chair, Congressman Haskell explained his current opposition on the ground that the bill "needed more study."

"How many more hearings do you want?" angrily inquired Lee Metcalf of Montana, Democrat, in this executive session of the committee. "This bill already has received exhaustive study. It is now so late in the session that if we send it back to the subcommittee for further study, as you suggest, it will kill the chances for action at this session of Congress. That's what some of you fellows really want, I guess. Look at these voluminous hearings," he added waving a transcript containing more than one thousand pages of testimony on school aid.

Democrats Frank Thompson, Jr., of New Jersey and Stewart Udall of Arizona joined the argument. "These arguments about further study," said Thompson, "are sheer sophistry. You Republicans are struggling as hard as I ever have seen anyone struggle to rationalize an untenable position. You were for this bill last year when President Eisenhower said he wanted it; now you are trying to wiggle out because the President is no longer for it. But the need of school construction is even greater now than it was last year. The shortage of classrooms has increased. I want to do something about it. This is the President's own bill, but as a Democrat I am supporting it to relieve the serious shortage of classrooms."

"Times have changed since last year," argued Republican Peter Frelinghuysen, Jr., of New Jersey. "For one thing we are in a business recession, and this of course must be considered in government spending for schools."

"The fact that we are in a recession is all the more reason why we should put through a school bill as fast as possible," shot back Metcalf. "School construction will mean more jobs."

Republican Congressmen, however, remained unmoved. Not a word of encouragement was received from the White House, as the roll was called to kill the bill to build schoolhouses for American children.

xix

YOUNG MAN WITH A WET FINGER

RICHARD MILHOUS NIXON is a young man with a wet finger in the wind. His course changes as the wind blows. He has been on all sides of many political fences. He has been a liberal, an extreme reactionary, a moderate; finally a liberal once again. He is able, shrewd, fast on his feet. He has imagination, verve, and energy. He has great courage—the courage to face a hostile mob of Latin-American voters, or a critical audience of TV viewers. But would he be able to lead the nation up the path of self-confidence and adequate defense to its onetime glorious rating as the world's greatest power?

The answer is not easy.

A study of the relatively short life of Richard Nixon shows that his very first vote was cast for Franklin D. Roosevelt and that he began his public life as a young attorney for one of the most liberal New Deal agencies, the Office of Price Administration. Yet in Congress he voted against labor, against price controls and all things savoring of the New Deal. His record shows that although he still lists himself as a Quaker he waged an intolerant, vicious, un-Quaker-like campaign to purge and punish men for their political faiths. It shows that he has been a stanch Taft isolationist, voting against foreign aid and arms for Korea, yet later the most vigorous campaigner for foreign aid and armed intervention even in Indochina.

The question is: Has Nixon grown? Has he changed with maturity? Or has he changed from expediency?

The record is complex. You have to know the man to get the answer.

In 1946, when Nixon was about to leave the Navy, he borrowed $150 from the manager of the Erco Company of Maryland, whose naval contract he was renegotiating as sole judge and jury for the taxpayer, flew back to California to answer a newspaper ad in search of a young man to run for Congress against the Democratic incumbent, Jerry Voorhis, and persuaded the millionaire residents of San Marino who inserted the ad that he was their man. Nixon was elected. The Erco Company, which loaned him the money, got a refund from the government on its naval contract. It was Richard Nixon's first conflict of interest. It was also his first experience with the political technique of guilt by association. Congressman Voorhis, who hated Communism, was so effectively smeared as a pro-Communist that he eventually moved out of California. This was the real birth of McCarthyism.

In Washington Mr. Nixon also kept his finger in the wind. The American people were just beginning to be suspicious of Soviet Russia, and Nixon, climbing aboard the Un-American Activities Committee, reaped headline after headline. Bert Andrews, shrewd correspondent for the New York *Herald Tribune*, took Nixon under his wing, introduced him to Whittaker Chambers, the ex-Communist who had tangled with the ex-State Department official Alger Hiss, and phoned Nixon as the young Congressman was taking a Panama Canal cruise at the taxpayers' expense, urging him to get off the boat and fly back. Nixon did so—again at the taxpayers' expense—and proceeded to make more headlines by "discovering" the famed pumpkin papers hidden in the pumpkin patch of Whittaker Chambers' farm near Westminster, Maryland. Andrews and Nixon, with a keen sense of what makes news, had arranged to have them "discovered" in a place sure to make news.

From this springboard the young Congressman from Whittier, California, ran for the Senate in 1950 in a campaign which had so much Republican money to spend that Nixon billboards were even placed across the Mexican border. In the earlier primary, however, Nixon was so anxious for funds and so uninhibited as to where he got them that he accepted a $5,000 check from "Mystery Man" Henry Grunewald, relayed through GOP Senate Committee Chairman Owen Brewster of Maine. The campaign repeated the technique used against Congressman Voorhis. This time Congresswoman Helen Gahagan Douglas, Democrat, was made to appear a Communist. She had sponsored such constructive legislation as the Douglas-McMahon bill creating the Atomic Energy Commission and the public-housing slum-clearance bill. She had voted for such anti-Communist measures as the Marshall Plan and military aid for Korea.

Nixon had voted against them. Nevertheless, Mrs. Douglas was made to appear the Communist, Nixon the heroic battler against Communism.

Mr. Nixon won, and thereafter he became a bulwark of the conservative, isolationist wing of the Senate. The year 1951 even found Senator Nixon an eager-beaver leaper aboard the Douglas MacArthur band wagon just at the time Governor James H. Duff of Pennsylvania was starting the boom for MacArthur's onetime subordinate, Dwight D. Eisenhower, then commander of SHAPE in Paris.

"What party does Eisenhower belong to?" Nixon asked when Duff tried to enlist the young Senator's support.

Just one year later, Nixon had accomplished the political miracle of jumping from the MacArthur band wagon to second place on the Eisenhower Presidential ticket. The jump was not entirely spontaneous. It had been carefully arranged once again by Dick's good friend, Bert Andrews of the New York *Herald Tribune*, who had sold Governor Thomas E. Dewey of New York and Paul G. Hoffman, the Marshall Plan Administrator, on the idea that Nixon was an up-and-coming young senator who could give a boost to foreign aid and who would be effective in stirring up anti-Communist ammunition against Adlai Stevenson. Nixon, Andrews argued, had investigated Hiss, while Stevenson had submitted a sworn affidavit supporting Hiss. The somewhat bewildered military man who had been catapulted from Paris to the smoke-filled rooms of Chicago to run for President took Dewey and Hoffman at their word. He accepted young Mr. Nixon as his Vice-Presidential running mate. At that time Nixon was only thirty-nine years old, had served only two terms in the House and eighteen months in the Senate, had voted for F.D.R., and had almost no background in the Republican Party. In seven short years he had jumped from lieutenant in the Navy to become the second-youngest Vice-President in American history. He accomplished the jump largely by keeping a wet finger in the wind.

As Vice-President of the United States, Richard M. Nixon reversed himself once again. He worked for foreign aid. He championed the rights of the Negro. As a Senator he had voted against civil rights. But now he stiffened Eisenhower's backbone when the President wavered over the Little Rock crisis. He antagonized his old conservative friends in the Senate by moving to scrap the filibuster and by championing a more drastic civil-rights bill than was finally adopted. And, having once voted for the Taft-Hartley bill, he made a rightabout-face and championed labor. Going to Rio de Janeiro to attend the inauguration of the President of Brazil, he made a prolabor speech—the Brazilian President having been elected by a labor party—which dumfounded Bill Daugherty, head of the Letter Carriers Union, who was a co-delegate. After he had won fame in the 1952 Presidential campaign as the champion of the Republican cloth coat, his wife acquired a coat of Afghan lamb pelts, a white ermine stole, and a mink stole. And having been elected to the Senate with benefit of generous funds from the China lobby, Nixon proceeded to tell the President of Indonesia and the Prime Ministers of India and Burma that he was in favor of recognizing Red China.

Perhaps no politician in recent years has changed the complexion of his political philosophy more rapidly and more successfully than Richard M. Nixon. A less friendly press would have torn him to pieces. The benign press of Mr. Eisenhower's first term smiled.

The life of Richard M. Nixon has oscillated from passage through turmoil to skating on very thin ice. He has managed both with amazing dexterity. From each brush with political death, after each agonizing gaze down into the chasm of political suicide, he has come back unperturbed and unscathed. Young men with less hardened nerves would have suffered a breakdown. Not Mr. Nixon.

His conflicts, his skirmishes, his near-escapes from political accident give important insight into his character and help answer the question as to whether this young man could lead his country back up the hill to power and prestige.

One early and quite significant conflict revolved around Nixon's law firm and a Rumanian refugee, Nicholae Malaxa, who turned up in the United States as the representative of a Communist trade mission but remained to promote a seamless pipe company, the Western Tube Corporation, in California. Significantly, Malaxa sought out Nixon's home town, Whittier, to become the site of his proposed factory, and Nixon's law partner, Thomas Bewley, to become secretary of this new $12,000,000 company. The Nixon law firm also became its attorneys.

The significance of this unusual association lay in the fact that Mr. Malaxa, as a prominent Rumanian industrialist, had been a stanch supporter of the fascist, anti-Semitic Iron Guard; had co-operated with the Nazis when his country was occupied by the Germans; and had gone into partnership with Albert Goering, brother of Hermann Goering. Subsequently, when the Communists took over Rumania,

Malaxa showed great dexterity and great lack of principle by winning their support. He was the only Rumanian industrialist whose factories were given back to him by the Communist regime. He even got himself appointed a member of a Communist trade mission to the United States. In New York he purchased jewelry from Tiffany's to send to Anna Pauker, then Communist Prime Minister of Rumania. And by an amazing combination of good fortune, political pull, or what have you, he was able to get $2,400,000 out of the Communist administration in Rumania. It was with this money that he proposed to erect a factory in Nixon's home town.

Despite Nixon's charges against Congresswoman Helen Gahagan Douglas and Congressman Jerry Voorhis that they associated with pro-Communists, and despite Nixon's claim to have divorced himself from his law firm, the young Senator from California became the champion and, in effect, secret, unofficial lobbyist for Malaxa in Washington. His friend Senator Pat McCarran of Nevada and his friend Congressman Pat Hillings of California obligingly included Malaxa's name in a bill to give permanent residence in the United States. The bill passed the Senate, but when it got to the House of Representatives, Congressmen Francis E. Walter of Pennsylvania, Democrat, and Kenneth B. Keating of New York, Republican, struck out Malaxa's name. Nixon's friend Congressman Hillings did his best to replace it, without success.

This was not all. On May 16, 1952, Malaxa's company applied to the National Production Authority for a certificate of necessity to build its seamless-tube factory in Whittier. A certificate of necessity is a highly prized, not easy to obtain specification that a plant is so important to the defense of the nation that it can write off the cost of construction in five years. The National Production Authority, however, did not consider Malaxa's Western Tube Corporation essential to national defense. No tax-reduction certificate was granted.

At this point Senator Nixon, whose law partner had been retained, got busy. He wrote a letter on the stationery of the Senate Labor and Public Welfare Committee to Manley Fleischmann, NPA administrator, telling him how essential Malaxa's plant was to the nation. To strengthen his position, Nixon shrewdly went to his senior colleague from California, William Knowland, and had him sign the letter also. The letter did the trick. Malaxa's application for tax reduction had lain in the NPA files for four months. After receipt of the letter, the NPA acted within a few days. The company organized by the man who had been on intimate terms with the Communist regime of

Rumania, and who had been the partner of Hermann Goering's brother, got a 60 per cent tax write-off on $10,299,667. This was in 1952.

Mr. Nixon denied having anything to do with his law firm. But photographs of the directory of the Bank of America Building, where his law firm has offices, showed that in 1952 Nixon, his partner, Bewley, and Western Tube occupied rooms 607-608-609. The Whittier telephone directory for the year 1952 also showed all three as having the same phone number. A lackadaisical press never bothered to dig out the facts regarding Mr. Nixon's pro-Communist friend; and Senate committees never investigate fellow Senators.

Another crisis in the life of Richard M. Nixon pertained to an influence peddler who had managed his election campaigns and is credited with devising the strategy of smearing political opponents, Murray Chotiner. A less versatile young man than Mr. Nixon would have been wounded by this association; he was not.

Murray Chotiner is the lawyer whom the petty criminals of the Los Angeles underworld seek out when they get into trouble. Almost every gambler and bookmaker in the Los Angeles area has retained Murray Chotiner or his brother at one time or another. The court records between 1949 and June 1, 1952, include 221 underworld cases handled by the Chotiners. The record also shows that they were extremely successful in getting the Los Angeles underworld off with light fines or suspended sentences.

Murray Chotiner came into the life of young Richard Nixon when Nixon first ran for the House of Representatives. Chotiner was credited with devising the brilliant idea of having Liberty Belles or Minute Women or paid telephone operators call voters in the district to ask, "Did you know that Congressman Voorhis had Communist sympathies? As a patriotic citizen, I thought I should warn you." Before questions could be asked, the caller hung up. The cost of this campaign was partly offset by none other than Mickey Cohen, notorious Los Angeles underworld czar, who got to know Chotiner when Nixon rented headquarters in a building owned by Mickey.

When Mr. Nixon came to Washington, Mr. Chotiner also came to Washington. On one important occasion he even came ahead of him. On January 4, 1953, Chotiner sent a check for $1,500 to the Statler Hotel in Washington as down payment for twenty-five rooms for Nixon's inaugural guests. From that point on, Chotiner made Nixon's office on Capitol Hill his office. He wrote letters "on behalf of Vice-

President Nixon" and was made associate director of the "Len Hall Campaign School" of the Republican National Committee. He lectured on campaign tactics to forty-eight Republican state chairmen just before they went to Denver to ask Eisenhower to run again. Between June 1, 1954, and January 23, 1956, he was paid $5,085 in expenses by the Republican National Committee.

A man this close to the Vice-President could not have operated without the co-operation of the Vice-President. Nevertheless, in 1956 the public suddenly discovered that Mr. Chotiner was using this position of prestige and power in exactly the same manner as John Maragon had used his position close to General Harry H. Vaughan, military aide to President Truman. The difference was that Maragon went to jail. Chotiner did not. Furthermore, he was far more successful. His operations were nothing short of amazing. He was able to intervene directly with Sherman Adams at the White House on behalf of his client, North American Airlines, and Mr. Adams, in turn, intervened with the Civil Aeronautics Board and thereafter reported in detail back to Mr. Chotiner. Mr. Chotiner also became the attorney for Sam and Herman Kravitz, clothing manufacturers blacklisted for cheating the Army and in serious tax trouble. Though the Kravitzes operated in New Jersey, they reached all the way across the continent to Beverly Hills, California, to hire an attorney with power in high places. Mr. Chotiner also became potent in switching TV licenses away from highly qualified applicants recommended by FCC attorneys, to his political friends in California. He also became attorney for the National Research Company. This firm was under serious scrutiny by both the Secret Service and the Federal Trade Commission for using a spread-eagle insignia similar to the seal of the United States to give the impression it was a government agency; nevertheless it continued to operate with the protection and counsel of Vice-President Nixon's former campaign manager.

Most interesting of all, Mr. Chotiner turned up as attorney for Marco Reginelli, notorious czar of the South Jersey numbers racket, previously listed by Truman's Attorney General, James P. McGranery, for deportation as a racketeer. Reginelli had a long record of larceny, receiving stolen goods, conspiracy to steal, and moral turpitude. But after he, too, reached from New Jersey across the continent to Beverly Hills, California, for a friend of Nixon's to represent him, he seemed to lead a charmed life. One charge against him involved transporting Mrs. Louise Abate from New Jersey to Florida in violation of the Mann Act. Mrs. Abate was subpoenaed to testify against Reginelli. One day later she was found dead. Because of the suspicious circumstances, the U.S. Attorney in Atlantic City, Raymond Del Tuffo, called in the FBI. The FBI promptly asked the Justice Department in Washington for authority to investigate, and although J. Edgar Hoover's request for jurisdiction was marked "Important and Urgent—Rackets," his letter was delayed inside the Justice Department until it was too late to collect evidence. The letter went to Rex Collings, chief of the general-crimes section, the man whom Murray Chotiner called upon when he intervened at the Justice Department on behalf of Reginelli. The letter was routed from Collings to Dave Luce, assistant to Warren Olney, in charge of the criminal division. Some place in between, the letter, despite the markings "Important and Urgent—Rackets," was lost.

Collings and Luce are both from California. Both were appointed on the recommendation of Vice-President Nixon.

The Vice-President at this point did not rise up in righteous wrath to demand the dismissal or the investigation of Luce and Collings. Nor did he disassociate himself from or disavow Mr. Chotiner. Instead, when a Senate committee chairmaned by Senator John L. McClellan of Arkansas sought to investigate Murray Chotiner's operations, Nixon's friends on the committee went out of their way to protect Chotiner. The same committee had excoriated John Maragon, General Harry Vaughan, Truman's military aide, and Colonel James Hunt, the five-per-center of Truman's day. It had made headlines in developing gifts of deep freezes and a mink coat. Later Senator McClellan was to make more headlines investigating the Teamsters Union and various labor officials. But when the campaign manager for Vice-President Nixon came before his committee, the Senator from Arkansas looked down benignly and assured Mr. Chotiner, "The chair will not require you to go further to say that the government was involved and had an interest in the litigation of the subject matter of your being retained."

When Robert F. Kennedy, the committee's counsel, sought to cross-examine Chotiner regarding his visits with government officials and the pressure he had used in protecting Reginelli from deportation, another friend of Nixon's objected.

"You're embarking on a fishing expedition," Senator McCarthy told Kennedy.

"No details," ruled Chairman McClellan, who in other cases had been fierce and unrelenting in his cross-examination of witnesses.

Thus did the Senate committee charged with investigating influence in government probe the influence peddler who had used the office of the Vice-President to write hundreds of letters stating, "I am writing you on behalf of Vice-President Nixon."

There was a very good reason why Joe McCarthy went to bat for Nixon. He owed him a heavy debt of gratitude, dating back to the early days of the Eisenhower Administration when Harold Stassen had publicly put McCarthy where he belonged in the controversy over Greek ships. Stassen had stated that it was not the job of a United States Senator, even Joe McCarthy, to make executive agreements with a foreign power or foreign shipowners. This was the job of the State Department. It was the first time anyone in the Eisenhower Administration had dared tangle with Joe McCarthy, and when Stassen rapped him over the knuckles Mr. Nixon promptly intervened. Nixon arranged a luncheon between McCarthy and John Foster Dulles, following which Mr. Dulles issued a public statement defending McCarthy. In the end it was Stassen who got spanked.

This occurred at a time when it was obvious that Eisenhower must have, and needed to have, a showdown with the rambunctious, irresponsible Senator from Wisconsin. Governor Dewey had advised Eisenhower, even during the 1952 election campaign, that he could not appease McCarthy, that an open break must come, and the sooner the better. Yet time after time Mr. Nixon intervened to prevent that break. When Eisenhower delivered a forthright speech at Dartmouth University, criticizing bookburning at American overseas libraries, and the Voice of America was about to broadcast that speech, suddenly Mr. Nixon intervened. Rushing to the White House, he stopped the Voice of America broadcast. He even persuaded the President to issue a statement that his Dartmouth speech meant no reflection on the junior Senator from Wisconsin.

Even after McCarthy had publicly excoriated John Foster Dulles and started to blast the Army which had produced the President of the United States, Nixon continued to appease McCarthy. It was he who arranged the secret chicken luncheon in the Senate at which Secretary of the Army Robert T. Stevens was summoned before a select group of pro-McCarthy Republicans and told to go back to the Pentagon and issue a statement apologizing to McCarthy.

The American public will not soon forget the Army-McCarthy hearings which followed. They will probably not forget the setback McCarthy gave to U.S. foreign policy, to the U.S. Army, and to the scientists of the nation. But they have forgotten the manner in which

Richard M. Nixon started McCarthyism back in California and stanchly upheld McCarthy's hand until the time he was censured by the Senate. McCarthy's life after that censure was not a happy one. He used to walk around the Capitol, a forlorn figure, a sheaf of press handouts under his arm, trying to persuade newsmen to use them. When Nixon addressed a big Republican rally in Milwaukee in the 1956 campaign, Joseph R. McCarthy, the Senator from Wisconsin, sidled into a seat on the platform along with other Milwaukee dignitaries—until Nixon's aides spotted him and hustled him out of the hall. A few minutes later, newspapermen found Joe sitting on the curb outside the auditorium weeping bitterly. Even his old friend Dick Nixon had deserted him.

Dwight D. Eisenhower had swallowed his compunctions about becoming a politician and had settled down to whistle-stopping across the United States with the verve and gusto of Harry Truman when suddenly on September 18, 1952, a bombshell hit his campaign train. It was learned that the man who aspired to be Vice-President of the United States, Richard M. Nixon, had received a personal expense fund of $18,235 from a "millionaires' club" in California. News of the bombshell percolated to candidate Eisenhower gradually. Passing through Des Moines, he might have read the news on page 8 of the Des Moines *Tribune*. Even if Eisenhower read the papers, which he does not, he would have had difficulty reading this sensational news story. It was buried. That night in Omaha he might have read the story in the Omaha *World Herald*, but he would have had to look at the very last page, and even then he would have received the impression that Mr. Nixon was the recipient of a trust fund from some admiring supporter. The headline read: "Beneficiary of Trust Fund."

Late that evening in Omaha the Eisenhower staff huddled in the rear end of the campaign train to decide what they should do about the bombshell. Candidate Eisenhower slept serenely. Not until next morning was the unpleasant news broken to him that the model young man of America had received over $18,000 to pay for his personal expenses while a senator in Washington. Both Ike and the worried advisers who huddled in Omaha began to wonder whether they should not have thought twice before picking a Vice-Presidential candidate who was only thirty-nine years old, had served in the Senate only eighteen months and in the House of Representatives only two terms, and had virtually no background in the Republican

Party. Fortunately for Nixon, they did not know that night in Omaha that he had also voted for Franklin D. Roosevelt, or they might have dumped him from the ticket altogether.

If there had been a careful investigation of Mr. Nixon, however, his Republican sponsors would have found some interesting financial developments which the average American citizen is not able to accomplish without benefit of either a personal expense fund, leftover campaign funds, or some outside financial help.

They would have found, for instance, that one year after Nixon was elected to the House of Representatives in 1946 the family bought a farm in York County, Pennsylvania. The farm was purchased in the name of Nixon's father and mother, price not known, and for a while Nixon used it for weekend trips from Washington. York County is probably the wealthiest farm area in the United States.

The Nixon family back in California had operated a grocery store, and as their son branched out in national politics they branched out with an adjacent restaurant and a U.S. post office. Though young Congressman Nixon was a Republican, he was able to wangle out of the Truman Administration a substation post office located right inside his father's grocery store. The senior Nixon drew a salary of only $600 a year, but the post office helped to entice customers into the store.

A few blocks down Whittier Boulevard, brother Don Nixon opened a swank new drive-in restaurant, replete with palm trees, an orange grove, and tables under the grove. As they drove in, customers gave their orders through a microphone, then picked up the food and took it out under the orange trees. The setup must have cost well over $100,000. The Nixon drive-in was begun when Richard was still a senator in Washington, but after he became Vice-President his brother Don suddenly seemed able to borrow money from all sorts of people and started four different restaurants. The expansion was so rapid that in 1957 he went into bankruptcy owing his creditors $380,905.87. Politics, it seemed, was a big help in borrowing money, but not much help toward business efficiency.

As a senator, young Mr. Nixon acquired a modest California bungalow in Whittier, and at about the same time a bungalow in Florida for his parents, plus a house in Washington for which he paid $41,000. It was this house, in the exclusive Westmoreland section of the nation's capital, which attracted considerable attention immediately after the public learned that their Vice-Presidential candidate was the recipient of a personal expense fund. Mr. Nixon hastened to explain that no part of the expense fund had gone to the purchase of the house and that it was heavily mortgaged.

The facts are, however, that prior to making this statement Mr. Nixon had confided to Peter Edson that without his expense fund he would not have been able to buy his home in Washington. Major General Burr Johnson, U.S. Army, retired, who sold Nixon the $41,000 home, stated that he received $20,600 in cash, which at that time was necessary under home-finance regulation X. What Mr. Nixon has never satisfactorily explained was how he was able to produce $20,600 in cash at the same time he had purchased another house in California and at a time when Mrs. Nixon, writing in *The Saturday Evening Post* September 6, 1952, just two weeks before the expense fund came to light, reported that her husband was so broke sometimes "there wasn't enough money to buy stamps to mail campaign literature." She referred, of course, to 1946. Yet with a Congressman's salary then only $12,500 and with two children to support, it would have taken a financial wizard to accumulate enough cash to be able to buy two houses and pay a cash deposit of $20,600 on one of them. When Nixon first came to Washington he paid $92 a month for a two-bedroom apartment. In further contrast, he has now parlayed his $41,000 home to a $70,000, twenty-two-room mansion overlooking Glover Parkway, furnished with so many gifts from foreign potentates that he even puts oriental rugs on the porch.

These are some of the financial facts in the background of Mr. Nixon which the Republicans who nominated him for Vice-President did not know about and which a complacent electorate in 1952 never did investigate.

Adlai Stevenson, during the 1952 campaign, made public his complete photostated income-tax returns. Newspapermen were allowed to scrutinize every detail, every deduction. Eisenhower did not do this. He selected portions of his returns and gave out a summarized financial statement. Mr. Nixon did even less. He gave a glamourized television report to the nation purporting to bare his financial breast. But to this day he has never permitted the press to see his tax returns. In the telecast he stated that his personal expense fund had been cleared by the law firm of Gibson, Dunn & Crutcher, but he did not mention the fact that this law firm also represented some of Nixon's biggest and most active donors. It was not unprejudiced. He also stated that the Price Waterhouse accounting firm had checked his expense fund and given him a clean bill of health. It happens that

Price Waterhouse got caught with such amazing discrepancies in checking the account of McKesson & Robbins drug company that they were forced to pay the company's stockholders $500,000 because of their oversight. In auditing the Nixon fund, Price Waterhouse appeared to be more careful. In the fine print of their statement, they noted they had not had time to examine all of the Nixon funds.

Mr. Nixon's self-examination with the help of self-appointed lawyers and self-appointed accountants in a coast-to-coast television broadcast was one of the most carefully prepared in political history. He rehearsed for a full day. All of the techniques he had learned as a major in public speaking at Whittier College, all of the gimmicks known to the television trade (supplied by three experts from the network) were brought into play.

It was a courageous broadcast, somewhat like Nixon's subsequent encounter with anti-American mobs in Venezuela. On the outcome of the broadcast depended his political life. Yet the cards were heavily stacked in his favor. Television technique and the anti-Truman temper of the times being what they were, the young candidate could not fail. No political broadcast, not even Madison Avenue's highest-rated commercial programs, got a bigger audience than that to which the future Vice-President reported on that September night in the heat of the 1952 campaign. General Eisenhower had announced in advance that he would listen carefully. He did. It was known, of course, what his reaction was to be. It mattered not that Mr. Nixon talked little about his finances, more about the cloth coats and his little dog. General Eisenhower promptly pronounced it a complete justification and flew to Wheeling, West Virginia, to embrace Mr. Nixon and welcome him back to his "clean as a hound's tooth" campaign. Mr. Nixon, flying from California to Wheeling, exhibited no joy over the necessity of taking the long trip. As the plane touched at the Wheeling airport, he groused to newspapermen, "This guy makes me fly clear across the United States." A minute later photographers snapped the two men in warm embrace.

More conflicts of interest have plagued the Eisenhower Administration than that of any other President in American history. A conflict of interest is when a government official puts himself in the position of working both for his own pocketbook and for the taxpayers. The founding fathers made it clear that a public servant cannot serve two masters. He cannot serve both himself and the public.

Ever since Senator Burton of Kansas was convicted of taking a fee from a constituent for handling a claim against the Post Office Department and resigned on June 4, 1906, the conflict-of-interest laws have been enforced with a fair degree of severity. But with the advent of the Eisenhower Administration they have not been enforced at all. High official after high official, from Secretary of the Air Force Harold Talbott to Sherman Adams, has been found on the payroll of private companies or benefiting financially from private sources at the same time they were being paid by the government. But none has been prosecuted. One reason: It would have been almost impossible, certainly inconsistent, to prosecute them when the Vice-President of the United States had been guilty of similar conflict.

During the Eisenhower Administration also there arose two important questions of whether the government should levy taxes upon a private fund spent on behalf of an individual. One was the case of Harry Bridges, the West Coast longshoreman leader, whose union and friends contributed money to fight his legal battles. The other was the case of James Hoffa, head of the Teamsters Union, whose union and friends also contributed money to fight his legal battles. After some hesitation, the Administration decided to tax Bridges and Hoffa for these funds. The hesitation was due to the fact that the Vice-President of the United States also received a fund contributed by people outside the government, for which he was not taxed.

The reason the laws of the United States forbid any private receipt of funds by a member of Congress is obvious. A senator or Congressman is supposed to represent all of his constituents. He is not supposed to represent one group which can afford to pay him privately. That is also why campaign contributions must be publicly registered. Thus, if a senator does vote for a group which contributes to his election, at least the public has a way of knowing it. But when money is paid secretly to a senator after his election, it amounts to a private subsidy by a private group to get that senator to vote for them, not for all the people. And when that senator performs specific favors for the individuals who pay him it is clearly a criminal offense.

In the rush of sympathy for Mr. Nixon which followed his dramatic television discourse, a lenient and one-sided press, with a few exceptions, never bothered to dig into the favors which Mr. Nixon had performed for those who contributed to his personal fund. The favors were many.

There was, first of all, the fact that Mr. Nixon's office intervened vigorously with the Justice Department to secure a $500,000 tax refund from the government for Dana Smith, the lawyer who collected the $18,235.

There was also the case of Mr. Dana Smith's gambling losses totaling $4,200 at the gaming tables of the Club Sans Souci in Havana. He paid his loss by check, then stopped payment on the check. Norman Rothman, manager of Sans Souci, then sued. Whereupon Senator Nixon wrote a letter to no less than the American Ambassador to Cuba, asking the Ambassador to intercede officially on behalf of Mr. Smith. Gambling is strictly out of bounds for an American envoy. He is charged with representing the United States of America on problems of a much higher level. The Ambassador informed Senator Nixon that there was nothing he could do about Mr. Smith's gambling debt.

There was also the case of two California oilmen, Tyler Woodward of Southern California Petroleum and William O. Anderson, who filed application for a lease to explore for oil on a military reservation, Camp Roberts, California, in 1949. They found that oil exploration was not permissible because a private individual cannot lease oil land on U.S. military property.

In 1950 Richard M. Nixon was elected to the Senate. In 1951 Woodward and Anderson contributed to his personal expense fund. And in 1951 he introduced a bill, S-1029, which would permit private individuals to stake out oil leases on military property.

The public, of course, had no way of knowing what Senator Nixon's motives were in introducing the bill to permit private exploration of U.S. military lands. Nor had they any way of knowing who had contributed to his expense fund, or even that he had one.

The public also had no way of knowing what influenced Nixon's voting record in the Senate. That voting record is extremely important, because it is almost diametrically opposed to what Nixon, as Vice-President, professes to stand for today; and it is also almost diametrically opposed to the New Deal ideas of Franklin D. Roosevelt, for whom Nixon voted before he had to worry about the San Marino millionaires who contributed to his expense fund.

The roll call of those donors and the manner in which they were interested in Nixon's votes is worthy of some space here if we are to gauge the character and qualifications of the young man who may be called upon to lead the United States in the future.

The contributors to the Nixon fund were not popcorn peddlers.

They were among the biggest-bracket businessmen in California. Here is the roll call of the donors, with the voting record of the man they subsidized in the United States Senate:

Fred H. Bixby, president of Alamitos Land Co.; director of the Security First National Bank; founder of the Fire and Marine Insurance Co.; member of a family which owns tremendous areas in Long Beach and controls the Jotham Bixby Co. and A.M.E. Bixby Co.

J. Benton Van Nuys, president of the Van Nuys Building Co., Van Nuys Investment Co., La Hacienda Co., First Safe Deposit Co.

The real-estate men who donated to Nixon's secret fund were active in trying to obtain the removal of rent controls and blocking Taft-Act public housing for slum clearance in Los Angeles. Here is how their man, Senator Nixon, voted on these questions:

June 20, 1951—Voted to cut public housing from 50,000 units to 5,000 units.

June 4, 1952—Voted to shorten rent controls by four months.

June 5—Voted for the amendment to take rent control out of the hands of the federal government and let local communities vote on the imposition of rent controls in critical areas.

June 12—Introduced, with Senator Knowland, an amendment to the defense bill aimed at sidetracking public housing altogether.

Many of Senator Nixon's secret donors were also oilmen or oil-equipment manufacturers, including some with government contracts:

Herbert Hoover, Jr., president of United Geophysical, director of Union Oil and of Southern California Edison.

Earle M. Jorgensen, chairman of the Jorgensen Oil Co. and director of the Citizens National Trust.

Rodney S. Burkee, president of the Lane-Wells Co., Petro-Tech Service Co., Lane-Wells Canadian Co.; director of Petroleum Equipment Suppliers Association and Sells Surveys, Inc.

Earl B. Gilmore, president of the A. F. Gilmore Co. and Kerman Cattle Co.; director of Technical Crafts Co. and Gilmore and Nolan, Inc.

William B. Hubbard, president of Anselma Oil Co. and Realitos Oil Co.; director of Cherry Rivet Co.

Thomas P. Pike, president of Pike Drilling Co. and Casualty Insurance Co.

Frank Seaver, president of Hydril Co., Doheny Stone Drill Co. and Texford Manufacturing Co.

Leland K. Whittier, vice-president of Belridge Oil, Rodeo Land and Water; a director of Western Oil and Gas Association and the Farmers and Merchants National Bank.

Edward R. Valentine, vice-president of Fullerton Oil; a director of the California Portland Cement Co.

Arthur S. Crites, who has both oil and real-estate interests at Bakersfield.

R. R. Bush, a Pasadena oilman, Tyler Woodward and William O. Anderson.

Here is how Senator Nixon voted in Congress to uphold the interests of the above oilmen who contributed to his secret fund:

On August 21, 1951, he voted for the basing-point bill which the oil companies favored.

In September, 1951, he voted against cutting the oil-depletion allowance from 27½ per cent to 14 per cent.

His most active work for the oil companies, however, related to tidelands oil. Nixon even sent copies of tidelands-oil literature out under his own frank, despite the fact he claimed he used the secret expense fund to mail letters and thus save the taxpayers mailing expense.

Another group of secret donors to the Nixon personal expense fund were executives of milk companies. They included:

Thorkild Knudsen, president of the Knudsen Creamery.

Alford Ghormley, vice-president of Carnation Milk and president of the Carnaco Equipment Co.

J. W. McKenzie, of Arden's Milk and Valley Maid.

The Bixby family, which has big milk-products investments.

Here is how the young Senator who was subsidized by the above executives voted when it came to cheese and dairy products:

On the question of restricting cheese and dairy products from France, Denmark, and other NATO countries, Nixon lined up with the dairy interests. The State Department urged that the Senate vote with our NATO allies. It argued that the amount of cheese entering the United States from Western Europe was relatively small and that a vote against foreign cheese would be used as a battle cry by the Communists. In latter years Nixon, as Vice-President, has urged the import of goods from NATO countries, but as a senator he voted with the milk-products men who had contributed to his secret fund.

Quite a number of bankers and executives of building-and-loan associations also contributed to the Nixon fund, including:

W. Herbert Allen, vice-president of the Title Insurance and Trust Co.

Arthur S. Crites of Bakersfield, vice-president of the Bakersfield Home Building Association and secretary and director of the Kern County Mutual Building and Loan Association.

Walker Smith, president of Smith & Sons Investment Co., the Red River Lumber Co., and Shasta Forests.

Charles Howard, president of Howard Securities Co.

Robert E. Hunter, director of Citizens National Trust and Savings Bank and the Pacific Finance Co.

Hulet P. Smith, Arcadia Mortgage Co.

On banking problems also young Senator Nixon went right down the line for those who had contributed to his fund. When the Senate voted on proposals to plug some of the loopholes in the tax law, Nixon voted for an amendment which actually widened one loophole by permitting mutual savings banks and building-and-loan associations to exempt their reserves from taxation up to 10 per cent.

The excuse for the Nixon expense fund, as explained to the American public on his famed telecast, was to defray the cost of his office expenses, thus saving the taxpayers money. What the young Senator did not tell the public, however, was that on his income-tax returns he had claimed a deduction in 1951 for office expenses totaling $1,294.05 beyond the $2,500 tax-free allowance given him by the government. Part of this claim on his tax returns was for $600 for taking constituents to lunch. In Nixon's 1950 tax returns he also claimed a deduction of $1,471 for office expenses, part of which was $260 for constituents' lunches. Yet the Price Waterhouse audit of his expense fund for those same years listed "meetings and lunches at California hotels, $410"; also "meals, taxicab fares and parking charges paid for visitors, $382.52"—all paid from his personal expense fund.

Obviously, the Price Waterhouse audit and the Senator's income-tax returns were in serious conflict. If expenses were paid from a special fund, they should not have been deducted from his taxes. The public, however, never knew what Nixon's income-tax returns were, and to this day he has not made them public.

It would seem likely, however, in view of Nixon's voting record during his brief term in the Senate, that those who contributed did so not merely for the purpose of defraying the young Senator's expenses, but rather because they figured on receiving legislative dividends for themselves.

That is the unwritten record of the Nixon personal expense fund.

It was also the beginning of the long list of conflict-of-interest cases which plagued the Eisenhower Administration and brought political morality in the United States to a new low.

There has been a great deal of speculation in the public mind as to whether Prince Richard was truly the anointed heir apparent of King Ike. What the public hasn't known, however, is that there is even more speculation in the minds of both Richard and Ike.

The first dread doubt that Richard M. Nixon was not exactly the man to run with him for Vice-President crept into Eisenhower's mind on his campaign train that morning after the news of the Nixon personal expense fund broke in Omaha. And although the candidate went along with the arguments of his advisers that the team could not be disrupted, that the course of expediency was not to shake public confidence, nevertheless those doubts have occasionally come back to haunt the man who finally made the "clean as a hound's tooth" decision. Probably only Nixon himself knows that the President really meant it when he announced to a press conference that Nixon was to go out and chart his course.

There have been moments of great personal crisis for Nixon between the dramatic telecast which re-established his place in the confidence of the public and the summer of 1956 when he was finally renominated as Vice-President. One of these was on the night of September 24, 1955, when the President suffered his heart attack in Denver. Nixon spent that night at the home of his close friend William P. Rogers, now Attorney General, searching his soul as to what steps he should take as President of the United States. Nixon has categorically denied reports published subsequent to that all-night vigil that he sought to become Acting President during Eisenhower's illness. Nevertheless, the fact is that Sherman Adams took a special trip to the hospital in Denver to make sure that Nixon did not become Acting President, after a meeting in the office of the Secretary of the Treasury, George Humphrey, where it was decided that Nixon would preside over Cabinet meetings and over sessions of the National Security Council but would receive no other powers. This was a face-saving device. The Cabinet and those who really run the White House were determined that the Vice-President should make absolutely no progress toward the fulfillment of his great ambition to become President of the United States.

The public did not know it, but there were many weeks between Eisenhower's heart attack in September 1955 and the spring of 1956 when Richard M. Nixon had no idea that he would ever again become Ike's running mate. The lowest point in his personal doldrums came in January of 1956 when Eisenhower called him to the White House and told him he had decided to run again. He also said that he thought Nixon should consider carefully what he should do. He felt that Nixon should realize that it might be harder for him to run as Vice-President and therefore he should chart his course accordingly.

Mr. Nixon took this to mean that he was not particularly welcome on the Republican ticket. For one month he moped. For one month he felt the bottom had dropped completely out of his rosy plans for the future. All the work he had spent building his public relations, erasing the memory of the personal expense fund, all the studied moves to keep himself on the front pages of the papers week in and week out, seemed to have been in vain.

Then, by a strange quirk of circumstances, he was rescued by what frequently motivates Washington—a personal feud. There are no two men in Washington who hate each other more than Sherman Adams, ex-Governor of New Hampshire, later No. 2 man in the White House, and Senator Styles Bridges, ex-Governor of New Hampshire, later No. 2 Republican in the Senate. One was all-powerful at the lower end of Pennsylvania Avenue; the other was all-powerful at the Capitol end of Pennsylvania Avenue. Their personal animosity has been carried so far that on one occasion Senator Bridges sent word to the White House that Sherman Adams was not to present the President's views at a meeting of Congressional leaders. Eisenhower bowed to the Bridges ultimatum.

This feud, perhaps more than any other factor, clinched the renomination of Richard Nixon. The first primary of any state in the Union takes place in New Hampshire. In 1956 no one had paid much attention to New Hampshire. No one expected any real contest on the Republican ticket. But Nixon, who knows the impact of surprise strength, huddled in advance with the man who sways the Republican organization in New Hampshire—Senator Bridges. They were old friends. In addition, Bridges was delighted to do anything to help a man whom Sherman Adams disliked. The result was an overwhelming surprise, and, as far as the public knew, a completely impromptu write-in for Richard Nixon in New Hampshire.

Dwight D. Eisenhower is a man easily impressed by strength, especially political strength, and this just about clinched Nixon's position on the ticket. To clinch it further, however, Nixon telephoned long-distance to a carefully selected group of Republican state chairmen and Republican national committeemen. He told them that the President had advised him to chart his course; therefore he was taking political soundings as to what that course should be. Any politician is flattered at receiving a call from a Vice-President; the reaction was almost unanimous that Nixon should run. When he took this score sheet to the White House and showed it to Eisenhower, there wasn't much Ike could do except go along—at least publicly.

Behind the scenes, however, the clique in the White House who opposed Nixon had one other trump card up its sleeve. He was Harold Stassen of Minnesota. In the end he did not prove much of a trump. However, even Mr. Stassen, brash and audacious as he is, did not stick his neck out and oppose Nixon publicly without private encouragement. That encouragement came first from Sherman Adams and Milton Eisenhower, the President's brother, and later to a limited degree from the President himself.

That it was doomed to failure was a foregone conclusion. By that time Nixon had too many trump cards in his own hand. He had too carefully cultivated state leaders. He had too many powerful friends in the Senate. And as far as the public knew he had the support of Dwight D. Eisenhower. The public had no inkling that the President had any misgivings about his boy.

So Richard M. Nixon was swept to victory once again on the Eisenhower ticket. But the fact remains that Prince Richard is still uncertain as to just where he stands with King Ike. In late 1957, Nixon was talking to Don Cook of the New York *Herald Tribune*. "You'll be seeing the President before you go back to Paris," Nixon said. "Be sure to talk to him about the importance of my taking a trip to Europe."

Nixon also knew that whenever Eisenhower had called the roll of promising young Republican candidates for President, as he has frequently done at his stag dinners, Nixon's name was omitted. His close friend, Attorney General William Rogers, has been mentioned; also Ambassador Henry Cabot Lodge, Clifford P. Case, Senator from New Jersey, and George Craig, former commander of the American Legion and former Governor of Indiana; but not the Vice-President of the United States. It may have surprised the public, therefore, but it did not surprise Nixon when on April 30, 1958, President Eisenhower told his press conference, "Mr. Nixon and I are warm friends. I admire him and I respect him. Now, when it comes to the successor, as far as I am concerned, the candidate will be named by the Republican Party, and I submit that I think that there are a lot of darned good men that could be used."

The most important question about the future of Richard Nixon is whether he would be good for the United States or whether he is good only for Richard Nixon. Those who have observed him close up in Washington agree that he has performed a notable service for the United States on his good-will missions abroad—until he pushed his luck too far and went to South America. There he undid much of the good will he had built up elsewhere. Although he won for himself acclaim for his courage, he also publicized dramatically and unforgettably the mistakes that his Administration had made in an area where we are supposed to have not merely good friends but also good neighbors. The trip may have helped Nixon politically, but it hurt the United States internationally.

Mr. Nixon also served as a gadfly to the President and the Pentagon to spur the missile race with Russia on to greater speed. But when he failed to persuade Eisenhower to abandon soothing syrup and tell the people the facts, Mr. Nixon lapsed into soothing syrup himself.

Mr. Nixon's most surprising and spectacular leadership has been in fighting for civil rights. As a member of the Senate Labor and Public Welfare Committee, he was one of only three senators who voted to keep the civil-rights bill bottled up in committee. He did not even want the civil-rights bill to go to the Senate floor for free and open debate. Senators had to vote the bill out over his head. Yet as Vice-President he incurred the enmity of Old Guard Republicans, including his good friend, Senator Bridges of New Hampshire, when at the beginning of the Eighty-fifth Congress in January 1957, he ruled that the long-accepted Senate Rule 22, making filibusters easy, was unconstitutional. In preparing this ruling, he worked behind the scenes with such Senate Democratic liberals as Humphrey of Minnesota and Douglas of Illinois. "If you give the right answer," advised Humphrey, "it may make another Abraham Lincoln out of you." Nixon listened and gave the right answer. Later, when President Eisenhower wobbled regarding a firm stand at Little Rock, it was Nixon who urged the sending of U.S. troops. Six months later when a Congressman from the Deep South, Frank W. Boykin of Mobile, Alabama, chided Eisenhower over Little Rock, Nixon told him, "It was an absurd mistake." Maxwell Rabb, White House aide for minority groups, now resigned, was given the blame.

Richard Nixon has progressed a long way on what Democrats call his "road to maturity." But how much of this is an astute public-relations build-up? How much represents real change?

A Washington dowager sitting beside Dean Acheson, the former Secretary of State, at dinner gushed, "Oh, I can't help liking the new Mr. Nixon. He seems so changed."

"Madam," replied Acheson, "for five million dollars you can change the public impression of almost anyone."

It is true that a lot of money has been spent on Dick Nixon's public relations. It is also true that he himself has performed an amazing feat of creating the new Mr. Nixon. He has been able to make the public forget that it was he who drove some of our most noted scientists out of office; that no later than 1954 he removed the security clearance of Dr. Edward U. Condon, the man who speeded development of the hydrogen bomb by one year. Though he made headlines by talking about his wife's cloth coat and Democrats' mink coats, he has now been able to exhibit his wife in mink and ermine stoles without public repercussion. Though he had to have an unofficial expense fund as senator, he now has an official Vice-Presidential expense fund nine times as great as that of Harry Truman. He is allotted $101,925, which helps pay for a staff of thirteen, including a colonel, a major, and a press agent—compared with $11,460 spent by Truman, Henry Wallace, and John N. Garner as Vice-President. Though a member of the American Legion and a frequent speaker at veterans' rallies, he has managed to lull veterans into forgetting the fact that, as a member of the Senate Subcommittee on Veterans' Affairs, he had the worst attendance record of any senator. When real work for veterans was to be done, Nixon was not present.

Just how did Mr. Nixon accomplish this miracle of public relations? The answer is by securing the advice of some of the best brains on Madison Avenue and by using the power and prestige of the Vice-Presidency. When you attend Cabinet meetings you obtain inside news. This is a valuable commodity. You can leak it to the newspapermen who can do you the most good. When you are Vice-President, and especially when your President is in poor health, it's your job to meet visiting dignitaries. It's your job to dedicate buildings, lay cornerstones, open charity drives. This means that automatically your name and picture are on the front pages of newspapers three or four times a week. The Vice-President has other prerogatives. He can recommend diplomatic appointments.

It was not entirely accidental that Philip M. Klutznick, president of B'nai B'rith, was appointed a delegate to the United Nations, even though Klutznick is a Democrat. Earlier Klutznick had arranged to present Nixon the B'nai B'rith national award—an award which automatically wiped out the stigma cast upon Nixon when, in purchasing his house in restricted Westmoreland Hills, he signed a covenant promising never to resell to a Jew.

It is no accident that Nixon always celebrates his wife's birthday on St. Patrick's Day, though she was actually born the day before. Her birth certificate, filed in Ely, Nevada, shows that she was christened Thelma Catherine Ryan, born 3:25 A.M. on March 16. But, though Mrs. Nixon left the Catholic faith, the nickname "Pat" and the birthday on St. Patrick's Day is a matter which her husband does not overlook with the Irish vote.

It was no accident, furthermore, that Vice-President Nixon took with him on a trip through Asia a battery of press-association newsmen. When Adlai Stevenson took a similar trip, not one newspaperman accompanied him. Cable tolls are high from the Pacific and press associations do not like to report on the routine junketing of a Vice-President. However, Mr. Nixon has friends in very high press places. They sent their men with him to the Orient.

On that trip the Vice-President arrived in Djakarta, capital of Indonesia, where he was to be entertained by Ambassador Hugh S. Cumming, Jr. It was a hot and sticky day. The American Embassy is not air-cooled, and as Mrs. Cumming was preparing for the reception a battery of television men with klieg lights unloaded their equipment at the Embassy.

"I am sorry," said Mrs. Cumming, "but we are not taking television pictures here. You will have to go away. Your lights are entirely too hot." They departed.

Later, when Mr. Nixon arrived, Mrs. Cumming remarked that she had saved him quite an ordeal by sending the television crew away.

"What!" exclaimed Nixon. He rushed to the telephone and ordered the TV crew to return.

Thus has the new Mr. Nixon been made.

Perhaps the greatest tragedy in Nixon's life is the fact that he has so yearned to be President that he has continually kept a wet finger in the wind. It is perhaps symbolic that his favorite poem is Walt Whitman's "Captain, My Captain," written after the assassination of Abraham Lincoln. Unquestionably, in reaching for the Presidency, Nixon has developed new abilities, new experience. The new Mr.

Nixon is not all mere public-relations build-up. If he were in the White House, he would be a better negotiator than Eisenhower. He is more brilliant, more flexible, has a tireless physique which can withstand the strain of a summit conference. Eisenhower cannot. Nixon can think fast, make quick decisions. But would he be too hasty in those decisions? Would he, in these days when American bombers are flying daily across the Arctic, use the strategy he expounded to the American Society of Newspaper Editors in April, 1954—that of sending American troops to Indochina? Or would he rely on braggadocio and bombast as he did in his speech in Cincinnati one week later when he said, "We warned the Chinese Communists that if they make overt moves across into Indochina that they will run the risk of retaliation from the United States against China. Result: The possibility of that overt move by the Chinese Communists has been reduced very, very definitely." The Chinese, not taking Mr. Nixon seriously, continued to move into Indochina. They possess most of it today.

Or would Mr. Nixon revert to type and once again purge innocent scientists? He stated to the *National Review* on December 14, 1957, that he had changed his mind not one iota regarding the purge of Dr. Robert Oppenheimer from government. Or would Mr. Nixon expand on the tactic used at San Mateo, California, in 1954, when a heckler asked, "Tell us a dog story, Dick"? Nixon ordered his personal goons to throw the heckler out of the hall.

Despite his ability, despite his brilliance, despite his amazing aptitude for molding public opinion, the United States of America is accustomed to being led by men whose character has been steeled in the battle of issues, not polished by the veneer of Madison Avenue. As Nixon's colleague from California, Senator William F. Knowland, once remarked: "I do not consider a Pepsodent smile, a ready quip, an actor's perfection with lines, nor an ability to avoid issues, as qualifications for high office."

The winds of public opinion are fickle. The President of the United States cannot lead the United States by keeping a wet finger in the wind.

XX

WAR OR PEACE

THE AUTHORS BELIEVE that the American people are equal to any challenge—if they know the facts. The facts today are that we have lost the initiative for positive victory in war. But have we lost the initiative for peace? Not irrevocably. The fires of peace have burned low, and it will take the desperate ingenuity of a freezing man blowing life into the dying embers of his campfire to restore the warmth of peace to this divided world. However, it can be done. It is a foregone conclusion from the preceding pages that America must remain strong. We must be able to negotiate from strength. Today we can't. They have the missiles, we haven't. In war the simple axiom is still true, that the winner is the side that gets there firstest with the mostest.

Today we have to face the fact that if Russia launched a war against the United States first she would win. If she got the drop on the United States by one hour, she would wipe out all the industrial cities of the Middle West, the Capital of the United States, and the great seaports along the Atlantic seaboard. Our B-47's could retaliate with severe punishment of Russian cities, but by that time it might be too late to revitalize America for perhaps a decade, perhaps forever. The question we may well ask, therefore, is why does not the Kremlin use this striking power now? Why does it not follow the advice of Nikolai Lenin, father of the Russian Revolution, who prophesied that Communism would triumph only after a terrible war in which the capitalist nations made their last desperate stand? Why does not Premier Khrushchev precipitate that war now when he may well have the upper hand? What is the reason that the Kremlin still continues to harp on peace?

Charles E. Bohlen, before retiring as American Ambassador to the Soviet Union, wrote a report which gives the probable answer. He made two points. One he made with reservations, the other without. He reported, with reservations, that the leaders in the Kremlin did not want war. They did not want war, first because they feared that any showdown with the United States would be too costly in Russian life and Russian resources and might conceivably mean the end of civilization. Second, the leaders of the Kremlin did not want war because they felt that in the long haul they could win a cold war; they could capture the trade, the minds, the political allegiance of most of the people of Asia, Europe, and perhaps even Latin America. Time, they concluded, was on their side. Perhaps they depended upon the stupidity of American foreign policy, on our concentration on golf, ease, and tranquilizers.

Ambassador Bohlen also reported—and this without reservations—that the great mass of the Russian people did not want war. They had suffered too much in the last war, had been taught by their masters in the Kremlin to hate war. Therefore, Bohlen reported, if the Kremlin should reverse itself and decide on war, it would take many months of propaganda by the leaders of Russia to reverse the thinking of their people and prepare them for war. Thus the United States would have warning of what was to come.

Ambassador Bohlen's report was based upon the fact that no civilian population, without exception, suffered more during World War II than that of Russia. Although France, the Netherlands, Belgium, were overrun by armies of occupation, their conquest took a few short days. The Nazi armies penetrated deep into Russia, fighting most of the way. Behind lay a shambles. Twenty million Russians lost their lives through battle, disease, and starvation. The memory of such suffering is not easily forgotten.

And the Moscow radio has not permitted this to be forgotten. Week after week it has pounded home the hopes for peace, the danger of war. And though the objective has been to warn the Russian people against the United States and steel them for sacrifices, the effect has been to make the Russian people believe the Kremlin's own propaganda. The Moscow radio has been a two-edged sword.

John Foster Dulles and some of the military advisers accompanying President Eisenhower to the Geneva Conference in 1955 were fearful that the new smiles exchanged by the President, Bulganin and Khrushchev might make it difficult for the United States to secure future military appropriations. This was not the case. Military appropriations were cut by Eisenhower's own Budget Bureau and his own Secretary of the Treasury. On the other hand, the fact that President

Eisenhower was able to meet on a friendly basis the Soviet leaders at Geneva created great good will for the United States. It helped dispel the Soviet myth that the United States was hell-bent for war.

To Ambassador Bohlen's reports might be added other developments, some of them taking place since John Foster Dulles, for political reasons, transferred our ablest ambassador from Moscow. There is the fact that the more Russia pushes education and develops a new intelligentsia, the more the Russian people question war's futility. As Allen Dulles has indicated, it is impossible to educate men and women to think about physics and biology without opening their minds to politics and disarmament, justice and freedom. The restlessness of the students at Moscow University, the conversations between American and Soviet students, between American and Soviet professors, all point to the fact that education has been a two-way street. It has increased Soviet science, but it has also increased Russian desire to know more about, and be friendly with, the outside world.

Also add to Bohlen's peace appraisal the satellite countries, where we have a great potential reservoir of friendship and the Kremlin has a long history of unrest.

Finally, add to Ambassador Bohlen's report the fact Russia and the United States have been allies in two great wars, have never opposed each other in any major war, and for one hundred years enjoyed a period of friendly co-operation during which the Russian fleet once protected San Francisco and New York from the threat of the British fleet. Most historians have neglected this crucial chapter in the history of the Civil War. President Lincoln had sent Bayard Taylor with a personal letter to Foreign Minister Gorchakov at St. Petersburg, asking for help. Lincoln at that time was desperately afraid England and France would recognize the Confederacy. So it was secretly agreed between Lincoln and the Czar that in case of such recognition Russia would ally itself with the North and attack the British fleet. Part of the secret understanding was the purchase of Alaska by the United States at a price to include the naval expenses of the Russian government for helping to defend New York and San Francisco.

Early in the fall of 1863, six Russian warships under the command of Rear Admiral Popov anchored off San Francisco while six additional Russian warships under Rear Admiral Lisovski visited New York. Gertrude Ederle when she swam the English Channel, Van Cliburn when he returned from his musical triumphs in Moscow, Charles Lindbergh when he flew the Atlantic got no warmer reception in Manhattan than the crew and officers of the Russian fleet. They were wined and dined, taken to Niagara Falls, toasted in bourbon; they visited Meade's headquarters in Virginia, were given a grand ball in the Academy of Music and when they got drunk were discharged immediately by the New York police. The Army of the Potomac even took a day off while Mrs. Lincoln set tongues wagging in the North, in the South and in the capitals of Europe by drinking a toast to the Czar. Neither the people of the North nor those of the South knew why the Russian fleet remained all winter in American waters, though the chancelleries of Europe understood well.

Admiral Lisovski finally confided to Admiral Farragut that he was under sealed orders, to be broken only "in a contingency that has not occurred, namely if war broke out between the United States and foreign nations." In San Francisco Admiral Popov was quite frank. He handed a note to Confederate raiders which read as follows: "The undersigned is instructed to inform whom it may concern that the ships of the above-mentioned squadron are bound to assist the authorities of every place where friendship is offered them in all measures which may be deemed necessary by the local authorities to repel any attempt against the security of the place." Since the people of San Francisco were profuse in the friendship offered the Russian fleet, the warning to Confederate raiders was not lost.

Thus the North weathered the most crucial year of the Civil War, thanks to an alliance with Russia. Without that alliance, the United States today might be functioning under two separate governments.

The only permanent insurance the American people can have against war with a country where the decision to make war can be arrived at by a dozen men is the insurance of people—people who don't want to fight. As far as the people of the Soviet Union are concerned, the problem of the United States falls into two categories—the people of the satellite countries and the people of Russia. It was to isolate the people of the satellite countries and the people of Russia so they could not be influenced by outside opinion that Joseph Stalin erected the Iron Curtain. He wanted to keep the power to make war in his hands. He wanted to be able to control both Russian thought and satellite public opinion. He feared the reaction of the Soviet bloc's people if they were able to compare the standard of living of their Western neighbors with their own.

There have now been revolutionary changes both along the Iron

Curtain and behind the Iron Curtain, both in regard to the people of the satellite countries and the people of Russia. How great those changes are one of the authors* learned on two trips—one along the edge of the Iron Curtain in 1951, the other behind the Iron Curtain in 1958.

For several years I had been hammering home the idea that the Iron Curtain was the weakest point in the Soviet Union's defense. If its people must be protected from the outside world, I suggested, then its people must be taught to resent that protection. Its people must learn that their rulers had something to hide, something to fear from contacts with the outside world. For several years also I had been hammering home the idea that if we were to bring peace to the world we must have friendship among peoples.

Thus was conceived the idea of the friendship-freedom balloons which I proposed to various officials of the Truman Administration in 1948. I got kind words but no response. The most encouraging words came from General Omar Bradley, Chief of Staff of the Army, who said, "If you can win friends for us behind the Iron Curtain, then my boys can go fishing." Finally, in the winter of 1951 I took a trip along the Iron Curtain, from Turkey in the south to Berlin in the north. On that trip I not only inspected the Iron Curtain but tried to organize committees of Europeans who would undertake to sign leaflets urging friendship with the people behind the Iron Curtain.

I found the Iron Curtain to be not iron but barbed wire—a long straggling line of rusty barbed wire rolled into tangled skeins like the trenches of World War I or the beaches of Normandy and Salerno in World War II. The road leading to the Curtain passed the Roman wells built by the Emperor Hadrian and was paved with stone laid when he went that way. Suddenly the road ended. Ahead was an iron gate bearing that international English word known to every tongue, "Stop." Beyond was another gate slightly rusty and dilapidated, bearing the words "Bulgaria" in both Roman and Cyrillic letters. This was the Iron Curtain. The gate was the outpost called Serhad, which in Turkish means both "the frontier" and "the neckline where one's head is chopped off."

Alongside the gate was a series of blockhouses—one on the Bulgarian side, a bit shabby, with a few windowpanes missing; and on the Turkish side two blockhouses, one near the gate, one set back

* The personal experiences referred to in this chapter are those of Mr. Pearson.

from the gate and connected with a series of trenches. I climbed stairs inside the thick-walled parapet to a tower from which a Turkish soldier stood scanning the landscape through field glasses. The sturdy walls, pierced with rifle slots, looked down on nothing more than winter barley fields, a team of water buffaloes pulling a John Deere disk drill—a tribute to the Marshall Plan—and a long barricade of barbed wire extending north. A herd of buffaloes grazing in Bulgaria did not know the difference between communism and democracy, between Russianized Bulgaria and American-aided Turkey. Aside from a Bulgarian guard in the tower on the opposite side who watched us with field glasses and occasionally ran to a telephone to notify headquarters about our party, there was peace and quiet on both sides of the Iron Curtain. It was so peaceful that two Turkish officers and I pulled our chairs out onto a stone platform just six feet away from the gate separating Turkey from Bulgaria. The weather was cold, but the sun was warm and we sat in the sunshine drinking coffee in full view of the Communist guards who peered down through rifle slots in their watchtower a few feet away and probably pondered, as we did, the whys and wherefores of the artificial barrier separating peoples who wanted peace. We lingered in the sun, talking about the days when the army of Sultan Bajazet battled with the armored knights of the Polish King and the Grand Marshal of France in the days when the Crusades swept across these same barley fields before the gates of Adrianople. For hundreds of years men had fought in a land which wanted peace, to control this gateway to the Bosporus. And still there was no peace.

North from Turkey I passed along the Albanian frontier. I had lived on that frontier after World War I, had traveled back and forth between Albania and Yugoslavia without interruption. But now the frontier was guarded as no other in Europe. Truckloads of Yugoslav troops passed in the night. We were stopped for passport identification every ten kilometers. Tito wanted no intercourse with pro-Russian Albania. The Iron Curtain was rigid and impenetrable.

Farther north, in Berlin, a city cut in two by the Iron Curtain, its penetration was a daily occurrence. Commuters between East Berlin crossed to West Berlin by streetcar, by taxi, or on foot. I walked across and had my picture taken under a signpost at the juncture of "Stalin Allee" and "Lenin Allee."

During this trip I talked to members of the Turkish Parliament and members of the Yugoslav Cabinet, to distinguished citizens in Germany, France, and England, about the idea of forming a committee of private citizens to send messages of friendship behind the Iron Curtain. I emphasized the importance of winning the people of both the satellite countries and Russia over to the idea of peace; and proposed that if there was no other way to communicate we should take advantage of the winds, which always blow in the upper altitudes from west to east, to send messages by balloon. I pointed out the importance of dramatizing the existence of an Iron Curtain to the people behind it.

I got nowhere. There seemed to be a fear on the part of people of Western Europe against antagonizing Moscow. The people of Turkey feared retaliation. They were too close to the border. The people of Germany likewise. Those I talked to in France and England weren't particularly interested. Only in Yugoslavia did I get a firm pledge of co-operation.

Six months later, however, I came back to Germany and, with the help of the Committee for Free Europe, finally began the first propaganda penetration of the Iron Curtain. Camped in a wheat field in Bavaria about a mile from the Czechoslovakian border on August 15, 1951, we released several thousand balloons filled with friendship messages to the people of Czechoslovakia. The messages urged no one to revolt. They merely told the people of Czechoslovakia that the people of the West had not forgotten them. And because we knew Americans were resented behind the Iron Curtain, the messages were signed by such international organizations as the Federation of Women's Clubs, the AFL-CIO for Canada and Latin America, and the International Federation of Free Journalists.

It was cold and drizzly in that German wheat field. The Czech border looked grim and foreboding. A battery of young Germans stuffed 2,200 leaflets into each balloon, held the balloon over a hydrogen tank until inflated, slipped a rubber band over the intake, and released the balloon. By gauging the winds, we were able to time the descent so the balloons dropped their messages in the more populated parts of the land. At first there was no reaction from behind the Iron Curtain. Complete silence greeted our barrage of friendship. Then as some 15,000,000 leaflets floated down on 12,000,000 people in an area no bigger than Virginia and West Virginia, suddenly there was a political explosion. Premier Zapotocky appeared on the floor of Parliament to denounce the messages. The magazine *Tvorba* carried a front-page cartoon showing Harry Truman releasing balloons. President Truman, of course, had nothing to do with it. Some of his people didn't even approve of the operation. But the Czech reaction, both public and private, indicated that we had accomplished the first purpose of our mission—reminding the Czech people that their government had erected an artificial barrier to prevent them from having contact with the outside world.

As the barrage of leaflets continued to Czechoslovakia and other satellite countries, we learned from refugees that some of the leaflets were placed in baggage racks on railroad trains, some tacked on telephone poles, and some even tacked up surreptitiously on government bulletin boards. Official Czech protests were based upon the claim that the balloons were a hazard to air travel; but probably the real reason for the protests was the fact that the governments behind the Iron Curtain were put in the ludicrous position of boasting the benefits of communism, yet simultaneously refusing to let their people compare those benefits with those of the Western world.

I do not know whether the 200,000,000 leaflets rained down behind the Iron Curtain during the ensuing years had anything to do with the eventual lifting of the Iron Curtain. Perhaps it helped. Probably, however, the Iron Curtain was lifted chiefly because the Communist regimes became more confident of their own success. Having achieved amazing scientific victories, having scored the greatest achievement in education in modern times, and having increased the production of consumer goods, they were not afraid to let their people compare notes with the outside world.

Seven years after releasing the first friendship balloon to the people of Czechoslovakia, I flew into Prague without a passport visa. It was May 1958. And in contrast to that August night on the border of Czechoslovakia seven years before when only an occasional refugee slipped between the sentries, no visa is now required for transit travelers through Czechoslovakia. However, not wanting to spend the night at the International Hotel at the airport, I asked special permission to go into Prague. This was an unusual request, but it was granted.

When I looked across the hotel courtyard next morning, I saw hanging in almost every window of the Hotel Alkorn the number-one badge of the traveling American—drip-dry shirts. American tourists were on the march behind the Iron Curtain.

In Bucharest I had been invited to address the Union of Rumanian Journalists. This in itself was something of a miracle. Or perhaps it was an indication of confidence in Communist progress and also of Iron Curtain desire for peace. How radical was this invitation to one who had led the first penetration of the Iron Curtain can be judged from the scream of editorial vituperation leveled at me by the Communist press some years before. Even before I had launched the first freedom balloons from the German-Czechoslovak border, *Pravda* August 31, 1946, proclaimed: "The Pearson news cocktail is a mixture of one or two generally known facts with a dose of anti-Soviet lying. . . . Pearson will resort to any means to sabotage the cause of peace." *Ogenek* January 22, 1950, told its readers: "Pearson is an unwavering adherent of the maniacal plans for the establishment of world domination by American monopolies." *Izvestia* September 11, 1946, reported: "If the magnates of monopolistic capital profiteer on wars, so also do their newspaper salesmen. Such a one is that veteran of slander, Drew Pearson." *Universul*, Communist Party organ in Bucharest, the city which I visited in 1958, proclaimed in June 1950: "The international organization of journalists has expelled from its ranks all journalists who have compromised themselves by carrying on racial and war propaganda. Drew Pearson, the zealous agent of Wall Street monopolies, is included in this role of infamy."

Eight years later the Union of Rumanian Journalists invited that same "zealous agent of Wall Street monopolies" to address its gathering. Furthermore, it carried almost in full the text of his speech which dealt with the American free press and the American press conference by which American journalists cross-examine the heads of their government—a procedure totally foreign to the Communist press. During the eight-year interval between the castigation of *Universul* and the welcome given the newspaperman whom it had nominated for the "role of infamy," my method of reporting had not changed. Nor had the facts I reported changed. But the point of view of those behind the Iron Curtain had changed. They had become more confident of their position, less subservient to an inferiority complex, and, in my opinion, more anxious to co-operate with the rest of the world toward peace.

Historians take judicial notice of the fact that peoples and countries do change. They change in their outlook toward other countries. There was a day when the Moslem faith was pledged to spread the word of the Prophet throughout the world with the flaming sword. There was a day when the armed might of the Christian world was mobilized under the cross of the Crusaders to stop the sword of Islam and recapture the Holy Places of Christ. Today the West considers the Terrible Turk its best friend in the East. Today Christian pilgrims visit the birthplace of Christ at Bethlehem under the protection of Moslem guards; and at one time a Moslem guard stood over the Church of the Holy Sepulchre in Jerusalem in order to keep Christian sects from stabbing each other at this holiest of Holy Places.

For almost one hundred years the United States and England were at odds; they fought two wars against each other, battled for trade, called each other names over Ireland, and approached the brink of another war in 1863, when the Russian fleet virtually kept them apart. Yet today no two firmer friends are to be found anywhere. The United States has fought two world wars against Germany, yet Germany is now one of the defense bulwarks of the United States on the continent of Europe. American armies fought the length and breadth of Italy from Salerno to the Po, and American bombers laid waste such priceless relics of history as the Monte Cassino Monastery. Yet today Italy and the United States stand as firm friends. So time can be the healer of many wounds.

My own personal experiences, first in penetrating the Iron Curtain and later traveling behind it, are important only as an indication that time has made changes and that wounds can be healed.

The history of American friendship with the satellite countries goes back a long way. It goes back to the day when the thirteen colonies were fighting against the tyranny of the British crown and when some of the satellites, particularly Poland, were fighting against the tyranny of the Russian crown. At that time Count Casimir Pulaski and Thaddeus Kosciusko came to America and fought from Brandywine to Yorktown and Savannah. Their ancestors in Poland had been fighting against the Russians for centuries, and some of their descendants are still resisting. While the present-day Poles may have forgotten this early link between their country and the United States, they have not forgotten the fact that thousands of their relatives live in Milwaukee, Chicago, Detroit, and Buffalo. One of the largest Polish cities in the world is Hamtramck in Detroit. Polish-Americans elect to the United States Congress John C. Kluczynski of Chicago, Thaddeus M. Machrowicz and John Lesinski of Detroit, Edmund P. Radwan of Buffalo, Clement J. Zablocki and Alvin E. O'Konski of Milwaukee and Mercer, Wisconsin. The letters, the exchange of food packages, the visits of relatives constitute an important link between the United States and Communist Poland. War between that country and the United States would not be easily undertaken or prolonged.

It was Czech-Americans from Pittsburgh, led by Thomas G. Masaryk, who founded the Republic of Czechoslovakia under the guidance of Woodrow Wilson in 1918. In Pittsburgh and Chicago the telephone directories still list almost as many Czechoslovak names as in the phone directory of Prague. In the little town of Lidice south of Chicago is a memorial to the heroes of Czechoslovakia murdered by Nazi tyrants in 1942. Every year on June 10 the Czechoslovakian National Council of America gathers to pay tribute to its patriots. In Cleveland and Youngstown live almost as many Hungarians as in the city of Budapest. Rumania has been the battleground for Russian armies, had a slice of its northern territory annexed by the Soviet Union, harbors many memories of friction with the Soviet, as against long and pleasant relations with the United States.

This is a background which cannot be forgotten overnight and which Moscow propaganda cannot entirely erase. It will not, however, serve as a base for fomenting satellite revolution. The tragic lesson of Hungary bore testimony to that fact. One of John Foster Dulles' greatest errors was his speech in Buffalo, September 14, 1952, promising Poles, Czechs, and Hungarians that Eisenhower, if elected, would in effect foment revolution behind the Iron Curtain.

But if the American people want to work at constructive friendship, rather than hold out impossible promises; if we want to help the people of satellite countries without any hope of return other than peace; if we are content to let them remain behind the Iron Curtain until they evolve their own independence, as eventually they must, then these peoples will come to be an even greater insurance policy for peace. No government in the Kremlin can afford war as long as over 76,000,000 non-Russians remain a threat of insurrection in time of war. This constitutes one of the greatest existing pressures for peace. It also is the reason why the Kremlin fought so hard to bring Tito of Yugoslavia back into the Moscow fold and treated him so savagely when it failed. It is probably the chief reason why ex-Premier Nagy and General Pal Maleter were brutally executed—as an example to other restless satellite leaders that they too might have to pay with their necks for any independence from Moscow.

To encourage satellite independence and extend the American insurance policy for peace, the State Department proposed to President Eisenhower and Senate leaders in the spring of 1958 that the President be given authority to extend American foreign aid to the satellite nations if he considered it in the best interest of the United States. This was an extension of Marshall Plan policy which originally was offered to Poland, Czechoslovakia, Hungary, and the other satellites, but which was abruptly turned down on the demand of Foreign

Minister Molotov. It was this decision, dictated by the Kremlin, not the satellites, in July 1947, which actually began the Cold War. A renewed offer of American aid ten years later, it was believed, might help to end the Cold War; and Senator John Kennedy of Massachusetts drafted an amendment approved by the State Department April 15, which would give the President the right to channel foreign aid behind the Iron Curtain. His amendment was accepted by the Senate Foreign Relations Committee without a peep from its most outspoken member, Senator Knowland of California. The first confidential print of the bill carried the State Department's official endorsement as follows: "The Executive Branch favors the foregoing Kennedy Amendment."

Then, out of the political blue, Knowland descended on the State Department with all his ponderous bulk, threatening to slash foreign-aid appropriations unless the Eisenhower Administration withdrew its approval of the Kennedy amendment. Since the Administration had originally urged the amendment and later drafted the revision, this was difficult. However, Acting Secretary of State Christian A. Herter panicked. He retreated as fast from the Kennedy amendment as he had from Harold Stassen's proposal at the San Francisco Convention of 1956 that he run against Vice-President Nixon. Deputy Under Secretary of State Douglas Dillon did not panic. And finally the State Department agreed as a compromise to favor the Kennedy amendment in principle but let Congress decide how to implement it. This decision, an olive branch to the Senator from California, was reported to Committee Chairman Theodore F. Green of Rhode Island on May 29, but it did not satisfy the leader of right-wing Republicans at all. Knowland was just returned from a primary vote in California which showed that the people of his state did not endorse him to be Governor of that state. He had been chided as "the Senator from Formosa" because of his steadfast support of Generalissimo Chiang Kai-shek. His policies had been castigated as out-of-date and outmoded. The belligerent Mr. Knowland, however, demanded an appointment with the President, immediately got it, and in effect blackmailed the President with the threat that he would cause trouble for the foreign-aid bill unless foreign aid was banned to the satellite countries.

Eisenhower surrendered. His surrender was a body blow to American efforts to write a further insurance policy for peace behind the Iron Curtain.

The pro-Eisenhower coalition in the Senate had long realized, as the State Department had realized, that all attempts to blockade and boycott the Soviet bloc had failed. We had placed an embargo on trade with Communist China. We had restricted shipments of strategic materials to Russia and the satellites. We had set up an elaborate system of trade licenses, plus requirements that our allies must not deal on certain key commodities behind the Iron Curtain. But despite all this, Soviet industrial might continued to expand. It brushed off the Western-world boycott as a fleabite. Official evidence of this growth was not only visible to even the shortsighted eyes of orthodox Republicans, but was recognized officially by the House Committee on Foreign Affairs with a report that "the Soviet rate of industrial growth for total production is considerably larger than that of the United States." Soviet-bloc production of steel jumped up to approximately the same level as American steel production during the depressed winter of 1958; while the big three aluminum companies of the United States were forced to reduce their prices two cents per pound because of Soviet aluminum competition in Western Europe. Edward L. Ryerson, former President of Inland Steel and head of an American steel-industry delegation touring the Soviet, came back to say, "We did not quite appreciate how much they've done in a relatively short time in the development of steel. The Russians have some steel operations superior to anything known in the United States." This was accomplished, of course, despite the American boycott.

Nevertheless, Senator Knowland, believer in a continued boycott against the satellites, emerged from his triumph over Eisenhower and on the White House steps, facing the statue of General Kosciusko, the Polish hero who had fought to free America, triumphantly announced in effect that America would not help Poland or her sister nations behind the Iron Curtain.

Remarked Senator George D. Aiken of the rock-ribbed Republican state of Vermont, "If we can't understand where the State Department stands, how can we expect our allies to believe in them?"

Thus ended an important chapter in an abortive American effort to ensure peace. Premier Khrushchev earlier that year had met with Premier Gomulka of Poland in a hunting lodge on the Russian border, where he had spent several days trying to convince Gomulka that Poland should not accept aid from the United States. Khrushchev had failed. But Senator Knowland of California, Republican Leader of the Senate, had reversed Khrushchev's defeat.

Since the end of World War II the United States has unfolded its heart and its treasury in the greatest exhibition of generosity ever known to man. It has given alike to friend and former foe. It has even offered to relinquish its monopoly of nuclear weapons. It has offered to permit inspection teams to scrutinize its factories and fly over its boundaries in the interest of disarmament if other nations would do the same. During this period the Soviet Union has engaged in terror, force, intrigue. Its leaders have admitted publicly that their former dictator was a ruthless tyrant. They have followed in his footsteps in Hungary by a bloody suppression of man's desire to govern himself. And they have vetoed proposal after proposal for disarmament inspection.

Yet all the barometers of world esteem show that American prestige is down, Soviet prestige is up. A Gallup poll taken in New Delhi, India, in January 1958 on the question of "which is doing more to help peace, Russia or the West?" showed Russia with a rating of 54 per cent, the West 18 per cent; 28 per cent were undecided.

Another Gallup poll taken in the capitals of the world in May 1958, just before Vice-President Nixon was stoned and spat upon in South America, showed that respect for the United States had decreased drastically. In France, our oldest ally in Europe, anti-U.S. sentiment outnumbered pro-U.S. sentiment by eleven to one. In eight NATO centers, dependent upon American support for their military defense, the poll showed that the prestige of the United States had gone down with 28 per cent of the people; had gone up with only 11 per cent.

Why this drastic decrease in view of all the American people have done for their fellow men? The answer, in our opinion, is twofold:

1. We have bungled our foreign policy, have permitted our affairs of state to be guided by old men intent on their golf or with one eye over their shoulder, watching the isolationists in Congress. For this the blame is ours alone.

2. It is not always deeds that count, but words; and in the battle of words the United States has lagged woefully. Part of the battle of peace is the battle of words. We must win friends in order to win the peace. We are the world's best advertising experts. We have been able to sell freezers to Eskimos and sun lamps to Hottentots, but we have not been able to sell American friendship even to the people whom we have helped with billions of dollars. Nikolai Lenin, Father of the Communist Revolution, wrote in 1905: "Propaganda is of crucial importance for the triumph of the Party." Lord Keynes, the labor economist of capitalistic Great Britain, put it another way:

"Soon or late it is ideas, not economic interests, which are dangerous for good or evil." If wars begin in the minds of men, as stated in the UNESCO charter, then hydrogen wars can begin only in hermetically sealed minds.

Yet the United States first ignored the importance of winning men's minds, then proceeded to berate and belabor those who pioneered our channels of propaganda. No man in recent political life has been so criticized as the late Elmer Davis, Director of the Office of War Information. And when William Benton, founder of a lucrative Madison Avenue advertising agency, became Assistant Secretary of State in Charge of Propaganda, he was verbally stoned out of government. He became the number-one target of the Republican National Committee, the radio networks, the press associations and those who put fear of government competition ahead of protection of country. So loath was Congress to permit the United States government to enter the battle of ideas that the debate on the Smith-Mundt Act, setting up the machinery for the battle of ideas, lasted 50 per cent longer than the debate on the highly controversial Taft-Hartley Act, both passed by the Eightieth Congress. Even after a Republican administration came into power in 1953, the gumshoeing emissaries of Republican Senator McCarthy, Roy Cohn and David Schine, proceeded to terrorize American libraries and information agencies abroad. And when finally the McCarthy era was over and it looked as if the United States Information Service would settle down to an unharassed life of constructive accomplishment, Senator Lyndon Johnson, the Democratic leader, flew into a rage because of ill-chosen political remarks by its chief, Arthur Larson. Once again, thanks to Johnson, the job of getting American deeds presented to the world through American words was sabotaged.

Nikita Khrushchev, sitting in Moscow, watching Congressman Walter of Pennsylvania try to erect new barriers against East-West exchange, watching Senator Knowland of California fight the Kremlin's battle by banning the same American aid to Poland which he, Khrushchev, had urged Premier Gomulka not to take, watching the Congress cut the U.S. propaganda budget to less money than he, Khrushchev, spent on jamming the Voice of America, must have thanked his lucky stars for American masochism. With all the moral weapons in our hands, we handed them to Khrushchev on a golden platter.

"If Communist propaganda can continue indefinitely in the West," remarked Christian Pineau when Premier of France, "while the West cannot spread its propaganda in Communist countries, then one day we shall all be subjugated." "Truth," said the London *Economist*, "is no longer the first casualty of war; it must be assassinated before war can be made." "If we can crack the Iron Curtain," said former Senator Benton of Connecticut, "it should be possible to create a world climate of opinion in which no nation would dare employ nuclear weapons to make war or use its stockpile to intimidate other peoples." Yet the United States continued to let the Soviet Union outsell us in the idea market places of the world.

Benton, the first Assistant Secretary of State for Propaganda, later the lone senator who had the courage to demand the censure of Senator McCarthy and was defeated for his pains, has prepared a program for getting American ideas across to the people of the Soviet Union. He recommends:

1. President Eisenhower to ask for the privilege of making a monthly talk to the Russian people over Soviet radio and television facilities—a talk which would emphasize our desire for peace. Reciprocal American facilities would be offered to Premier Khrushchev to address the people of the United States.

2. The Soviet proposal for a special session of the General Assembly of the United Nations to discuss disarmament should be accepted—but with the proviso that the deliberations be fully reported by the Soviet press and radio to the Russian people.

3. An American offer to permit Russia to operate a radio station in Washington if they will permit us to operate one in Moscow.

4. Hammer home the point that if Russia will agree to a rigid system of nuclear disarmament, the United States is prepared to spend all that we save on disarmament, as much as ten billion dollars annually, to help the economic development of less favored nations.

5. Request the Soviet to take all of the American students they can accommodate at their universities. We need young people who speak Russian. Our students in Russia would be ambassadors for the American way of life. The tidal wave of American youngsters, numbering three million more, will descend on American colleges by 1970, with college administrators seeing little hope of doubling their facilities. Tuition and living costs at foreign universities are much less; and a quarter of a million young Americans enrolled in Russian universities every year would be a vitally important bridge for understanding and peace.

6. An exchange of American Congressmen with members of the Supreme Soviet. This could be the most fruitful exchange of all.

American Congressmen visiting Russia have come back with new understanding of American-Soviet problems.

7. The United States should untangle its own red-tape curtain. It should simplify the cumbersome maze of regulations which make the American immigration curtain more vexing than that of Russia. "In my judgment," says Benton, "it is infinitely more important to reach the Russian people than to reach the moon." This is his formula for doing it.

Even the best propaganda machine, however, cannot cover up mistakes, as Ambassador George Allen, chief of the U.S. Information Agency, tacitly admitted in a television interview shortly after taking office. American policy must be sound; it must be alert. It cannot retreat; it cannot be handled in slipshod manner. It cannot ask Chancellor Adenauer of Germany for a letter to President Eisenhower suggesting that the American people contribute old clothes to refugees from East Germany in 1953 and then allow that letter to gather dust so long at Eisenhower's fishing camp near Denver that the State Department was both ashamed to issue the dated letter and ashamed to ask Adenauer for an updated copy. Nor can our foreign policy be conducted in such lackadaisical fashion that one month is permitted to elapse between Premier Bulganin's letter of December 10, 1957, asking for a summit conference, and Eisenhower's reply. Old men do not always think fast or act fast. And during that month, a peace-hungry world thought only that Russia wanted peace, that the United States did not care enough about peace to reply. The diplomats of Washington called Bulganin's letter insincere propaganda.

"I haven't read it," was Secretary Dulles' comment. He added that he had not discussed it with President Eisenhower.

But millions of people all over Asia, Africa, and Europe did read the Bulganin letter and did discuss it. They particularly read the warning: "For the first time in history . . . in the event of war, neither of the great powers will be in a privileged position that would ensure it from becoming from the very outset a theater of military operation."

And they discussed Bulganin's plea: "What can all this lead to? The United States, we believe, will gain nothing by it militarily. It will not become less vulnerable, while the danger of war will increase."

It was not until January 12, 1958, that President Eisenhower finally got around to answering Bulganin; and by this time Bulganin had sent him another letter dated January 8, reminding him, in effect, that a month had passed without a reply and that Russia was still working for peace. Though Bulganin's letter should have been answered in exhaustive detail, Eisenhower replied, January 20, in a curt forty-word note.

Marshal Bulganin came back February 1 with another letter, and it took Eisenhower fourteen days to answer. The Kremlin knew in advance what Washington's answers would be—a series of anguished noes. That doubtless was why they kept writing. The latest techniques of Madison Avenue were behind the Russian letter barrage, as Bulganin and Khrushchev sent note after note to Eisenhower. Madison Avenue at its worst was behind the Eisenhower replies as he replied with almost frozen repetition, "No." It took the Eisenhower Administration four months, eight letters and three notes to wake up to the fact that it might be smart to answer the Russians a little faster. Finally, as Khrushchev proposed that the United States join with Russia in ending nuclear tests, Secretary Dulles, appearing at his press conference April 9, almost glowed with pride over the fact that the Eisenhower Administration had managed to get off a reply to Moscow in only four days.

Even the President at his press conference admitted that his Administration could have fielded the Eisenhower notes with more speed and suggested putting a psychological expert in the State Department. However, two psychological experts had long been stationed in the White House—C. D. Jackson of *Life*, *Time*, and *Fortune*, and later Nelson Rockefeller, who had done an excellent job under Roosevelt. They might have penetrated the Iron Curtain, but neither could penetrate the lackadaisical atmosphere of the White House. Discouraged, they resigned.

Meanwhile, Russia's announcement of a unilateral ban on H-bomb tests scored the number-one propaganda victory of 1958. It almost equaled the number-one victory of 1957—launching the sputnik. The steady drumbeat of Bulganin notes urging a summit conference and the banning of missile bases in Europe had pictured the United States as a warmonger, Russia as the disciple of peace. How badly the United States muffed the ball on banning H-bomb tests was known only to a few people. But as early as September 11, 1956, President Eisenhower and the National Security Council had decided to propose almost exactly what Moscow proposed in April 1958. One week later, however, Eisenhower's political advisers warned that Adlai Stevenson had already made speeches proposing the end of H-bomb tests. They advised that it would be a political mistake to play into Stevenson's hands by going ahead with the Security Council's decision of September 11.

Accordingly, Eisenhower reversed himself. On September 19, he came out with a vigorous statement attacking Stevenson's H-bomb proposal as "a theatrical gesture." In speech after speech thereafter he attacked the Stevenson plan as political grandstanding, insinuated that Stevenson was not qualified to discuss atomic energy. Suddenly, on October 26 the President stormed into the National Security Council and angrily lectured members about leaks to the press. He complained that the September 11 decision to ban H-bomb tests had become known to newspapermen, and he was ordering a full investigation.

White House embarrassment over Stevenson's nuclear proposal was such that politics was even injected into the Public Health Service's survey of radioactivity. All summer, state officials had cooperated with Public Health officials regarding the spread of strontium 90, the poisonous aftermath of bomb tests which creeps into the bones of young children. Suddenly the survey was called off. It was terminated so precipitously that on September 26, 1956, Assistant Surgeon General Otis L. Anderson wrote state health officials: "Field sampling operations in connection with radiation surveillance network will terminate at the close of business Thursday, September 27, 1956." Twenty-four hours is an extremely abrupt cancellation notice, but the race for President was on.

Previous surveys had showed increases of radioactivity as high as fifteen to twenty-five times normal by some Public Health monitoring stations. An increase of ten times normal, according to the Atomic Energy Commission, is considered the alarm point.

Thus have the foreign affairs of the United States been conducted, regardless of our professed desire for peace.

A cultural-exchange treaty has now been signed between the United States and the Soviet Union. It gives further evidence that the leaders of the Kremlin are not afraid to let their people rub shoulders with the West, compare standards of living of the two countries. On the whole, the exchange has gone well. There has been warmth and cordiality between Russians and Americans. Soviet citizens visiting the United States have shown a genuine desire for friendship, while Americans visiting Russia have been deluged with attention. There are still those, both in and out of government, who have thrown monkey wrenches into the friendship machinery. W. Paul O'Neill, a member of the State Department Office of Cultural Exchange, advised against sending the Harlem Globetrotters to Moscow for fear the Russians might learn new basketball tricks. He even expressed the opinion that it was not wise to put the Moiseyev Ballet on Ed Sullivan's television program because their smiles were so contagious the American people would come to believe the Russian people were friendly. And when Alvin C. Eurich of the Ford Foundation, returning from a survey of education in Russia, recommended that the State Department give an entry permit to Professor A. D. Alexandrov, head of the University of Leningrad, the same Mr. O'Neill put sand in the gear box. Professor Alexandrov is the top mathematical physicist of the world, the Russian scientist who is working on plans to reach the moon. But six months passed and Eurich got no reply from the State Department regarding a visa for Professor Alexandrov. The Professor meanwhile had gone to Canada to exchange information with Canadian scientists, but was not permitted to come to the United States for similar exchange on the vital problems of space. Finally, the authors telephoned Mr. O'Neill to ask the status of Professor Alexandrov's visa. Mr. O'Neill simply did not remember the case. He had filed it and forgotten it—apparently not considering the admission of the top Russian physicist and expert on space problems to be worth thinking about twice.

Although not part of the Soviet exchange treaty, exchanges with the satellites have also bogged down in the State Department. When the Rumanian government sought to send Peter Dimitrou to the United States to study farm problems his application was kept waiting a month and he was finally told that he could remain in the United States only sixty days. As the sixty-day period neared its end, Dimitrou asked for permission to remain another thirty days, inasmuch as he was buying ten million dollars' worth of American seed corn and agricultural machinery. But that made no difference to the State Department. Dimitrou was ordered to leave immediately. He departed on his sixtieth day despite the fact that he had the endorsement of Roswell Garst, the Coon Rapids, Iowa, farmer who has done more for people-to-people friendship with the Soviet bloc than any other one person. Reverse treatment was given to Dr. Nicholae Lupu, the distinguished Rumanian doctor who helped organize the conference of internal medicine held in Philadelphia in the spring of 1958. The American Legation in Bucharest delayed Dr. Lupu's visa until so late that his report on internal medicine had to be read in Philadelphia for him.

On the other hand, an American architectural exhibit on "The American Way of Life" was shown in the three leading cities of Rumania; an exhibit on Walt Whitman also toured Rumania, while the Philadelphia Orchestra received a tremendous ovation in Bucharest.

When five Russian veterans of that historic meeting of American and Russian troops on the River Elbe in April 1945 came to Washington, they received a tremendous ovation at the baseball park and were flabbergasted to learn that American veterans could take thirty years to pay for a home, with no down payment, and that American amputees received free automobiles. And when two Moscow cartoonists, Vitalii Goriaev and Ivan Semeonov, started on an extended tour from Washington to California, their trip was suddenly canceled by the Soviet government apparently because they had become too friendly and too talkative. They had admitted to Americans that they never drew cartoons critical of Soviet officials and said there must have been a mistake about Nikita Khrushchev's famous remark that the Communists would "bury the West."

When Van Cliburn, the Texas piano prodigy who won the highest musician honors Moscow could bestow, came to Washington, the cultural-exchange program suddenly broke down—at least on the American side. Cliburn had received a ticker-tape ovation up Broadway and another ovation when he played at Carnegie Hall. But when he came to Washington, President Eisenhower was playing golf at Gettysburg, and Senator Lyndon Johnson of Texas, who had once stopped debate on the Senate floor to publicly introduce blond, buxom Jayne Mansfield, did not bother to welcome his fellow Texan. The Soviet Embassy did welcome Cliburn with open arms; the State Department did not.

"Where will you ever find another country like Russia?" exclaimed Madame Mamedov, the Russian cultural attaché. "Not only do we give an American the first prize, but we are happy about it.

"I warn you not to get in a picture with me," she added, as the photographer started shooting. "If you run for Congress it will ruin your career."

Thus runs the course of people-to-people friendship between the U.S.A. and the U.S.S.R. As far as the people are concerned, it has run well. As far as officials are concerned, it has sometimes limped.

But considering the fact that the two countries have been making faces and calling each other names for thirteen years, the new policy of smiles has been disturbed by surprisingly few frowns.

In deciding whether the United States can live in peace beside the Soviet Union, we have to study not merely the warm and genuine welcome given to such American visitors as violinist Isaac Stern, pianist Van Cliburn and the Philadelphia Orchestra, and the reception given by Americans to Minister of Agriculture Matskevich and other Russians, but we also have to study the actual instances of working co-operation between the two nations. The friction between Moscow and Washington has been headlined, the co-operation has not. Co-operation does not make headlines. When the Russian military attaché gets arrested for passing through a stop sign in the Maryland suburbs it is front-page news in the Washington *Post.* When American scientists co-operate with Russian scientists in the Antarctic, it gets obscure mention on the inside pages. Nevertheless, one of the most fascinating examples of international co-operation has been taking place in the Antarctic, where, according to Admiral George Dufek, Commander of the U.S. Navy in the Antarctic, "there is complete harmony, co-operation, and cordiality between the Russians and Americans. The Russians have an observer with us in Little America; we have an observer with them. When we visit their base we receive a hearty welcome, are invited to dinner and receive other tokens of hospitality. We bring photographic apparatus and take all the pictures we like. It is the same way when they come to visit us. When a Japanese ship got into trouble, the Russians went out to help. When a Russian ship got into trouble, we went out to help."

Admiral Dufek could have added that the American government has proposed that the Russians take over one of our bases as a loan and operate it themselves; while the Russians have offered to turn over some of their bases to New Zealand, Britain, Argentina, and Chile.

Or consider the experience of Harry J. Anslinger, Commissioner of Narcotics for the United States, who has been elected on the motion of Soviet Russia to be chairman of the International Board of Narcotics Control. Commissioner Anslinger pays tribute to the Russian delegates for giving him complete co-operation and for taking the lead in forcing various countries of the world to ban illicit narcotics. The United States and the Soviet Union, according to

Anslinger, support each other on every move to control narcotics.

The oldest story of American-Russian co-operation, of course, is the control of seals in the Bering Sea. Ever since 1905, when seals faced extinction, the United States and Russia have worked together to protect the breeding grounds and regulate the slaughter of seals.

Against these examples of co-operation and friendship are balanced the fact that a fleet of Russian submarines frequently lurks off the American coast, while American bombers constantly cross the Arctic on practice flights to within an hour or two of the Russian coast. There was also the bitter demonstration against the American Embassy in Moscow after we landed Marines in Lebanon, when a crowd, obviously well organized, marched four abreast to smash the windows of the Embassy with bricks that suddenly appeared from nowhere.

These are the precarious factors which make for war. These are the factors which make it so imperative that both nations work at peace.

Nothing can take a nation down the road to war quicker than vacillation. Nothing is more likely to confuse a potential enemy than inability to differentiate between tough words that have conviction behind them or tough words that are mere bluff. Of such uncertainties wars are made. And as the United States of America passed the middle of the twentieth century it veered toward indecision, vacillation, equivocation and compromise. It followed a policy of talking big and carrying a little stick.

Said Senator William Fulbright of Arkansas, January 12, 1958, in comparing the nation's drift into civil war in 1858 with our current drift toward disaster: "President Buchanan, a tired and amiable man with tired policies, continued to spread the campaign of his own confusion over the land. Today what was true in 1858 is again true, but on a vastly larger scale and in vastly menacing form. . . . The peril of the nation increases daily because of the way the incumbent administration has dulled and continues to dull the nation's awareness of the danger it faces. . . . We have developed the chronic habit of not following through."

The confusion, the peril increased despite Senator Fulbright's warning. It reached a climax with the landing of United States Marines in Lebanon in July 1958 and with Moscow's demands for a summit conference immediately thereafter. Confusion in the Near East had been building up for a long time. As usual, it was built on vacillation. John Foster Dulles had pulled the rug out from under the British in Suez early in 1953 by privately confiding to the new revolutionary regime in Egypt that the United States was pressuring the British to leave; so the British, their bargaining power gone, did leave without even a written agreement safeguarding their century-old investment in Suez. Shortly thereafter, Mr. Dulles had dangled the golden promise of the Aswan Dam before Colonel Nasser even at a time when he knew Nasser was importing huge quantities of arms from Russia; and he refused to let Secretary of Agriculture Benson depress Egyptian cotton by dumping American surplus cotton, even though Nasser at that very moment was bartering Egyptian cotton for Russian arms. Finally when the Russian–Egyptian arms deal created too much Western resentment, especially among Jewish contributors to Eisenhower's 1956 election campaign, Mr. Dulles suddenly yanked the promise of the Aswan Dam away from Nasser with such abruptness that Nasser, to save face, seized the Suez Canal. Mr. Dulles seemed surprised. He seemed even more surprised when the British and French, after repeated advance warnings, moved to retake the Canal which had once belonged to them. At this point, Mr. Eisenhower and Mr. Dulles personally demanded, and in no uncertain terms, that the British and French get out and get out immediately. They did—but with great loss of prestige to themselves and to the West generally. President Eisenhower had been running for re-election on a platform of peace when suddenly he found there was no peace. So he put personal politics at home ahead of Allied unity abroad, and rescued Colonel Nasser as he was cringing in a bombproof shelter in a Cairo suburb, fearful of assassination by his own Army officers.

All this contributed to the confusion of our Allies and to the abortive landing of U.S. Marines in Lebanon in July 1958. It also brought us nearer the point where we faced either war with Russia, tacit surrender to Russia, or realization that a complete overhaul of our national policy is necessary.

It was just one year and nine months after Eisenhower had peremptorily telephoned the Prime Minister of England on November 5, 1956, to demand the evacuation of British troops from Suez that Eisenhower telephoned the British Prime Minister again, July 14, 1958, to urge that Britain join the United States in sending British troops back into the Near East.

What had happened suddenly to reverse the policy of the United States? Briefly, the Kremlin–Nasser timetable for taking over the

Near East had been clicking right on schedule, with little pro-West Lebanon next on the list for subversion and revolt. For weeks, arms and agents imported from Syria and Egypt had been fomenting hatred and dissension between Moslems and Christians. For weeks also, Mr. Dulles had urged Lebanon not to call on the United States for help under the Eisenhower Doctrine. Then suddenly he woke up to find that the Kremlin timetable had jumped ahead of schedule. In Iraq, King Faisal had been murdered, the body of Premier Nuri Said dragged through the streets, and a pro-Nasser revolutionary government had taken over a country supposed to serve as a pro-Western buttress against Russia.

The news was telephoned to Allen Dulles, head of Central Intelligence, at 2:00 A.M., July 14. Later that morning, he and his brother, the Secretary of State, came to the White House. The situation was grave. In twenty-four hours the entire Near East might fall into the hands of the colonel whom Eisenhower had saved from a bombproof shelter in the suburbs of Cairo a year and nine months before.

The history of nations, the erosion of national prestige, the build-up for wars sometimes turn on minor human equations. They can also be decided on the spur of the moment. Three times in his administration Dwight D. Eisenhower had called out troops—at Little Rock, Arkansas; in the Caribbean when a Venezuelan mob threatened Vice-President Nixon; and in Lebanon. In each case the decision was hasty and one which he later regretted. In the case of Lebanon, one factor that influenced Eisenhower which he did not know about was a telephone call from Constantine Brown of the Washington *Star* to two senators, Styles Bridges of New Hampshire and William Knowland of California, urging that the answer to revolution in Iraq should be the landing of U.S. troops in Lebanon.

Bridges and Knowland are the two top-ranking Republicans in the Senate. They are nationalistic, inclined to be isolationist, definitely conservative. When they appeared at the White House that same morning to attend the swearing-in ceremony of John McCone as chairman of the Atomic Energy Commission, they took occasion to advise Eisenhower that vigorous action was needed in the Near East. Eisenhower can and has jumped through foreign-policy hoops for these two Republican Senators. Their word, added to the doleful word of John Foster Dulles, tipped the scales.

The President got Prime Minister Harold Macmillan on the scrambled transatlantic telephone and told him the United States was prepared to send troops to Lebanon. Would England in turn send troops to Jordan? The conversation was pitched in far different tone than the call to Prime Minister Anthony Eden in November 1956, when Eisenhower had used such unprintable language in demanding that Britain pull its troops out of Suez that Eden became physically ill and shortly thereafter resigned.

Macmillan told the now polite President of the United States that he would put his request before the cabinet and call back. He did so around noon. The answer was in the affirmative. Britain would send troops to Jordan.

It was decided to move immediately and move vigorously, not with the idea of saving President Chamoun in Lebanon, but of preventing a stampede to Nasser in Jordan and Saudi Arabia, and as a gesture of reassurance to Turkey and Iran. It was also decided the United States would send far more troops than necessary in case they should be needed in Iraq.

To this end, Turkey mobilized two divisions on the Iraqi border and was ready to send them direct to Baghdad. All it asked was that the U.S. Air Force provide cover. Turkey was champing at the bit and rarin' to go. She never did. The United States changed its mind.

On the morning of July 15 troop-carrying units of the U.S. Sixth Fleet appeared off Beirut. The Marines landed. There were no incidents. A few boys swam out to meet the boats. Bathers on the beach waved. The lackadaisical reception gave no inkling of the storm that was to come. It gave no inkling of the mental torment to be suffered by the man who had made the decision to intervene with troops in the Near East.

Just a few hours after the Marines landed, Dwight D. Eisenhower began to get cold feet.

A phone call from Henry Cabot Lodge, Ambassador to the United Nations and a very close friend of Ike's, told of sour reaction in New York. Dag Hammarskjöld, Lodge reported, was furious. The UN Security Council would not be likely to support the United States; would not take over our troops as part of the UN police force.

A series of cables and ambassadorial representations began to trickle into Washington. Eisenhower paced the floor snapping at aides, calling for full and frequent reports on Near East developments. A dozen times in one day he had General Andrew Goodpaster call the Pentagon. Several calls were to order the Pentagon to restrict information to the press. American troops were still pouring in on the beaches of Lebanon, yet the President already was anxious to have them out.

Chancellor Konrad Adenauer of West Germany registered a stiff private protest. American troops, he pointed out, were being airlifted from NATO bases in Germany without his knowledge or consent. Premier de Gaulle of France was angry that he had not been consulted. He was even more disgruntled after a French cruiser with 1,800 French troops aboard was kept in the outer harbor of Beirut, not permitted by American authorities to send its men ashore. Protests came from such NATO allies as Norway, Denmark and Belgium. Baron Silvercruys, the Ambassador of Belgium, called on Under Secretary of State Herter to warn that the United States had put itself in the position of using force to protect American oil companies.

"If Near East oil were cut off from Belgium," said Under Secretary Herter, "you would be the first to be asking the United States for oil."

Greece, which had been saved from starvation and guerrilla warfare by American aid, demurred at letting American planes refuel in Athens en route to Turkey. Saudi Arabia, whose King Saud had been wined and dined by Eisenhower in order to secure the renewal of the great U.S. air base at Dhahran, simply ignored the American request to use that base for American military planes. Prince Faisal informed the American Ambassador that his cabinet could not understand the American request. It was an Arab alibi for not getting around to answering it. Saudi Arabia would not even permit its oil to be shipped to Jordan nor permit American planes to fly over its deserts to carry that oil to Jordan. Austria protested vigorously when American transports carrying troops flew over a corner of the Austrian Tyrol; and Nikita Khrushchev in Moscow encouraged Chancellor Raab in his threat to shoot down American planes if they continued to fly over Austria.

Suddenly it became all too apparent that the vast network of allies the United States had labored so long to build and strengthen was but a shell. In Europe, only the British Commonwealth and Italy stood firm.

There was a day when reaction would have been different. But that day was before Russia launched its first sputnik; before it became known that Russia had an arsenal of intermediate-range ballistic missiles. It was also before the United States in the eyes of much of the world had come to be considered a second-class power.

Eisenhower's decision to land in Lebanon was made without consulting any of the Near Eastern advisers in the State Department. It was made without consulting the American Ambassador in Lebanon, Robert McClintock, who had repeatedly warned against any landing and who even said that he would row out in a small boat to prevent troops from going ashore. The Lebanese Ambassador in Washington also cautioned against American intervention. After the troops landed they were given orders by President Chamoun not to intervene in the Lebanese civil war, not to police the Syrian border, not to do anything except sit. So many troops poured into Lebanon that they got in one another's way. Moslem resentment against the United States flared. When Ambassador Robert Murphy arrived in Lebanon to work out a compromise and permit a graceful evacuation of American forces, he found President Chamoun jumpy, irrational and even incoherent. Back in the United States, Henry Cabot Lodge at first declined to give a speech before the UN Security Council accusing the United Arab Republic of stirring up revolt in Lebanon. It was only after Secretary of State Dulles called him and virtually ordered the speech that Lodge acquiesced.

Dwight D. Eisenhower was still pacing the White House floor, still worrying how he was to get American troops out of Lebanon, when Nikita Khrushchev dropped on the unsuspecting world his proposal for a summit conference.

The invitation was couched in the belligerent tones of a victorious nation summoning a defeated nation to an armistice.

"The Soviet Union," warned Khrushchev, "possesses atomic and hydrogen bombs, an Air Force and a Navy, plus ballistic missiles of all types, including intercontinental ones."

These were not the words of a nation which wants peace. Yet they were true. Eisenhower knew they were true and the world knew they were true, even if the American people did not. A weaker nation sometimes has to sit down at the conference table whether it wants to or not. The United States, thanks to soothing syrup and tranquilizing pills, thanks to bickering and budget-cutting, thanks to putting profits ahead of patriotism, was no longer able to negotiate from strength.

XXI

OUR THREE ALTERNATIVES

ANY COLD ANALYSIS of the American position in the world today must reach the unpleasant conclusion that we have three alternatives. We can precipitate a preventive war and hope to win it. We can reconcile ourselves to becoming definitely and permanently a second-class power. Or we can tighten our belts for a long and self-sacrificing attempt to prove that capitalism is better than communism; that our science can be better than communist science, our education better than communist education, our dedication more determined than that of the Soviet Union.

We don't believe the American people will long hesitate in making this choice.

The first alternative—preventive war—is, of course, suggested in the Gaither report as a new national policy. But in nearly two hundred years of American history it has never been adopted, and we believe the American people will recoil at adopting it today. Certainly the world would recoil after we adopted it. Atomic war is too cruel, too risky, too likely to set the entire world on fire, too likely to wipe out vegetation, animal life, human life for years to come. Even if we won a preventive war, victory in modern war has come to mean an obligation by the victor to reconstruct the vanquished.

The second alternative—resignation to the permanent status of second-class power—is not one which the American people will accept with their eyes open. They have accepted it hitherto because they have been lulled into a condition of comatose overconfidence. They have believed with John Foster Dulles that all we had to do was sit by and wait for the day when the walls of the Kremlin came tumbling down. "They have made very little progress in the last few years," Secretary Dulles told the Senate Foreign Relations Committee on February 26, 1956, at a time when Russia was developing sputniks and ballistic missiles; was concentrating on scientific education and increased industrial output. "The fact is," said Mr. Dulles, "that they have failed and they have got to devise new policies."

The real fact is, Mr. Dulles notwithstanding, that Russia has not devised any new policies. The further fact is that we will have to revise ours—if we do not want to go the way of the Greek Empire and the Roman Empire, the British Empire and all other governments which have put material comfort ahead of self-sacrifice, the welfare of a few ahead of the welfare of many.

We will have to prove that capitalism is what the United States Chamber of Commerce says it is, and what the authors think it can be. This will not be easy. The United States Chamber of Commerce is the first to wave the flag regarding the virtues of capitalism but the first to run in the opposite direction when it comes to high taxes to pay for the cost of protecting capitalism. It is the first to undercut the capitalistic system by persuading Congressmen to vote against legislation to keep American education abreast of Russian education.

If the American people are going to shun the first two alternatives, as we believe they will, there are two basic safeguards we will have to adopt to ensure peace. They are:

1. Keep strong—militarily, economically, spiritually.
2. Win the people of Russia to be friends of the United States.

These may seem easy goals to attain, but they are not. To remain strong means high taxes, long hours, controls on wages and prices against inflation, the stern sacrifice and the sustained patriotism of wartime. Russian newspapers are filled with pictures of workers who establish the best production records—in peace. American newspapers feature photographs of bathing beauties—in peace. Jenkin Lloyd Jones, publisher of the Tulsa *Tribune*, coming back from Russia in 1958, reported that the Soviet subsisted on propaganda. That is true. Soviet propaganda and Soviet education have been so successful that police controls, at first necessary to enforce communism, have been taken off. Communist education has been so intense and economic gains so great since the czar that the majority of Russian people have come to believe in communism. We are not going to change this overnight. We may never change it. But we can show that our system is better, though we will have to exert superhuman energy, determination and dedication.

We cannot go in for $75 medicine cabinets, $6,000 coffee tables and $350,000 reflecting pools at our Air Force Academy. Effete furniture and luxurious buildings will not win the battle of capitalism vs. communism. Vicuña coats given to high officials in return for favors in high places will not help the battle. The Sherman Adams scandal, the unprecedented number of gifts to President Eisenhower, our unparalleled number of recent conflict-of-interest cases have put us in the same category as European governments, where the public has lost faith in democracy. Class distinction, materialism, lack of idealism have been making Europe decadent. In the past we have stood apart. The Adams gifts, the array of presents to Eisenhower, the income-tax favoritism under both Truman and Eisenhower were not important in a material sense, but disastrous in a morale sense. They gave Americans the same blasé disrespect for government that has bogged down Europe. Dishonesty has spread to other walks of life—to labor and business. Half a billion dollars a year is now stolen by American businessmen, an average of $2,000,000 for every working day; not the way to demonstrate the superiority of capitalism.

The United States of America was founded by men of principle and spirituality. They were willing to suffer great hardship for these principles. They came a long way over uncharted seas to a rugged wilderness to practice their spiritual beliefs. They set the highest standard of honesty and spirituality, and willingness to sacrifice for that honesty and spirituality, the world has ever seen. We will have to get back to their standards if we are to win the great competition with communism.

History shows that Rome was not defeated by outside invaders as much as it defeated itself. France was not overrun by the Nazis merely because the Nazis were strong. France was overrun because it was weak, because ease, corruption, lack of leadership had sapped the core of France. The decadence of Rome, the defeatism of France have already set in with the American people. Both can be reversed. But it will take heroic steps to accomplish that reversal, and to go one step farther and win the friendship of the Russian people.

It is not enough that we publish a catalogue of good intentions. We will have to select certain laboratory tests for peace, then, if these are successful, extend those successes to other areas. Here are some concrete steps the United States could take along the now dimly lighted road to peace:

A United States of Europe. The landing of American Marines in Lebanon has already demonstrated how thin a shell is our NATO alliance. Meanwhile, the Benelux countries have demonstrated that it is possible to make a start toward a European confederation. The revival of West German nationalism and the revival of French de Gaullism make it all the more imperative that there be a United

States of Europe. Such a confederation could solve the problem of East and West Germany, could replace a military NATO with a police force for peace. An army conscripted in the United States to fight the battles of Europe will never be effective. The sooner we weld the remnants of NATO into a United States of Europe, the better.

Education and people-to-people friendship. Education gives the greatest hope of all for peace. The more the peoples of the West get to know the peoples of the East, and vice versa, the less chance there is of any attack on the United States. The more education there is in Russian schools and universities, the more rebellion there will be against highhandedness toward the United States. In 1958, 4,000 Americans out of 173,000,000 were studying Russian. In Russia about 14,000,000 were studying English. To win friends we have to speak the other nation's language. A crash program to teach Russian in American schools and universities should be the first order of a people-to-people friendship program.

Control of outer space. This is a new field with no previously built-in prejudices. It is a field where the scientific mind, rather than the political mind, might prevail. It could offer a start toward Russian-American co-operation.

Two summit meetings per year between the heads of state of the United States and the Soviet Union. There is no reason why the Premier of Russia and the President of the United States should not meet at regular intervals just as stockholders of a giant corporation meet in Wall Street. The problems that are unsolved in one meeting would go over to the next. It is not necessary to preface these meetings with protracted haggles over what will be on the agenda. As long as the leaders of the most powerful nations in the world are talking at regular intervals, the guarantee is implicit that they will not be fighting. As long as negotiations continue in a labor dispute, there is hope of settlement. The same principle can apply to conversations between the U.S.A. and the U.S.S.R.

A public-works plan for the world. Soviet Russia has now proved that she has a competent and sizable number of engineers and is turning out even more than the United States. Let them cooperate with American engineers in a public-works program similar to that proposed for the Near East, to develop the great wasted water-power projects of Africa, the unharnessed sun of the African, Asian, and American deserts, the Danubian and other waterways of Europe, in a comprehensive plan to improve the power, the food supply, the transportation, and the living standards of the world.

But most of all the United States has to recover the initiative for peace. Either we spend billions to become moles underground, or we learn to live in peace with each other above ground. Either we burrow out mountainsides for underground factories, build great warehouses for the storage of wheat in the caves of Kansas and Kentucky, learn to live in subways like underground rabbit warrens; or we learn the art of living as friends. There is no other alternative.

We will have to work at peace just as intensively as we have worked at preparing for war. We will have to exercise great patience, great understanding. There are no brass bands playing as we march down the road to peace. There are many setbacks. There are such setbacks as the execution of Hungary's ex-Premier Nagy, the crackdown on Yugoslavia's Tito, the restlessness of China, the hardening of the Soviet line in the summer of 1958. These are outward signs of internal strife which, while setting back the cause of peace, could promote it further in the end. Disruption inside the Kremlin may work in our favor—if we are prepared.

That preparedness must include not only the end of military inefficiency and the harnessing of scientific brainpower, but a Renaissance of the principles that made this country great.

The great Presidents of the United States have never hesitated to use moral suasion to influence the affairs of men. Jefferson, Lincoln, Wilson, and Roosevelt shook the world with their sermons on freedom and human brotherhood. Their words penetrated to the farthest corners of Europe, were discussed over the campfires of soldiers in the Urals and the Carpathians. I have heard Bulgar prisoners discussing the speeches of Woodrow Wilson with Serbian guards and Albanian conscripts, squatting in tents in the mountains of central Serbia. It was the idealism of his words, his promise of the future, that made them say, "*Nacho Vilson taku,*" meaning "Wilson would not have it so."

The stirring ideals of the American people can ring out again if we choose to think less of fear, more of peace. We have been so busy with the McCarthy obsession of looking under our own beds for Bolshevik bogeymen that we have not had time or else were afraid to lift our voices in hope, peace, and friendship. Or, we have been so complacent, so self-satisfied with turning out 6,000,000 automobiles a year to Russia's 100,000, so busy buying tranquilizing pills and worrying about golf scores, that we could not see that the Soviet was no longer peddling communism as something akin to misery, but as something connected with success. American foreign policy is still based on the idea that we are a supreme military power. Unfortunately, we are not. It is still based on containment. We can no more contain Russia today than the Ku Klux Klan could stage a march through Harlem on St. Patrick's Day. Asia and Africa know this and most of Europe knows it even if Senator Knowland and the right wing of the Republican Party do not. That's why our allies are worried; that's why large parts of Asia and the Near East have deserted.

We need to formulate a new foreign policy based on more humility, based on more energy, based on the idealism of Jefferson, Lincoln, Wilson, and Roosevelt. If Russia can emerge from the age of peasantry despite the cumbersome handicap of communism, then the American people can achieve greater miracles with the efficiency of capitalism.

We repeat: The emergence of Russia from the wheelbarrow age to the atomic age is the greatest miracle of modern times. And while the American who says this publicly is likely to be blasted as pro-Communist by the Un-American Activities Committee, yet if America doesn't recognize this fact, it is likely to get blasted off the face of the earth. Too long have we put self-interest ahead of national interest, ease before duty, luxury before sacrifice, golf before decisions, Thunderbirds before missiles, Madison Avenue camouflage before truth.

We cannot sit back and wait for bickering inside the Kremlin to deliver Russia into our hands. The walls of the Kremlin are not like the walls of Jericho. They will not come tumbling down after seven statements by John Foster Dulles. Nor will they yield to a civilization in which an Elvis Presley makes more than the President of the United States, in which truck drivers in Chicago are paid more than many schoolteachers, in which one third of all prescriptions filled at drugstores are for tranquilizing pills. The road to Miltown is not the road to victory over the vigorous and unscrupulous government that rules Russia. We cannot win the battle for freedom or the great goal of peace if we keep our heads in the sands of ignorance.

The ingredients of greatness, however, have not gone out of the bones of the American people. They are equal to great challenge—if they know the facts. They have risen to great heights during crises of the past. They can rise again.

About the Authors

DREW PEARSON *was born in Evanston, Illinois, and educated at Phillips Exeter Academy and Swarthmore College. Following a period of relief work with the American Friends Service Committee, he taught at the University of Pennsylvania and Columbia University. He was a roving foreign correspondent for several years before settling in Washington. His first book,* Washington Merry-Go-Round, *written with Robert S. Allen, led to the daily newspaper column of that name, published since 1932, and currently syndicated in the Washington* Post, *the New York* Mirror, *the Chicago* American, *the Los Angeles* Mirror, *and more than 600 other newspapers. He has sponsored the Friendship Train, helped to organize the Freedom Balloon campaign, and in 1948 was named Father of the Year. Though he works under high pressure at his office in Georgetown and his Maryland dairy farm, his quiet, almost retiring personality shows no trace of the hard-boiled reporter.*

JACK ANDERSON, *a native of Salt Lake City, studied at the University of Utah and George Washington University. He began working with Drew Pearson in 1948, following two years with the* Stars and Stripes *in Chungking and Shanghai, China. He is the co-author, with Ronald May, of* McCarthy: The Man, the Senator, the Ism.